How Israel Was Won

How Israel Was Won

A Concise History of the Arab-Israeli Conflict

Baylis Thomas

LEXINGTON BOOKS
Lanham • Boulder • New York • Oxford

LEXINGTON BOOKS

Published in the United States of America
by Lexington Books
4720 Boston Way, Lanham, Maryland 20706

12 Hid's Copse Road
Cumnor Hill, Oxford OX2 9JJ, England

Copyright © 1999 by Lexington Books

British Library Cataloguing in Publication Information Available

Library of Congress Cataloging-in-Publication Data

Thomas, Baylis, 1932–
    How Israel was won : a concise history of the Arab-Israeli conflict /
Baylis Thomas.
        p.   cm.
    Includes bibliographical references (p.) and index.
    ISBN 0-7391-0063-7(cloth : alk. paper) — ISBN 0–7391–0064–5
(pbk : alk. paper)
        1. Israel—History. 2. Arab-Israeli conflict. 3. Palestine—
History—1917–1948. 4. Israel—Politics and Government. 5. Middle
East—Politics and government. I. Title.
DS126.5T495   1999
956.94—dc21   99-10673
                                                    CIP

Printed in the United States of America

♾™ The paper used in this publication meets the minimum requirements of American
National Standard for Information Sciences—Permanence of Paper for Printed Library
Materials, ANSI/NISO Z39.48–1992.

Contents

Chapter 1 – Early Zionism Before the Balfour Declaration   1

The First Zionist Congress in 1897 proposed establishment of a Jewish state through the influence of foreign governments. Herzl failed to gaining a state in Palestine through British or German influence over the Ottoman Empire. With the approach of World War I, Britain sought justification for a permanent military presence in Palestine. Support of Jewish claims in Palestine, in conflict with Arab claims, created tensions and the justification needed.

Chapter 2 – World War I and the Balfour Declaration (1917)   9

Britain pledges a grant of Arab national independence over Greater Syria (including Palestine) to Sharif Hussein in exchange for help in defeating the Ottoman Empire (MacMahon-Hussein letters, 1915). Britain also pledges to war ally, France, control over parts of Greater Syria (Sykes-Picot Agreement, 1916). Britain further pledges a homeland in Palestine to the Jews in exchange for their help in ending U.S. neutrality in WWI (Balfour Declaration, 1917). Britain plays on verbal ambiguitities in an attempt to satisfy its conflicting promises to the Arabs and Jews.

pact. Britain withdraws; the state of Israel is declared despite UN prohibitions.

External threats: (1) Third World disapproval of Israeli "imperialist" collusion with Britain and France in the Suez War, and (2) PLO and Fatah terrorism. Internal threats: (1) a faltering economy, (2) ethnic conflict between Oriental and European Jews, (3) violation of Arab-Israeli citizens and Israeli self-criticism over lost idealism, and (4) public exposure of Kastner collaboration with Eichmann.

Arab nations are domestically destabilized and polarized by the Cold War. Eisenhower fails to win over Arab nations because of U.S. hostility to Arab nationalism. Kennedy falls under Jewish suspicion because he fails to oppose Arab nationalism. Kennedy reopens the Palestinian refugee issue and presses for repatriation in exchange for U.S. arms to Israel. Johnson arms Israel, as do Britain, France and Germany. The Soviets (and the United States) arm the Arab countries.

Israel attacks Jordan (Qalqilia and Samu) and publicly threatens invasion of Syria. Egypt is drawn in by Soviet-sponsored Syrian-Egyptian mutual defense pact. Nasser requests partial removal of UN forces along Sinai border to show readiness to protect Syria. An apprehensive Israeli public thinks the prime minister weak. Israeli military insists on an easily-won war. Nasser is seen as a coward by Arab nations and as responsible for domestic economic failure. He closes the Strait of Tiran to Israel. Johnson presses for diplomacy, judging Israel to be invulnerable and lacking reason for war. The Soviets threaten Israel about attack of Syria or Egypt. Impending U.S.-Egyptian talks alarm Israel about Egyptian prestige. Israel invades Egypt.

Israel destroys the Egyptian air force on the ground in three hours on false claim of having been attacked. Jerusalem, the Sinai Desert and West Bank are captured in three days. The UN demands a cease-fire and the Soviets threaten Israel about further aggression. Israel, stymied by U.S. disapproval of carrying the war into Syria, attacks a U.S. intelligence ship monitoring Israeli movements. Israel invades the Golan Heights and calls its attack on the U.S. ship a "mistake." The Soviets cut ties and threaten war on Israel. Israel completes sweep in six days. Israelis killed, 759; Arabs killed, up to 30,000. Refugees from Syria, the West Bank and the Sinai, 323,000.

The UN Resolution 242 calls for return of captured Arab lands in exchange for peace treaties with Israel. Israel balks, retaining the Sinai, West Bank and Golan Heights. The PLO proposes a single Arab-Jewish democratic state over all of Palestine. Egypt seeks return of the Sinai, attacks a disorganized IDF and advances east across the Suez Canal (Yom Kippur War). Syria temporarily pushes Israel out of the Golan Heights. Israel recaptures the Golan and the Suez Canal. A U.S. nuclear alert follows a Soviet threat of intervention because of Israeli cease-fire violations. The Arabs withhold oil in protest over U.S. support of Israel, shocking the world.

Chapter 17 – The PLO, the West Bank and the Lebanon Wars (1982)   209

The PLO, head-quartered in Lebanon, proposes a Palestinian state in the West Bank and Gaza and supports a Moslem majority in a civil war in Lebanon against an Israeli-supported Christian minority government (1975-1976). Israel, after returning the Sinai to Egypt in exchange for a peace treaty, looks to control the West Bank and smash its PLO leadership in Lebanon. West bank territory is confiscated for Jewish settlements and political and military oppression intensifies. Israel invades Lebanon on pretext of ending PLO terrorism and routs rival Syrian forces along the way. Reagan sides with Israel against the PLO and Soviet-supported Syria. The IDF inflicts massive losses on the PLO, Palestinian refugees, Shi'ite Lebanese villages and Beirut residents (30,000 to 40,000 killed). Begin, Shamir, Sharon and Eitan are apportioned blame for massacres in Sabra and Shatilla Palestinian refugee camps.

Chapter 18 – Likud's Greater-Israel Dream and the Intifada (1988)   243

Reagan (1982 peace plan) challenges Begin's claim to need Jewish settlements for Israeli security and criticizes his notion of Palestinian autonomy. U.S. peace-keeping forces in Lebanon align with Christian government forces, but suicide bombings lead to U.S. withdrawal. In 1984, Begin is replaced by Shamir who then alternates with Peres as prime minister. Defense Minister Rabin's "iron fist" policy fails to suppress a 1988 Palestinian grassroots uprising, the *intifada,* which Hamas and Islamic Jihad support (the PLO later). Arafat declares a Palestinian state (West Bank and Gaza) which is recognized by 100 countries including the Soviet Union, China and India – not the West. Shamir refuses to talk about Palestinian autonomy (not sovereignty) during the intifada. The 1991 Gulf War leads to the decline of the PLO and intifada when Palestinians support Saddam Hussein for his promise to fight for their rights.

Chapter 19 – The Oslo Accords and the Demise of the Peace Process (1998) 263

Rabin replaces Shamir in 1992. He continues settlement expansion and closes off the occupied territories in early 1993. Foreign Minister Peres, in secret negotiations with a weakened Arafat, prepares to make autonomy concessions in exchange for Arafat's curbing of Hamas and recognition of Israel. These Oslo Accords hold promise of relief from an oppressive occupation but are viewed by Palestinian critics as a surrender to Israeli rule. Netanyahu replaces the assassinated Rabin in 1995, insisting that Hamas be crushed as a condition for further peace negotiations. But Arafat faces loss of Palestinian support if he severely curbs Hamas. Netanyahu imposes punishing sanctions on Palestinians and the peace process falters, 1998.

Three levels of government: (1) official, (2) "invisible," and (3) military. The official government is run by a strong cabinet and weak parliament. Political power is concentrated in the central committee of the political party and prime minister. Israeli courts are constrained by the absence of a national constitution, safeguard of civil rights. The "invisible" government (Histadrut, Jewish Agency and Jewish National Fund), now less powerful than formerly, controls matters of industry, labor, health, immigration, housing and land use to the advantage of Jewish citizens. The military government enforces defense (martial) law in a discriminatory manner, controlling the personal freedom, property, civil rights and land use of Arab-Israeli citizens.

Zionism reflects a universal ideal of nationalism, that associated with democracy, liberalism, the value of the common man, the people's right to self-determination and freedom from domination. Paradoxically, nationalism is also associated with the illiberal exclusion of minorities and the imperialistic conquest of alien peoples. For questions arise about who is included in "the people" and how far their "self-determination" may encroach upon that of outsiders. Further, nationalism is based on a belief in the existence of prized traits shared equally by members of this people but not by others considered less endowed or entitled. Thus, nationalism is associated with both democracy and xenophobia, with both self-defense and conquest. Zionism embraces this paradox.

Maps

For Donald Neff

Acknowledgments

I am profoundly grateful for the encouragement and thoughtful suggestions offered by Ronald Bleier, Mason Cooley, John Haney, Norma Hurlburt, Steve Ostrowski, and Steve Stearns throughout this study. The generous editorial help of Seymour Kleinberg and Alison Thomas, as well as the patient and sustaining support of publishing consultant Richard Rowson, are deeply appreciated.

Gratefully acknowledged is permission granted to quote from:

(1) *Collusion Across the Jordan: King Abdullah, the Zionist Movement and the Partition of Palestine,* Avi Shlaim. Copyright (c) 1988 by Columbia University Press.

(2) *A History of Israel: From the Rise of Zionism to Our Time,* Howard M. Sachar. Copyright (c) 1979 by Alfred A. Knopf, Inc.

(3) *Warriors For Jerusalem: The Six Days That Changed the Middle East,* Donald Neff. Copyright (c) 1988 by Amana Books.

All books are reprinted with the permission of the publisher.

Introduction

The demand for a Jewish state has popularly been seen in relation to the Holocaust – both as a response to the Holocaust and as a safeguard against any future Holocaust. The founding of Israel has thus carried great moral weight and those Arabs who have stood in the way have provoked enmity in much of the Western world. Historically, Palestinian Arabs have objected to a Jewish state on grounds that they have been forced to pay with their homes and land for a Holocaust perpetrated by Europeans who have made no sacrifice of land nor even altered their immigration quotas for Jews.

Palestinians have come to be seen as agents attempting further injury of Jews rather than as a people themselves injured as a secondary consequence of the Holocaust. The notion that Palestinian and Arab national resistance to Zionism was an extension of the Holocaust has been dubbed by one Israeli historian, Avi Shlaim, the "Holocaust syndrome."[1] According to this description, the conflict in the Middle East is experienced as a replay of World War II anti-Semitism and murder of Jews – an understandable but misleading transposition of events from one time, place and circumstance to another.

The Holocaust syndrome has affected Israeli policies through a preoccupation with internal security and the development of an invincible fighting force capable of countering what seemed an Arab Goliath. In the context of this syndrome, Jewish aggression has been understood as defensive and as a corrective to the tragic helplessness of Jews during World War II. Of paramount importance has been the establishment of a Jewish state on land cleared of Arabs and open for the rescue and permanent sanctuary of worldwide Jewry.

The Holocaust syndrome has also shaped popular misunderstanding of

Middle East events in the West. For example, Nobel Peace Prize winner Elie Wiesel reflected popular perceptions when he explained that the Jewish people, seeking fair and peaceful accommodation, were greeted with warring Arabs: "When Israel accepted the United Nations partition plan, it was thus the only nation ever to recognize a Palestinian state. Arab armies responded with war."[2] Readers who feel the weight of the Holocaust have little reason to question this misleading statement.

Viewing the Middle East conflict through the Holocaust filter is to distort history – to take partial truth as whole. For example, the Jews *did* officially accept the 1947 UN proposal for partitioning Palestine into two independent states, one Jewish, one Palestinian, yet not before making secret arrangements to *subvert* that UN proposal. Historians now know that David Ben-Gurion and King Abdullah of Transjordan made a secret non-aggression pact (blessed by Britain) in which: (a) the Jews would permit Transjordan to invade Palestine (in a pretense of "saving" the Palestinians from the Jews) and annex that territory designated by the UN for the Palestinian state; and (b) in exchange, Transjordan would not invade any territory earmarked by the UN for the Jewish state.[3] Since Transjordan had the only Arab army in the Middle East of any military significance, Ben-Gurion was assured that the Jewish state would be safe in a larger war and that an independent Palestinian state would not come into existence.[4] Ben-Gurion and Abdullah were dividing up Palestine between themselves without a fight.

Transjordan honored this non-aggression pact in the 1948 war. Its forces never entered or attacked any territory which the UN had designated for the Jewish state.[5] Rather, Israel broke the pact by invading and annexing large portions of territory earmarked for the Palestinian state, territory that Transjordan had expected to annex. Ben-Gurion's acceptance of the UN partition proposal and his pact with Transjordan were interim devices, tactical steps toward gaining all of Palestine: "Establish a Jewish State at once, even if it is not in the whole land. The rest will come in the course of time. It must come."[6]

To say that "Arab armies responded with war" is a further popular misperception that fits with the Holocaust syndrome but glosses over many historical facts – not merely that Transjordan did not respond with war. The armies of the surrounding Arab nations were, altogether, of "negligible importance."[7] They knew that they could at best put up a show for domestic consumption, not seriously fight Israel. Moreover, they entered Palestine with an intent to stop Transjordan from annexing Palestinian land since that would have upset the intra-Arab balance of power.[8] Egypt, Syria and Lebanon welcomed last-minute U.S. proposals to avert war with Israel and, thereby, foil Transjordan's takeover of Palestine. Ben-Gurion rejected these U.S. truce proposals.[9] War against the weak Arab states was part of a strategy to enlarge Israeli boundaries beyond those already designated by the UN.[10]

The image of Arabs terrorizing Jews also fits the template of the Holocaust syndrome. The reverse idea of Jews terrorizing Arabs seems to make little sense except as somehow defensive or retaliatory. Yet historians tell us that Jewish terrorism, with Haganah assistance, was the chief cause of panic and flight of 750,000 Palestinians to refugee camps in 1948.[11] Thousands of starving refugees were shot as they attempted to return to their homes. After five years of languishing in refugee camps as outcasts in Syria, Lebanon and Jordan, Palestinians began small-scale reprisal sabotage in Israel.[12] After seventeen years in a refugee camp, Yasser Arafat, a schoolboy during the 1948 war, organized the Fatah movement for excursions into Israel.

These few examples from 1948 are unexceptional. Yet they were the initial disquieting facts I encountered as I began this study, an attempt at a fair and concise integration of the scholarship on the history of the Arab-Israeli conflict. Certainly the Holocaust had influenced *my* assumptions about what I would find. How could those past unspeakable horrors *not* stir visions and expectations about the Middle East? Who, or which media, questioned the virtue or necessity of an aggressive Jewish self-defense or did *not* cheer the fighting Jew? The world *needed* atonement for World War II complicity in having left the Jews helpless before their fate. At the same time, that world was grateful to stand the Arabs in their stead, shifting responsibility to an alien and historically disparaged people.

Memory has a way of becoming a political instrument, selectively shifting attention to those current events which seem consistent with concerns and expectations arising from the past. The memory of the Holocaust made the Jewish colonization of Palestine seem like a defensive operation and raised the specter of Nazi aggression when the Palestinians resisted that colonization. Moreover, such analogy of past and present events becomes an oracle about the future. This oracle then justifies present actions and even creates a duty to the future to prevent past events.[13] In reality, the Jewish colonization of Palestine was the operation of a resourceful, internationally favored people against a less politically advanced, organized or equipped people.

Memory takes part for whole; it creates myth from fragments of truth. We know this from our own history in which American pioneers are portrayed as victims of vicious attack rather than as victimizing colonizers. The white man's conquest of the West comes to be depicted as an unintended by-product of a brave *defense*. Once the indigenous population "somehow" ends up dispossessed and marginalized, the outcome is ascribed to their senseless greed and fanatical intransigence. This is the justifying myth of not only the American and Zionist colonizations but also of colonization efforts by most nations.

This study integrates the classic as well as revisionist historical scholarship on the Arab-Israeli conflict, primarily that of American, British and Israeli historians. This scholarship has profited from relatively recent declassified government documents coming from both Israel and the United States. Looking beneath the Holocaust syndrome and the popular myths, this integrated history describes the political outlook and intentions of the antagonists as well as their behavior "on the ground," and examines the critical role of the Cold War antagonists on the outcome of the Arab-Israeli struggle.

Notes

1. Avi Shlaim, *Collusion across the Jordan* (New York: Columbia University Press, 1988), 437.

2. *New York Times,*(letter to the editor), June 23, 1988.

3. Shlaim, *Collusion,* 110ff.

4. Transjordan had a British-trained army of less than 5,000 compared with the Jewish Haganah army of 50,000. Simha Flapan, *The Birth of Israel* (New York: Pantheon, 1987), 151.

5. Shlaim, *Collusion,* 239. Fighting did occur in Jerusalem, a holy city for both Arabs and Jews that was designated by the UN as an international city, i.e., neither Jewish nor Palestinian land.

6. Ben-Gurion quote cited in Shlaim, *Collusion,* 17. "Even if it involved the partitioning of Palestine . . . [Ben-Gurion] worked on the assumption that a partial Jewish State would not be the end but only the beginning. The plan was to bring into this state all the Jews it could possibly hold, to build a Jewish economy, to organize a first-class army and then [quoting Ben-Gurion] 'I am certain we will be able to settle in all the other parts of the country, whether through agreement . . . or in another way,' " 17.

7. Flapan, *Birth of Israel,* 192. The Arabs' military capacity was "beneath

criticism" according to General MacMillan, commander in chief of the British forces in Palestine. Ibid.

8. "The invasion of Palestine by Arab armies . . . was not aimed at destroying the Jewish state. It was intended to prevent Abdullah [Transjordan] from annexing the Arab part of Palestine." Flapan, *Birth of Israel,* 151. Clark Clifford put it simply to President Truman: "What is really at play in Palestine is a contest between various Arab States and rulers to attach to themselves Arab Palestine or a part of it. . . . Any remaining contest for territory will be, not between Jews and Arabs, but between Arabs and Arabs; not for Jewish territory, but for the part of Palestine assigned to the Arab state." Clifford papers, box 13 *Truman Library* (May 9, 1948), *Truman Library.* "It may be argued that the Arab League's decision to intervene was rooted not in a common interest to save Palestine for the Palestinians or to defeat Zionist ambitions but in inter-Arab fears and rivalries." Avi Shlaim, *The Politics of Partition* (New York: Columbia University Press, 1990), 160.

9. Flapan, *Birth of Israel,* 150.

10. "The Jewish Agency refusal [of truce proposals] exposes its aim to set up its separate state by force of arms – the military action after May 15 [1948] will be conducted by the Haganah with the help of the terrorist organizations, the Irgun and LEHI [Fighters for the Freedom of Israel], [and] the UN will face a distorted situation. The Jews will be the real aggressors against the Arabs, but will claim that they are only defending the borders of the state, decided upon . . . by the General Assembly." U.S. diplomat Robert McClintock in *Foreign Relations of the United States: Annual Report* May 4, 1948 (Washington: U.S. State Department, 1971), 894-5.

11. The most infamous source of panic and flight was the Irgun massacre of 254 men, women and children in the village of Deir Yassin. But there were at least twenty other large-scale massacres (fifty or more civilians each) in 1948, according to the former director of the Israeli army archives, cited in Norman Finkelstein, *Image and Reality of the Israel-Palestine Conflict* (London: Verso, 1995), 110. Israeli historian Benny Morris concludes, "In general, in most cases the final and decisive precipitant to flight was a Haganah, IZL [Irgun], LHI [Stern Gang] or IDF [Israel Defense Force] attack or the inhabitants' fear of such attack. . . . Ben-Gurion clearly wanted as few Arabs as possible to remain in the Jewish State. He hoped to see them flee. He said as much to his colleagues and aides . . . [though] no expulsion policy was ever enunciated. . . . He preferred that his generals 'understand' what he wanted done." Benny Morris, *The Birth of the Palestinian Refugee Problem, 1947-1949* (Cambridge: Cambridge University Press, 1987), 292-4.

12. Ariel Sharon's commando raids on refugee camps in Gaza and in Arab villages in 1953 provoked retaliation. Jonathan Shimshoni, *Israel and Conventional Deterrence: Border Warfare from 1953 to 1970* (Ithaca: Cornell University Press, 1988), 74. Moshe Dayan, chief of Israel's army, was attacking Arab villages in 1954 "to help prod this or that Arab state into a premature war with Israel . . . in which Israel could realize such major strategic objectives as the conquest of the West Bank

or Sinai." Benny Morris, *Israel's Border Wars, 1949-1956: Arab Infiltration, Israeli Retaliation, and the count-down to the Suez War* (Oxford: Clarendon Press, 1993), 178-9.

13. See *Haunted by History: Myths in International Relations,* Cyril Buffet and Beatrice Heuser, eds. (Oxford: Berghahn, 1998). The editors quote a dictionary definition explaining how the political myth "consciously, in the form of well-aimed propaganda, seeks to give an imaginary definition of a mission. That which is shown in the image may in the distant past have played a role close to reality, but is now supposed to justify present actions through an imaginary duty to the future and make it invulnerable to criticism" (ix).

Chapter 1

Early Zionism Before the Balfour Declaration

The search for legitimacy through European imperial power

When Theodor Herzl proposed the idea of a Jewish state in *Der Judenstaat* in 1896, the idea was rejected by most Jews in both Europe and America. Jews in Palestine were also opposed to the territorial and political goals of Zionism out of fear that Jewish immigration would disturb their good relations with both Moslem and Christian neighbors. Moreover, an attempt to establish a Jewish state in Palestine would very likely heighten oppressive controls of the Ottoman government then ruling Palestine.

Nevertheless, a core of Jews led by Herzl called the First Zionist Congress in Basel, Switzerland, in 1897 to facilitate the goal of a Jewish state. Four means were agreed upon: (1) the promotion of Jewish immigration to Palestine; (2) the "organization and binding together of the whole of Jewry" through appropriate means; (3) the "strengthening and fostering of Jewish national sentiment and consciousness"; and (4) the taking of steps toward "obtaining [foreign] government consent" for the objectives of Zionism.[1]

The Congress agreed that their major goal was the last, the gaining of consent of powerful governments. Herzl approached several European governments, each having its own imperialist designs on and, to different extents, influence over a vulnerable Ottoman Empire. That empire had been weakened by wars with Greece and Persia as well as by worldwide ostracism for atrocities committed against Bulgarian revolutionaries in 1875 and the Armenians in 1894 and later. The empire was also suffering internal stresses related to the Kurdish independence movement and Arab discontent in Palestine.

Herzl, a highly assimilated Austrian Jew, considered that Germany was best suited to influence the Ottoman government. He approached Kaiser Wilhelm II in 1898 in the hope that "at one stroke we should obtain a completely legalized internal and external status [in Palestine]." It was his belief that "the suzerainty of the Porte and the protectorate under Germany ought to be adequate legal under-pinning" for a Jewish state in Palestine.[2]

Yet the timing was poor. Before the Young Turk national revolution of 1908-1909, German influence was limited and the approach failed. Then in 1901 Herzl tried to negotiate directly with the sultan for "an open agreement by which an autonomous Jewish colonization of Palestine on a large scale might take place."[3] This also failed despite an attractive offer of Jewish financial assistance to an Ottoman Empire then in great need.

Herzl turned to Britain and found the year 1902 to be more favorable. Jewish refugees from pogroms in Russia were flooding England and were presumed to threaten the English standard of living. Faced with this "problem" and, at the same time, needing white settlers to colonize Africa and other possessions, Britain thought it might solve both problems by sending Jews to British colonies.[4] Herzl argued precisely that point: that Jewish colonization could serve British imperial interests.

Specifically, Herzl sought Cyprus and the Egyptian Sinai peninsula, both under British control. The Sinai in particular could serve as a steppingstone to Palestine. "When we are under the Union Jack at El Arish [Sinai coast], then Palestine too will fall into 'the British sphere of influence,'" Herzl told Joseph Chamberlain, the British colonial secretary. However, the British consul-general (the de facto viceroy of Egypt) would not agree about either Cyprus or the Sinai.

Zionist fortunes improved in 1903. Chamberlain offered the Jews an East African area (approximately present-day Kenya) within a larger tract (misnamed Uganda). Herzl accepted this proposal at the Sixth Zionist Congress in 1903, arguing that, while "Uganda" was not Palestine, it could, as an "auxiliary colonization," provide a "national and state foundation" as well as relief for unfortunate Jews fleeing pogroms in Russia.

Opposition to the East Africa proposal came, ironically, from Russian Jews. They were more touched by the religious mysticism of Palestine than were the secular Jews of Western Europe. A violent split developed within the Zionist movement. In the end, objection to Jewish colonization came from British settlers in East Africa and the British government withdrew its African proposal.

Shared supremacist views; divergent colonialist goals

The British and the Zionists shared a colonialist stereotype concerning the inferiority and docility of Arabs and a justifying notion that no significant culture nor productive use of land existed in Palestine – hence the Zionist slogan, "A land without people for a people without land."[5] Other Jews cautioned against viewing the Arabs as so insignificant. Asher Ginzberg (pen name, Achad Ha'am) cautioned Zionists in 1893 about their dismissal of both Turks and Palestinian Arabs:

> We are accustomed to believing, outside Israel, that the Arabs are all desert savages, a people like donkeys, and that they neither see nor understand what is happening around them. But that is a great mistake. We are accustomed to believe . . . .that the Turkish government is so weak and so savage . . . that for a little money we could do what we like there, and that in addition we will be protected by the representatives of the European kingdoms. But that too is a great mistake.[6]

Gershon Shafir concludes that the Jews "were not ignorant of the Palestinian Arabs, but in their assessment of the balance of forces estimated that the Palestinian Arab population could put obstacles in the way of Jewish rebirth in Eretz Israel but ultimately was not capable of arresting the process."[7]

While Britain and the Jews shared supremacist views, their colonialist interests in the Middle East differed. British colonialism was largely *economic* – a matter of exploiting natural resources, utilizing local labor and selling finished goods to the colonized people. The Jewish idea was *territorial* – obtaining land and removing Arab labor from it. "The Zionists constantly dangled before their European interlocutors this possibility of using Jewish colonization," yet they had no intention of offering the British the use of Arab labor.[8] The goal of establishing an all-Jewish state required removal of the Arab population, an aspect of Jewish colonization that did not serve British interests. On the other hand, Jewish-Arab *conflict* in Palestine would necessitate British troops and enable the British to both protect the Suez Canal and provide buffer against the French in Syria.

When the British withheld support and non-Zionist Jews in Palestine opposed the Zionist plan, Herzl turned to business connections and charity. Here he met with some success. The Anglo-Palestine Bank was opened in 1903, the Jewish National Fund began land purchases in 1905 and the Palestine Land Development Fund readied settlement land for foreign buyers in 1908. Influential American Zionist organizations raised money.[9] By 1914, about 2 percent of all of Palestine had been purchased and the number of Jewish settlers had risen to 12,000. This created a total Jewish population of about 60,000, compared with an Arab population of 644,000.[10]

Opportunities and conflicts arise from World War I for both Jews and Arabs

In 1914 the outbreak of war precluded Jewish colonization in Africa. Zionists in Britain and the United States now "bent their efforts toward obtaining a guarantee from the Allies that, in the event of Ottoman defeat, Palestine would be recognized as a Jewish commonwealth open to unrestricted immigration."[11] British Home Secretary and Zionist sympathizer Herbert Samuel worked in 1915 to convince Prime Minister Herbert Asquith that a Jewish state in Palestine (envisioned as a protectorate within the British Empire) would "enable England to fulfill in yet another sphere her historic part of the civiliser of the backward countries."[12] However, Samuel thought that the *immediate* establishment of an autonomous Jewish state was too dangerous, given the population disparity: "The dream of a Jewish State, prosperous, progressive and home of a brilliant civilization, might vanish in a series of squalid conflicts with the Arab population." Yet he believed that a Jewish state with a Jewish majority could eventually develop out of a British protectorate.[13] The prime minister remained unconvinced.

There were, however, two other major impediments to the Zionist cause in Palestine. First was the fact that in 1915 the British made declarations to Sharif Hussein of Mecca (guardian of Islam's holiest places) that as reward for Arab rebellion against, and help in defeat of, the Ottoman Empire in World War I, Britain would stimulate national independence in the whole Arab-speaking world.[14] Though Palestine was not specifically mentioned by Sir Henry MacMahon, high commissioner in Egypt, this declaration on behalf of the British government clearly implied Palestine. As historian Christopher Sykes has observed, anyone reading MacMahon's words defining the boundaries of the Arab-speaking world "could not suppose otherwise than that Palestine was part of it."[15] Because of this MacMahon-Hussein agreement, the Arabs rebelled and attacked Ottoman forces in support of the Allies (led by Sharif Hussein's second son, Feisal, subsequent king of Iraq, and by T. E. Lawrence ("Lawrence of Arabia").

The second obstacle to the Zionist cause in Palestine was a British-French agreement (the Sykes-Picot agreement) made in 1916, a half year after the MacMahon-Hussein agreement. By this agreement the whole Arab world north of present-day Saudi Arabia was to be divided (after World War I) into *French and British zones of control*, theoretically in the context of an Arab confederation.[16] Britain would directly control present-day Iraq, Kuwait, Jordan and southern Palestine while France would directly control southern Turkey, Syria and northern Palestine. However, because of competing Russian Orthodox and Roman Catholic interests in Palestine, the Sykes-Picot agreement devolved into a compromise in which Britain, France, Russia and Italy would jointly share in an Allied Condominium over Palestine. The Jews in Palestine were to have the same civil, religious and political rights as other groups.[17] This was *not* what either the Zionists or Palestinian Arabs wanted. Each wanted its own independent state.

This European Condominium agreement about post-war control of Arab territory contradicted the MacMahon-Hussein agreement and when the Arab world learned about it in the winter of 1917-18, the response was shock.[18]

The sudden importance of Palestine and the Jews to Britain

Zionist fortunes blossomed in 1916 when Lord George Curzon reported to the new Lloyd George government on the importance of *exclusive* British control over Palestine. The international regime sharing control of Syria (and Palestine) with France, Russia and Italy was deemed unacceptable. Britain wanted to have an exclusive and permanent military garrison in Palestine after the war in order to protect the Suez Canal and its air routes to India.

It was true that Britain already had effective military control over Palestine. Yet Prime Minister David Lloyd George knew he could use this fact neither as a basis for excluding France nor for staking a British postwar claim to Palestine – a violation of Woodrow Wilson's principle of nonacquisition of territory by war. So an "idealistic" rationale was needed for cutting out France and other allies from Palestine. The Zionists held the answer. If an attempt was made to impose a Jewish state on Palestine, this would *predictably elicit Arab hostility* which, in turn, could justify a British military/peacemaker presence in Palestine.[19] And if it happened to come to pass that a Jewish state was established in Palestine, then this, too, would serve British ends. "From a purely British point of view, a prosperous Jewish population in Palestine, owing its inception and its opportunity of development to British policy, might be an invaluable asset as a defense of the Suez Canal against attack from the north and as a station on the future air routes to the East."[20] Britain also feared that Germany had the same idea, for German Zionists were arguing that a Jewish state could be a bastion of German influence in Palestine.[21]

Britain was galvanized in favor of the Zionists.[22] Pro-Zionist British undersecretary Mark Sykes (of the Sykes-Picot agreement) also changed his view about sharing Palestine with the French or others. He now devoted himself to the marriage of Zionist and British interests, and this materialized in 1917 in the form of the Balfour Declaration – a second shock to, and betrayal of, the Arabs. The Balfour Declaration required repudiation not only of agreements with France, Russia and Italy but also of earlier agreements with the Arabs.[23]

Sykes's son, the historian Christopher Sykes, concluded that "Zionism . . . found itself closely bound to imperialism . . . depended for its foundation and early growth on the success of British imperialism, and in the twentieth century that meant the failure of Arab nationalism."[24]

Notes

1. W.T. Mallison, Jr., *George Washington Law Review* 32 (June 1964), 983.

2. Theodor Herzl, *Complete Diaries,* Marvin Lowenthal, ed. and trans. (New York: Dial Press, 1956), 105.

3. James W. Parkes, *A History of Palestine from 135 A.D. to Modern Times* (New York: Oxford University Press, 1949), 271.

4. Richard P. Stevens, "Zionism as a Phase of Western Imperialism," in *Transformation of Palestine,* Ibrahim Abu-Lughod, ed. (Evanston: Northwestern University Press, 1971), 35-6.

5. This standard wilderness myth – that a land is empty or inhabited by only a few or an unproductive people – implies that the land to be colonized is settled, not conquered. This myth, applied to Palestine as well as colonial North America, South Africa and Eastern Europe during World War II, has been examined by Norman Finkelstein in *Image and Reality of the Israel-Palestine Conflict* (London: Verso,

1995), chapter 4, and is described below in Appendix B. Golda Meir alluded to a related myth concerning the political emptiness of Palestine: "It wasn't as if there had been in Palestine a Palestinian people that felt itself as such, and that we drove out to take its place. They didn't exist!" Quoted in. Ilan Halevi, *A History of the Jews* (London: Zed Books, 1987), 171. The phrase, "human dust," regarding Palestinian Arabs, was a common Zionist expression at the turn of the century (193, n.3).

6. Halevi, *A History*, 169.

7. Gershon Shafir, *Land, Labor and the Origins of the Israeli-Palestinian Conflict, 1882-1914* (Cambridge: Cambridge University Press, 1989), 204.

8. Shafir, *Land, Labor*, 167.

9. Between 1914 and 1917, $10 million was donated.

10. Stevens, "Zionism," 40.

11. Stevens, "Zionism," 42

12. John Bowle, *Viscount Samuel* (London: Gollancz, 1957), 170. Samuel argued further that Britain would have to choose among five possible outcomes: (1) France might annex Palestine, threatening British lines of communication to the East; (2) Palestine might remain backward if returned to Turkey; (3) the internationalization of Palestine might provide a stepping-stone for a German protectorate; (4) a Jewish state might be immediately established; or (5) a British protectorate over Palestine might be established (his preference).

13. "It is hoped that under British rule facilities would be given to Jewish organizations to purchase land, to found colonies, to establish educational and religious institutions, and to co-operate in the economic development of the country, and that Jewish immigration, carefully regulated, would be given preference, so that in the course of time the Jewish inhabitants, grown into a majority and settled in the land, may be conceded such degree of self-government as the conditions of that day might justify." Bowle, *Viscount Samuel*, 175-7.

14. It was stated in MacMahon's letter: "Great Britain is prepared to recognize and support the independence of the Arabs" (MacMahon-Hussein correspondence, 24 October 1915). That is not to say that Britain intended to vacate the Middle East. Arab independence would be realized from within some form of protectorate system to be run by the British. Christopher Sykes, *Crossroads to Israel* (Cleveland: World Publishing, 1965), 27, 63. The French-controlled territory west of Damascus extending up the Mediterranean coast to the Turkish frontier (present-day Lebanon) was to be exempted from the Arab domain.

15. Sykes, *Crossroads*, 63.

16. Britain entered into this agreement out of fear that France would demand control of all of Palestine. In 1915, France already had economic and cultural rights in Syria (at that time including present-day Lebanon) and since the "Holy Land" was an integral part of the Syrian administration, France appeared to have a legitimate claim to Palestine. To secure against such losses in Palestine and elsewhere, Britain

entered into the Sykes-Picot agreement.

17. Howard Sachar, *A History of Israel: From the Rise of Zionism to Our Time,* Vol. I (New York: Knopf, 1986), 93-4.

18. It has been argued by some historians that this arrangement did not *clearly* violate the MacMahon-Hussein agreement since British support for Arab independence had never precluded foreign "facilitation." However, when Arab nationalists objected to the Sykes-Picot agreement, the British and French falsely asserted that foreign control of Arab lands freed from Ottoman rule, as called for by Sykes-Picot, was merely an "offer" of "such support and efficacious help as will ensure the smooth working of Governments and Administrations which those populations will have elected of their own free will." Sykes, *Crossroads,* 29.

19. Sachar, *History,* Vol. I, 96.

20. Sachar, *History,* Vol. I, 100.

21. Sachar, *History,* Vol. I, 97.

22. Britain may have felt indebted, some say, to Chaim Weizmann, British Zionist leader and chemist, for contributions to the chemistry of war explosives.

23. The British reneged on their commitment to Sharif Hussein, constructing "an absolutely indefensible interpretation of MacMahon's key letter" that Palestine was excluded from the agreement. This interpretation involved duplicitous semantic play, false translations and claims that Palestine was west of the district (Vilayet) of Syria, when in fact it was south. When the Arabic text of these letters surfaced in 1923, something the British had taken great pains to avoid, the deception was exposed. The Arab argument about the MacMahon letters was "undoubtedly on extremely firm ground." Sykes, *Crossroads,* 63-4.

24. Sykes, *Crossroads,* 26.

Chapter 2

World War I and the Balfour Declaration (1917)

Britain seeks Jewish help to end U.S. neutrality and urge Russia to fight

Apart from its desire to gain control of Palestine by playing peacemaker in a Zionist push for statehood, Britain had the immediate problem of winning World War I. Here again the Jews had a use. The Allies (Britain, France, Russia, Japan, Belgium and Serbia) had been fighting since 1914 against the Central Powers (Germany, Austria-Hungary and the Ottoman Empire) and Russia was near collapse two years into the war. The Allies desperately needed the help of the then-neutral United States. An exaggerated though popularly held belief was that American Jews would be pivotal in influencing the United States to enter the war. Accordingly, Britain had additional motivation for offering the Jews a national home in Palestine. The Jews might, in exchange for British support of Zionism, press the U.S. government to enter the war on the British side. With fears that Germany was about to do the same, Britain sought to make an immediate declaration. The Jews agreed to this quid pro quo:

> The Zionist leaders gave us [Britain] a definite promise that, if the Allies committed themselves to giving facilities for the establishment of a national home for the Jews in Palestine, they would do their best to rally Jewish sentiment and support throughout the world to the Allied cause.[1]

The Balfour Declaration, 1917

There were, however, sticking points concerning British support for a Jewish national home in Palestine. Firstly, the Sykes-Picot agreement would have to be repudiated, as would agreements with other allies about sharing control of the Middle East. However, France had good reason to acquiesce. If Russian Jews, in exchange for a promise of a national home, would press the Russian government to keep fighting, then the Germans, occupied on the Russian front, would be unable to redirect their forces against France.[2]

A second sticking point was that world Jewry was divided about the desirability of a Jewish state in Palestine. In the United States, Jewish opinion generally favored a state in Palestine while British and Palestinian Jewish opinion was more anti-Zionist.

Complex negotiations were undertaken in Britain among three groups: (1) the British government; (2) pro-Zionist Jewish groups (Chaim Weizmann, Lord Rothschild and Nahum Sokolow of the World Zionist Organization); and (3) anti-Zionist Jewish groups (Edwin Montagu, British secretary of state for India, and Claude Montefiore, private citizen). In the United States, Supreme Court Justice Louis Brandeis also supported the Zionist position while former president of the Pennsylvania Court of Common Pleas, Mayer Sulzberger, argued that it was undemocratic to impose the will of Jewish outsiders on Palestinian Arabs.

The conflict was intense. Anti-Zionist Jews debated Zionists on grounds that a political state violated Jewish values as well as the legal rights of Christian and Moslem Palestinians not represented or consulted in the negotiations. On the other hand, Zionists claimed to speak for the "Jewish people" and to have the ability to deliver worldwide Jewish support for U.S. entry into, and Russian perseverance in, the war.

The preliminary positions of the parties were as follows: (1) The British Foreign Office drafted a declaration proposing the establishment in Palestine of "a sanctuary for Jewish victims of persecution." (2) The Zionist draft by Chaim Weizmann and Mark Sykes (British undersecretary) stressed British recognition of Palestine as "the National Home of the Jewish people" and made reference to a "grant of internal autonomy to the Jewish nationality in Palestine" along with "freedom of immigration for Jews."[3] The British foreign Secretary, Arthur Balfour, a self-described ardent Zionist, then rewrote the Foreign Office statement so that it differed only slightly from the Weizmann-Sykes draft.[4] (3) Montagu, a British Jew and anti-Zionist, objected: "I assume that it means that Mohammedans and Christians are to make way for the Jews . . . you will find a population in Palestine driving out its present inhabitants, taking all the best country. . . . Palestine will become the world's Ghetto."[5] He argued further, (*a*) that racist concepts like the "Jewish people" would impair the rights of Jews in their home countries by implying that Jews are a people apart and (*b*) that the pushing of Christians and Moslems out of Palestine would be grounds for increased anti-Semitism around the world. Montefiore also objected to Zionist phrases about "Jewish nationality" and "Jewish race" as typical anti-Semitic thinking.

Weizmann was put on the defensive. He and Sykes backed down in their demand for Jewish autonomy in Palestine. The British government wrote a subsequent draft (Milner-Amery) that watered down the Zionist/Balfour version. Rather than Palestine being *the* home of the Jewish people, the Milner-Amery draft proposed that *a home in Palestine* be established and, further, that nothing should be done that might prejudice the civil and religious rights of non-Jewish communities. This version of the Balfour Declaration, backing away as it did from the idea of a Jewish state over all of Palestine, incorporated anti-Zionist Jewish sentiments through the clause about the rights and interests of non-Jews.[6]

Weizmann felt that this Milner-Avery draft "crippled" the Zionist goal. Nevertheless it stood as the near-final version of the Balfour Declaration. In final form the British secretary of state for foreign affairs, Arthur Balfour, stated in his famous 1917 Declaration to Lord Rothschild:

> His Majesty's Government views with favour the establishment in Palestine of a national home for the Jewish people and will use their best endeavours to facilitate the achievement of this object, it being clearly understood that nothing shall be done which may prejudice the civil and religious rights of existing non-Jewish communities in Palestine or the rights and political status enjoyed by Jews in any other country.

The British attempted to achieve a balance between the conflicting interests of Zionist and anti-Zionist Jews through imprecise language about "a national home" in Palestine. They believed that this language was sufficient to enlist Jewish help to end U.S. neutrality (and keep Russia fighting) while vague enough to satisfy anti-Zionist Jews and avoid *clear* violation of Britain's 1915 MacMahon commitment to Arab independence in Palestine. In one document Britain was attempting to fulfill its quid pro quo arrangements with both the Zionist Jews and the Arabs. This juggling act with incompatibles haunted Britain and the fate of the Middle East for the next thirty years.

U.S. reaction to the Balfour Declaration

Italy and France approved the Balfour Declaration in February 1918. The United States made no immediate response.[7] Woodrow Wilson supported the idea of a Jewish national home in Palestine in conformity with his humanitarian idea of a sanctuary for Jews persecuted in Russia[8] – though few Russian Jews wished to go to Palestine.[9] Wilson did not accept the Zionist plan that Palestine, in whole or part, become a Jewish state. He saw Jewish statehood in terms of British/Jewish colonial domination over Palestinian national self-determination, yet wanted persecuted Jews to have some sanctuary. In early 1918 he stated with regard to Palestinian Arab self-determination:

> The other nationalities which are now under Turkish rule should be assured an undoubted security of life and an absolutely unmolested opportunity of autonomous development. . . . Peoples may now be dominated and governed only by their own consen. . . . People and provinces are not to be bartered about from sovereignty to sovereignty as if they were mere chattels and pawns in a game, even the great game, now forever discredited, of the balance of power.[10]

Wilson and even some American Zionists opposed Weizmann's brand of unmitigated, ideological Zionism. Weizmann argued fervently for a Zionist interpretation of the Balfour Declaration, claiming that "in spite of the phrasing, the intent was clear."[11] He chose to ignore the fact that the Declaration had been designed for anti-Zionist as well as Zionist Jews. He thought that the meaning of the Balfour Declaration could be manipulated, claiming that "it would mean exactly what we would make it mean – neither more nor less."[12]

Opposing Weizmann's statist interpretation of the term *national home* was Wilson's close friend and chief representative of the American Zionists, Justice Brandeis. Brandeis felt that Jews should concentrate on economic development within a possible British protectorate in Palestine. Explicit statist efforts seemed to him maladaptive. Weizmann countered that Brandeis's form of Zionism was "Zionism without Zion." At Brandeis's request, Wilson approved the Balfour Declaration as it was worded but he boycotted Weizmann and the next Zionist Congress in 1921.[13]

History and play on the wording national home

The equivocal phrase *national home* was Britain's compromise between Zionist and anti-Zionist Jews and was designed to keep the Arabs fighting against the Ottoman Turks – implying that they need not worry about a Jewish *state*. The phrase encouraged at one moment, denied at another, the idea that *national home* meant *national state*. Winston Churchill, the colonial secretary, played both sides through this ambiguity.[14]

The equivocal word (*Heimstatte*) had first been suggested by Max Nordau (early associate of Herzl) to avoid speaking of a Jewish state (*Judenstaat*) and was adopted at the First Zionist Congress in 1897 as an intentional "circumlocution that would express all we meant, but would . . . avoid provoking Turkish rulers. . . . It was equivocal, but we all understood what it meant. To us it signified 'Judenstaat' then and it signifies the same now."[15] Weizmann's closest collaborator, Nahum Sokolov, wrote disingenuously in 1918, "It has been obstinately repeated by anti-Zionists that Zionism aims at the creation of an independent 'Jewish State.' But this is wholly fallacious. The 'Jewish State' was never a part of the Zionist programme."[16]

Arab reaction to the Balfour Declaration

Nevertheless, the equivocal phrase *national home* alarmed some Arab nationalists. The Balfour Declaration, coming on top of the discovery of the secret Sykes-Picot agreement – a secret kept from the Arabs until the Turks were defeated – was a double shock to these Arabs. To placate them, the British and French issued a misleading, mollifying declaration (November 1918) affirming "the setting up of national governments and administrations [in Syria, Palestine and Iraq] that shall derive their authority from the free exercise of the initiative and choice of the indigenous population."[17] In truth, the population of Syria had little choice in the French-controlled administration. Nor was there choice in Palestine. In a behind-the-scenes internal government memorandum in 1919, Balfour stated: "In Palestine we do not propose even to go through the form of consulting the wishes of the present inhabitants of the country"[18] – a contradiction of the 1918 Declaration and the Balfour Declaration stricture against prejudicing the rights of non-Jews:

> The four great powers are committed to Zionism and Zionism, be it right or wrong, good or bad, is rooted in age-long tradition, in present needs, in future hopes, of far profounder import than the desires and prejudices of the 700,000 Arabs who now inhabit that ancient land.[19]

Sharif Hussein (of the MacMahon-Hussein agreement) *accepted* the Balfour

Declaration as a humanitarian gesture toward Jews, believing the declaration not to be in conflict with Palestinian Arab self-determination, for the British were assuring him that Palestine would become part of a larger Arab state ("Syria").[20] British representative D. G. Hogarth was reassuring the king in January of 1918 that Britain would honor the MacMahon pledge. Hussein was told that Jewish immigration to Palestine was to occur only "in so far as is compatible with the freedom of the existing population, both economic and political. . . ."[21] Hussein also believed the 1918 Anglo-French Declaration about the choice of the indigenous population. Hence, under the assumption that the Balfour Declaration meant what it said and that Jews, in friendship and cooperation with Arabs (as Hogarth put it), would deliver their legendary economic support and political influence on behalf of Arab independence, Hussein "welcomed Jews to all Arab lands."[22]

Prince Feisal, second son of Sharif Hussein and leader of the Arab rebellion against the Ottoman Turks, went even further toward the Zionists. Weizmann and Feisal, "mindful of [their] racial kinship and ancient bonds," signed a formal agreement on January 4, 1919, to take a common stance at the peace conference. They agreed that Palestine would have guaranteed status as an enclave of "Zionist Jews" while the rest of Syria would be an Arab state. The Jews were to have a right to free immigration and settlement of the land while Arab tenant farmers would be safeguarded on their plots and assisted in their economic development.[23] Feisal added a codicil: "provided that the Arabs obtain their independence. . . ." Feisal was more interested in Zionist diplomatic help in *removing the French* from Syria than he was in preventing immigration of Jews into Palestine. He preferred this "Semitic" understanding to the League of Nations' mandate system that soon would formalize European dominance over the Middle East.

But Weizmann backed out. To make a common front at the peace table with Arabs against French domination in Syria would have alienated the British, who had specific commitments to the French in the Middle East. Weizmann decided to seek a Jewish state in Palestine through the route of British imperial power rather than make common cause with Arabs. Stranded, Feisal terminated relations with the Zionists and came to view the "Jewish National Home" as merely a subprovince within a larger Arab kingdom.[24]

The following year, 1920, Feisal assumed the kingship of Syria, in conflict with Britain's ally, France. When Feisal's older brother, Abdullah, threatened to defend him against the French, Britain made Abdulla amir of territory east of the Jordan River (Transjordan) and installed Feisal as a puppet king in Iraq.

Palestine was thereby separated from Transjordan by the stroke of Colonial Secretary Winston Churchill's pen.[25]

Survey of sentiment in Palestine – the King-Crane Commission, 1919
President Wilson appointed the King-Crane Commission to sound out the wishes of the Palestinian people liberated from Ottoman rule. In its report the commission first quoted President Wilson:

> The settlement of every question, whether of territory, of sovereignty, of economic arrangement, or of political relationship [should be] upon the basis of the free acceptance of that settlement by the people immediately concerned, and not upon the the basis of the material interest or advantage of any other nation or people which may desire a different settlement for the sake of its own exterior influence ormastery.[26]

The commission further observed:

> If that principle [self-determination] is to rule, and so the wishes of Palestine's population are to be decisive as to what is to be done with Palestine, then it is to be remembered that the non-Jewish population of Palestine – nearly nine-tenths of the whole – are emphatically against the entire Zionist program. To subject a people so minded to unlimited immigration and to steady financial and social pressure to surrender the land, would be a gross violation of the principle just quoted, and of the peoples' rights, though it kept within the forms of law.[27]

The commission then recommended:

> It can hardly be doubted that the extreme Zionist Program must be greatly modified. For "a national home for the Jewish people" is not equivalent to making Palestine into a Jewish State; nor can the erection of such Jewish State be accomplished without the gravest trespass upon the "civil and religious rights of existing non-Jewish communities in Palestine." The fact came out repeatedly in the Commission's conference with Jewish representatives, that the Zionists look forward to a practically complete dispossession of the present non-Jewish inhabitants of Palestine, by various forms of purchase.[28]

The King-Crane Commission did not reject the Balfour Declaration, only its Zionist interpretation. With 90 percent of the population emphatically against the Zionist program, the commission concluded that that program could only be carried out by force of arms.[29] Of course this conclusion was not news to the British, who had counted on the need of a "force of arms" to justify their presence as a military buffer – all the while watching over the Suez Canal and countering French influence in Syria.[30] A Jewish state or "home" needing military guard against Palestinian hostility provided the raison d'etre.[31]

President Wilson opposed these colonialist intrigues but finally was forced to compromise. He acceded to a new legal invention, the League of Nations "mandate" system, that extended, at least for the while, European domination over the Middle East.

Notes

1. Richard P. Stevens, "Zionism as a Phase of Western Imperialism," in *Transformation of Palestine,* Ibrahim Abu-Lughod, ed. (Evanston: Northwestern University Press, 1971), 49.

2. Russia did not keep fighting. Germany negotiated a peace treaty (Brest-Litovsk) with Russia in 1918 in order to focus on the war in Western Europe.

3. Leonard J. Stein, *The Balfour Declaration* (New York: Simon and Schuster, 1961), 468-9.

4. Christopher Sykes, *Crossroads to Israel* (Cleveland: World Publishing, 1965), 6. Balfour was both pro-Semitic and anti-Semitic. He embraced ideas about the superiority of Jews but, as an assimilated Jew, was negative about Jewish exclusiveness regarding community life and intermarriage. Stein, *The Balfour Declaration,* 164-5.

5. Great Britain, Public Records Office, Cab. No. 24/24 (August 23, 1917). Cited by W.T. Mallison, Jr. "The Balfour Declaration: An Appraisal in International Law," in *Transformation of Palestine.* Ibrahim Abu-Lughod, ed. (Evanston: North-western University Press, 1971), 74-6.

6. Stein, *The Balfour Declaration,* 522.

7. Being at war with Germany, but not Turkey, the United States chose not to interfere with matters related to Turkish sovereignty, as the Balfour Declaration clearly did.

8. For example, fifty Jews were killed in the infamous Kishinev massacre of 1903. Pogroms in Russia related to anti-Semitism, governmental discouragement of local nationalism among Russia's heterogeneous peoples and tsarist opposition to the Jewish socialistic movement. Perhaps 2 million Jews fled west between 1890 and 1920.

9. Russian Jews preferred to go to the United States or Europe where full civil and political rights had been in force since the mid-1800's.

10. U.S. Department of State, *Papers Relating to the Foreign Relations of the*

United States [1918], Vol.I, Suppl. 1 (Washington, D.C., 1933): 16, 112. Cited in Mallison, "The Balfour Declaration," 104-5.

11. Cited in Mallison, "The Balfour Declaration," 96.

12. Cited in Mallison, "The Balfour Declaration," 86.

13. Rufus Learsi, *Fulfillment: The Epic Story of Zionism* (Cleveland: World Publishing Co., 1951), 191.

14. Colonial Secretary Winston Churchill pretended in 1919 to "clarify" the term in order to assuage the fears of the Moslem-Christian Associates, pointing out that "Palestine [was] to be '*a* national home' not '*the* national home', a great difference in meaning. The establishment of a national home does not mean a Jewish Government to dominate the Arabs." Government Memorandum, August 1919, Documents on Foreign Policy, 1st series, Vol. IV. Cited in Sykes, *Crossroads to Israel*, 50.

15. Sykes, *Crossroads to Israel*, 11.

16. Sykes, *Crossroads to Israel*, 11.

17. Sykes, *Crossroads to Israel*, 5.

18. Sykes, *Crossroads to Israel*, 5.

19. Sykes, *Crossroads to Israel*, 5.

20. Sharif Hussein saw, as did the Jews, that riding British imperialism was the key to national self-determination in the Middle East. But being the majority and indigenous population, Arabs saw no need to eliminate the Jewish minority.

21. Sykes, *Crossroads to Israel*, 29.

22. Sykes, *Crossroads to Israel*, 30.

23. Howard Sachar, *A History of Israel: From the Rise of Zionism to Our Time*, Vol. I (New York: Knopf, 1986), 121.

24. Sachar, *History,* Vol. I, 122.

25. Transjordan did not become independent until 1946. It was severed from Palestine in 1923 while still a part of Britain's League of Nations mandate. For the history of British and French goals in the Middle East – importantly keeping out the Russians – see David Fromkin, *A Peace to End All Peace: Creating the Modern Middle East, 1914-1922*. New York: Henry Holt, 1989.

26. U.S. Department of State, *Papers Relative to the Foreign Relations of the United States* [1919], Vol. XII (Washington, D.C., 1947), 793.

27. U.S. Department of State, *Papers Relative* [1919], 793.

28. U.S. Department of State, *Papers Relative* [1919], 792.

29. In 1919 the Jewish population in Palestine was 65,000, or just under 10 percent of the total. A minority of this minority favored the establishment of the Zionist plan. In the 1922 census, Palestine was 11 percent Jewish, 9 percent Christian, and 80 percent Muslim. Sykes, *Crossroads to Israel*, 12; J.C. Hurewitz, *The Struggle for Palestine* (New York: Schocken, 1976), 27; Sachar, *History*, Vol. I, 130.

30. Sykes, *Crossroads to Israel*, 75.

31. Sachar, *History*, Vol. I, 119.

Chapter 3

The League of Nations Mandate System (1922)

The Mandate System: European control of the Middle East

The spoils of war have traditionally been garnered through protectorships over or direct annexation of occupied territory. Britain and France expected protectorships to ensure their permanent control over military and foreign affairs in the Middle East. On the other hand, President Wilson sought independence for liberated subject nationalities and rejected the idea of protectorships. He was forced to compromise. The form of that compromise was a new legal entity fashioned by the League of Nations called the "mandate."

A mandate differed from a protectorate in that: (1) the mandate authority (the controlling state) had a primary obligation to *facilitate the self-government* of the territory's inhabitants; (2) the mandate was to be *temporary*, to terminate when the inhabitants were ready for independent statehood; and (3) the mandate authority was *accountable* to the League. Former German and Ottoman colonies were ranked by their degree of readiness to assume self-government. The "Class A" territories in the Middle East (Syria, Lebanon, Iraq and Palestine) were considered to be nearly ready for self-government, i.e., statehood. All Class A territories except Palestine did, in fact, become states when the mandate powers withdrew.

The mandate system only partially satisfied Wilson's ideal of nonacquisition of territory by war and national self-determination. By permitting delay of national independence for a territory's indigenous people, it perpetuated European dominance for an indefinite future.

Obstacles to Britain's exercise of mandate authority in Palestine

Britain's high commissioner, Herbert Samuel, had complete administrative and legislative authority over Palestine. He was responsible for establishing nationality (citizenship) laws and for gaining the cooperation of Jews and Arabs in sharing administrative functions. The obstacles to cooperation and establishment of self-government in Palestine were, however, formidable.

First, the Palestinian Arabs rejected the mandate system outright. They demanded an independent state with a democratic, parliamentary form of government, an idea rejected at the San Remo Peace Conference of 1920.[1] Some Arab leaders were willing to acquiesce to a U.S. but not British mandate authority.

Second, Britain insisted that the Balfour Declaration be introduced into the text of the mandate. Arab acceptance of the mandate meant acceptance of the Balfour Declaration. Further, Arab acceptance of a British-imposed constitution in Palestine, also grounded in mandate authority, would have meant the same. Consequently, Arabs opposed both the mandate system and any potential constitution deriving from it.[2]

Third, the Jews would not accept the concept of a democratic self-government in Palestine since 90 percent of the population was not Jewish. Democratic government would be acceptable only after massive Jewish immigration or removal of the Moslem and Christian populations.[3]

Fourth, if a Jewish *national home* meant a state existing for Jews, as some Arabs suspected, then that state would violate Article 2 of the mandate requirements to "safeguard the civil and religious rights of all the inhabitants of Palestine, irrespective of race and religion." A Jewish state, whether theocratic (religious law dictating civil law) or ethnic/racial (the government preferentially advancing Jewish interests) would deny equal treatment, opportunity and rights to Moslems and Christians.

The impossible mandate

Fundamentally, the mandate embraced irreconcilable goals. Had Jewish *national home* meant Jewish *community within Palestine,* then democratic self-government *would* have been possible and acceptable to Palestinian Arabs. But that was not what it meant to either Jew or Arab. The equivocal phrase could mask but not alter the fact that a Jewish state and national self-determination for Palestinian Arabs were incompatible. Indeed, a Jewish state conflicted with the whole rationale of the mandate system, i.e. establishment of democratic

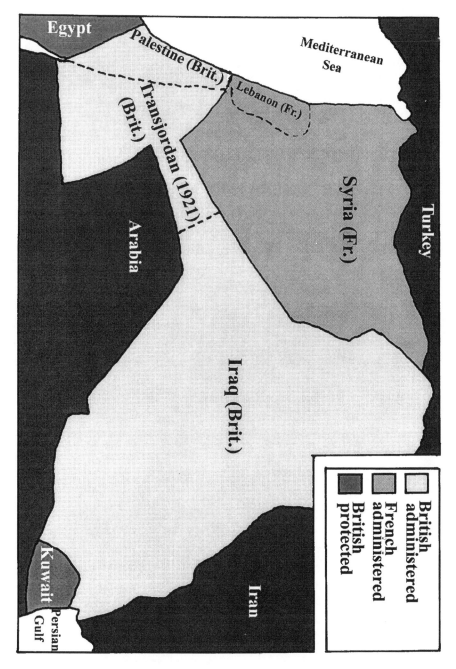

1920 San Remo Allocation of Mandates

self-government by an indigenous population.

It was not this contradiction, however, that led to the collapse of the mandate. Initially it was the bitter struggle of Arab nationalists against Jewish immigration and land purchases that precluded cooperation and created violence in Palestine – a violence which the British had correctly anticipated, and needed, to justify their presence. But what the British had not anticipated was that the violence would be directed against *them*, first by the Palestinian Arabs in the 1930s and then by the Jews in the 1940s. This violence against British authority delivered the coup de grâce to the mandate.

Conflict over immigration and displacement from the land

The Zionists knew that whatever the British might do for them in Palestine, a Jewish state, like any state, would require both people and territory. In Palestine they had neither.[4] A Jewish state, should it come into existence by fiat, would be unable to rule over a vast Moslem and Christian population that together owned virtually all the land in Palestine. Consequently, "it was of utmost importance . . . that the Jews should come to outnumber the rest of the population, and to acquire ownership of most of the land. Only when these objectives were realized would the Zionists demand self-governing institutions for the country as a whole."[5] The mandate text ambiguously supported Jewish immigration.[6]

Palestinian Arabs were unable to stem the waves of Jewish immigration and strategic land purchases. From 1917 to 1935 the Jewish population rose from about 60,000 to over 400,000.[7] In 1935 alone there were more than 60,000 new immigrants.[8] To accommodate this influx, the Jewish Agency (Jewish leadership in pre-state Palestine) and the Jewish labor organization ("Histadrut") boycotted Arab labor.[9]

The quantity of land purchased by Jews was not vast (7.6 percent by 1949) but that land was the most fertile as well as being strategically chosen to comprise the nucleus for a Jewish state.[10] More than $360 million for land purchases poured in from the Diaspora between 1919 and 1936.[11] A resulting inflation of land values made it relatively easy to buy land from poor peasants or foreign owners of large tracts at prices exorbitant by local standards. Ottoman land reform in the Tanzimat period also produced unfair opportunities for Zionists to purchase land from absentee landlords. Sales were often kept secret so that Palestinians could avoid the opprobrium of being "land sellers" to Jews.[12] "Palestinian Arab politicians [as well as notables and religious leaders] who were landowners selling land to Jews did not dwell on the land issue lest their own deep involvement become part of public discussion."[13] This "cooptation of Arab elites [*effendi* class] was achieved by means of careful distribution of favors, privileges, and special dispensations."[14] It was not difficult to displace a semi-feudal people long under Ottoman rule, heavily taxed, indebted at usurious rates (between 50 and 120 percent per year) and working the land without clear title.[15]

But mounting social problems and unrest were created by this enlarging population of landless Palestinians (some 30 percent of the rural population by 1930).[16] Arab nationalists were unable to stop land sales and the British were unable to protect Arab peasants from eviction. Partly this was due to Arab peasant mistrust and fear of British authority, resulting in failure to make appeal.

Palestinian Arab terror in 1929

Though Jewish immigration and land purchase alarmed Arab nationalists, violence was not sparked until the 16th Zionist Congress in Zurich in 1929. Closely watched by Palestinian leaders, this congress was a major international event that featured a spectacular array of eminent Jews, including Albert Einstein. At this congress the Jewish Agency was transformed into an essentially Zionist organization.[17]

Ze'ev Vladimir Jabotinsky, a commanding personality (sometimes dubbed "the father of Jewish terrorism") gave a speech to the 16th Congress which threw the Arabs into a panic, stating directly that a national home meant a Jewish state and that a Jewish majority would be achieved by the "great colonizing masses." Arabs were convinced that the Jews were mounting a worldwide conspiracy and a massive attack on them.

Days after the Zionist Congress, Jabotinsky's followers held an anti-Arab demonstration in Jerusalem, loudly demanding ownership of the Western (Wailing) Wall, a religious shrine for Arabs and Jews alike, and took an oath to defend it at all costs. Large numbers of Arab peasants came into Jerusalem with clubs and knives, perhaps organized by nationalist leaders. The police and the British army proved inadequate to maintain order. Murders occurred in Jerusalem and Haifa. An infamous, brutal massacre of sixty Jews, including children, with fifty wounded, took place in Hebron. Other atrocities were committed in Safed where twenty Jews were murdered. Order was not restored for two weeks. In the course of this uprising, 133 Jews were killed, 339 wounded; 116 Arabs were killed, 232 wounded – largely by the police, not by the Jews.

Britain's Shaw Commission investigated. It was concluded that the main cause of the uprising related to the landless and discontented Arab class created by Zionist expansion. The commission recommended that immigration be controlled to prevent repetition of the mass immigration of the mid-1920s and that eviction of Arab tenants be rigidly held in check until a thorough land survey could be completed.[18]

Further Arab violence in 1936

Several years later, between 1932 and 1935, Arab frustration over stateless-ness and Jewish immigration again moved toward violence. Hitler was in power in Germany and 145,000 Jews immigrated to Palestine, an unprecedented number. At the time no one anticipated the Holocaust, yet a Jewish national home was a pressing need. At the very least, Palestine was a symbol of self-help and self-respect at a hideous moment of national degradation for European Jews.

It seemed to Palestinians that Hitler was being used as a pretext: that Jewish immigration was not so much a humanitarian cause as a Zionist exploitation of Nazism to establish a Jewish state at their expense. Regarding this perception, Sykes has observed: "It had this important element of truth: that from the very beginning of the Nazi disaster the Zionist leadership determined to wrest political advantage from the tragedy."[19] The Palestinians argued that only 12 percent of the immigrants were actually coming from Germany, the same proportion as before Hitler came to power. Moreover, they observed that the British, with their larger and richer country, had permitted fewer than 3,000 Jewish immigrants in the same period. Not being Europeans, the Palestinians saw themselves as in no way responsible for the breakdown of civilization in Europe and felt wrongly forced to forego national independence just because Europe refused to help the Jews.

At this time the British high commissioner made an attempt to institute a constitution and a democratizing representative council in Palestine. Palestinian Arabs, skeptical, nevertheless inclined toward acceptance. The Jews rejected the effort. The Palestinians continued to press for national sovereignty and a halt to Jewish immigration and organized a countrywide strike and boycott of Jewish goods that only heightened their own economic suffering.

Once Jewish immigration went beyond the number legally permitted by the British, the Palestinian Arabs gradually broke into armed rebellion in 1936. In the first weeks, Jews were the target of atrocities. For the next three years the

British army was the target.[20] The British employed eighteen battalions and two squadrons of RAF airplanes to bomb Palestinian villages, killing 5,000-10,000 people by 1939.[21]

The 1937 Peel Commission concluded, as had other British commissions, that it was the Jewish Agency's Zionist intention to establish a state, not just a national home, that was largely responsible for Arab violence. The commission saw no chance of Arab-Jewish national reconciliation. It recommended an end to the British mandate and a partitioning of Palestine into separate Jewish and Arab states, the latter to be united with Transjordan.[22] Both states would be required to make military alliances with Britain in conformity with British strategic interests.

The Palestinian Arabs rejected this plan because it called for a Jewish state. Unsure, the Jews debated about whether to hold out for all of Palestine now or to accept the Peel Commission's proposed boundaries as a first step. As David Ben-Gurion stated it, "The debate has not been for or against the indivisibility of Eretz Israel. No Zionist can forgo the smallest portion of Eretz Israel. The debate was over which of two routes would lead quicker to the common goal."[23]

Changing British geostrategic needs suddenly favor the Palestinian cause

The conflict between Palestinian Arabs and Jews took a sudden turn with the onslaught of World War II. British strategic interests in Palestine shifted radically. Britain now needed oil from surrounding Arab nations to conduct war and thus needed to reverse the hostility in the Arab world toward Britain's violent quashing of the Arab rebellion in Palestine. Britain sought this chiefly by rejection of a Jewish state in Palestine. The shocked Jews suddenly found themselves undermined by imperial British power, much as the Arabs had by the Balfour Declaration. It remained obvious to both Arabs and Jews that British geopolitical needs were the key to self-determination. Now the Jews were in sorry shape.

Notes

1. This conference specified treaty conditions between the Allies and Turkey.

2. Weizmann proposed that the mandate declare unequivocally that Jews alone had a right to Palestine, but his phrase "the historic rights of the Jews to Palestine" was excluded from mandate language. W.T. Mallison, Jr. "The Balfour Declaration: An Appraisal in International Law," in *Transformation of Palestine,* Ibrahim

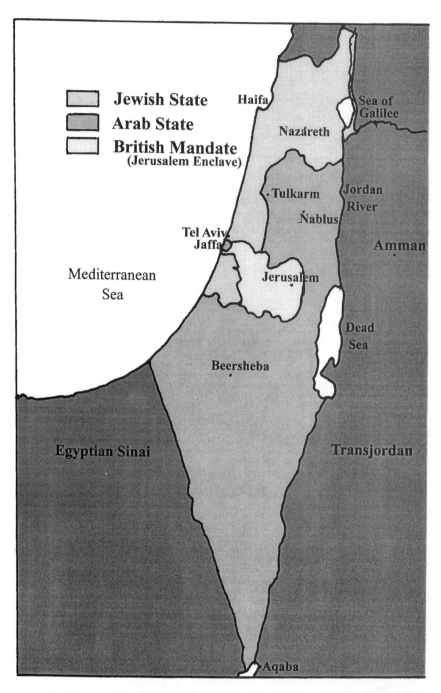

Jewish State
Arab State
British Mandate
(Jerusalem Enclave)

Haifa
Sea of Galilee
Nazáreth

Mediterranean Sea

Tulkarm
Jordan River
Ñablus

Tel Aviv
Jaffa

Amman

Jerusalem

Dead Sea

Beersheba

Egyptian Sinai

Transjordan

Aqaba

1937 Peel Commission Plan

Abu-Lughod, ed. (Evanston: Northwestern University Press, 1971), 98.

3. J.C. Hurewitz, *The Struggle for Palestine* (New York: Schocken, 1976), 21.

4. At the time of the Balfour Declaration (1917) there were 55,000 to 65,000 Jews in Palestine, up from 12,000 in 1845, 5 to 10 percent of the total population. Less then 1 percent of the land in Palestine was owned by Jews. Howard Sachar, *A History of Israel: From the Rise of Zionism to Our Time*, Vol. I (New York: Knopf, 1986), 113; Christopher Sykes, *Crossroads to Israel* (Cleveland: World Publishing, 1965), 12; Hurewitz, *The Struggle for Palestine*, 27.

5. Hurewitz, *The Struggle for Palestine*, 21.

6. Embracing incompatible goals, the mandate necessarily contained ambiguous provisions as to how to achieve those goals. It sought both to facilitate Jewish immigration "under suitable conditions" and to limit Jewish immigration so as to "ensure that the rights and position of other sections of the population are not prejudiced."

7. Hurewitz, *Struggle for Palestine*, 27. From 1917 to 1920, the Jewish population increased from 60,000 to 280,000.

8. Peel Commission Report, Parliamentary Papers, Cmd. 5893 (H.M.S.O., 1938).

9. As a result, for the same jobs, Arab workers were paid one-third to one-half as much as Jewish workers in 1935. N. Weinstock, "Le sionisme contre Israel" (Paris: F. Maspero, 1969) translated in Association of Arab-American University Graduates Information Paper No. 15 (Detroit, Michigan, April 1975). In his Royal Commission report of 1930, Sir John Hope Simpson wrote, "The principle of the persistent and deliberate boycott of Arab labor in the colonies is not only contrary to the Mandate, but it is in addition a constant and increasing source of danger to the country." The boycotting of Arab labor had a longer history – in 1912, Yemenite Jews were imported to compete with Arab labor. Baruch Kimmerling, *Zionism and Economy* (Cambridge, Mass.: Schenkman Publishing, 1983), 50.

10. Of those land sales to Jews which were officially recorded, 142,000 acres were sold by 1920, 355,000 acres by 1939 and 500,000 acres by 1948. Yehoshua Porath, "The Land Problem as a Factor in Relations among Arabs, Jews and the Mandatory Government," in *The Palestinians and the Middle East Conflict*, Gabriel Ben-Dor, ed. (Ramat Gan, Israel: Turtledove Publishing, 1979), 509; Kenneth W. Stein, *The Land Question in Palestine, 1917-1939* (Chapel Hill: University of North Carolina Press, 1984), 3-4.

11. Hurewitz, *Struggle for Palestine*, 30.

12. "Jewish philanthropic or public organizations – such as the Palestine Jewish Colonization Association (established and owned by Baron Edmund de Rothschild, and later known as PICA), Palestine Land Development Co. and the Jewish National Fund (the last two established by the World Zionist Organization) – offered to buy lands at prices substantially above their market value, the big Arab landowners were eager to take advantage of this unexpected windfall and sold large tracts to the Jews." Porath, "The Land Problem," 508.

13. Stein, *The Land Question*, 66.

14. Ian Lustick, *Arabs in the Jewish State* (Austin: University of Texas Press, 1980), 203.

15. Palestinians were often unable to prove ownership because registry of land in Palestine had subjected the owner to service in the Ottoman army. A.L. Tibawi, *A Modern History of Syria* (London: Macmillan, 1969), 176.

16. Royal Commission's Hope-Simpson Report, cited in Sykes, *Crossroads to Israel,* 115.

17. Originally the Jewish Agency had been an administrative organization which, in cooperation with the British government of Palestine, was to assist in the establishment of a national home. But at the 16th Zionist Congress in Zurich in 1929, the Jewish Agency became, through internal subterfuge, an essentially Zionist organization and, by 1937, totally Zionist.

18. Sykes, *Crossroads to Israel,* 113.

19. Sykes, *Crossroads to Israel,* 137.

20. In the initial six months of fighting, 187 Moslems, 10 Christian Arabs, 80 Jews, and 28 British were killed. Sykes, *Crossroads to Israel,* 150.

21. The Arab rebellion was largely against the British, though some actions were taken against the Jews, especially their property. By and large the Jews did not take to arms. However, unofficial Jewish terrorist organizations did arise, most notably the Orde Wingate-led Special Night Squads and the Jewish terrorist organization, the Irgun, which detonated land mines in the Arab fruit market, killing seventy-four in July 1938. During the three-year rebellion, estimates ranged from 5,000 to 15,000 Arabs dead, some fraction of which was due to conflicts between competing Arab nationalist groups.

22. Transjordan was a large, sparsely populated tract east of the Jordan River, originally considered part of mandated Palestine but made into a separate state in 1923 by Britain. The Peel Commission also recommended a neutral enclave around Jerusalem and Bethlehem under continued British mandate.

23. Sykes, *Crossroads to Israel,* 174.

Chapter 4

Britain Curbs Jewish Statehood and Immigration (1938–1942)

Britain's new strategic needs

While the British government accepted the 1937 judgment of Lord Peel's commission that the Arabs and Jews could not be reconciled, it rejected the commission's recommendation to partition Palestine into two separate states. Yet storm clouds were gathered over Europe and Britain was anxious to find a way to end Arab-Jewish tensions. To this end, Britain called a conference of Arabs and Jews (the St. James Palace Conference) in the first weeks of 1939 and proposed a binational (joint) state. Neither Arab nor Jew accepted the proposal and the conference ended in failure on the day Hitler's army invaded Czechoslovakia, March 17, 1939.

To wage war against Germany, Britain needed oil from the surrounding Arab countries. The task of winning Arab loyalty was formidable indeed since Britain had harshly quashed the Palestinian Arab rebellion (1936-1939). Moreover, the Germans were pointing out that it was Britain and France that had deprived Arab countries of their independence, not Germany.

Britain's White Paper of 1939

To court the Arabs, the British took several turnaround steps. The first, during the St. James Palace Conference, was to publish an accurate translation of that long-suppressed 1915 MacMahon-Hussein correspondence that pledged Arab national independence in "Syria" (including Palestine). Using the face-saving, minimalist language of diplomacy, the British now conceded that they "were not free to dispose of Palestine without regard for the wishes and interests of the inhabitants of Palestine."[1]

Britain's second step was to publish the famous White Paper of 1939 – an instrument which, in one stroke, undermined Zionist demands for a state. The white paper had three major provisions:

(1) A *state of Palestine was to be established* within ten years. The British declared their intention to follow the "spirit of the Mandate system" by developing self-governing institutions in a state in which Arab and Jew would jointly share governmental authority. A specifically Jewish state was ruled out unequivocally.

(2) *Jewish immigration was to be limited.* An indefinite increase in Jewish immigration that was "against the strongly expressed will of the Arab people" was judged to be tantamount to "rule by force" and contrary to the spirit of the mandate. Consequently, only 75,000 Jews would be allowed to immigrate over the next five years – partly as "a contribution towards the solution of the Jewish refugee problem."

(3) *Land sales would be limited.* The British would regulate the sale of land with a view to mitigating the problem of the "considerable landless Arab population."

The White Paper of 1939 further expressed regret over "misunderstandings" about some phrases in the MacMahon correspondence and made provision for safeguarding holy places, for the special position of a Jewish national home (not a state) and, of course, for agreements concerning British commercial and strategic military interests.

The Jewish rebuttal was that: (1) the primary purpose of the mandate was to secure the establishment of a Jewish national home, not to develop self-governing institutions,[2] and (2) that self-government should come only after demographic change through Jewish immigration and land purchase.[3]

Reactions to the 1939 White Paper

The Arabs had mixed reactions. They saw various loopholes concerning immigration and the "special position" of a Jewish national home. They saw in specific provisions about "self-governance" too much British influence and denied, on fundamental grounds, the right of Britain to dictate the terms of Palestinian Arab national sovereignty.

The Jews decried Britain's "betrayal" of them and "appeasement" of the Arabs. Given the way Zionists construed the Balfour Declaration, they had good reason. The fact remained that both Arabs and Jews had relied, to differing extents, on British imperial power as the giver of all things. As such, both were vulnerable to disappointment. While both made claims about their "rights" as *the* indigenous people of Palestine – the Jews, by promise of God; the Arabs, by virtue of millennial occupation[4] – both knew that British imperial power was the key to statehood.

Arab attitudes toward Britain during World War II

Britain's 1939 release of the MacMahon-Hussein letters and the White Paper was reasonably successful in its primary goal of keeping Palestinian Arabs and the surrounding Arab countries neutral with regard to the war. Undoubtedly the Arab countries were attracted by a German pledge of Arab independence after the war, but Britain matched that by further courting of Arabs – recognizing the independence of Syria and Lebanon in 1941. However, the British never succeeded in winning the Arab heart. While the Arab rebellion in Palestine had ended, that had been due more to a matter of economic exhaustion and fractional disorganization than a coming to terms with the British. The Arab enlistees in Britain's wartime army were unenthusiastic fighters. On the other hand, Jewish enlistees had a real need to fight with the British against the Nazis. They were mindful, too, that their cooperation might induce Britain to scrap the infamous 1939 White Paper.

Strain between Britain and the Jews over a Jewish army

Nevertheless, relations between the Jews and the British were not easy. Strain existed over the question of an independent Jewish army. While some Jews had joined the British army, the Jewish Agency wanted a Jewish army under its own flag, not only to fight the Nazis but to later compel by force a Zionist solution on Palestine as need be.

Britain judged the military value of Jewish help to be insufficient to outweigh the political liability of inciting Arab upset at the prospect of an official Jewish army. Moreover a Jewish army would, it was thought, probably increase Jewish terrorism against Palestinian Arabs.[5] Britain thus rejected the idea of a separate Jewish army. The Jewish Agency responded by trying to organize committees in the United States and Britain to help establish a Jewish army but was unsuccessful.[6] Still, military training in the British army and a sequestering of British arms proved to be invaluable to the Zionist cause after the war. Some 43,000 British-trained Jews from Palestine were under arms by the end of 1942, most selected by the Jewish Agency. Many later became members of the Haganah, an illegal Jewish army under mandate law.[7]

Strain between Britain and the Jews over immigration

Immigration was a key to the creation of a Jewish state and, of course, a source of distress to the Arab population for that reason. Yet the flight of the Jews from Nazi persecution forcefully introduced humanitarian considerations into the conflict. Britain was strictly enforcing the immigration policy announced in the 1939 White Paper in order that Arabs recognize that Britain was not giving away Palestine to the Jews. The Jews strenuously objected.[8]

The background of this clash dated from the year before. At the 1938 international conference at Evian, France, thirty-one nations met to determine their mutual readiness to accept refugees (mostly Jewish). Neither the United States nor Britain acted honorably, each limiting immigration to only 100,000 Jews over the next three years. The tiny Dominican Republic offered as much. It is true that at that time the number of potential refugees in need of rescue seemed limited to possible victims of Germany's Nuremberg Laws (about 600,000 Jews). No one guessed that nearly six million European and Polish Jews, as well as an equal number of Polish Catholics, Slavs, Gypsies, homosexuals and political prisoners, would be gassed, shot or starved to death.[9] In retrospect the limited international offers of rescue are painful to behold, if not morally offensive. The Evian Conference was a sorry showing.

If Evian demonstrated the parochial interests and selfishness of the civilized nations, the Zionists themselves were not free of blame. They made no outcry at Evian, wanting Jews to be settled in Palestine, not in Britain, the United States or elsewhere.[10] What Evian did support was the Zionist demand for immigration into Palestine – Palestine as the only answer to Hitler.[11] At the same time Evian gave support to an Arab objection that large Western nations would not inconvenience themselves with a relatively small number of refugees – whereas that refugee population was large enough to substantially alter the population and politics of Palestine. The British had little rebuttal.

Jews press for immigration, land and a Jewish commonwealth, the Biltmore Program(1942)

To reverse restrictions imposed by Britain's white paper,[12] the Jews employed several strategies. They applied diplomatic pressure on Britain, the United States and the Soviet Union; they stirred American public opinion by falsely but effectively suggesting that the British sank or turned back Jewish refugee ships.[13] But the chief strategy against the white paper was a clear and bold act of political rebellion in 1942, the Biltmore Program. The Jews demanded the *immediate establishment of a Jewish commonwealth over all of Palestine with full control over immigration.* This program, drafted at the Biltmore Hotel Conference in New York, was Ben-Gurion's bid to overthrow the British White Paper of 1939 through American influence, and more specifically, that of the world's largest and wealthiest Jewish community. While Chaim Weizmann argued more cautiously for gradualism and against immediate statehood, the Biltmore Program did gain significant American public support.[14]

Later that year, in mid-1942, reliable information from the Polish government in exile about the Nazi death camps was reaching the West. The issue of Jewish statehood would have had great and immediate consequence had there been some way of getting Jews out of Europe. Tragically, there wasn't.

Notes

1. Great Britain, Parliamentary Papers. Cmd. 5974. Report of a Committee to consider correspondence between Sir Henry MacMahon and Sharif of Mecca in 1915 and 1916. (London, March 16, 1939), 10-11. Cited in J.C. Hurewitz, *The Struggle for Palestine* (New York: Schocken, 1976), 99.
2. The Passfield White Paper of 1930 denied this interpretation of the primary purpose of the mandate and explicitly stated that the policy was one of "equality of obligation" to Arabs and Jews.
3. Hurewitz, *Struggle,* 21, 104. The Jewish argument seems to imply acceptance of the Arab position that an existing people have a right to self-governance. But the Jewish argument goes on to suggest that it is legitimate to deprive an existing population of self-government while seeking to change the nature of that population.
4. The Jewish claim to be *the* indigenous people of Palestine, and thereby in rightful possession of Palestine, unwittingly validated that same form of argument advanced by Palestinian Arabs. As descendants of Abraham, the Arabs could, like the Jews, make a biblical claim to Palestine as a land promised by God to Abraham

and descendents – Arabs descending from Ishmael, Jews from Jacob, both of them Abraham's sons. However, Arabs considered their historical and continuous occupation of Palestine to be the stronger claim.

5. The British feared that their failure to control Jewish terrorism would turn Palestinian Arabs against them. Accordingly, the British induced the Irgun to desist from hostilities toward Arabs and to provide intelligence on enemy agents in exchange for lenient treatment of arrested Irgunists. In 1940, the British released imprisoned Irgunists, including Abraham Stern, who went on to form a more radical terrorist group, the Stern Gang.

6. Most American Jews thought it best that military units remain part of the British army. Non-Zionist Jews in Britain considered that a Jewish army would add to the difficulties of winning the war and suspected it was politically motivated for a future fight for a Jewish state.

7. Some 4 percent of the Jewish population served in the British armed forces, and another 5 percent performed police and Home Guard functions. The British also trained 1,500 Jews as saboteur-commandos (later, the elite "Palmah" unit of the Haganah) for use in the event of German occupation of Palestine. The Haganah was a loose militia in the 1920s, became more disciplined in the 1930s and its use by the British during World War II conferred on it a kind of quasi-legality.

8. The British also believed that illegal Jewish immigration into Palestine from Germany, with the consent or initiative of the Gestapo, was designed to embarrass the British with the Arabs. Britain thought that Germany could be sneaking German-Jewish intelligence agents and saboteurs into Palestine.

9. Martin Gilbert, *The Macmillan Atlas of the Holocaust* (New York: Macmillan, 1982), 11. "In addition to the six million Jewish men, women and children who were murdered at least an equal number of non-Jews was also killed . . . by deliberate, planned murder."

10. The attempt at Evian to provide emigration for Jews "was in no sense congenial to the spirit of Zionism. The reason is not obscure. If the thirty-one nations had done their duty and shown hospitality to those in dire need, then the pressure on the National Home and the heightened enthusiasm of Zionism within Palestine would both have been relaxed. This was the last thing that the Zionist leaders wished for." Christopher Sykes, *Crossroads to Israel* (Cleveland: World Publishing, 1965), 188-9.

11. At the height of the refugee problem during the middle of the war, when Roosevelt proposed to find a permanent solution for displaced Jews on a worldwide basis, Zionists bitterly attacked his proposal to open the doors of many nations to Jewish refugees after the war. Ernst, Morris, *So Far So Good* (New York: Harpers, 1948), 175.

12. Ways were found to circumvent the White Paper restrictions on land sales in prohibited areas. Sykes, *Crossroads to Israel,* 215n. 19.

13. For example, the British refused entry into Palestine of the illegal refugee ship

La Patria with intention of sending it on to the British island of Mauritius. For political reasons the Jewish Agency wanted it to land in Palestine and, through the Haganah, blew a hole in the ship – presumably intending only to disable the engines. It sank at a cost of 252 lives. The Agency declared the sinking to be an act done by the passengers as a mass suicidal protest against the British. Despite many claims otherwise, no cases are known in which refugee ships were sent back to Axis-occupied countries after April 1939. Sykes, *Crossroads to Israel,* 225-7.

14. In effect the Biltmore Program constituted a declaration not only that the White Paper was invalid but, by brushing aside the notion of a national home and the rights of non-Jews, that the Balfour Declaration, too, was invalid.

Chapter 5

Britain Withdraws from Palestine (1948)

U. S. strategic interests in the Middle East

By 1943 Britain and the Jews were at serious odds. The Biltmore Program had gone nowhere; Jewish groups were smuggling in immigrants and engaging in terrorist attacks aimed at pushing the British out of Palestine. The British sought U.S. help, thinking the United States had sufficient influence to control Jewish immigration and terrorism. But the Jews, too, sought U.S. help, thinking that the United States had sufficient influence to remove the British from Palestine. Both were partly wrong because neither side appreciated the existence of opposing forces *within* the United States between the government and the people.

The *U.S. government* (particularly the State, War and Navy Departments) wanted control of Middle Eastern oil, military bases, commercial air routes and communications, and had no desire to alienate Arab nations by supporting Zionist demands for increased immigration. Until the war, Saudi and Kuwaiti oil had been mostly a commercial matter to American oil companies. Suddenly oil was a vital resource for national defense. The U.S. government went into political high gear. Between 1943 and 1947, the United States poured $50 to $100 million in lend-lease, loans and credits to ensure the stability of the Saudi government and the U.S. position there. Saudi Arabia became a virtual U.S. protectorate. It was equally evident to Britain and the Soviets that whatever the claims and counterclaims about a right of self-determination in Palestine, it was imprudent to alienate Arab countries by supporting the Zionist cause.

On the other hand, the *U.S. public* was behind the Zionists. A growing awareness of the Holocaust, coupled with the Zionist claim that a Jewish state was the only appropriate response to that Holocaust, touched the U.S. public. Both Franklin Delano Roosevelt and Thomas Dewey supported the Zionist program in their 1944 presidential campaigns. State legislatures were adopting pro-Zionist resolutions and both the public and Congress called for a Jewish state. Jewish terrorist groups seeking to end British rule felt free by 1943, once Rommel was defeated in North Africa and posed no threat to Palestine, to directly attack the British. They found sponsorship and financing from the U.S public.[1]

Because U.S. strategic interests conflicted with public sentiment, President Roosevelt followed in the duplicitous footsteps of the British thirty years before, campaigning as a pro-Zionist while secretly assuring the king of Saudi Arabia that he would not support the Jews against the Arabs.

Britain and the United States conflict over immigration in Palestine

When Roosevelt died in April 1945, Harry S Truman inherited the strategy of encouraging both sides. Aware of the need not to inflame Arabs, he nonetheless repeatedly recommended to the British that they admit into Palestine 100,000 Jewish refugees (known as displaced persons, or DPs), carefully refusing to offer the U.S. military help that would have been needed to impose that immigration on an objecting Arab population. Britain had promised the Palestinians that it would stop illegal immigration and feared that Jewish immigration would simply increase the ranks of Jewish terrorists attacking British facilities and forces. The Haganah was already fighting the British.

The British accused Truman of moralizing to them about refugees in order to play politics with the U.S. Jewish vote. Britain argued more generally that the accommodation of European DPs was a humanitarian and worldwide issue involving non-Jews as well as Jews – not a narrow Zionist political issue of getting Jews to Palestine.[2] To be fair, Truman was aware of this and did, in fact, try to aid both non-Jewish and Jewish DPs by advancing a policy designed to expedite changes in U.S. immigration laws. But these laws, designed to impede immigration and under the control of Congress, were not easy to revise. More to the point, the U.S. public and Congress, preferring the Palestine solution, resisted Truman's efforts to increase U.S. immigration.[3] America's enthusiasm for Jewish immigration did not translate to U.S. soil. As one historian observed, "It seems that history will record a regret that politicians and publicists in

America who clamored for an enormous Jewish exodus to Palestine did not give the same support to Mr. Truman's [U.S. immigration] initiative in December, 1945."[4]

Jewish terrorism, the means of nationalism in the Middle East

The British, frustrated by Truman's pressuring of them to admit more Jews into Palestine, were far more outraged by Jewish terrorism. This terrorism was aimed at ousting the British in order to facilitate Jewish immigration in a de facto Jewish state. Britain responded with an ultimatum: it would not admit Truman's recommended 100,000 immigrants "unless and until" the Haganah (some 60,000 strong by now)[5] disbanded and surrendered its arms. The Jewish Agency, too, was to cooperate in apprehending Jewish terrorists.

But in 1946, the illegal Haganah was increasingly in collusion with Jewish terrorist groups – notably, the Irgun and LEHI (Fighters for the Freedom of Israel and former Stern Group) led by Menachem Begin and Yitzhak Shamir, respectively.[6] Britain was virtually at war with these groups. Large-scale arms trafficking, involving Ben-Gurion himself, was defended by fellow leaders of the Jewish Agency.[7] When the Jewish community refused help in apprehending terrorists, the British instituted harsh Emergency (martial) Laws[8] that legalized military courts, curfews and so on – making of Palestine a virtual police state. Eventually, the British took to terrorist actions themselves.

Jewish attacks took a significant toll on British authority and capability in Palestine. Ten of the eleven bridges connecting Palestine with surrounding nations were blown up, virtually isolating the country. A British radar station and fifteen planes were destroyed. The LEHI destroyed anything British, including oil refineries and military installations. It also assassinated Lord Moyne, a British minister, wrongly thinking him anti-Zionist.[9] British troop movements were paralyzed by hundreds of dynamitings of the rail system by the Palmah.[10] By 1946 the Irgun had doubled its size and was destroying any facility needed by the British to govern Palestine, such as police stations, utilities, and railroads. British officers were taken hostage to get terrorists' death sentences commuted. Led by Begin, the Irgun blew off a wing of the King David Hotel in Jerusalem that housed the British government Criminal Investigation Division, killing ninety-one (sixty-three non-British). Acre Prison was dynamited in order to free forty-one convicted terrorists. By the end of 1946, Jewish terrorists had killed 373 people, 300 of them civilians.

Arab terrorism

The British were less concerned about Palestinian Arab terrorism because it was largely directed against its own community – Arabs who sold land to Jews. Financially drained and stung by their unsuccessful revolt against the British in 1936-1939, the Arabs were slow to reorganize. Unlike the Jews, they had little belief that Britain could be defeated. Consequently, they had no clear opponent or focus. Their political leaders stood rigidly and exclusively on the ground of self-determination as plaintiffs before British imperial power – a power that at one time controlled one-quarter of the world's population. They could not imagine that British power could be undermined, as the Jews were trying to do. Nor did Arab terrorism ever attain that immunity from international criticism which Jewish terrorism achieved as a kind of displaced response to the Holocaust. In the West, the very idea of Jewish terrorism was paradoxical because it suggested that the victim and victimizer were one. Arab terrorism never gained this aura of immunity to criticism.

The failure of the British to suppress Jewish terrorism was a growing signal to the Palestinian nationalists to organize militias. Yet Palestinian leadership was in disarray. The British had exiled the Palestinian nationalist leader, Grand Mufti of Jerusalem Haj Amin el Husseini, as well as other political leaders.[11] Still, disorganized, poorly funded, competing groups began to form: the al-Najjadah which eventually hoped to match the Haganah, and the al-Futuwwah, a rival group connected with the Husseini Arab nationalists. The size of these militant Arab forces is not clear. However, over the next two years, these forces (including all local Palestinian volunteers as well as volunteers from outside countries), collectively grew to something less than 23,500 by May 1948 (when the British withdrew and fighting for Palestine between Arab and Jew began in earnest). Palestinian forces smuggled arms across the border from surrounding Arab countries. The Haganah had a manpower of nearly three times that of the Palestinian nationalists and had secret munitions factories within Palestine.

Factors behind the success of Jewish terrorism

If the Palestinian Arabs learned that revolt against the British does not pay, the Jews learned a decade later that it does – the difference being that in 1936 the British were resolved and strong enough to suppress any insurrection, whereas by the mid-1940s they were near collapse following World War II. Moreover, Jewish terrorists had learned the importance of professional training in the British army and had financial support from the American public.

But Jewish resolve and outlook also contributed to the success of Jewish militancy: (1) ruthless Nazi methods seemed to justify ruthless methods on behalf of the Jews; (2) Jewish terrorism, linked with the cause of Jewish immigration, acquired a humanitarian image; and (3) British conscience, or at least concern for reputation in dealing with Jews, provided Jewish terrorists with wider latitude.

Britain's last-ditch diplomatic efforts to bring peace to Palestine – the Morrison-Grady (federated provinces) Plan
Unable to afford the military, political and financial costs of battling Jewish terror and facing growing Arab indignation about continuing Jewish immigration, Britain made a last-ditch attempt at a Jewish-Arab political compromise: the Anglo-American Committee of Inquiry. In April 1946 this committee proposed that: (1) 100,000 Jews be permitted to immigrate into Palestine – to satisfy Truman; (2) restrictions on Jewish land-purchases be eased, and (3) Palestine become a *UN Trusteeship* which, upon further negotiation, would either become (*a*) a *unitary* state for Arabs and Jews together, (*b*) a binational *federation of two states* with British or UN oversight, or (*c*) *two independent sovereign states.* Truman liked the 100,000 proposal and the binational federation idea.

Britain and the United States agreed to restudy these proposals at the ministerial level. The final result was the Morrison-Grady Plan. This called for the immigration of 100,000 Jews to Palestine and the *federalization* of Jewish and Arab *provinces* under a time-limited British trusteeship – two semi-autonomous provinces (like American states) exercising control over their own intra-community affairs. The British would rule over Jerusalem and the Negev Desert and govern the federation in matters of defense, foreign relations, customs, and so forth. Truman would obtain his proposed immigration of 100,000 Jews and Britain would obtain what it always wanted: control over Palestine and military bases in the Negev. One British official summarized the plan: "It is a beautiful scheme. It treats the Arabs and Jews on a footing of complete equality in that it gives nothing to either party, while it leaves us a free run over the whole of Palestine."[12] The Arabs and Jews both rejected the Morrison-Grady Plan.

David Ben-Gurion, head of the Jewish Agency, then proposed his own plan, a modification of the 1942 Biltmore Program: Most of Palestine and some areas in Transjordan would become a Jewish state whereas densely populated

Palestinian Arab areas would go to Transjordan.[13] Truman grew "intensely resentful" and negative toward this Jewish campaign he considered to be counter to both U.S. and Arab interests. He threatened to withdraw from negotiations altogether, leaving the British and the Zionists to "sort out the mess by themselves."[14] Disfavor toward Jews was festering around Begin's recent Irgun terrorist bombing of the King David Hotel.

In something of a panic, the Jewish Agency met in Paris.[15] Opinion was divided as to what Truman would tolerate. The alternatives: (1) demand a Jewish state over *all* of Palestine (i.e., the Biltmore plan with Ben-Gurion's modification), (2) partition into "two sovereign states" as the Peel Commission had proposed in 1937, or (3) the Morrison-Grady "autonomous provinces" plan that left the British in charge and sovereign statehood deferred.

The first alternative, the Biltmore plan, was manifestly a violation of Palestinian rights and frontally opposed to equivalent Palestinian demands for a state over all of Palestine. It would be equally unacceptable to the West. The second alternative, *partition* into two sovereign states – with both the UN and the British out of the picture – was preferred by the Jewish Agency, though it fell short of gaining all of Palestine.[16] The agency doubted that Truman would accept a two-state solution, however. The third alternative, the Morrison-Grady Plan proposing provinces, was felt to be too indefinite about eventual Jewish statehood. Yet it seemed the best tactic – acceptance of the Morrison-Grady provinces plan as a roundabout negotiating basis for a "viable Jewish state."[17] The agency proposed this, additionally demanding the Negev.[18]

It was not to be. Truman wavered but for a number of reasons finally rejected the Morrison-Grady Plan.[19] The British also rejected the Jewish Agency's proposal. They wanted the Negev themselves for a military base to protect the Suez Canal.[20]

Britain's efforts sabotaged: U.S. elections and Zionist extremism

The failed Morrison-Grady Plan was Britain's last hope of restoring order in Palestine. The British threw up their hands after sustaining two additional major blows: the first related to Truman, the second to Zionist extremism.

On October 4, 1946, Truman finally took the position of supporting the *partitioning* of Palestine into *two states* along with an immediate immigration of 100,000 Jews (the Yom Kippur statement). This plan completely excluded the British from Palestine. The decisive factor in his decision was "the Democratic Party's need to mobilize the Jewish vote in the impending congressional elections."[21] The British were infuriated that Truman made his Yom Kippur statement while Arab-Jewish negotiations were still in progress in London.

The second blow came at the World Zionist Congress in December 1946. Chaim Weizmann, a relatively moderate Zionist, was defeated by the extremist/activist Zionism of Ben-Gurion and Rabbi Silver, president of the Zionist Organization of America.[22] "Just as the Yom Kippur statement had convinced Foreign Minister Ernest Bevin that he would never be able to rely upon Americans to moderate the Zionists' demands, so the [Zionist] congress indicated the clear triumph of the extremist camp."[23]

On February 14, 1947, the British government decided to refer the whole problem of Palestine to the United Nations. Britain would withdraw from Palestine. There seemed to be no other way to end a draining war with the Jews. Britain would retain some influence in the Middle East through its client state, Transjordan.

Notes

1. Jewish terrorists were financed through bank-robbing and extortion in Palestine, and, in the United States, by the Hebrew Committee of National Liberation and the Political Action Committee for Palestine. But most of the funds for illegal immigration and Jewish terrorism came from Americans. The *New York Times* refused at first to run fund-raising Irgun ads (submitted by the "American League for a Free Palestine") until Jewish-owned department stores boycotted the paper in 1947. Alfred Lilienthal, "Book on *Times'* Editor," *Washington Report on Middle East Affairs* (June 1989), 22. "The pro-terrorist advertisements in the American press provoked bitter reaction in Britain." J.C. Hurewitz, *The Struggle for Palestine* (New York: Schocken, 1976), 278, 300.

2. Observing that non-Jews were also victims of Nazism and that Palestine was not a solution for them, Britain sent DPs to camps in North Africa and Cyprus rather than Palestine, where 18,000 Jews, half illegal immigrants, were already entering each year.

3. A draft report of the Goldberg Commission stated, "What is certain is that the exclusive concentration on Palestine as a solution, coupled with its intrinsic pessimism as to the other alternatives, distracted the Zionist movement as well as large segments of American Jews from giving serious attention to various rescue plans offered by the advocates of separating rescue from political or ideological considerations." Noam Chomsky, *The Fateful Triangle: The United States, Israel*

and the Palestinians (Boston: South End Press, 1983), 94. Rabbi Stephen Wise, a prominent American close to Roosevelt opposed a 1943 congressional effort to set up a commission "to effectuate the rescue of the Jewish people of Europe" because it failed to demand that Britain open up Palestine to Jews.

4. Christopher Sykes, *Crossroads to Israel* (Cleveland: World Publishing, 1965), 287.

5. Hurewitz, *Struggle for Palestine,* 239, 280. By way of comparison, the British had about 80,000 troops in Palestine, about one-tenth of the total British army at that time – an army exhausted from World War II.

6. The "Irgun" (also called "Etzel") was the Irgun Zvai Leumi or National Military Organization. The "Stern Gang," later called the "Fighters for the Freedom of Israel" or LEHI, was begun by Abraham Stern, an Irgun revisionist. In 1943 the LEHI was commanded by Yitzhak Shamir, Israel Scheib and Narhan Yellin-Mor.

Looking at Nazi Germany *before* the Holocaust, it is more understandable that both Palestinian nationalists and Jewish terrorists sought to cooperate with Germany against the British. The Palestinian leader, the grand mufti of Jerusalem, saw Germany in 1933 as a potential ally against the Jews and Britain. The LEHI, seeking to rid Palestine of the British in 1941, also offered to cooperate with Germany. Mark Tessler, *A History of the Israeli-Palestinian Conflict* (Bloomington: Indiana University Press, 1994), 230. LEHI proposal published by B. Michael, *Ha'aretz,* January 31, 1983.

7. Moshe Sharett, the second prime minister of Israel, was imprisoned in Latrun in Palestine. Ben-Gurion and Moshe Sneh fled to France to avoid arrest. France was a haven for Jewish terrorists, e.g., Yitzhak Shamir. Menachem Begin lived underground with a price on his head.

8. Laws still in force in Israel and the occupied territories today.

9. Lord Moyne was assassinated in Cairo in 1944, the killing planned and approved by Yitzhak Shamir. Donald Neff, *Warriors for Jerusalem* (Brattleboro, Vt.: Amana Books, 1988), 357.

10. The Palmah ("striking unit") was the nucleus of the later elite commando force of the Haganah. Hurewitz, *Struggle for Palestine,* 128.

11. Even by 1945, the Arab community in Palestine had not recovered from the economic losses of the 1936-1939 civil war. The political leadership, outlawed by the British, had fled the country during World War II and tried to make alliances with the Axis. The Arab Higher Committee ceased to function in Palestine. Efforts made in 1945 to resuscitate this body were blocked by the exiled mufti, still forbidden by the British to return to Palestine.

12. Howard Sachar, *A History of Israel: From the Rise of Zionism to Our Time.* Vol. I (New York; Knopf, 1986), 271.

13. Michael J. Cohen, *Palestine and the Great Powers, 1945-1948* (Princeton: Princeton University Press, 1982), 139. This plan was destined to form the basis for the Jewish-Abdullah 1947 collusion against an independent Palestinian state.

14. Truman remarked, "Well, you can't satisfy these people. . . . The Jews aren't going to write the history of the United States or my history." Rabbi Silver's public

boasting about his influence on the President made Truman "livid." Quotes from Cohen, *Palestine*, 129, 132.

15. David Niles, pro-Zionist adviser to Truman, urgently warned the Jews that Truman would "wash his hands" of the Palestine issue unless the Jews came up with a reasonable plan. Cohen, *Palestine*, 142.

16. Some leaders, e.g., Rabbis J.L. Fishman (Maimon) and Stephen Wise, were willing to settle for partition rather than all of Palestine out of guilt for having voted down the 1937 Peel partition plan, which, by establishing a Jewish state in part of Palestine, conceivably might have spared some Jews the Holocaust. "Wise confessed to his 'harrowing sense of guilt' over his 1937 vote against partition." Cohen, *Palestine*, 143.

17. That is, a province "designated to become a Jewish state" which would have full administrative and economic autonomy, including control over immigration. Cohen, *Palestine*, 145.

18. This 35 percent, added on to the 17 percent assigned to the Jewish province under the Morrison-Grady Plan, would give the Jews (one-third of the population) more than half of Palestine and the most fertile land.

19. For a description of the reasons, see Steven L. Spiegel, *The Other Arab-Israeli Conflict* (Chicago: University of Chicago Press, 1985), 23.

20. Britain had recently agreed to withdraw forces from Egypt proper.

21. Cohen, *Palestine*, 164, 165, 170. "The administration understood that Governor Dewey intended to make a major speech on the subject, and . . . Truman now felt it vital to say something." In the opinion of Rabbi Silver, head of the American Zionist Organization, Truman's statement was simply a "smart pre-election move." Truman declared to some diplomats (1945): "I'm sorry, gentlemen, but I have to answer to hundreds of thousands who are anxious for the success of Zionism: I do not have hundreds of thousands of Arabs among my constituents." Spiegel, *Other Conflict*, 19.

22. "For Weizmann, violence negated the precepts of Jewish morality." Silver "controlled Jewish purse strings." Cohen, *Palestine*, 180-2.

23. Cohen, *Palestine*, 182-3.

Chapter 6

UN Proposal for Partition (1947)

Territories on which the League of Nations imposed mandates were to become sovereign states upon termination of those mandates. By the end of World War II, all mandate areas had reverted to sovereign states except Palestine. When Britain announced its intention to withdraw, Palestine should have become a sovereign state. But the League of Nations as an institution had lapsed in 1946.[1] Thus, legal questions arose regarding Palestine as a sovereign state. Did the recently established United Nations have any legal authority to impose or alter League of Nations provisions?[2]

The Arabs sought a ruling in International Court but the court refused to rule. The United Nations Ad Hoc Committee on Palestine (Subcommittee Two) also considered testing the matter in International Court but finally decided not to. The Arabs protested this subversion of statehood and UN assumption of authority over Palestine. Their protest took the form of a refusal to meet with the United Nations Special Committee on Palestine (UNSCOP) in June of 1947 when UNSCOP was making local inquiries in Palestine into the Arab-Jewish conflict. UNSCOP went ahead and in September communicated to the UN its majority recommendation: a *partition* of Palestine into two independent states, one Jewish, the other Palestinian-Arab. Jerusalem would be designated an international city.

The Palestinian Arabs rejected the partitioning plan as an infringement of their self-determination as well as on demographic and logical grounds. They argued that the Jewish state which the UN was proposing comprised 56 percent of Palestine, yet the Jewish population (including illegal immigrants) comprised only 31 percent of the population. They pointed to the logical inconsistency of a plan that rejected the idea of all of Palestine being an Arab state because that state would contain a Jewish minority (31 percent), yet accepted the idea of a Jewish state that would encompass an even larger Arab minority (46 percent) within its borders.[3] Moreover, the Arabs objected that 80 percent of the territory designated for a Jewish state was owned by Arabs, that it would garner seven-eighths of Arab citrus groves and that it included major population centers. The territory remaining for an Arab state would be impoverished and dependent on subventions and relief from the Jewish state or elsewhere.[4] The British foreign secretary considered the UN-proposed boundaries to be manifestly unfair to the Palestinian Arabs, noting that many saw them as "little more than a joke."[5] The Arabs further objected that they were effectively prevented from participating in UN subcommittee negotiations concerning the boundaries and conditions of partition.[6]

It is true that the UN attempted to alleviate some of the obvious economic unfairnesses by recommending a *two-year transitional period* during which (*a*) neither side would declare statehood and (*b*) a cooperative *economic union* should exist (to increase the economic viability of the Palestinian-Arab state to be). Ben-Gurion rejected the provision for economic union and drew up his own proposal, which U.S. Secretary of State George Marshall judged to be "designed to establish economic separation."[7]

To the Western world, partition seemed an even-handed and objective compromise solution. To the Palestinian Arabs it was no compromise at all. They argued that compromise involves giving up something you *already* have – and that in this case Arabs were expected to give up more than half their lands while the Jews have no land to give up.[8] In their view, the "compromise" the Jews were being asked to make was to give up all of what they *wanted* – all of Palestine.[9] Partition was all gain for the Jews and only loss for the Arabs.

The Arabs also rejected partition because they believed it to be a ruse – a tactical step by the Jews to gain all of Palestine. The Zionist Organization of America had, indeed, voted at the end of October 1946 for a Jewish state over all of Palestine. In 1947 it was a widely held Arab belief throughout the Middle East that "partition would be used by the Jews for ultimate expansion and establishment of a Jewish state in the whole of Palestine."[10] In part this was based on Ben-Gurion's expressed views about partition back in 1937:

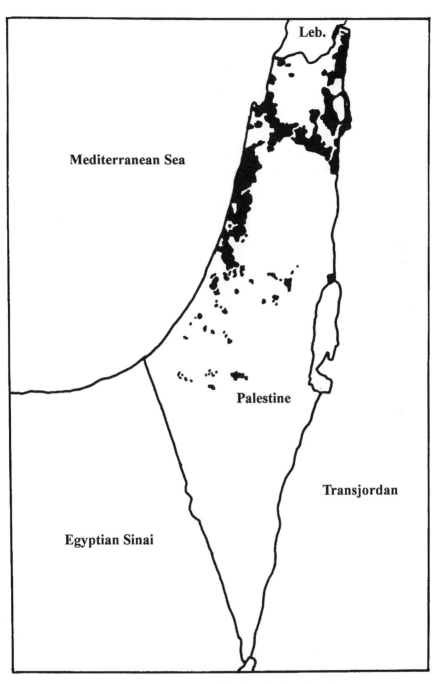

Jewish Land Ownership in Palestine (1947)

The debate has not been for or against the divisibility of Eretz Israel. No Zionist can forego the smallest portion of Eretz Israel. The debate was over which of two routes would lead more quickly to the common goal.[11] [Also in 1937] After the formation of a large army in the wake of the establishment of the state, we will abolish partition and expand to the whole of Palestine.[12]

The 1942 Biltmore plan directly expressed this goal.

Jewish terrorist groups rejected the UN partition plan because it denied to them all of Palestine. However, the Jewish Agency had good reasons for officially accepting partition, at least as a steppingstone: (1) it offered the first *international* recognition of the legitimacy of a Jewish state in Palestine, and (2) they believed they had made arrangements with Transjordan that would preclude the UN-proposed independent Palestinian Arab state.

The Jewish Agency, Transjordan and Britain subvert the UN partition plan

The Palestinian-Arab state proposed by the UN partition plan was, on its own, neither economically nor militarily viable. Therefore it constituted tempting spoils for both Transjordan and the Jews once Britain withdrew. Of course the Jews could not formally take over the UN-designated Arab state-to-be while at the same time officially supporting a *two-state* solution. Moreover, on the practical level, it would have been impossible for a Jewish state to gulp down an Arab population more than double its size.[13] Thus, the best immediate solution was to allow King Abdullah of Transjordan to annex the Palestinian areas otherwise designated by the UN for the Palestinian-Arab state. Certainly Abdullah had no desire to fight the Jews. In fact he was friendly with them and only wanted land as part of his expansionist "Greater Syria" scheme.[14]

On November 17, 1947, a week before the UN was to vote on partition, Golda Meir and King Abdullah made a secret *mutual nonaggression pact:* In exchange for Transjordan's noninterference with the establishment of the Jewish state, the Jews would allow Transjordan's territorial acquisition of Arab Palestine. "Abdullah secured Jewish agreement for annexing the populated Arab part of Palestine adjacent to his kingdom [the West Bank] . . . [and] promised that he would never attack the Jews or join with other Arabs in frustrating the establishment of a Jewish state."[15] Meir and Abdullah agreed that their "common enemy" was the grand mufti of Jerusalem (Haj Amin el Husseini), the fanatical leader of Palestinian nationalism.[16] Meir assured Abdullah that while the Jews could not offer him active assistance in occupying Palestinian-Arab land, the king could do there as he pleased.[17]

What of course Abdullah and the Jews were setting up, while seeming to support the UN partition plan, was its defeat. Palestine would be partitioned into a Jewish state and an enlarged Transjordanian state – the independent Palestinian Arab state aborted. The Jews and Transjordan were dividing Palestine between themselves without a fight. Transjordan, pretending to "save" the Palestinians from advancing Jewish forces, would invade and annex Palestinian territory; the Jews would have their state without interference. The Jews were not only neutralizing the only significant military force in the Arab world,[18] Transjordan, they were eliminating a potentially hostile Palestinian Arab state.

Britain, the patron of Transjordan, blessed this secret mutual non-aggression pact. Behind a mask of official "neutrality" toward the UN partition proposal – in order not to offend the surrounding Arab states – Britain wished for partition as a necessary step leading to its client's annexation of Arab Palestine. "The real aim behind British policy was the consolidation and extension of Abdullah's power."[19] The Meir-Abdullah pact, coupled with the partition proposal, provided that power. It appears that the United States quietly acquiesced to this Jewish-Transjordanian collusion in violation of the UN partition plan.[20]

The Palestinian Arabs, struggling against the partition, falsely assumed that the territory allotted them by the UN was secure. They did not know that the independence of that territory had been subverted a week before the UN vote.

The Big Three support partition

Britain, the United States and the Soviet Union each wanted access to Middle East oil, military bases, commercial airlines routes and the Mediterranean Sea. Each was divided over what strategy to use both to fulfill its interests and counter those of its rivals. As it happened, each viewed partition favorably, at least as a temporary device.

Britain: Partition, at the very least, was a viable way out of the struggle with Jewish terrorism. Britain could not afford the struggle, having been economically sapped by World War II. Indeed, Palestine illustrated the need of a new global strategy altogether: rather than maintaining troops in colonies all over the world, Britain would encourage self-determination in those colonies – at least as long as trade agreements and security pacts (military access) remained intact. If internal disputes existed, as in Palestine, then partition (or federation) would be encouraged. Britain was moving from an empire to a commonwealth system. This already began in 1945 when the socialist/egalitarian labor government of Clement Atlee replaced the conservative/imperialist government of Winston Churchill. Atlee announced, in the course of one week, his intention to relinquish control of India, end financial and military commitments to Turkey and Greece, and turn the Palestine problem over to the UN.[21]

The U.S.S.R.: The Soviets favored partition in their search for influence in the Middle East. They had been frustrated by Truman's effective containment policy – the Truman Doctrine supporting conservative, anti-communist governments in nations circling U.S.S.R. borders (notably Iran, Turkey and Greece).[22] Palestine seemed a potential gateway for the Soviets once British withdrawal was in the air. Soviet hostility to Britain and the Zionism that Britain once supported no longer needed to be directed at Zionism once Britain withdrew. On the contrary, the existence of a modern Jewish state, freed of British influence, would *undercut* any British justification for remaining in or reentering Palestine. Moreover, the expected violent clash of Jews and Arabs in Palestine could open doors for Soviet influence or intervention – the same logic the British had used three decades before. It seems that these two ideas – a Jewish state without a British presence and a flaring of Arab-Jewish hostilities in which the Soviets might intervene – led the Soviets to vote in *favor* of partition, much to the surprise of the West and the Zionists.

The United States: At first, Truman had been careful not to express a position about the Middle East, being torn between (*a*) the advice of the State Department, the Defense Department and U.S. business interests not to alienate Arab oil,[23] and (*b*) the sentiments of a pro-Zionist U.S. public moved by the Holocaust and a Congress under pressure from a powerful Jewish lobby.[24] He was pulled in many conflicting directions by other factors as well. Truman was exasperated with Jewish propaganda and pressure groups, yet impressed with the gentlemanly and temperate counsel of the towering Chaim Weizmann. His back was up over increasingly belligerent Palestinian Arab statements and moves to raise illegal armies, yet he believed they had cause. He was pressed by the Democratic National Committee chairman to make pro-Zionist statements as a way to raise campaign funds, yet he was not solely a cynical politician. He was confronted by the incongruity of representing a democratic government "of, for, and by" the people, yet offering support to a Jewish state designed in principle for the benefit of Jews only. Some accused him of yielding to Jewish partisan interests at the sacrifice of U.S. national interests. Eleanor Roosevelt urged on the American delegation at the UN the view that *world* interests demanded partition as the only course of action that could demonstrate UN effectiveness.[25]

Eventually, in his October 1946 Yom Kippur speech, Truman endorsed the "basic principles" of partition, though largely for domestic political reasons, as described in chapter 5.

On November 25, 1947, the UN Ad Hoc Committee approved the partition report, but it was one vote short of the necessary two-thirds for passage in the General Assembly. Through filibuster the Zionists managed to gain a four-day delay because of the Thanksgiving weekend – to be followed by a General Assembly vote. The Zionist lobby went into high gear. Truman instructed the State Department not to use threats or improper pressure on foreign delegations, but did so himself.[26] Moreover, great economic and political pressure was immediately applied by U.S. government officials on nations dependent on U.S. aid and business.[27] The resolution recommending partition of Palestine was passed by the UN General Assembly on November 29, 1947.

What this meant was *not* that the UN had just created two new states – the UN, being a peace-keeping organization only, is not so empowered. But that vote reflected international approval for the formation of two states after a two-year transitional period. The Jews declared statehood six months later (May 15, 1948), the day the British left Palestine. The world powers, including the United States and the U.S.S.R., immediately gave diplomatic recognition – creating for Israel the status of a world-recognized state.[28]

Other factors favoring adoption of partition

It is clear that the strategic interests and rivalries of the Big Three played a primary role in the partitioning of Palestine. But other currents existed beneath or beside the strategies of the imperial powers: (1) the influence of the Holocaust; (2) the influence of Western perceptions about Jewish and Arab racial and cultural differences; and (3) shifting application of the principle of self-determination from Arabs to Jews.

Concerning the Holocaust, historian Michael Cohen has noted:

> It has been asserted that the United Nations partition resolution was Western civilization's gesture of repentance for the Holocaust, that the establishment of the state of Israel in some way represented the repayment of a debt owed by those nations that realized they might have done more to prevent or at least limit the scale of Jewish tragedy during World War II. There is much to be said for this thesis. Compassion for the victims of Nazism and the survivors languishing in the DP camps undoubtedly played an integral, albeit intangible role in the psyches of postwar politicians.[29]

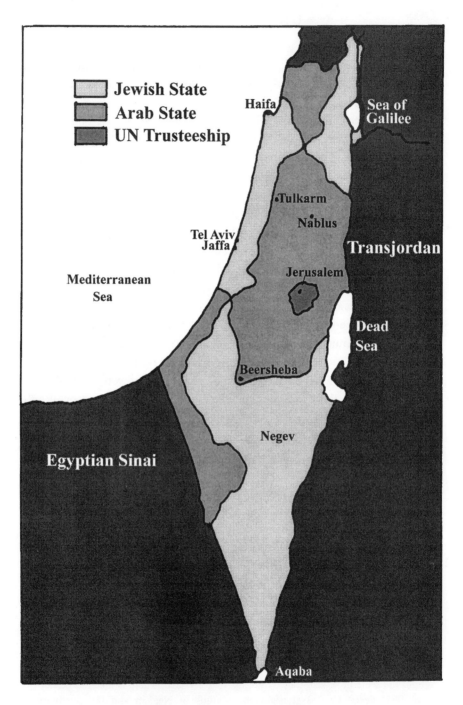

Jewish State
Arab State
UN Trusteeship

Haifa

Sea of Galilee

•Tulkarm

Nablus

Tel Aviv
Jaffa

Transjordan

Jerusalem

Mediterranean
Sea

Dead
Sea

Beersheba

Negev

Egyptian Sinai

Aqaba

1947 UN Partition Proposal

Cohen notes, however, that this "gesture of repentance" was insufficient to give the Jews a state on that first and uncoerced UN vote of November 25. The extra votes required for passage were based on "mundane material factors" such as financial pressure exerted on nations dependent on U.S. aid. Thus, the factors of compassion and guilt, while undoubtedly playing a role in passage of partition, were insufficient for a two-thirds majority in the General Assembly.

The effect of the Holocaust on governments had its limits. This was because (*a*) the Allies may not have felt that they could have done more for the Jews, especially after 1939 when Europe was virtually closed and the war had desperately to be won; (*b*) the Zionists themselves were not considered blameless, in that humanitarian concern for Jews took a second place for Zionists in America;[30] and (*c*) Jewish terrorism, while popularly depicted as guerrilla warfare ("freedom fighters") for the sake of aiding immigration, inspired revulsion in postwar politicians. Truman wrote to Eleanor Roosevelt in August 1947, "I fear very much that the Jews are like all underdogs. When they get on top they are just as intolerant and as cruel as the people were to them when they were underneath."[31] There was both disapproval and compassion for the Jews and certainly blame to be shared all around.

Concerning Western perceptions of Jewish and Arab racial and cultural differences, the creation of a Jewish state through partition was favored in the West partly because the West saw Judaism as fundamental to Christianity, and Islam as alien. And even if the anti-Semites in the West considered Jews to be "clever cheats," the Arabs were worse – "sodomites and punitive barbarians." Jewish culture, too, had far greater appeal in its order, efficiency and social philosophy. The West also thought of the Jews as the virtuous underdog – attracted by "the gallant little people with a great and tormented past . . . pioneers taming the wilderness . . . planners using science to increase production . . . collective farmers . . . [the] terrorist making his gesture in the face of authority – all images of a new world . . . hopeful, violent and earnest."[32] Arabs, on the other hand, were feudal serfs embracing a fanatical religion, nomads living in tents without science, education or sense of nationalism – *alien* people like the American Indians. What was there in Palestine, the Jews and the West asked, that is not *improved* by the addition of a Jewish state?

Finally, there was the shift in the application of the principle of self-determination from Arab to Jew. The Wilsonian concept of self-determination embraced the right of a people who *inhabit a land* to govern that land. On the other hand, was it not obvious that the persecuted and homeless Jews also had a right of "self-determination" while *not* inhabiting a land? This new definition of "self-determination" gained a kind of moral force because of World War II. By applying this idea of self-determination to a landless people, Truman gave legitimacy to Jewish self-determination in Palestine, a legitimacy previously associated with Palestinian Arabs:

> I was fully aware of the Arabs' hostility to Jewish settlement in Palestine, but, like many Americans, I was troubled by the plight of the Jewish people in Europe. The Balfour Declaration, promising the Jews the opportunity to establish a homeland in Palestine, had always seemed to me to go hand in hand with the noble policies of Woodrow Wilson, especially the principle of self-determination.[33]

Truman avoided the question that self-determination was designed to answer: that a people do not have a right to declare dominion over lands inhabited by others. In the service of this avoidance, he, like the Jews, acted as though Palestine was not inhabited, or not importantly so. Thus, it was available to be "fairly" partitioned between Arabs and Jews. For Truman, like Wilson, the principle of self-determination was a noble ideal. But that ideal, in the context of landlessness, was an abstraction that failed to consider the concrete particulars concerning existing inhabitants – what Henry James referred to as "the dear little deadly question of how to do it."

Nor did Truman, or any other U.S. president since, seriously consider that the American democratic model of diverse groups living under a common flag, with religious freedom and equal civil rights for all, might actually find application in the Middle East.

Notes

1. The League did not operate during the war and was dissolved in 1946.

2. The United Nations was designed to replace the League of Nations. Its founding members were nations declaring war on the Axis by March 1945.

3. Walid Khalidi, *Before Their Diaspora* (Washington D.C.: Institute for Palestine Studies, 1984), 305-6.

4. The 1937 Peel Commission had acknowledged this lack of viability and recommended that the Jewish state pay yearly subventions to the Palestinian Arabs as a kind of payment for injury resulting from the assignment of the most fertile lands to the Jewish state. Christopher Sykes, *Crossroads to Israel* (Cleveland: World Publishing, 1965), 169.

5. Communication of the chief of the Palestine Administration to the Colonial Office. Michael J. Cohen, *Palestine and the Great Powers, 1945-1948* (Princeton: Princeton University Press, 1982), 272.

6. The Arabs had boycotted the June 1947 UNSCOP inquiry but wished to participate in the Ad Hoc Committee on Palestine's *subcommittees* of October 1947. They were excluded from Subcommittee One, responsible for studying and modifying the boundaries and other specifics of partition. The UN Ad Hoc Committee on Palestine placed only pro-partition, pro-Jewish countries (including the United States. and U.S.S.R.) on this subcommittee. The chairman of the Ad Hoc Committee, though limited in his freedom of choice concerning assignment of delegates to various committees, "was criticized severely for composing them exclusively of delegates who already supported the schemes that were called upon to consider." The Arabs were included only in Subcommittee Two, dealing with the minority report (unitary Arab plan), which was not taken seriously. Cohen, *Palestine*, 284.

7. Cited in Simha Flapan, *The Birth of Israel* (New York: Pantheon, 1987), 42.

8. Palestinian historian Walid Khalidi summarized the Arab side of the argument: "But whereas in 1937 partition had been recommended by the royal commission of an imperial power it was now the ostensibly disinterested verdict of an impartial international body. This endowed the concept with the attributes of objectivity and even-handedness – in short, a compromise solution. But a compromise by definition is an arrangement acceptable, however grudgingly, to the protagonists. The 'partition' of Palestine proposed by UNSCOP was no such thing. It was Zionist in inspiration, Zionist in principle, Zionist in substance, and Zionist in most details. The very idea of partition was abhorrent to the Arabs of Palestine and it was against it that they had fought their bitter, desperate and costly fight in the years 1937-39. Also, 'compromise' implies mutual concession. What were the Zionists conceding? You can only really concede what you possess. What possessions in Palestine were the Zionists conceding? None at all. . . . It surely goes against the grain of human nature to expect the party that would suffer this reversal to enter into the transaction just because some third party, itself affiliated to the potential aggrandizer, chose to befog the issue by calling this transaction a 'compromise.' One might say all this is very well except that it ignores the power factor. True enough, but if we are talking about power, then we should say so and not pretend that we are talking about compromise." *From Haven to Conquest* (Washington, D.C.: Institute For Palestinian Studies, 1987), lxix-lxx.

9. Cohen, *Palestine*, 174.

10. Communication of British Ambassador Campbell to the Foreign Office. Cited in Cohen, *Palestine*, 197.

11. Sykes, *Crossroads to Israel*, 174. Regarding the UN partition plan, Ben-Gurion also made it clear that his aim for Jerusalem, despite its designation as an international zone, was for it to be Jewish. He considered that the UN borders of the state were not final since partition was, for him, a tactical step toward expansion. See Flapan, *Birth of Israel*, 32.

12. Ben-Gurion to the Zionist Executive, also in 1937. Flapan, *Birth of Israel,* 22.

Ben-Gurion frequently made speeches depicting all of Palestine as belonging to a Jewish state, e.g., July 4, 1947, before the UNSCOP inquiry committee. Ben-Gurion's biographer concluded: "Partition lines were of secondary importance in Ben-Gurion's eyes because he intended to change them in any case; they were not the end but only the beginning." Avi Shlaim, *Collusion across the Jordan* (New York: Columbia University Press, 1988), 16, summarizing Michael Bar-Zohar, *Ben-Gurion: A Political Biography* (in Hebrew), Vol. I. (Tel Aviv: Am Oved, 1975), 356-8.

13. Ben-Gurion kept open the route for future expansion into Arab areas by refusing to define the boundaries of the Jewish state when declaring Israel's independent statehood.

14. Transjordan and the Jews were traditionally friendly and for political reasons the Jews, like the British, gave Transjordan annual subsidies. They could easily enter into a political and strategic partnership. Abdullah's "Greater Syria" was to comprise Transjordan, Syria, Iraq, Lebanon and Palestine, creating a Hashemite empire that could be legislated conjointly by Arabs and Jews but would fall under King Abdullah's executive rule.

15. Avi Shlaim, *The Politics of Partition* (New York: Columbia University Press, 1990), 100. Abdullah kept his promise, fighting the Jews only in Jerusalem (neither Jewish nor Arab territory by the UN plan) and in Arab areas which the Jews invaded. Shlaim, *Collusion,* 239.

16. The mufti was the common enemy because of his absolute refusal to make any accommodation to the Zionist cause. He was exiled by the British from Palestine in 1938, fled to Germany and collaborated with the Nazis. His supporters threatened rival Palestinian leaders seeking accommodation and were behind the assassination of King Abdullah.

17. Howard Sachar, *A History of Israel,From the Rise of Zionism to Our Time,* Vol. I (New York: Knopf, 1986), 322. Also Flapan, *Birth of Israel,* 39. See Shlaim, *Collusion,* 115, for the text of Sasson's summary to Sharett of the Meir-Abdullah meeting.

18. Transjordan had the only significant Arab army in the Middle East, a small fighting force of only 4,500, but British financed and well trained and led by British officers.

19. Shlaim, *Collusion,* 220. "[Foreign Secretary] Bevin, who is portrayed by Zionist historians as irreconcilably opposed to the establishment of a Jewish state, appears, by February 1948, to be resigned to the inevitable emergence of a Jewish state. It is hardly an exaggeration to say that he colluded directly with the Transjordanians and indirectly with the Jews to abort the birth of a Palestinian Arab state." 139.

20. The United States wavered but finally opposed Transjordan's "Greater Syrian" expansionist plans for Syria and Lebanon because of protests from Saudi

Arabia, Syria and Egypt. But the United States, while not knowing specifically of the Jewish-Transjordanian pact, did not oppose that part of the Greater Syria plan in which Transjordan would incorporate Arab Palestine. In fact, the United States assumed that the secret talks of May 1, 1948, between Jewish and Transjordanian military officers "indicated operational coordination between the Zionists and Abdullah." The United States made no objection. The Jews denied U.S. suspicions. See Cohen, *Palestine,* 374; Flapan, *Birth of Israel,* 253, n. 28, 177.

21. Like Palestine, India was partitioned into two states, India and Pakistan. The ensuing bloodshed took more than one million lives.

22. The Truman Doctrine of March 1947 aimed at supporting nations which otherwise might fall under the influence of Soviet communism. In Greece, after the Nazis left and after Britain tried unsuccessfully to establish a royalist (if not fascist-oriented) government, the United States supported the government's war against a communist-led peasant, and worker-based nationalist movement. 160,000 died, 800,000 were made refugees.

23. The U.S. government helped American airline companies gain air rights in Iraq, Egypt, Lebanon and Syria. Oil interests were of even greater economic importance. American petroleum companies owned 42 percent of Middle East oil supplies by 1947 but sought even larger holdings, as well as pipeline rights across Arab territories.

24. The American Zionist Emergency Council orchestrated lobbying and pressure groups throughout the country with a large budget and fourteen professionally staffed departments. It was extraordinarily effective in the congressional, judicial, and executive branches of government as well at the local level of Kiwanis and Rotary Clubs.

25. The conflict between Arabs and Jews seemed irresolvable. Yet the UN *needed* for its own survival an appearance of being able to resolve international conflicts. Conflict resolution was the raison d'être of the UN.

26. Cohen, *Palestine,* 295.

27. The warnings by two U.S. Supreme Court justices, as well as Clark Clifford's influence, succeeded in reversing the Philippine vote. Presidential aide and pro-Zionist David Niles and Secretary of State Edward Stettinius successfully twisted the arm of Liberia. Henry Morgenthau, Jr., pressured Cuba. A former undersecretary of state induced Haiti to change its vote. Bernard Baruch convinced France by threatening to cut off U.S. aid. Bribes were paid to Latin American delegates. The Soviet vote swept in the votes of the Ukrainian and Byelorussian Soviet Republics, Czechoslovakia, Poland, Bulgaria, Rumania and possibly Yugoslavia. See Cohen, *Palestine,* 296-8; Steven L. Spiegel, *The Other Arab-Israeli Conflict* (Chicago: University of Chicago Press, 1985), 30; Shlaim, *Collusion,* 117.

28. In contrast, in September of 1948 when Egypt declared an "all-Palestinian government" over Palestine, the major world powers ignored it. Thus, apart from Syria, Lebanon and Iraq, the Palestinian state failed to attain recognition.

29. Cohen, *Palestine,* 292-3.

30. Truman stated that he tended to blame the intractability of the Palestinian problem on the "extreme American Zionists." Cohen, *Palestine,* 293.

31. Cohen, *Palestine,* 293.

32. Albert Hourani, a Lebanese scholar-historian and Oxford don, quoted in Sachar, *History,* Vol. I, 295.

33. Harry S Truman, *Memoirs: Years of Trial and Hope* (Garden City, N.Y.: Doubleday, 1956), 133.

Chapter 7

Civil War (December, 1947 to May, 1948)

Following passage of the UN partition resolution on November 27, 1947, local fighting broke out in Palestine. No published study has established and apportioned blame for the hostilities which gradually escalated into full-scale civil war. It would seem, however, that the hostilities were "almost spontaneous."[1] Violence was inevitable since the international community, while voting for partition, failed to implement it with UN peace-keeping forces. So between November 28, 1947, and May 14, 1948 (*before* the British withdrew and the Jews declared statehood), fighting was largely between local forces – a civil war between Palestinian Arabs and Jews. After May 14 the war became an *international* conflict between Israel and the surrounding Arab nations (see chapter 8).

The UN partition resolution: Political decision without teeth

Once passed by the UN, the partition plan took on an aura of legitimacy and fair compromise. While it was not entirely clear whether the UN had the legal authority to *forceably* implement partition, there certainly was hope in the West that it would do so.[2] This was not to be. For one, the United States had no wish to contribute to UN forces where Soviet forces would also be involved. Secondly, there was an international reluctance to forceably impose partition on a land overwhelmingly Arab, particularly when Arabs were protesting partition on grounds of their right of self-determination – the very right the UN claimed to champion.

In truth, the UN partition resolution did not resolve but rather *fueled* the conflict by polarizing both sides – filling the Jews with joy and justification, the Arabs with outrage and panic. The protagonists openly faced each other without benefit of either an international peace-keeping buffer or an effective British military force that had afforded a degree of protection to both Arab and Jew.[3]

An imbalance of fighting forces

The UN-proposed Arab state was not economically viable or militarily defensible. It constituted, thus, a political and military vacuum easily filled by Transjordanian or Jewish intervention. Moreover, local Arab fighting forces were very limited at the time, consisting of approximately 3,000 volunteers led by the mufti's nephew. The surrounding Arab countries (the Arab League), fearful of the British troops still in Palestine, offered little meaningful military help to local Palestinians. The League did send in some irregulars (the so-called "Arab Liberation Army"), a disorganized and unmotivated army of 2,000 to 3,000 primarily Syrian mercenaries.[4] The leader of this army, Fawei al-Kaukji, condemned the local Palestinians for "getting in the way" but was himself "little short of a menace to his own side," according to the British minister.[5] Al-Kaukji actually collaborated with the Haganah to undermine the local Palestinians. An additional group of 2,000 Moslem Brotherhood volunteers came from Egypt.[6]

The added presence of Syrian and Egyptian forces supplementing local Palestinians forces has left a popular impression of significant resolve and intervention by the surrounding Arab League nations, but the total Arab force was less than 10,000. The outside forces were largely for show. They engaged in spotty ineffectual actions in Palestine and, in combination with Palestinian volunteers and terrorist factions, comprised an Arab fighting force that was neither competent nor coordinated in late 1947.[7] Because the Palestinian Arabs had no governmental authority and lacked the power to conscript men, they had nothing faintly resembling the leadership of the Jewish Agency and its military wing (the Haganah and terrorist groups). Still, once the British withdrew in May 1948, the combined Arab forces probably doubled.

The Jewish fighting forces consisted of the Haganah and Jewish terrorists:

> The Haganah had been forged during the war [World War II] into a well-organized illegal army of an estimated 60,000 troops with a striking force, a static defense force and reservists. In these units belonged most of the enlistees from the Jewish Brigade and other branches of the British armed forces, now being demobilized gradually. Moreover the equivalent of one

year's compulsory military training for high-school seniors was inaugurated in November 1945. Considerable military supplies acquired during the war years had been distributed throughout the community.[8]

Historians as well as actual military participants at the time have made different assessments of Jewish military strength in 1947, ranging from 30,000 including reservists, to 60,000 not including reservists.[9] Partly, these variable estimates have to do with the *changing* balance of forces – immigration of Jewish fighting-age men and foreign volunteers steadily increasing while Palestinian Arabs fled (some 200,000 by May 15, 1948).[10] Whatever the estimates, Israeli historian Simha Flapan concludes that Jewish forces never outnumbered Arab forces, neither during the civil war phase of the war nor after May 1948 during the international war.[11]

Ben-Gurion had reason to feel confident. He saw little real threat from local Palestinian Arabs. Because he understood at the time that the Palestinian Arabs could not effectively attack the Jews or even defend themselves against attack, he felt free to devote Jewish forces to continued attack of the *British*, whom he believed might, despite their scheduled evacuation on May 15, need to be forced out of Palestine. He knew, too, that the only significant Arab force outside Palestine was Transjordan's army (the Arab Legion), which, as described in the previous chapter, had been neutralized by a mutual non-aggression pact.

Ben-Gurion considered that he had the leeway to place political considerations above military ones. For example, he posted the Haganah around the *periphery* of UN-designated Jewish territory – leaving the Jewish settlements within exposed to Palestinian attack.[12] He was demonstrating to the world an important political point: that Jewish territory, as allotted by the UN, was viable and self-maintaining. For both political and military reasons Ben-Gurion also chose to defend rather than abandon thirty-five Jewish settlements in territory earmarked by the UN for an Arab state – settlements that could later be used as both defensive barriers and potentially offensive bases.[13]

The political use of the Haganah did carry initial costs for some Jewish citizens, particularly those in Jerusalem. Because the Haganah was stretched thinly around the periphery of the Jewish state-to-be and was protecting and supplying Jewish settlements in UN-designated Arab territory, it was incapable of concentrated military action. Nor was the Haganah fully mobilized and equipped at the very first.[14] Consequently, the Palestinian Arabs were relatively more effective in the first months of fighting after November 27, 1947. They could, for example, easily control highways in Arab areas of Palestine.

Jerusalem, tucked into Arab territory and dependent on highway transportation for food, water and supplies, was besieged by bands of Palestinian guerrillas in January 1948. Convoys to the city were blocked.

Still, limiting the use of the Haganah made military and political sense. Had the Haganah aggressively escalated, the British, still in charge of law and order, might as aggressively have curtailed them as they had the Arabs in 1936. More importantly, there was concern that escalation of fighting might cause the United States to press for an abandonment of the UN partition plan in favor of a UN *trusteeship* over Palestine, precluding the establishment of a sovereign Jewish state. Ben-Gurion faced a dilemma: possible international disapproval were he to escalate the violence, or seeming weakness that might lead to belief in the international community that a Jewish state was not militarily viable. Either alternative could encourage the UN to revert to trusteeship.

In December 1947, Ben-Gurion chose the more militant course. He announced a policy of "aggressive defense" that involved the destruction of Arab homes and expulsion of Arabs in territory designated for the Jewish state.[15] The fighting escalated in volleys of retaliation and counter-retaliation. For example, on December 30, 1947, the Irgun threw a grenade at Arab workers in a Haifa refinery, killing six and wounding forty-two (a violation of an established non-aggression agreement between Arab and Jewish workers).[16] Arab workers retaliated by killing forty-one Jewish workers. The Haganah retaliated against that retaliation by attacking a nearby Arab village (Balad al-Shaykh), killing fifty to sixty, including women and children.[17] A few days later the Irgun killed 26 Arab citizens in Jaffa with a car bomb and another twenty-five with explosives in Jerusalem. In March 1948, three parked British army trucks exploded in Jerusalem, killing fifty Jews, an act suspiciously suggestive of British-Arab collaboration. In the three large towns (Tel Aviv, Haifa and Jerusalem) most terrorist attacks were initiated by the Irgun after January 1948. They succeeded in instilling panic in large sections of the Arab community.[18] A pattern developed in which the Irgun or LEHI would initiate an attack, the Arabs would retaliate, and the Haganah, while condemning the action of Jewish terrorists, would further embark on inflaming Jewish "counter-retaliation."

The United States reverses its position on partition, favoring UN trusteeship

On March 19, 1948, after three and one half months of increasingly intense, largely terrorist fighting – at a time when the Palestinian Arab blockade of the Tel Aviv-Jerusalem highway had seriously interrupted supplies to Jerusalem –

the United States announced in favor of a temporary UN trusteeship. U.S. motives were mixed: (1) the aforementioned fear that U.S. and Soviet forces would be drawn into the conflict;[19] (2) a U.S. State Department concern that a Jewish state might assume a communist coloration, given its Russian Jewish-socialist-kibbutzim roots – thereby handing the Soviets a victory; (3) a U.S. State Department belief that the Arab countries would accept more Jewish immigration under a trusteeship; and (4) concern for reducing violence and assuring the safety of the Jews.

The Jews were incensed by U.S. "backsliding" toward trusteeship. Delay of statehood (not the fighting of Arabs) was seen as the "next Holocaust." Moreover, since Ben-Gurion had knowledge of what the United States only suspected (the Jewish-Transjordanian non-aggression pact), he had far less reason to be concerned about the dangers of escalation than did the United States. Accordingly, Ben-Gurion pressed forward militarily before the United States could organize a UN vote on trusteeship. He would demonstrate not mere military self-sufficiency but a capacity for *definitive victory* and declare statehood at the earliest possible time.[20] Statehood would "depend on our ability to emerge victorious." This aggressive stance was possible because arms were arriving in two weeks (on April 1) from Czechoslovakia and the Jewish military forces continued to grow rapidly.[21] This new aggressive military plan was called "Plan Dalet."

Plan Dalet: Defeat of Arabs in civil war and flight of the Arab population

Plan Dalet was not limited to expulsion of Arabs living within UN-designated Jewish territory. It included the seizure of Arab areas in Galilee (northern Palestine) and the corridor between Tel Aviv and Jerusalem (areas designated by the UN for the Arab state-to-be or for an international free zone). All Jewish settlements in UN-designated Arab territory were to be secured, rather than evacuated, with corridors reaching out to create a solid, continuous and enlarged Jewish territory. "The aim of the plan was annexation [of Arab territory] – the destruction of Arab villages was to be followed by the establishment of Jewish villages in their place."[22]

This plan violated both the UN partition resolution and the secret non-aggression pact with Transjordan. Consequently, the military actions were, at first, left to unofficial forces, the Irgun and LEHI. These groups, officially condemned by the Jewish Agency for their terrorism, were permitted to operate largely without check.[23]

Ben-Gurion was aware of the risks attached to attacking Arab villages and cities within areas designated by the UN for the Arab state: (1) the British, still present, might intervene militarily, (2) the UN might condemn Jewish actions, and (3) Transjordan might, from its side, break the non-aggression pact – since the Jews were violating it. On the other hand, success would enlarge Jewish territory beyond UN-apportioned areas *and* demonstrate Jewish capacity for definitive victory.

The Plan Dalet goal of creating a corridor between Tel Aviv and Jerusalem was a top priority. Arab control of the Tel Aviv-Jerusalem highway was strangling Jerusalem. By March 25, 1948, the besieged city was under food and water rationing. By capturing Palestinian Arab villages along the east-west highway, the siege of Jerusalem could be broken and Arab Palestine divided in half. Accordingly, 1,500 Haganah troops using smuggled Czech arms opened the Jerusalem highway at Castel in Arab Palestine in Operation Nachshon. In this fight the local Husseini Palestinian nationalists, led by the mufti's cousin, Abd al-Qadir al-Husseini, were refused a resupply of arms by Fawzi al-Kaukji (a.k.a. al-Qawukji), fractious leader of the Arab Liberation Army – now collaborating with the Haganah against local Palestinians.[24] When al-Husseini was killed, his death led to the complete collapse of local Palestinian forces.[25] Three days later (April 4, 1948) the Arab Liberation Army was itself dealt a humiliating and fatal defeat while attacking a kibbutz on the Jenin-Haifa highway.[26]

Thus, it was evident by early April that the Palestinians and the Arab Liberation Army irregulars could not defend themselves against the Jews. "Once the tide had turned in their favor, the Jews no longer felt constrained to remain within the narrow and awkward boundaries laid down for them by the UN cartographers. . . . The only practical constraint on Jewish expansion stemmed from their understanding with Abdullah to let him take the Arab parts as defined by the [UN] resolution."[27] By violating the agreement not to attack Arab territories, Ben-Gurion risked a Transjordanian retaliation and even precipitation of an international war that might *include* Transjordan on the Arab side. Yet the Jews now had a powerful fighting force. Perhaps Abdullah couldn't be counted on anyhow, being under pressure from the Arab League to attack Jewish areas as proof of non-collusion with the Jews.[28] On the other hand, if Abdullah kept his word (as in fact he did),[29] then the Jews would profit. Firstly, the Arab countries would be militarily divided by their opposition to Transjordan annexation in Palestine (as in fact they were). Secondly, the Jews could exploit intra-Arab conflict by violating the non-aggression pact, invading and annexing Arab territory themselves (as in fact they did).[30]

Further Jewish terrorism

On April 9, 1948, just after the defeat of the Palestinians and Arab Liberation Army in Operation Nachshon, a watershed event occurred that accelerated the flight of Palestinian Arabs from Palestine. It created a massive refugee problem that hardened relations between the Jews and Abdullah. The Haganah had razed the villages of Castel, Hulda and Deir Mohsin along the Tel Aviv-Jerusalem highway as part of Plan Dalet. Another Arab village outside Jerusalem, Deir Yassin, was attacked by the Irgun and LEHI, headed respectively by Menachem Begin and Yitzhak Shamir.[31] Two hundred fifty-four men, women and children were murdered, some mutilated and thrown down wells.[32] Some villagers were taken by truck to Jerusalem for a victory parade through the streets then returned and shot against a wall. Several weeks later, Palestinian terrorists killed seventy-seven Jewish civilians in reprisal, followed by Jewish counter-reprisals. Terrorism accelerated on both sides.[33]

The Jewish Agency denied all responsibility for Deir Yassin. It denounced the Irgun in a telegram to Abdullah – yet ratified in the next days an agreement of cooperation between the Irgun and Haganah. The news of Deir Yassin (spread largely by Arabs) flashed across Palestine. Ben-Gurion was concerned that the massacre would inflame Abdullah or force him to align with the surrounding Arab countries, thereby enlarging the war and turning the UN political tide against partition: "A major contention of official Zionist propaganda was that peaceful relations between Arabs and Jews were possible [and] . . . one of the main objectives of . . . policy. Any sign of deterioration, any incident liable to plunge Palestine into a bloodbath, naturally encouraged the opponents of partition."[34]

It was a watershed event because the fate of Deir Yassin, a village having strictly observed a non-aggression pact with the Haganah, demonstrated decisively that such non-aggression pacts, common between Arab villagers and the Haganah, could not be relied on. "More than any other single event, it was responsible for breaking the spirit of the civilian population and setting into motion the mass exodus of Arabs from Palestine."[35]

After this event, "entire Arab communities were fleeing in terror even before Jewish forces overran their homes."[36] The capture of Haifa (a half-Jewish city) two weeks later and the attack on Jaffa (the largest Arab city in Palestine) in May created 145,000 additional refugees fleeing in fear for their lives. By the end of

May 1948, soon after the Jews declared statehood, 370,000 Arabs were fleeing from Jewish held territory to other countries as homeless refugees.[37]

This mass exodus of Palestinians presented the Zionists with what Chaim Weizmann later called a "miraculous simplification of the problem." But that same exodus also destroyed Truman's rationale for the establishment of the Jewish state – a state that was supposed to *solve* the European refugee problem, not to create a new refugee problem. By the end of the civil war period there were many more Arab refugees in the Middle East than there were Jewish refugees remaining in Europe.

Ben-Gurion rejects UN and U.S. truce proposals

In April and May 1948, the United States abandoned its trusteeship proposal of March and focused attention on arranging a truce. In parallel, the UN Security Council set up a truce commission (April 23, 1948) to end the local fighting, stop displacement of Palestinian Arabs and head off a full-scale Jewish-Arab international war. Ben-Gurion was "vigorously opposed to any kind of truce"[38] lest it lead to trusteeship, extension of the British mandate or otherwise jeopardize a Jewish state.[39] Israel's fate, in Ben-Gurion's view, depended more on getting military equipment than on what happened at truce negotiations at Lake Success.[40] Moreover, he was confident by April 1948 of having both U.S. support and Jewish military superiority in the event of any international war. UN military experts shared his appraisal.[41] The Arab countries felt otherwise:

> Despite the agreement in principle they had reached in favor of official intervention in Palestine, they [the Arab countries] still preferred a solution which would would make it unnecessary for them to be drawn into war. They wished to avoid an armed conflict and thereby deny Abdullah the opportunity to pursue his expansionist aims.[42]

So when the UN Security Council voted for a truce in the civil conflict between the Palestinian Arabs and the Jews on April 17, 1948 (one month before the end of the British mandate), Egypt voted in favor and Syria was prepared to agree.[43]

Certainly the Arab countries were torn. They were not financially or militarily able to fight a war in Palestine, yet were trapped by their own belligerent rhetoric and domestic opposition to partition in Palestine.

Public opinion in Arab countries was greatly alarmed by the news of the Deir

Yassin massacre and the flight of tens of thousands of Arabs from Jaffa, Haifa, Tiberias, and other towns. The prevailing belief was that the Irgun was gaining more and more power in Palestine. There was tremendous pressure on the Arab rulers to do something to save their Arab brethren in Palestine from murder, plunder, and expulsion.[44]

And yet, according to a cable from the American ambassador in Cairo: "The Arabs would now welcome almost any face-saving device if it would prevent open war. Might even accept de facto partition through acquiescence to march of Abdullah's troops to Jewish-Arab frontier."[45]

In late April 1948, the U.S. State Department independently pressed for a truce. The United States was alarmed that with the British soon to be gone, the Jews and Arabs would *both* declare statehood and enter into an arms race that would precipitate a conflagration involving many foreign countries (not unlike the Spanish civil war). The State Department persuaded the Arab nations to accept, off the record, a Jewish immigration of 48,000 per year, a prior sticking point and condition demanded by Ben-Gurion. The United States also considered pledging assistance to the Jews if, after the truce, the Arabs were to invade. By now accepting these conditions that Ben-Gurion had previously insisted on, the Arab nations sought to avoid war in Palestine.

But the Jews turned down the U.S. proposal, knowing that the local Palestinians and Syrian irregulars were demoralized. Weapons from Czechoslovakia and France were coming in past the British troops who were now concerned only with leaving Palestine without casualties. With a stockpile of war surplus arms in Europe and a capacity to make munitions locally within Palestine, the Jews were prepared to take their chances.[46] Moreover, generalized war would provide King Abdullah with the opportunity to invade Palestinian areas in appearance of saving the Palestinians from the Jews – in which case, the Jews would have, through Abdullah, a way to control the Palestinian Arabs. Alternatively, the Jews could simply ignore the pact with Abdullah and advance on and acquire Palestinian territory in a lopsided war.

The United States was disturbed by Jewish recalcitrance to accept a truce. Truman warned that if the Jews refused the truce without reasonable grounds, they need not expect anything else from the United States.[47] U.S. diplomat Robert McClintock issued a stern critique of the Jewish position:

The Jewish Agency refusal [of the truce] exposes its aim to set up its separate state by force of arms – the military action after May 15 will be conducted by the Haganah with the help of the terrorist organizations, the Irgun and LEHI, [and] the UN will face a distorted situation. The Jews will be the real aggressors against the Arabs, but will claim that they are only defending the borders of the state, decided upon . . . by the General Assembly.[48]

Through diplomatic channels, without official public pronouncement, the Arab countries (with the exception of Transjordan) accepted the U.S. truce proposal on May 3, 1948.[49] The secretary general of the Arab League sought to convince Abdullah to support the truce, but this last ditch effort by the Arab League was futile since truce would have wrecked Abdullah's annexation plan. The Jews stood firm since a truce would have forced them to accept the UN-drawn boundaries for a Jewish state. Ben-Gurion's stated reason for refusal was that a truce would give the Arab armies time to prepare themselves to invade.[50]

Jewish public sentiment in Palestine was also against a truce, even though it would have prevented an expected outside Arab invasion. The Jews clearly dominated the fighting and were excited about their defeat of local Palestinian and volunteer fighting groups. Spectacular victories in Galilee, the surrender of Arabs in Jaffa and the flight of Arabs from Haifa, all created an atmosphere of enthusiasm and confidence, along with much anti-Arab ultranationalistic propaganda. The Jewish Agency, while condemning Jewish terrorism, was increasingly utilizing that terrorism for its own purposes, and the Haganah (under Agency control) was blowing up Arab villages with abandon. Even the more liberal, antiwar parties in Jewish Palestine were against a truce, believing it to be merely a way to prevent the creation of the Jewish state. Ben-Gurion was determined to take the military route, supported by a broad wave of public enthusiasm.

Meir threatens Abdullah about joining a coming Arab invasion

The Jews had created a problem for themselves by violating their own non-aggression pact with Transjordan. Mutual suspicion was in the air. It was reasonable for Abdullah to suspect by late April that the Jews intended to take all of Palestine and leave him with nothing to annex. Seeming to presage such a total takeover was: (1) the occupation or destruction of Arab villages earmarked for Transjordan by the Meir-Abdullah agreement, (2) the conquest of Haifa and Jaffa by the Haganah and Irgun, and (3) a broken truce in Jerusalem.[51] The Jews were also making unequivocal assertions that Jerusalem was to be all Jewish.[52]

In light of the Jewish invasion of Arab territory and the Deir Yassin massacre, which resulted in refugee problems for the Arab nations, the Jews had reason to suspect that Abdullah might be unable to resist pressure from the Arab League to protect Palestinian Arabs. Ben-Gurion had Golda Meir meet again with Abdullah on May 10, 1948 – by some accounts to determine his intentions, by others, to threaten him.[53] As at their first meeting in November 1947, Abdullah again raised his favorite idea: *a union of Palestine (in its entirety) with Transjordan,* with a 50-percent Jewish parliament and executive cabinet – a kind of Judeo-Arab republic/kingdom. Meir flatly refused and reminded him of their non-aggression pact designed to split Palestine into a Jewish state and Arab territories to be annexed by Transjordan.

Anxious to avoid military conflict, Abdullah then suggested that the Jews cede to him some *Jewish* territory in order to dispel a growing Arab League suspicion about Jewish-Transjordanian collusion.[54] Perhaps, then, he could even convince the Arabs to accept partition.[55] He argued that without such territorial concessions, he simply appeared to be collaborating with the Jews rather than championing Palestinian Arab independence. Meir answered that there could be no question of territorial concessions[56] and that if Transjordan fought the Jews, the Jews would no longer be bound by UN-designated borders. Each would take whatever was in his power to take – notwithstanding the fact that the Jews had already captured UN-designated Arab territory.[57] Ben-Gurion's advisor paraphrased Meir's threat: "If you join the invasion, we will take off the velvet gloves."[58]

Abdullah indicated that he had no intention of reneging on their pact but that new events like the atrocity at Deir Yassin had brought outside Arab pressure on him – necessitating a change in *tactics* but not a change in original plan.[59] Meir's response was a proposed Transjordan-Jewish peace treaty that would bar entry of Transjordan into Palestine! Abdullah would be permitted to send a governer to rule Arab parts – only later would these parts be recognized by the Jews as annexed to Transjordan.[60] Acceptance of such a proposal would have immediately ruined Abdullah's legitimacy in the Arab world.

Abdullah expressed his regrets about the coming bloodshed and destruction. The Jews were prepared to respect borders, Meir maintained, as long as there was peace. But in the event of war they would fight everywhere and with all their increasing power. She reported back to the Jewish provisional cabinet that "the meeting had been friendly and that Abdullah did not really want to fight, he feared defeat and was more afraid of his fellow Arabs than of the Jews. But he had become entangled and could not extricate himself."[61]

Consequent precipitation of the international war

> In Zionist historiography the [second Meir-Abdullah] meeting is usually
> presented as a valiant but utterly futile and unsuccessful attempt to avert the
> outbreak of war [with Transjordan and other Arab countries]. . . . The Zionist
> charge against Abdullah is that he revoked his pledge not to attack the Jewish
> state and threw his lot with the rest of the Arab world. This charge helped to
> sustain the legends that grew up around the 1948 war of a carefully
> orchestrated and monolithic all-Arab invasion plan directed at strangling the
> Jewish state at birth. . . . First- or second-hand accounts of the meeting,
> however, do not cast Abdullah quite so unambiguously in the role of villain
> and traitor. . . .[62]

Abdullah had to deal with the Arab world. He needed face-saving concessions
to gain credibility and to enable other Arab countries to back away from
formidable domestic rage about a Jewish takeover of Palestine.[63] He was
realistic enough to know that while he might be able to make a dent here and
there, he could not successfully fight the Jews.[64] Nor could he simply make a
peace treaty and do nothing while the Jews captured the whole of Jerusalem and
Palestinian refugees streamed into Arab countries. He needed an appearance of
war, at least some mock battles, and this Meir would not give him.

One historian ascribes this refusal to Meir's inflexibility:

> Mrs. Meir . . . was totally lacking in . . . political subtlety . . . she clung with
> the utmost tenacity . . . .to the unnatural and arbitrary borders of the 1947
> partition resolution. There was not the slightest hint of flexibility about the
> posture she struck. It should not have been beyond the realm of possibility to
> preserve the spirit of the November [1947] agreement by adopting new tactics
> – by staging mock battles, for example – to enable Abdullah to pose as a great
> Arab nationalist while at the same time averting a real military clash.[65]

However, this explanation presupposes that Meir *intended* to avert a war. In
fact, war was *the* means and justification for expansion beyond the UN-assigned
borders. The "inflexibility explanation" ignores the facts that: (1) the Jews had
rejected U.S. and UN truce efforts to avert international war in the weeks before;
(2) the mood for international war and victory already existed within the Jewish
community since Plan Dalet (December 1947); (3) a rapidly enlarging arsenal of
Jewish weapons gave Ben-Gurion confidence about Jewish military superiority;
and (4) a continuing cause for mass exodus of Palestinian Arabs was essential to

make the Jewish state "Jewish."[66]

Indeed, Ben-Gurion's statesmanship has been seen to consist precisely in his courage and vision to *reject* a truce, declare a Jewish state and proceed to international war – not to make peace with or save the face of Arab countries.[67]

The British mandate ended on May 14, British troops withdrawn. That same day the Jews declared the state of Israel – though without delineating its boundaries. The Arab countries were incensed by this provocatively early declaration of statehood (contrary to UN recommendation) but the United States and U.S.S.R. immediately gave diplomatic recognition. An international war involving Israel and the Arab nations was now expected – a war in which Israel would increasingly invade UN-designated Arab territory.

Observations

Reviewing the complex history of this period, several things are notable:

(1) Public opinion and, to a considerable extent, propaganda were powerful determinants of Middle East events – along with factors of military power and international climate. American public opinion was pushing for a Jewish state, regardless; Jewish public opinion in Palestine favored an immediate military rather than political solution; and Arab public opinion was aroused by belligerent Arab government rhetoric. Propaganda and nationalistic fervor combined to create a vortex which drew all parties into an international war – and an eventual unstable one-state solution in Palestine.

(2) The motivations of the conflicting parties were complex and hardly as pure as popularly represented. There is little basis for popular simplistic constructions such as: "When Israel accepted the United Nations partition plan, it thus was the only nation ever to recognize a Palestinian state. Arab armies responded with war."[68] This statement ignores the fact that the Jews clearly intended the demise of a sovereign Palestinian Arab state through economic crippling and collusion with Transjordan. Unquestionably, the Arab countries chose to invade. Yet the Jews avoided truce-making steps which could have taken advantage of Arab desires to avoid war with Israel (and conflict with each other).

(3) None of the conflicting parties seemed to think seriously about the *future* of Arab-Jewish relations. At the time it must have felt honorable and necessary to Arab nations to struggle against Jewish and Transjordanian expansion. It must also have seemed wise to the Jews to play to advantage and accept war, leaving future Arab-Jewish relations to take care of themselves. Yet the time was

one of last fading chances that the struggle in Palestine would be faced as a matter of negotiation, if not justice, rather than might – something that neither side pursued with any vigor.

Notes

1. Michael J. Cohen, *Palestine and the Great Powers, 1945-1948* (Princeton: Princeton University Press, 1982), 303.

2. Question was raised about whether the UN had the legal authority to impose a political solution such as partition. Perhaps it was because the United States wanted to *not* forceably implement partition that the U.S. ambassador to the UN argued, "The Charter of the United Nations does not empower the Security Council to enforce a political settlement. . . . The Security Council's action . . . is directed to keeping the peace and not to enforcing partition." However, the U.S. State Department legal advisor disagreed. Cohen, *Palestine*, 351-2.

3. Neither Arab nor Jew wished to encounter the well-trained British forces, which did attempt to protect and disarm both sides. The British were inconsistent in this peace-keeping function, more often favoring the Arabs (the Jews being judged uncooperative and terroristic). There is reason to believe that British soldiers, at the local level, favored the Arabs with information about facilities available for occupation upon British evacuation. Still, through intelligence collection, the Jews learned about and obtained their share of such facilities. British soldiers would sometimes sell guns and ammunition to Arabs, just as Allied soldiers would sell to Jews during the war. The British were decreasingly concerned about protecting either side once evacuation began.

4. The Arab Liberation Army was composed of about 2,000 to 3,000 men in early 1948, increasing to 6,000 to 8,000 by April 1948. Avi Shlaim, *Collusion across the Jordan* (New York: Columbia University Press, 1988), 155.

5. "The Palestinians were not even requested to carry out guerrilla operations against the Jewish forces or to perform any combat-support missions." Shlaim, *Collusion,* 202.

6. Howard Sachar, *A History of Israel: From the Rise of Zionism to Our Time,* Vol. I (New York: Knopf, 1986), 300.

7. Also fighting were a few Arab soldiers who had been with British army during World War II and some remnants of Arab terrorist societies long suppressed by the British. The British had suppressed the Arab Higher Committee, the central Palestinian Arab political institution, but allowed it to re-form in 1945. AHC chairman and Grand Mufti of Jerusalem Haj Amin el Husseini was barred from Palestine in 1938, though his cousin and deputy, Jamal Husseini, returned to Palestine in 1946.

8. Hurewitz, J. C., *The Struggle for Palestine* (New York: Schocken, 1976), 239.

9. Sachar, *History*, Vol. I, 300; Cohen, *Palestine*, 320. The low estimate comes from Lawrence Collins and Dominique Lapierre, *O Jerusalem* (New York, Simon and Schuster, 1972), 410: "At the outbreak of the war [civil war phase] the Israeli forces, numbering 30,000 men, had experience and enthusiasm but lacked equipment. Over one-third of the soldiers were without rifles. The Israeli forces had very little long-range armament, neither cannon nor mortars, few antitank weapons, and only light aircraft. However, there were massive stores of modern weapons, including tanks, aircraft, artillery and small arms, that had been purchased abroad and were awaiting transfer to Palestine [upon British departure on May 15].".". Included were 30,000 rifles, 5,000 machine guns, 200 heavy machine guns, 30 fighter aircraft, several B-12 bombers, 50 cannons 35 antiaircraft guns, 12 heavy mortars, and large stores of ammunition. Simha Flapan, *The Birth of Israel* (New York: Pantheon, 1987), 193-4.

10. Fred Khouri, *The Arab-Israeli Dilemma* (Syracuse, N.Y.: Syracuse University Press, 1985), 68. At first, middle-class business and political leaders left in conviction that partition was a fait accompli. Rural Palestinians left later in panic about Jewish terrorism.

11. See Flapan, *Birth of Israel*, 195-6.

12. No Jewish settlements, however deep in Arab territory, fell to Arab attack. Hundreds of Arab settlements fell to Jewish attack. One exception: Etzion, a Jewish settlement in a UN-designated Palestinian area, fell to Transjordan on May 12, 1948. This Transjordanian attack was preceded by an Etzion settler/soldier ambush of vehicles and roadblock to stop Transjordan from defending an Arab quarter in Jerusalem (Katamon) under Jewish attack. Shlaim, *Collusion*, 180, 215.

13. Netanel Lorch, *The Edge of the Sword: Israel's War of Independence, 1947-1949* (New York: Putman, 1961), 34, 49-50.

14. The Jews had arms distributed throughout settlements but the Haganah itself was initially in short supply. The Jews had munitions-making machinery in Palestine – supplied by the British during World War II – but were barred from production while the British were still in charge. The Jews also had large stocks of war surplus arms in Europe. These had to be smuggled into Palestine. The United States had an embargo on arms sales to either side. The British could still sell to Arab countries, so the Arab League was able to supply the Arab Liberation Army with rifles – though it refused to supply local Palestinians.

15. Ben-Gurion states, "We adopt the system of aggressive defense; with every Arab attack we must respond with a decisive blow: the destruction of the place or the expulsion of the residents along with the seizure of the place." David Ben-Gurion, *War Diary: The War of Independence, 1948-1949* (in Hebrew) [December 19, 1947] G. Rivlin and E. Orren, eds. (Tel Aviv: Ministry of Defense, 1982), 58. Cited in Flapan, *Birth of Israel*, 90.

16. Flapan, *Birth of Israel*, 95.

17. Cohen, *Palestine*, 308.

18. Cohen, *Palestine*, 308.

19. George Kennan of the Truman administration argued that the United States should relieve itself not only of the threat of Soviet participation in enforcement of partition, but of the stigma attached to the United States for having pushed through a partition plan of dubious legality by applying irregular pressures on other countries. Cohen, *Palestine*, 346-7.

20. Ben-Gurion was aware that he could declare statehood if the UN were to revert to trusteeship, but would thereby lose international recognition essential to statehood.

21. Illicit immigration continued, increasing manpower. Conscription of all 18 to 25-year-olds was imposed four months before.

22. Flapan, *Birth of Israel*, 42.

23. Christopher Sykes, *Crossroads to Israel* (Cleveland: World Publishing, 1965), 352.

24. He held a bitter personal grudge against al-Husseini and also seemed to believe that Palestine should be joined to Transjordan, not be independent, as the mufti desired. Repeatedly he sought deals with the Jews. Shlaim, *Collusion*, 155.

25. Shlaim, *Collusion*, 159.

26. The leader of the Arab Liberation Army had proven himself incompetent in an earlier battle at Tirat Zvi and sought to restore his image by trying (without clear success) to get the Jews to hand him a victory as a price for collaborating with them. Mishmar-Haemek was that attempt.

27. Shlaim, *Collusion*, 159.

28. Abdullah's propaganda against the Jews, designed to disguise the Jewish-Transjordanian pact, was viewed by some Jews as evidence of his intentions to break that pact.

29. Apart from Jerusalem, which was not covered by the Jewish-Transjordanian agreement, "the Arab Legion respected the partition borders and made no attempt to seize Jewish territory." Shlaim, *Collusion*, 239.

30. Flapan, *Birth of Israel*, 136. "In fact, Ben-Gurion himself had no intention of remaining loyal to his negotiators' commitment to Abdullah. He did not expect Abdullah to give up any part of Arab Palestine voluntarily. He notes in his dairies repeatedly the necessity of a head-on clash with the Arab Legion. He hoped to smash the Legion and force Abdullah to accept territorial concessions"(137) – as happened.

31. It is unknown whether either of these leaders did more than plan this massacre. Begin later justified the Irgun's action by claiming that the villagers were warned to flee. Menachem Begin, *The Revolt: Story of the Irgun* (New York: Nash Publications, 1977), 163.

32. Shlaim, *Crossroads*, 164; Mark Tessler, *A History of the Israeli-Palestinian Conflict* (Bloomington: Indiana University Press, 1994), 291.

33. Sykes, *Crossroads*, 351-2. Arab villagers committed an atrocity on May 13. They murdered 124 Jewish settlers from the Etzion bloc. The Arab Legion had attacked the Etzion bloc after the settlers, on several occasions, ambushed the Legion's communication units on the highway. The Legion turned the settlers over

to some local Arab villagers. Other massacres committed by the Haganah or Jewish terrorists included those in the Arab villages of Khissas, Sassa, Nasr al-Din, Ain al-Zeitoun, Er-Rama and Duweima. The forced expulsion of 70,000 Arabs from Lydda and Ramleh was ordered by Ben-Gurion and executed by Allon and Rabin. Tessler, *History of Conflict*, 293, 297.

34. Shlaim, *Collusion*, 164-5.

35. Shlaim, *Collusion*, 164.

36. Jacques de Reynier, chief Red Cross representative. Sachar, *History*, Vol. I, 334.

37. Flapan, *Birth of Israel*, 89ff.

38. Flapan, *Birth of Israel*, 165. American Zionist leader Rabbi Silver also opposed a truce (168).

39. Ben-Gurion opposed peace efforts by tactical stalling over a truce condition prohibiting immigration into Palestine of individuals capable of bearing arms.

40. Flapan, *Birth of Israel*, 166.

41. Flapan, *Birth of Israel*, 166.

42. Shlaim, *Collusion*, 189. See discussion in Flapan, *Birth of Israel*, 175-81.

43. The Syrians would have agreed as long as the truce included the condition that new persons capable of bearing arms were prohibited from entering Palestine. Both Jews and Arabs were importing fighting personnel from outside countries.

44. Flapan, *Birth of Israel*, 181.

45. U.S. State Department, 867N 01/5-1378 cable 513 from Cairo, May 13, 1948. Cited in Flapan, *Birth of Israel*, 181.

46. "They [the Jews] seemed confident on the basis of recent military successes and the prospect of a 'behind the barn' deal with Abdullah, that they could establish their sovereign state without any necessity for a truce with the Arabs of Palestine." George Marshall to Ernest Bevin. Quoted in Shlaim, *Collusion*, 190.

47. Flapan, *Birth of Israel*, 173. Yet Truman himself created the condition that made Jewish acceptance of the truce unlikely. For he secretly promised Weizmann that he would recognize the Jewish state whenever it was declared, making it clear he was on the side of the Jews. This helped undermine the U.S. State Department truce effort.

48. U.S. diplomat Robert McClintock. U.S. State Department, *Foreign Relations of the United States:Annual report* [May 4, 1948] (Washington, D.C. 1971), 894-95. Cited in Flapan, *Birth of Israel*, 174.

49. Robert Lovett, assistant secretary of state, informed American representatives in Arab countries that the Arab League and Iraq had accepted the truce proposal. U.S. State Department, 501 BB Palestine/5-548, cables 575, 589. Cited in Flapan, *Birth of Israel*, 174.

50. There was no evidence for thinking that the Arabs would profit from a truce *more* than the Jews. Gen. Yigael Yadin argued that a truce would be of greater help to the Jews. When a truce came a month later, after the Arab invasion, the Jews attained a massive superiority in equipment and manpower just because of that truce.

51. A broken cease-fire in Jerusalem at the end of April following Deir Yassin was chief among the events that stirred Abdullah's mistrust of Jewish intentions. Shlaim,

Collusion, 452. A cease-fire was arranged between the Haganah and the Arab Higher Committee, but before it was technically in effect, the Haganah captured an Arab section of the city (Katamon) and refused to return it.

52. This was made clear in a secret meeting on May 1 between officers from the Haganah (Shlomo Shamir) and the Arab Legion (Desmond Goldie).

53. Meir could have wondered about a single pact violation that Transjordan committed on April 28, 1948. The Arab Legion had attacked Kibbutz Gesher in Jewish territory after the settlers tried to take over a British police fortress. Abdullah, like Ben-Gurion, could not, for reasons of secrecy, always inform those under him of the Jewish-Transjordanian pact. "Under these circumstances it was not always possible to prevent lower-level violations of the agreement." Shlaim, *Collusion,* 178.

54. Flapan, *Birth of Israel,* 141.

55. Shlaim, *Collusion,* 205. Also, Avi Shlaim, *The Politics of Partition* (New York: Columbia University Press, 1990), 160-1.

56. The idea of the Jews ceding territory to build Abdullah's credibility had already been rejected before the meeting.

57. Shlaim, *Politics of Partition,* 161.

58. Yehoshua Palmon, Ben-Gurion's advisor on Arab affairs and Haganah intelligence officer, quoted in Shlaim, *Collusion,* 213.

59. Shlaim, *Collusion,* 211.

60. Cohen, *Palestine,* 334.

61. Cohen, *Palestine,* 334.

62. Shlaim, *Collusion,* 210-11.

63. Herzog to Myerson, May 7, 1948, in Israel State Archives and Central Zionist Archives, Political and Diplomatic Documents, December 1947-May 1948 (Jerusalem, 1979), 755-7. Cited in Shlaim, *Collusion,* 187.

64. He had rejected international truce efforts at this time, not because he wanted to fight, but because he wanted a warlike circumstance in which he could justify annexation of Arab Palestine as its savior.

65. Shlaim, *Collusion,* 213-4.

66. "Deep in his heart, he [Ben-Gurion] rejoiced at the flight of the Arabs from the areas allotted to the Jewish state. His calls on them to stay and promises of a just and humane treatment resulted from tactical considerations not from his fundamental position." Shlaim, *Collusion,* 165.

67. Dan Kurzman, "Can Arafat Be Ben-Gurion?" *New York Times,* September 18, 1988, 23

68. Elie Wiesel, "A Mideast Peace – Is it Possible?" *New York Times,* June 23, 1988, A23.

Chapter 8

International War (May, 1948 to December, 1948)

Arab against Arab

Contrary to popular impression, when Israel declared statehood on May 15, 1948 and set itself for international war, it faced neither a monolithic Arab invasion nor an Arab world primarily interested in its destruction. The chief Arab military power in the Middle East, Transjordan, had no intention of tangling with a large and now well-equipped Israeli force.[1] Moreover, Transjordan had already come to terms with the Jews through their mutual non-aggression pact. Certainly the Arab countries other than Transjordan (most notably Egypt, but also Syria, Iraq, Saudi Arabia and Lebanon) wanted to force Israel to some sort of terms. Yet they were equally interested in thwarting what they suspected was Transjordan's expansionist plan to annex UN-designated Arab Palestine. Egypt feared that if such annexation were to occur, Transjordan would give land to their British patron for military bases in Gaza and the Negev. Syria, too, feared that it would be the next casualty in Transjordan's Greater Syria plan. "Indeed, it may be argued that the Arab League's decision to intervene was rooted not in a common interest to save Palestine for the Palestinians or to defeat Zionist ambitions but in inter-Arab fears and rivalries."[2]

To dampen political fractiousness at home, Arab governments decried the displacement of their Palestinian "brothers" by Europe and the Jews, even though they had little intrinsic interest in Palestinians and wished to avoid war altogether. Domestic outrage about the terrorizing of Palestinians forced authorities to represent themselves as ready saviors, but the greater reason to intervene was suspicion of Abdullah's intentions to alter the rivalrous balance of Arab power in the Middle East by taking over territory in Palestine. Clark Clifford, Truman's White House aide, put it simply in a May 9, 1948, memorandum to the President:

> What is really at play in Palestine is a contest between various Arab States and rulers to attach to themselves Arab Palestine or a part of it . . . any remaining contest for territory will be, not between Jews and Arabs, but between Arabs and Arabs; not for Jewish territory, but for the part of Palestine assigned to the Arab state.[3]

Abdullah sabotages efforts at Arab military unity

For intra-Arab political reasons, Abdullah was elected commander-in-chief of all Arab forces planning to invade Palestine. But since he wanted no other Arab forces in Palestine besides his – so he alone could appear to be "saving the Palestinians from the Jews" – he refused to make any plans for the coming invasion. Certainly he knew that the Jews were too strong for any Arab force.[4] And the other Arab countries, suspicious of Abdullah, refused to allow him even to inspect their forces, supposedly under his command. This disorganization is not altogether inexplicable since the Arab countries, other than Transjordan, hoped that the UN would intervene. On May 11, four days before the British were due to leave Palestine, the Arab countries had no concrete military plan. Practical leadership fell to a weak deputy figure. Finally an operations officer drew up a plan coordinating the forces of different Arab countries. Abdullah modified this plan, then ignored and finally wrecked it. "Within a matter of days . . . it became clear that the notion of a commander-in-chief and a unified command was nothing but a fiction since none of the countries bothered to consult or coordinate their activities."[5] Abdullah's plans involved *non-cooperation* with the other Arab countries, as called for in his non-aggression pact with the Jews.[6] And his expansion into Arab Palestine, instead of attacking the Jews, took the form of thwarting other Arab military efforts.

David and Goliath

The international phase of the 1948 war has been filtered through the David and Goliath iconography with regard to the size of opposing forces and belief that Israel was on the defensive – that war was an unalloyed military necessity rather than an outgrowth of expansionist goals.

Concerning the relative size of military forces, Ben-Gurion claimed that "700,000 Jews are pitted against 27 million Arabs – one against forty."[7] The Arab countries equally indulged in wild propaganda about the magnitude of their threat to Israel. For example, the secretary general of the Arab League declared: "This will be a war of extermination and a momentous massacre that will be spoken of like the Mongol invasions and the Crusades."[8] This hyperbole about

Arab strength, coming from *both* Jews and Arabs, could not alter the fact that the Arab Goliath was suffering from extreme poverty, domestic discord and internal rivalries. Nearly all the Arab countries were in imminent danger of internal collapse. Except for Transjordan, they needed their armies at home to deal with severe internal political crises – there were coups d'états and rebellions in Syria, Egypt, Iraq and Lebanon within the year.[9] No amount of chest-beating or belligerent government speeches could heal these domestic fractures. Appraising the danger to Israel from these surrounding Arab countries, U.S. Secretary of State Marshall concluded:

> Internal weaknesses in various Arab countries make it difficult for them to act. Iraq [can only send] a handful of troops; Egypt [has] insufficient equipment for police duty at home; jealousies between Saudi Arabia and the Syrians, on the one hand, and the Hashemite governments of Transjordan and Iraq, on the other, prevent the Arabs from making the best use of existing forces. . . . Syria, Lebanon and Saudi Arabia are militarily unimportant.[10]

The U.S. ambassador to the UN similarly observed that intervention by any Arab state other than Transjordan would be of "negligible importance."[11]

Though historians debate the numbers, whether estimates come from Jewish, British or Arab sources, it is clear that "the Israelis were not outnumbered,"[12] The largest estimate of the total Arab force at the beginning of the international war (May 15, 1948) is 23,500.[13] The Transjordan army of 5,000 was, of course, neutralized by the non-aggression pact and partly directed toward *opposition* of other Arab forces.[14] The lowest estimate of Israeli forces on May 15, 1948, as reported by Ben-Gurion, was 30,574.[15] A more realistic figure is double that: 60,000 to 70,000 trained soldiers, not including several thousand extremist Irgun and LEHI fighters.[16]

The Israeli public and even some military leaders were concerned about what was perceived as an impending monolithic Arab invasion. They only heard the Arab speeches and knew nothing about the Israeli-Transjordanian non-aggression pact. But Ben-Gurion knew that Israeli territory needed little defense against Arab attack and in fact Israeli territory went largely unchallenged during the war. Fighting with Transjordan did occur in Jerusalem (in the UN zone) but not in Jewish territory – Abdullah kept to the pact:

> The fighting broke out in Jerusalem precisely because it was not covered by any kind of agreement or understanding between the two sides. Everywhere else, as we shall see, the [Transjordanian] Arab Legion respected the partition borders and made no attempt to seize Jewish territory.[17]

Abdullah had no interest in joining in or leading an unrealistic and disastrous show of support for Palestinian nationalism which, in his view, was both whimsical and contrary to his plans for annexing Arab Palestine. Moreover, he was instructed by British Foreign Minister Ernest Bevin: "Do not go and invade the areas allotted to the Jews."[18] The actions of Transjordan, as a British client state, reflected on Britain in desperate need of U.S. postwar approval and support.

The Arab invasion: Stalemate and truce

Three and a half weeks of fighting resulted in a stalemate on all fronts, at which time (June 11, 1948) a UN truce was declared. The three primary fronts were: Tel Aviv, the Nablus "Triangle," and Jerusalem-Latrun.

Tel Aviv front: One Egyptian brigade cautiously proceeded up the southern coast toward Tel Aviv, the largest Jewish city in Palestine. Another brigade headed toward the West Bank to block Transjordan – draining off nearly half of Egypt's limited military energies.[19] Yigael Yadin, Israeli commander of operations, had intimate knowledge of the Tel Aviv terrain and attacked the Egyptian forces from the rear on the night of May 29.[20] Surprised and in disarray, the Egyptians were ordered by Cairo to halt their advance. The Egyptians had initially caused the Jews some anxiety, but after fifteen days they were paralyzed in their position on the coast – Tel Aviv was never again in jeopardy.[21]

Nablus Triangle front (area between Nablus, Tulkarem and Jenin in the northern Arab territory, 35 miles north of Jerusalem): The Iraqis and Israelis fought a major battle here, Transjordan failing to assist the Iraqi advance as agreed. Unaccountably an Israeli brigade failed to mount an attack at Tulkarem, resulting in a stalemate.[22]

Jerusalem-Latrun front: This was the principal battleground of the international war. A coveted religious and strategic prize for both Arabs and Jews, this area was not covered by the Meir-Abdullah non-aggression pact. Fighting had previously occurred in Jerusalem during the civil war and a truce was in force. When the Jews declared statehood on May 15, 1948, they immediately broke this truce. "A well-planned and vigorous Israeli offensive, Operation Pitchfork, was launched to seize all Arab and mixed zones in the new city and form a solid Jewish area all way up to the Old City walls."[23] About 5,000 Arabs were evicted from their homes. Within the Old City (largely Arab), the Jewish Quarter of 1,700 residents, the site of an ancient Hebrew Temple, was lightly armed. Though indefensible, Israel chose to hold on to the Jewish Quarter and use it as a springboard for capturing the entire Old City.[24]

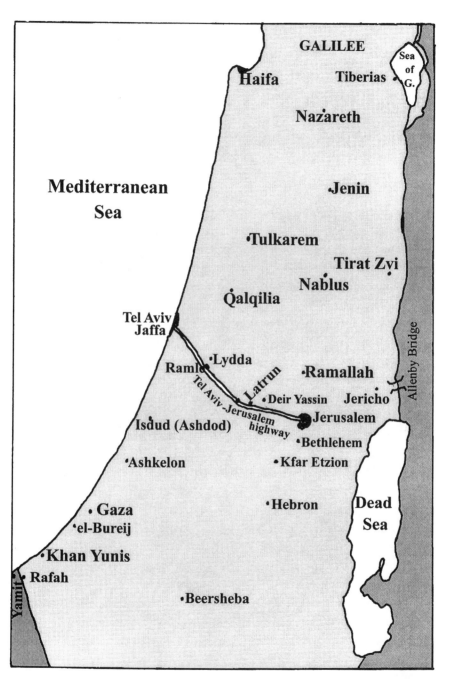

Central Palestine (1948)

Glubb Pasha, commander of Transjordan's Arab Legion, gave strict orders not to fight in Jerusalem.[25] Not only was that Britain's wish, but his 4,500 man army was insufficient to both defend the Old City and hold positions under Israeli attack in Arab territories.[26] Glubb, like Abdullah, had hopes of limiting hostilities to a *semblance* of war with the Jews in conformity with the non-aggression pact.[27] When Palestinian Arab irregulars defending the Old City were unable to stave off Operation Pitchfork, they made desperate appeals to Transjordan. Glubb resisted, hoping that the UN would arrange a new truce in Jerusalem. Abdullah was torn. He needed to gain credibility with the Arab nations by saving Palestinians from the Jews but did not wish to risk displeasing the British by engaging the Jews, especially in an area under UN jurisdiction. He hesitated, then intervened. The Israeli advance on the Old City was blocked and a stalemate resulted. By this action, Abdullah gained some prestige among his mistrustful "allies," having at least saved the Moslem Holy Places in Jerusalem.

The battle moved west from Jerusalem to Latrun along the Tel Aviv-Jerusalem highway in UN-designated Palestinian Arab territory. This highway was critical for supply of food and water in Jewish Jerusalem, as during the civil war. Glubb occupied an empty fortification in Latrun, controlling the highway, and defended it against fierce Israeli attacks. Ben-Gurion pressed for victory, fearing that a UN truce set for June 11 would come before Glubb had been removed.[28] Many Jewish casualties resulted but supplies got through to Jerusalem.

Truce violations seal the outcome of the international war

Though the fighting stopped, neither side fully observed the stipulated conditions of truce, namely, no new arms or troops. The Arabs added forces but largely frittered away their time in political wrangles. Israel added, retrained, reorganized and re-equipped its forces. Large quantities of modern weapons, especially tanks and aircraft from the Soviet bloc, France and private American sources, were illicitly imported.[29] The British, on the other hand, were forced by the UN to halt all arms sales to Arab countries. Consequently, after a month's truce, the Israeli army was transformed into a major modern fighting force while the Arab forces fell even further behind in number, quality, equipment and organization. Israel's fighting force was about twice that of the combined Arab nations.[30]

The truce was the turning point of the war.[31] The rest of the fighting was mainly a mopping-up operation in which Israel picked off or pinned down the forces of each Arab nation separately.

Bernadotte proposes a political union of Arab and Jew

During the truce period (on June 27), UN mediator Count Folke Bernadotte proposed a new and surprising settlement plan. Ignoring the original UN partition plan for independent Jewish and Palestinian Arab states, he recommended a *single* economic and political union over all of Palestine *and* Transjordan. Separate Jewish and Palestinian territories would work for common economic betterment, operate common services and coordinate foreign policy. This plan, eliminating altogether the idea of separate Arab and Jewish states, began to seem a practical way to stop the fighting and make the vulnerable Palestinian Arab state part of a larger Arab entity. This plan was roundly rejected both by the Arab countries and Israel, depriving the Jews, as it did, of a sovereign state, and effectively giving Arab Palestine to Transjordan – precisely what the surrounding Arab countries feared most.[32] Palestinian Arabs were never consulted.

Ten more days of fighting

His settlement plan rejected, Bernadotte sought but failed to negotiate an extension of the truce beyond June 11. The fighting continued ten more days before the UN imposed a second truce (July 18). During those ten days Israel seized the initiative in the Jerusalem-Latrun area (Operation Danny), where, in Ben-Gurion's view, the war was to be won.[33] Transjordanian forces were running out of ammunition and were denied resupply by their "allies" (Egypt, Syria and even Britain).[34] A second UN truce kept Egypt in position along the coast but the remaining Arab countries hardly mattered: "The Iraqi, Syrian and Lebanese armies had scarcely succeeded in crossing the frontier."[35]

Israel bombed Cairo with three heavy Flying Fortresses secretly imported from the United States. The campaign against Palestinian Arab citizens escalated with increasingly tough warnings and brutal means, creating another 100,000 refugees.

Bernadotte's second peace proposal and his assassination

During the second truce period, Ben-Gurion sought to write his own peace terms, cutting off any role for UN mediator Bernadotte. He saw that the Arab states, licking their wounds and unable to make common cause, were in a weak negotiating position and could be threatened by any further Israeli action. And yet on September 16, 1948, Bernadotte, with the support of the United States and Britain, proposed a *second* settlement plan for Palestine. Abandoning his earlier idea of a union of Palestine and Transjordan, he embraced the *two-state* partition idea, but with the Arab state territory joined with Transjordan. New geographical boundaries (to make more compact states) were proposed, e.g.,

Galilee, in fertile northern Palestine, would go to the Jewish state, while the Negev Desert would go to the Transjordanian state.[36] Jerusalem would retain its special status under UN supervision. Also under this plan, Arab refugees would have the right to return to their homes, with adequate compensation for any who might choose not to return. The Great Powers were fully behind this idea of an independent Jewish state and annexation of Arab Palestine by Transjordan.

Of course, Transjordan accepted the plan and the other Arab states rejected it. Israel also rejected it, wanting all of Galilee and all the Negev. Ben-Gurion saw little reason why he should accept UN-set boundaries when Israel was militarily able to expand its boundaries at will.[37] He knew, too, that the UN was quite unprepared to dispatch forces to Palestine to prevent Israel's expansion.[38]

The day after submission of the peace-settlement plan, the LEHI, led by Yitzhak Shamir, assassinated Bernadotte to show the world that Israel would not tolerate UN dictation of its borders. "The outside world, however, was shocked by this brutal manifestation of Zionist fanaticism, and the failure of the provisional government of Israel to apprehend the suspects dealt a death blow to its authority and credibility abroad. Yitzhak Shamir, one of the architects of the assassination, remained at large. . . . Bernadotte became a martyr in the cause of peace . . . [and his] report acquired the quality of a sacred political testament."[39]

Empty declaration of a Palestinian Arab state over all of Palestine

The Arab countries took strong exception to Transjordan's being the prime beneficiary of the Bernadotte plan.[40] Egypt and Transjordan were now overt enemies. In an effort to counteract Transjordan, as well as to placate public opinion back home about Egypt's failure to protect Palestinian Arabs, Egypt and the other Arab League countries declared a *Palestinian Arab government over all of Palestine*. The state was to be independent, sovereign and democratic, centered in Gaza and headed by the exiled mufti, leader of Palestinian nationalism.

Of course this state had no money, no civil service and no army of its own. Created under the auspices of the Arab League – largely to keep Transjordan from annexing Arab Palestine – it was all but ignored by the Great Powers and Israel.[41] Farcical in the eyes of the international community, the idea of a state over all of Palestine did move local Palestinian Arabs toward political consciousness and aspiration. They even revived their Holy War militia in an effort to aid Egypt's military efforts to block Transjordan's occupation and annexation of the Hebron area. This Palestinian militancy was, of course, a danger to Transjordan's plan to control Arab Palestine. Accordingly, Transjordan ruthlessly suppressed the Palestinian forces. This action completely blew the cover off Transjordan's pretense of support of Palestinian nationalism. It also ended all hope of an autonomous Palestine state.[42]

The All-Palestine state failed, not simply because it gained no recognition from the West but because it was born of Arab discord – discord between Transjordan and Egypt and between Transjordan and the Palestinians.

Israel renews the fighting

Ben-Gurion rejected Bernadotte's proposal that the Negev Desert go to Arab Palestine.[43] "Military force, in Ben-Gurion's view, would be decisive in settling the borders of the Jewish state and the future of Jerusalem."[44] Egypt was extending peace overtures, but Ben-Gurion was resolved to remove Egyptian forces remaining in the Negev.[45] Because a UN truce was in force, Ben-Gurion's plan required clandestine movement of Israeli troops and equipment into the Negev (Operation Yoav, October 1948) and, in addition, required some justification for attacking Egypt.[46] To this end, Israel fired on some of its own unarmed supply trucks provisioning a Jewish settlement in the Negev. UN observers concluded that Egyptian forces must be responsible. This provided Israel with a pretext to bomb Egyptian forces. When these Egyptian troops tried to evacuate the Negev on ships off the coast, Israeli underwater demolition teams sank the ships, with major loss of life. Transjordan, at loggerheads with Egypt, refused help. The Egyptian army was trapped and shattered.

Ben-Gurion considers taking all of Palestine

In late October, Israel conducted private quasi-armistice talks with Abdullah while, at the same time, making preparations for a large-scale offensive against his forces. Having already mopped up the Galilee area, Israel was capable, militarily, of pushing Transjordan and Iraq out of Palestine,[47] and thus taking all of Palestine.

The limits were not military. They came from international disapproval of Israeli-broken truces and expansionism into Arab areas. A November 4, 1948, UN resolution called for the withdrawal of all forces in the Negev to the October 14 positions as they had been prior to Operation Yoav. The UN threatened to take unspecified measures if either side failed to comply and Ben-Gurion could feel the pressure.

Moreover, questions were being raised within Israel by other leaders about the wisdom of further expansion into Arab Palestine: Could Israel control the vast number of Arabs who would fall under its rule if it were to take all of Palestine? And what chance, then, was there for peaceful coexistence with Transjordan now occupying Arab areas?[48] There was also some concern that

Britain might enter the war in defense of Transjordan if Israel attacked Tranjordanian forces in Palestine.[49] Would it not be better to allow Transjordan to annex Arab Palestine where it could control Palestinians angry over their homeless, stateless condition? And if Israel took the rest of Jerusalem, would there not exist a danger that the international community would compel Israel to accept internationalization of the *whole* city?

Ben-Gurion backed away from grander war plans in favor of more limited military campaigns and objectives.[50] On the one hand, he accepted a cease-fire in Jerusalem on November 29, 1948. On the other, he attempted to destroy all remaining Egyptian forces in the *Egyptian Sinai* (Operation Horev, December 22, 1948). When Israel entered the Sinai, Britain and the United States issued ultimatums and severe warnings, and Israel withdrew its troops from al-Arish.

Trying to arrange a peace

From cease-fire to peace settlement is a progression. A *cease-fire* ends hostilities, a *truce* lays down additional military conditions (e.g., no additional weapons), an *armistice* lays down provisional agreements about political and territorial control (e.g., new borders), and a *peace treaty* formalizes, through contract, a permanent mutual acceptance of all conditions. Israeli-Arab negotiations never spanned this distance.

Israel and Egypt arranged a *cease-fire* on January 7, 1949, and an *armistice* in February 1949, through the offices of Ralph Bunche, UN negotiator and ex-assistant of Bernadotte. Israel agreed to an Egyptian military presence in the Gaza Strip, the release of some Egyptian soldiers at Faluja and a small demilitarized zone at al-Auja (on the northern Sinai-Negev border). Israel still controlled the northern Negev and remained in position to capture the southern Negev held by Transjordanian troops – positions frozen by UN resolution. During March 1949 armistice talks with Transjordan, Israel invaded the southern Negev (Operation Fait Accompli), an operation which "created new facts which neither the UN nor Transjordan nor Britain had the power to change."[51] Coercion of Transjordan's Arab Legion was similarly employed on the West Bank through an Israeli Defense Force (IDF) display of troops conspicuously outnumbering the Legion ten to one (Operation Shin-Tav-Shin). In this way, Israel extracted large concessions of West Bank land. Britain and the United States did nothing to halt Israeli gunpoint diplomacy.[52] When the UN rebuked Israel for Operation Fait Accompli, Ben-Gurion overruled his generals (e.g., Yigal Allon) who were anxious to take the whole of the West Bank, the Triangle and all of Jerusalem. Armistice talks ended in early April 1949. Israel had obtained the southern Negev and large cuts in the West Bank.

Territorial consequences of the 1948 Arab-Israeli war

Israel was in possession of the bulk of Palestine – its UN allotment of 56 percent had now been increased to 77 percent of Palestine.[53] Palestinian Arab territory was cut in half, from 44 percent to about 23 percent of Palestine. Some 360 Arab villages and fourteen Arab towns within Israel had been destroyed without loss of any Jewish village.[54] Concerning Palestinian Arabs once living on territory now held by Israel, 85 percent had fled (726,000 out of an estimated 859,000).[55] Of the total Palestinian Arab population, 70 percent were refugees.

The Israeli public was ecstatic, in no mood to accept armistice agreements and resentful that 4,558 Israeli soldiers and 1,150 civilians had been killed.[56] While Ben-Gurion's armistice agreements came under criticism from both Israel's political left and right,[57] further expansion would have been imprudent given the climate of international disapproval.

Notes

1. Avi Shlaim, *Collusion Across the Jordan* (New York: Columbia University Press, 1988), 239. King Abdullah always had a realistic appreciation of the extent of Jewish military power. He kept to the non-agression pact with Israel. Fighting did take place in Jerusalem where the Meir-Abdullah pact had no application. Most Israeli troop losses occurred during invasion of UN-designated Arab territory. In the words of Transjordanian general Glubb Pasha: "The Trans-jordan Government had never intended to involve itself in any serious military operations at all, and it was fully aware from the first that partition was inevitable. I missed no opportunity to inform them that Trans-jordan had not sufficient resources to wage war on the Jewish state and the Prime Minister assured me frequently that he understood this." "The Trans-jordan Situation," August 12, 1948, British Foreign Office report 371/688-22, Public Records Office (London), cited in Shlaim, *Collusion,* 271-2.

2. Avi Shlaim, *The Politics of Partition* (New York: Columbia University Press, 1990), 160.

3. Clark Clifford papers, box 13 (May 9, 1948), Truman Library. Cited in Michael J. Cohen, *Palestine and the Great Powers, 1945-1948* (Princeton: Princeton University Press, 1982), 381-2.

4. Abdullah alone was clear-sighted: "The Jews are too strong – it is a mistake to make war." Shlaim, *Collusion,* 196.

5. Shlaim, *Collusion,* 197.

6. Shlaim, *Collusion,* 202.

7. Simha Flapan, *The Birth of Israel,* (New York: Pantheon, 1987), 189.

8. Flapan, *Birth of Israel,*192.

9. "The Syrian Cabinet, reshuffled in August 1948, was replaced with difficulty in December, only to be arrested at the end of March 1949 when the army staged a coup d'état. In Iraq a new Cabinet came to power in January [1949] and only the

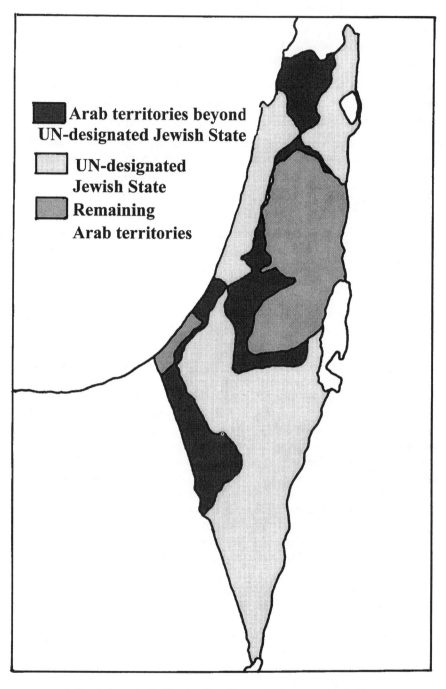

Palestinian-Arab Territories Captured in 1948 and 1949

ability of the new Premier . . . staved off serious trouble. In Egypt the government was forced in December 1948 to outlaw the ultranationalist Muslim Brethren, who maintained close relations with al-Hajj Amin [the exiled mufti]; a few weeks later the Brethren retaliated by assassinating the Prime Minister. In Lebanon the crisis was delayed until the summer of 1949 when the government had to resort to mass arrests of the quasi-Fascist Syrian National Party members and the execution of its leader to avert open rebellion." J.C. Hurewitz, *The Struggle for Palestine* (New York: Schocken, 1976), 318-9.

10. *Foreign Relations of the United States: Annual Report, 1947,* 983 (Washington: U.S. State Department, 1971). Cited by Flapan, *Birth of Israel,* 191.

11. Flapan, *Birth of Israel,* 192.

12. Jon and David Kimche, John Bagot Glubb, and Walid Khalidi, respectively. Their comparison of troop figures is cited in Flapan, *Birth of Israel,* 196.

13. Breakdown of Jon and David Kimche figure, cited by Flapan, *Birth of Israel,* 196.

14. Transjordan's Arab Legion had a force of less than 5,000, whereas the Haganah was 50,000 strong, according to Flapan, *Birth of Israel,* 151.

15. Ben-Gurion, *War Diary,* 428.

16. Fred Khouri, *The Arab-Israeli Dilemma* (Syracuse, N.Y.: Syracuse University Press, 1985), 71, 546 n.5. "Different authorities have estimated the total number of persons in the Israeli armed services on May 15 as from 35,000 to 80,000." Discrepancies exist because Israel added greatly to its manpower: *(a)* some 30,000 new immigrants selected carefully with the war effort in mind entered Israel between May 15 and August 9, 1948; and *(b)* foreign volunteers made up 18 percent of Israeli forces. Khouri, *Dilemma,* 71, 72.

17. Shlaim, *Collusion,* 239.

18. Shlaim, *Collusion,* 136.

19. Flapan, *Birth of Israel,* 151.

20. Yadin was a geologist; the Egyptians were using school children's maps.

21. Shlaim, *Collusion,* 271.

22. Some observers have thought the stalemate due to a balance of forces.

23. Shlaim, *Collusion,* 239-40.

24. David Shaltiel, *Jerusalem 1948* (in Hebrew) (Tel Aviv: Ministry of Defence, 1981), 173-5. Cited in Shlaim, *Collusion,* 240.

25. Glubb was in close accord with Abdullah – "His objective was to gain control over the Arab areas of Palestine in order to prevent their capture by the Israelis and ultimately to annex them to Transjordan." Shlaim, *Collusion,* 244.

26. "The Arab Legion had crossed the Jordan on May 15, with the approval of the British government, to help the Arabs defend the area of Judaea and Samaria [West Bank] allotted to them. We were strictly forbidden to enter Jerusalem, which had been declared by the United Nations to be an enclave or to enter any area allotted to the Jewish state in the partition plan. Our plans were therefore strictly in accordance with the orders of the United Nations and the approval of the British government." Glubb, quoted in Sir John Bagot, *The Changing Scenes of Life: An Autobiography* (London: Quartet Books, 1983), 148.

27. "Even at this late hour, Glubb had lingering hopes of limiting hostilities to a

semblance of war – a few skirmishes, a few token forays, and then allowing the dust to settle." Shlaim, *Collusion*, 239.

28. UN mediator Count Bernadotte, president of the Swedish Red Cross and a negotiator for Jewish lives in World War II, arranged a month's truce (June 11). Britain pressed for a cease-fire because its client engaged the Jews in a battle that effectively threatened a UN internationalization plan for Jerusalem to which Britain was officially committed.

29. An entire Czech airfield was used for a shuttle of arms and planes to Israel. Transports delivered dismantled fighter planes, artillery, armored vehicles, guns and ammunition. During the truce, Ben-Gurion approved Irgun's purchase of an American LST landing ship, tank vessel (the *Altalena*) to bring men and weapons from France. When the Irgun and Haganah fought over the weapons, the vessel burned and 82 Jews were killed. Howard Sachar, *A History of Israel:From the Rise of Zionism to Our Time,*Vol. .I (New York: Knopf, 1986), 328, 330.

30. During the truce, Arab forces in Palestine increased from about 25,000 to between 35,000 and 45,000, as compared with the 60,000 to 100,000 for Israel. *New York Times*, July 8, 10, 11, 1948; and Jon and David Kimche, *A Clash of Destinies* (New York: Praeger, 1960), 223.

31. Even before the truce (May 22), aircraft and cannons were arriving in Israel and Ben-Gurion called this "the beginning of the turning point." "We should [now] prepare to go over to the offensive," he told his general staff ten days after the Arab invasion (May 24). Flapan, *Birth of Israel,* 198. But the further massive buildup of men and weapons during the truce was the dramatic turn-around event of the war.

32. Syria saw in this plan Transjordan's becoming a Jewish colony – an even greater menace than the partitioning of Palestine.

33. Ben-Gurion planned to break Transjordan's army and capture Jerusalem and its environs. "If we win there, we will have won altogether." *War Diary* (June 18, 1948). Cited by Shlaim, *Collusion*, 262.

34. Britain was seeking to preserve its image with the U.S. and at the UN.

35. Shlaim, *Collusion*, 271

36. This was a reversal of the 1947 UN partition plan in which the Jews would get the Negev and the Arabs would retain parts of Galilee.

37. "In my view, it is not unlikely that, in the event of a military decision, we would succeed in . . . [securing] the Negev in our hands; in liberating the rest of New Jerusalem; in capturing the Old City; in seizing the entire central and western Galilee; and in enlarging the frontiers of the state in a number of other directions." Ben-Gurion [speech, September 27, 1948], *When Israel Fought in Battle* (in Hebrew) (Tel Aviv: Am Oved, 1975), 267. Cited in Shlaim, *Collusion,* 305.

38. The British Foreign Office offered an explanation for why *both* the Arab League and Israel favored a Palestinian Arab state rather than annexation by Transjordan: "Egypt does not want any other Arab state [notably Transjordan] to increase in relative power and importance, and [regarding Israel] an Arab Palestinian state would be a hopeless proposition and render the next step in Jewish expansion a very easy one." The Foreign Office also explained why neither the Jews nor the Arabs would negotiate a settlement through the UN: "The Jews are frankly expansionist and refuse to put forward any terms, for fear they should ask for less than changing

circumstances and the inefficiency of the United Nations may enable them to grab. The Arabs see little hope of practical help, either from us or from the United Nations." Sir Hugh Dow to Bernard Burrows, August 23, 1948, Foreign Office 371/68584, Public Records Office (London). Cited in Shlaim, *Collusion,* 290.

39. Shlaim, *Collusion,* 293. Shamir was one of the chief architects. Four hundred were temporarily imprisoned but never brought to trial. Yehoshua Cohen, friend of Ben-Gurion, is widely believed to be the trigger man. Sachar, *History,* Vol. I, 334.

40. "Azzam Pasha [secretary general of the Arab League], the Mufti and the Syrian Government would sooner see the Jews get the whole of Palestine than that King Abdullah should benefit." Glubb Pasha to Bernard Burrows. September 22, 1948, Foreign Office 371/68861, Public Records Office, London. "So overwhelming was Arab resistance to Transjordan's enlargement that the British argument that a weak Palestinian government would enable the Jews to gain control over the whole country made no impression." Shlaim, *Collusion,* 297, 325.

41. Israel vacillated. Under obligation by the UN 1947 partition plan to accept *some* kind of independent Palestinian-Arab state, Israel thought it likely that any such state would be weak and economically dependent on Israel, a facter in future Israeli expansion plans. See Moshe (Shertok) Sharett, *At the Gate of Nations, 1946-1949* (in Hebrew) (Tel Aviv: Am Oved, 1958), 307-9. Cited in Shlaim, *Collusion,* 302.

42. See Shlaim, *Collusion,* 296-303.

43. The United States supported the plan and any Israeli disapproval of UN boundaries.

44. Shlaim, *Collusion,* 304.

45. In September, Israeli representative Elias Sasson and Egypt's minister came to an understanding. Egypt accepted the State of Israel as a fait accompli and agreed to withdraw its troops from all of Palestine. However, Egypt wanted control over the Gaza Strip and some areas of the Negev in order to protect itself from a Transjordanian acquisition in southern Palestine in which British bases might be established. Ben-Gurion rejected these peace feelers. Shlaim, *Collusion,* 316-7.

46. Operation Yoav: Sachar, *History,* Vol. I, 339-40; Shlaim, *Collusion,* 320-1.

47. Shlaim, *Collusion,* 341.

48. Moshe Sharett, Israel's foreign minister (later prime minister) differed with Ben-Gurion about the wisdom of military goals without Clausewitzian consideration of well-defined political purposes. Shlaim, *Collusion,* 344.

49. Israel's various truce violations were of concern to Britain since it had treaty obligations to protect Transjordan. The UN was debating these truce violations and Ben-Gurion feared UN sanctions and hostile British actions in the guise of enforcement of UN resolutions. Shlaim, *Collusion,* 357-8.

50. Later he would bemoan not having done so. Shlaim, *Collusion,* 309.

51. Shlaim, *Collusion,* 404.

52. Wells Stabler, an American official in Transjordan, conveyed to Secretary of State George Marshall the rank injustice of U.S. passivity toward the blackmailing of Transjordan. Shlaim, *Collusion,* 414. Cuts forced on Transjordan separated many Arab farmers from their soil and later became a source of endemic border violence.

53. "The November 29 [1947 UN] decision had given the Jewish state 14,920,000 dunams; now we have 20,662,000 dunams in our control." Ben-Gurion, *War Diary* (August 2, 1949). This 20,662,000 dunams is 77.4 percent of Palestine. Donald Neff *Warriors for Jerusalem* (Brattleboro, Vt.: Amana Books, 1988), 23.

54. Flapan, *Birth of Israel*, 235.

55. Hurewitz, *Struggle for Palestine*, 319-20.

56. More Israeli soldiers were killed outside Israel in attacks on Arab Palestine than in defense of Israel. Flapan, *Birth of Israel*, 198-9.

57. On the right, Menachem Begin, invoking Munich, rejected the partitioning of Palestine with Jordan. On the left, the Communists and Mapam saw a Jordanian West Bank as an invitation to British and American influence in Palestine. Shlaim, *Collusion*, 430.

Chapter 9

Uneasy Settlement of the 1948 War

No progress was made toward a peace settlement at the ill-fated April-September, 1949 Lausanne Peace Conference. That was because none of the humiliated Arab countries wished to officially acknowledge their defeat and because Israel had no need to make peace. As Ben-Gurion put it, "I am prepared to get up in the middle of the night in order to sign a peace agreement – but I am not in a hurry and I can wait ten years. We are under no pressure whatsoever."[1]

Given Israel's military power, there was no need to return Palestinian Arab territory that the pact had earmarked for Transjordan. Nevertheless, King Abdullah resisted submitting to Israeli terms, pointing out to Israeli Foreign Minister Moshe Sharett that it was the Jews who had violated their secret understanding and caused the fighting. Abdullah reminded Sharett that he had never wanted to go to war and that it was the Irgun's Deir Yassin massacre and the Israeli breach of the Jerusalem cease-fire that had forced him to take action.[2] Moreover, he pointed out that at no point during the war had he tried to penetrate the frontiers of the Jewish state. Israeli historian Avi Shlaim judges: "It would have been difficult to challenge Abdullah's version of events and Sharett made no attempt to do so."[3] No progress toward peace was made. Ben-Gurion could wait, since a peace settlement now would only hamper possible future military expansion into remaining Arab Palestine.

Meanwhile, what was to be the fate of Palestinian Arab territory not yet held by Israel? Ben-Gurion vacillated.[4] On the one hand, an *advantage* to an independent Palestinian state, as called for by the UN, would be its weakness and financial dependence on Israel – likely a puppet state of Israel.[5] And support for that state would improve Israel's international image now suffering from refusal to permit Palestinian refugee return. On the other hand, the *danger* of a Palestinian state was that this return to the original UN partition plan might stimulate international demands for a return to UN-designated boundaries.

Suppose the territory were to be annexed by Transjordan? The *advantage* of that would be that Abdullah would be better able than Israel to control Palestinians angry over their loss of home, property and statehood. The *danger* was that Abdullah, intent on his "Greater Syria" plan for political union of Transjordan, Syria, Iraq and Arab Palestine, might fight Israel if Israel later attempted to seize that Palestinian territory.[6] Britain, too, might aid in that fight in accordance with its treaty obligations to defend Transjordan.

Best Route: Transjordan annexes Palestinian Arab territory (the West Bank)

Israel and Transjordan shared the same goal: suppression of Palestinian nationalism. Annexation of Arab Palestine by Transjordan seemed, finally, to be the best route. It fit with British and U.S. interests as well. Britain would retain, through its client, influence in the Middle East and Palestine. And the United States saw annexation by Transjordan as the shortest route to end the war – particularly desirable because Transjordan was a reliable U.S. ally against communism in the Middle East. Of course, the UN partition resolution was being completely ignored.

In this climate, Transjordan held general elections throughout Transjordan and Arab Palestine. The Palestinians, aware that an independent state was out of the question, indicated that union with Transjordan would be acceptable.[7] Transjordan made a show of equal representation to Palestinians by expanding its parliament, but all key cabinet positions were assigned to Transjordanians.

Palestine was now divided between Israel and the "Hashemite Kingdom of Jordan." Transjordan, lying east of the Jordan River, was now to be called "East Jordan" or simply "Jordan." The annexed Arab territory in Palestine west of the Jordan River was now to be called "West Jordan" or simply the "West Bank." These new names and the deletion of the name "Palestine" from maps marked the official demise of the 1947 UN partition resolution. Britain gave official recognition to this annexation. Israel did not.

The UN continued to call for the internationalization of Jerusalem, so Israel and Jordan hurriedly made common cause, agreeing to divide the city between them. Ben-Gurion openly defied the UN as well as the Catholic Church, the Soviet Union and the Arab League, each of whom had claims to property and shrines in Jerusalem.

1950-1951 – Israel raids and proposes to take the West Bank and the Sinai

Relations between Israel, Jordan and Egypt deteriorated further in 1950. A leading military hawk and protégé of Ben-Gurion, Moshe Dayan, was responsible for further forced expulsion of Arabs along the armistice borders. He conducted "reprisal" raids against Jordanian villages on presumption that these villages were supporting Palestinian "criminal infiltrators" entering Israel. "The Israeli public was full of righteous indignation and quite oblivious to the fact that most of these infiltrators were refugees who had been brutally driven out of their homes and now wanted to rebuild their lives."[8] Dayan's philosophy was that Israel ought to "threaten the Arabs and to constantly escalate the level of violence so as to demonstrate her superiority and to create the conditions for territorial expansion."[9] Needless to say, no further peace talks occurred.

Then in 1951, King Abdullah ("the dog who sold Palestine to the Zionists") was assassinated by dissident Palestinian nationalists. Ben-Gurion again considered invasion of the West Bank and the Egyptian Sinai. "Not content with the contingency plan to capture the West Bank, Ben-Gurion began to consider the possibility of seizing the entire Sinai Peninsula, all the way up to the Suez Canal."[10] He approached Britain with his proposal for "the expulsion of the Egyptians from Sinai to make way for British bases there and to turn the Suez Canal into an international waterway."[11] Additionally, he proposed that Britain take over Jordan, that "Israel's border should be the Jordan [River], while Britain took Transjordan."[12] Britain demurred and Ben-Gurion "had to abandon the idea of Sinai until five years later [the 1956 Suez War] . . . and the capture of both Sinai and the West Bank was left to Ben-Gurion's successors sixteen years later [the 1967 Six Day War]."[13]

Blame for the failure of peace

Israel blamed the British for the failure to achieve a lasting peace settlement with Jordan. Sir Knox Helm, British minister in Tel Aviv, agreed that the British could have done more to prepare the way for peace.[14] Still, Israel made no concessions whatsoever that could have enabled Jordan to save face and dispel an impression in the Arab world that it had sold out to Israel in order to annex Arab Palestine.[15] Elias Sasson, an Israeli official and expert on Arab affairs, thought there was a good deal of truth to the American, French, and British perception that Israel was responsible for the failure to establish the peace. He summarized the Jewish stance:

Firstly, the Jews think they can achieve peace without any price, maximal or minimal. They want to achieve *(a)* Arab surrender of all the areas occupied

today by Israel; *(b)* Arab agreement to absorb all the refugees in the neighboring countries; *(c)* Arab agreement to border adjustments in the centre, the
south and the Jerusalem area to Israel's exclusive advantage; *(d)* the
relinquishment by the Arabs of their assets and property in Israel in exchange
for compensation which would be evaluated by the Jews alone and which
would be paid, if at all, over a number of years after the attainment of peace;
(e) de facto and *de jure* recognition by the Arabs of the state of Israel and
its new frontiers; *(f)* Arab agreement to the immediate establishment of diplomatic and economic relations between their countries and Israel, etc., etc.[16]

The 1948 war gained much for Israel and Jordan. Nervous, at times conflicting,
these allies had succeeded (as the British and French had before them) in fulfilling
their respective desires to divide up Arab territory between themselves in the service
of expansion. Palestinian nationalism was averted.

The refugee problem and denial of right of return

There were 370,000 Palestinian Arabs made homeless during the civil war phase
of the 1948 war. By the end of the international phase (summer of 1949), another
356,000 Palestinian Arabs had fled Israeli-held territory – a total of three-quarters of a
million.[17] A third of these refugees (256,000) fled to outside Arab countries (100,000
to Lebanon, 75,000 to Jordan, 70,000 to Syria and 11,000 to Egypt and Iraq).[18] The
remaining two-thirds (470,000) found temporary refuge in the West Bank, Gaza and
Jordan. The 188,000 in Gaza were forced by both the Egyptians and Israelis to live
in a degraded state.

The Israeli government refused repatriation except in minor instances and
recommended that all refugees remain in or be sent to surrounding Arab nations.[19]
The Israeli disclaimer of responsibility for the refugee problem was grounded in the
misleading claim that the Jews had accepted partition while the Arabs had not – that
the Arabs, not the Jews, were therefore responsible for the war and the creation of the
refugee problem. A spokesman for the Arab states countercharged that Israel alone
was responsible for "driving three-quarters of the lawful population of Palestine from
their homes."

Both arguments had flaws. The Jews had hiddenly rejected the partition of
Palestine through the Meir-Abdullah collusion. Nor was Jewish support for partition
necessarily aimed at a *peaceful* resolution or avoidance war since the Jews rejected
U.S. and UN truce efforts in early 1948.

But even if the Jews were guiltless about the need for war, did they not bear
responsibility for the flight of Palestinians through terrorism and forced expulsion?

Not initially. The causes of the Arab exodus were complex and related to the kind of war it was.[20] For example, in the earliest stages, the Arabs were not necessarily *forced* out. Some Palestinian leaders and professional-class Arab inhabitants (e.g., of Haifa and Jaffa) *voluntarily* left before the war, not wishing to live under the inevitability of Jewish rule. At first the Jews actually attempted to *stop* departures, fearing international censure for their attacks on Arab city populations. On the other hand, research has shown that the subsequent mass exodus was *not* caused in any significant degree by Arab military authorities as some Jewish apologists have alleged.[21]

Unquestionably, the panic and mass exodus were related to: (1) the forcible expulsion of citizens and the bulldozing of Arab homes that began during the civil war with Plan Dalet (early March 1948); (2) the April 1948 Deir Yassin massacre, widely advertised, that convinced Palestinian Arabs of the worthlessness of local non-aggression (neutrality) agreements with the Jews; (3) the increasingly brutal expulsions during the international phase of the war; and (4) the collapse of public services, commerce, employment and famine. Israeli historian Benny Morris concluded, "In general, in most cases the final and decisive precipitant to flight was Haganah, IZL [Irgun], LHI [Stern Gang] or IDF [Israel Defense Force] attack or the inhabitants' fear of such attack."[22]

Arguments about who was immediately or distantly responsible for the flight are not, however, directly relevant to issues about whether there should be *repatriation.* The international community addressed this matter in 1948 through UN Resolution 194 (par. 11), affirming the Palestinian Arabs' right of return:

Resolved that the refugees wishing to return to their homes and live in peace with their neighbors should be permitted to do so at the earliest practicable date, and that compensation should be paid for the property of those choosing not to return and for the loss of or damage to property which, under principles of international law or in equity, should be made good by the Governments or authorities responsible.[23]

Israel's admission to UN membership was partly contingent on acceptance of Resolution 194 and Israel pledged to enforce it.[24] Israel also signed the 1949 Lausanne Protocol asserting that the *original* UN plan calling for a Palestinian Arab state – a potential homeland for Arab refugees – was a basis for peace negotiations.[25] After admission to the UN, Israel reneged on its pledge and refused Palestinian Arabs the right of return. Rather, it passed a 1950 Law of Return providing worldwide

Jewry with that right.[26]

Truman was upset. Israel's refusal to allow the return of even a portion of Palestinian refugees, say 200,000 to 250,000, caused the president to intervene personally. He expressed serious disappointment about Israel's failure either to make any territorial concessions or to accept return of refugees. Unless there was a positive change, he said, the U.S. government will regretfully be forced to the conclusion that a revision of its attitude toward Israel has become unavoidable.[27] Ben-Gurion did not budge.[28] The U.S. State Department's coordinator of Palestine refugee affairs recommended withholding $49 million in loans – to no effect.

The "in-gathering," a massive exchange of populations

Consistent with Zionist goals was the removal of Palestinian Arabs, prevention of their return and replacement with worldwide Jewry. The first problem was solved by the mass flight during the war. The second problem was prevention of their return. Ben-Gurion's position was unequivocal: "Their return must be prevented . . . at all costs."[29] The remaining problem was need for Jewish immigration. As Ben-Gurion made clear in 1937: "We must expel Arabs and take their places."[30] Massive immigration of Jews was needed in order to take physical possession of territory won through war. Without immigration there could be no settlement of the land – settlement constituted true conquest.[31] Thus, immigration was even more urgent than gaining more land. Moreover, occupation of Arab fields and homes by Jews would preclude their return.

Israel replaced Palestinian refugees with nearly an equal number of Jews from foreign countries: 50,000 from German and Austrian World War II DP camps; 200,000 from Eastern Europe who were smuggled into DP camps and then sent to Israel; 250,000 Oriental Jews from Islamic countries (e.g., Iraq, Yemen, Syria, Turkey, and Libya), most airlifted at Israeli expense. Many of these Oriental Jews were now suffering persecution in retaliation for Israel's expulsion of the Palestinians. By the end of 1950, 350,000 Jews had immigrated or been brought to Israel at Israel's expense; by mid-1951 the total was some 648,000. The Jewish population of Israel had doubled by 1952, changing from a predominantly European to a half-Oriental character.[32]

Inevitably, indiscriminate encouragement of Jewish immigration created economic and human disaster for many new arrivals. Two-hundred-thousand Jews took over Palestinian homes left standing after the war, but there were nearly 100,000 Jews living in tents in early 1951.[33] These predominantly Oriental Jews had no employment, subsisted on a slim dole in unalleviated squalor and were shipped to remote territories cut off from their normal social environment and families. By 1952, embittered and exhausted, many of those who had been imported, those with relatives in a Western country, left Israel. About 223,000 remained in shantytowns on the outskirts of Haifa, Tel Aviv and Jerusalem, finding occasional part-time employment. The attempt to induce immigrants to farm in remote territories by means of gifts of land was unsuccessful. Many returned penniless to the city. The political policy of supporting the immigration of foreign Jews and excluding Palestinian refugees effected a transfer that left both populations living in squalid conditions.

The emerging Israeli state: Dove or hawk?

There was conflict in Israeli government circles about the importance of considering the needs of Arabs and seeking peaceful coexistence. Abba Eban observed about Ben-Gurion, "He hardly knows there is an Arab world – Sharett does know."[34] Foreign Minister Sharett saw a need for peace and normal relations with Arab neighbors. He described the military "adventurism" of Dayan as a mere show of appetite for expansion and a willingness to harm others in an arbitrary fashion.[35] Ben-Gurion and Dayan criticized the diplomatic methods of Sharett, the dovish foreign minister and his assistant, Elias Sasson, and wanted to bring all of Palestine (and beyond) under Jewish rule.[36] Sharett wished to make concessions that would have made a formal peace agreement possible.

Public sentiment and government thinking were dominated by militant policy. The security of Israel was paramount and seen in terms of exclusion of Arabs, massive Jewish immigration, sophisticated weaponry and freedom from international pressure or opinion. This mind of the militant right reflects, in the view of Israeli historian, Shlaim, a "Holocaust syndrome – a tendency to view the Arab threat in light of the destruction of central Europe's Jewry by the Nazis . . . and the consequent determination to base Israel's security not on goodwill of outsiders or paper guarantees but on her own strength, on defensible borders, and on military deterrence."[37] A "complex that the Arabs want to destroy us" precluded the possibility that Israel would seek peaceful coexistence and become a "normal state" in the Middle East.[38]

And yet, there was no question, militancy had proved highly effective. The Jews had a state; Israel was the major military power in the Middle East; it had the money and power of the United States behind it; and it even had the diplomatic backing of the Soviet Union. Nahum Goldmann, past president of the World Zionist Organization, summarized the Israeli mentality that resulted from its military success:

> [Success had] a marked psychological effect on Israel. It seemed to show the advantage of direct action over diplomacy. . . . The victory offered such a glorious contrast to the centuries of persecution and humiliation, of adaption and compromise, that it seemed to indicate the only direction that could possibly be taken from then on. To brook nothing, tolerate no attack, but cut through Gordian knots, and to shape history by creating facts seemed so simple, so compelling, so satisfying that it became Israel's policy in its conflict with the Arab world.[39]

The new self-image was that of the "fighting Jew" – the Jew who through force would prevent another Holocaust, this one perpetrated by Arabs. The old passive Jew was gone. The ghetto mentality, with rigid maintenance of impenetrable borders through weaponry and intimidation, was not gone.

Notes

1. Avi Shlaim, *The Politics of Partition* (New York: Columbia University Press, 1990), 343, citing an interview in the *Herald Tribune,* July 1949.

2. Abdullah-Sharett meeting, May 5, 1949. Transjordan's foreign minister shared Abdullah's position: "[Tawfiq] Abul Huda [a Tranjordanian statesman] had not wanted to go to war either and remained faithful throughout to the limited strategy for which he had obtained Britain's secret endorsement. It was Israeli attempts to capture the Old City that brought about the clash between the Arab Legion and the Haganah." Shlaim, *Politics of Partition,* 334.

3. Shlaim, *Politics of Partition,* 334.

4. Shlaim, *Collusion across the Jordan* (New York: Columbia University Press, 1988), 503.

5. A puppet Palestinian government was feasible because the Palestinian Arabs were antagonistic toward Transjordan,and because Israel had in its employ Nimer al-Hawari, the former commander of al-Najjada, an Arab paramilitary organization. Al-Hawari claimed to speak for the Palestinian refugees and through him Israel could support a Palestinian government-in-exile. This government could resist annexation by Transjordan and create a small Palestinian state. Shlaim, *Collusion,* 506-7.

6. Transjordan's long-time hope of controlling Syria increased in feasibility because of a bloodless coup in Syria on March 30, 1949. The Iraqis, from the same Hashemite family as King Abdullah, increased the chance of a political union with Transjordan.

7. Shlaim, *Collusion,* 556.

8. Shlaim, *Collusion,* 570.

9. Shlaim, *Collusion,* 571.

10. Shlaim, *Collusion*, 611.

11. Shlaim, *Collusion*, 611.

12. Shlaim, *Collusion*, 611.

13. Shlaim. *Collusion*. 612.

14. Shlaim, *Collusion*, 603.

15. Shlaim, *Collusion*, 561. Arab League countries were highly critical of Jordan for seeking a formal peace settlement with Israel. On the other hand, Jordan needed to come away from the settlement table with an appearance of diplomatic success to establish that it was not simply a collaborator.

16. Sasson to Shmuel Divon, June 16, 1949, 2447/2, Israel State Archives. Cited in Shlaim, *Collusion*, 474, 596.

17. According to Hurewitz, 726,000; according to the UN Economic Survey Mission, 777,000. J.C. Hurewitz, *The Struggle for Palestine* (New York: Schocken, 1976), 321; Simha Flapan, *The Birth of Israel* (New York: Pantheon, 1987), 216.

18. Statistics: Hurewitz, *Struggle for Palestine*, 320-1. Statistics for a slightly earlier period, are compatible – from Howard Sachar, *A History of Israel: From the Rise of Zionism to Our Time*, Vol. I (New York: Knopf, 1986), 334-5, and Christopher Sykes, *Crossroads to Israel* (Cleveland: World Publishing, 1965), 356. The General Refugee Congress (a Palestinian group headed by al-Hawari) issued figures similar to those cited. Shlaim, *Collusion*, 490.

19. Israel's Middle East Department opined: "Those with the highest capacity for survival and adjustment will manage by a process of natural selection while the rest would be crushed. Some of them would die and most of them would turn into human dust and the waste of society, and join the most impoverished classes in the Arab countries." The Palestinian Refugee Problem, 2444/19, Israel State Archives. Cited in Shlaim, *Collusion*, 491.

20. This does not mean that the Israeli leadership was not desirous of removing the Arab population. "Ben-Gurion clearly wanted as few Arabs as possible to remain in the Jewish State. He hoped to see them flee. He said as much to his colleagues and aides in meeting in August, September and October. But no expulsion policy was ever enunciated and Ben-Gurion always refrained from issuing clear or written expulsion orders; he preferred that his generals 'understand' what he wanted done. He wished to avoid going down in history as the 'great expeller' and he did not want the Israeli government to be implicated in a morally questionable policy." Benny Morris, *The Birth of the Palestinian Refugee Problem, 1947-1949* (Cambridge: Cambridge University Press, 1987), 292-3.

21. Morris, *Palestinian Refugee*. Also see Sykes, *Crossroads to Israel*, 354.

22. Morris, *Palestinian Refugee*, 294. Weizmann's description of the Arab flight as a "miraculous simplification of Israel's task" implied that it had happened incidentally, that human intervention had not played a part. Sachar, *History*, Vol. I, 439.

23. UN General Assembly Resolution 194 (III), 3 GAOR (186th Plen. mtg.), 1948. The Universal Declaration of Human Rights was adopted by the UN on December 10, 1948, stating in Article 13(2), "Everybody has the right to leave any country, including

his own, and to return to his country" (General Assembly Res. 217A, UN Doc. A/810, at 71, 1948). See also the International Covenant on Civil and Political Rights, adopted by the UN (General Assembly Res. 2200, 21 UN GAOR, supp. (no. 16) 52 UN Doc. A/6316, 1966), and the United Nations Sub-commission on Prevention of Discrimination and Protection of Minorities, which adopted the "Draft Principles on Freedom and Nondiscrimination in Respect of the Right of a Person to Leave and Return to Any Country, Including His Own" (Resolution 2[XV] 1962). These UN principles were the same grounds upon which Jews in the Soviet Union asserted their right to leave.

24. General Assembly Res. 273 (III), UN Doc. A/818 and Doc. S/1093 (1949). The Arab countries would not accept Resolution 194 because they viewed it as a recognition of Israel's right to exist. Flapan, *Birth of Israel*, 218.

25. Shlaim, *Collusion*, 469; Flapan, *Birth of Israel*, 214.

26. This violates Articles 1(4) and 2 of the International Convention on the Elimination of All Forms of Racial Discrimination, adopted by the UN to prevent separate rights for different racial or ethnic groups (adopted January 4, 1969, 660 UNT.S. 195.).

27. Flapan, *Birth of Israel*, 214.

28. Later, Israel did offer to repatriate 100,000 refugees as a tactical move to improve its international image. However, the low number and conditions attached to this offer were considered unreasonable at the UN. Shlaim, *Collusion*, 472-3.

29. Ben-Gurion, *War Diary: The War of Independence, 1948-1949* (in Hebrew) [speech at meeting of provisional government, June 16, 1948] G. Rivlin and E. Orren, eds. (Tel Aviv: Ministry of Defence, 1982), 525. Cited by Flapan, *Birth of Israel*, 105.

30. Flapan, *Birth of Israel*, 103.

31. Summary of Ben-Gurion's view from Shlaim, *Collusion*, 438.

32. All statistics in this paragraph are from Michael J. Cohen, *Palestine and the Great Powers, 1945-1948* (Princeton: Princeton University Press, 1982), 56-7, and Sachar, *History*, Vol.I, 395-403.

33. Sachar, *History*, Vol. I, 404.

34. Shlaim, *Collusion*, 589.

35. Shlaim, *Collusion*, 572.

36. In addition to Palestine and the Sinai, Ben-Gurion had a scheme to annex part of Lebanon up to the Litani River (the current "security zone") and turn the rest of Lebanon into a cooperative Maronite state. Shlaim, *Collusion*, 392.

37. Shlaim, *Collusion*, 437.

38. Meir Pail interview. Shlaim, *Collusion*, 437.

39. Nahum Goldmann, *Sixty Years of Jewish Life: The Autobiography of Nahum Goldmann* (New York: Holt, Rinehart and Winston, 1969), 289-90.

Chapter 10

Border Turmoil in the Name of Israeli Security (1948-1955)

Palestinian refugees seeking to return to their homes were depicted as *criminal* infiltrators – language seeming to justify the use of force to bar them from Israeli for security reasons. The Zionist demographic goal of removing and keeping out Palestinians was now inextricably woven into a security argument.

The use of harsh force against infiltration was also directed against Arab villages *inside* Jordan, Syria and Egyptian-controlled Gaza. This served other strategic goals, as well, namely, expansion into and intimidation of the surrounding Arab nations hosting refugee camps. Ben-Gurion believed that Arab nations, unless further intimidated, would in the long run seek retaliation in a "second round" of war:

> What is our reality: the Arab nations have been beaten by us. Will they forget that swiftly? 700,000 men have beaten 30 million. Will they forget this insult? It has to be assumed that they have a sense of honour. We shall make efforts for peace – but for peace two sides are required. Is there any certainty that they will not want to have their revenge on us? Let us recognize the truth: we won not because our army is a performer of miracles but because the Arab army is rotten. Is this rot bound to persist? Is an Arab Mustafa Kemal not possible?[1]

This notion that returning Palestinians were criminal infiltrators or terrorists supported by Arab countries was necessary to the Israeli strategy of intimidation. "The Israeli government . . . wrongly . . . assumed, or at least claimed, that the Jordanian authorities condoned or even encouraged these clandestine border crossings."[2] But to the extent that Arab governments sought retaliation, it was more passive than that – more economic than military, including boycotting of Israeli products, blockading of ships, cutting communications. In fact, until 1954, Arab governments largely *curbed* entry of Palestinian civilians into Israel – including those merely seeking to return home.[3]

Israel pursued a "reprisal" policy designed not only to deter Palestinian refugees from reentry and to deter through intimidation a "second round" of Arab-nation revenge but also to consolidate and assure territorial gains along Israel's ill-defined borders. Pretext "reprisal" actions culminated in 1954-1955 with attempts to conquer territory in Jordan's West Bank. Large tracts of no man's land around Tiberias near the Sea of Galilee were seized. Plans were laid to invade the Egyptian Sinai.

Research on Palestinian criminal infiltration

Researcher Jonathan Shimshoni concludes that not until five years after being exiled in 1948 from their homes did Palestinian Arab refugees, living in deplorable and hopeless refugee camps in Syria and Gaza, begin infiltrating Israel with intentions of sabotage and revenge.[4] Serious incidents were limited to twenty-five in the four years following the 1948 war.[5] Howard Sachar ascribes some of the incidents of "infiltration" (border crossings) to the ill-defined nature of the borders themselves: The frontiers "between Israel and Jordan . . . cut off Arab villages from their fields and wells. Almost nowhere was the frontier clearly marked. Local Arabs . . . began crossing the artificial boundaries to reclaim their possessions. Some even attempted to harvest their old fields . . . moved into Israel to rejoin their families . . . or simply did not know the precise demarcation of the armistice line."[6]

More recently, Israeli historian Benny Morris learned from Israeli archives that barely 10 percent of the actual "infiltration" incidents between 1949 and 1956 were politically motivated or involved sabotage – most were clearly attempts by destitute refugees to return home, harvest crops, recover livestock or simply see their fields once more. Morris concludes that fear of hunger was the primary motive for risking Israeli bullets and that it was largely *in response* to Israel's iron-fist policies that politically motivated and violent infiltration arose after years of living in Gazan, Jordanian and Syrian refugee camps.[7] Israel set land mines along the unmarked borders and Gen. Yigal Allon established "free fire zones" in which Palestinian refugees were "shot without interrogation." This shoot-to-kill policy, born of the 1948 war, continued until 1956. Bodies were often booby-trapped in order to kill other infiltrators who came to retrieve them. Prisoners were sometimes tied to trees and shot, as were some of the wounded.

By early 1955, somewhere between 2,700 and 5,000 Palestinian refugees had been blown up by Israeli mines or shot (the vast majority unarmed citizens).[8] Whether those killings inspired Palestinian terrorism or inhibited it, between 1949 and 1956, some 200 to 250 Israeli civilians had been killed by terrorists.[9]

Israeli raids on Arab states and territories in the early 1950s

By October 1955, Ben-Gurion was ordering Dayan to prepare to capture the Strait of Tiran and possibly the Gaza Strip and the northern Sinai – a conceptual leap intended to solve territorial and military-strategic problems, not merely to combat Palestinian guerrilla raids.[10] Some of the hostilities *beyond* Israel's borders leading up to this order were as follows:

Gaza: The Gaza Strip (administered by Egypt) is a four-mile wide strip of coastal land, densely populated before the 1948 war with some 60,000 Palestinians. In 1948 an additional 250,000 refugees arrived. Unemployed, these refugees lived in "unalleviated misery . . . vegetating helplessly in the squalor of their UNRWA [UN Relief] shantytowns."[11]

There were surprisingly few border incidents until after Israel's August 1953 attack on the el-Bureij refugee camp near Gaza.[12] Two IDF commando ("101") squads commanded by Ariel Sharon infiltrated the camp without provocation. When discovered, they shot their way out, killing twenty Palestinians, injuring sixty, and creating panic.[13] The refugees rioted and demanded weapons from Egypt for retaliation. By April 1954, they had organized themselves enough to exchange small tit-for-tat attacks and counterattacks across the Gaza border with Israeli forces.

There were occasional Egyptian and Israeli IDF skirmishes as well. Nevertheless, the Gazan border was relatively quiet. This may have been because Arab-moderate Moshe Sharett replaced David Ben-Gurion as prime minister for two years.[14] Israel's attacks in the Gaza Strip became more measured and Sharett refused permission for large-scale military operations against Egypt as requested by Defense Minister Pinchas Lavon and Chief of Staff Moshe Dayan. Then, in November 1955, Ben-Gurion was back in office. The IDF, searching for weapons and Fedayeen at Khan Yunis in Gaza, killed at least 275 Palestinians and, days later, another 111 at nearby Rafah.[15]

Jordan: In October 1953, some Arab terrorists infiltrated Israel with a mind to sabotage and murder. A mother and two children were killed by a grenade, probably the work of Arab refugees from Syria. Jordan condemned the act and offered Israel assistance in apprehending the perpetrators. Nevertheless, Lavon and Dayan ordered Sharon's commando unit to dynamite forty-five homes in Qibya (Jordan). This killed sixty-nine civilians, half of them women and children, trapped in their homes.[16] Ben-Gurion falsely claimed it to have been the private work of Jewish settlers victimized by Arabs. The UN Security Council condemned Israel and the United States withheld $75 million in grants.

In 1955, the Jordanian-Israeli front was relatively quiet – eight Israeli and eighteen Arab deaths. In September 1956, in response to a guerrilla attack that killed six Israeli soldiers, Israel killed sixteen Jordanian soldiers at Qariya. Raids and counter-raids reached their zenith when Israel launched a massive retaliation against the Jordanian police fortress at Qalqilia. Tanks, artillery and eventually planes were used in a savage battle that approached full-scale warfare. Destroyed were 850 houses, most in retaliation after the fighting had stopped.

Egypt: In the summer of 1954, Israel infiltrated Egypt, initiating terrorist bombings in Cairo and Alexandria. The targets were selected so as to appear to be the work of Egyptian, anti-Western terrorists, e.g., British and U.S. information centers, movie theaters, consulates and public buildings. The purpose was to bring scorn on Egypt in an effort to sabotage Egyptian-British talks about the Suez Canal and Egyptian-U.S. weapons negotiations. When the terrorists were caught, Israel called it an anti-Jewish, "Nazi-inspired" Egyptian plot. Moshe Dayan, Shimon Peres (then director-general of the defense ministry) and Benyamin Gibli (chief of army intelligence) were implicated in the forging of documents to falsely blame Defense Minister Lavon in what became known as the "Lavon Affair." Egypt convicted and executed two of the Israeli terrorists in February 1955. Ben-Gurion, again defense minister that February, pressed for a "retaliatory" invasion of Egyptian army headquarters in Gaza. Israel blew up train depots and water-pumping stations, killing thirty-nine Egyptian troops and wounded thirty-two others, upon claim that the Egyptian troops had infiltrated Israel. The UN Security Council censured Israel and U.S. Secretary of State John Foster Dulles protested bitterly to Prime Minister Sharett.[17]

This attack heralded a new revolutionary era in Israeli-Egyptian relations.[18] Ben-Gurion had designed the assault to: (1) demonstrate to Cairo the military supremacy of the IDF; (2) punish Egypt for having hanged the two Jewish terrorists caught in the Lavon Affair; and (3) "mobilize the raid into a brink-manship relationship." One month after the February raid on Egyptian army headquarters, Defense Minister Ben-Gurion tried to convince the Israeli cabinet to permit the army to conquer the whole of the Gaza Strip and hold it for bargaining purposes.[19] Sharett barely succeeded in blocking the plan. What was not in doubt was that Ben-Gurion and Chief of Staff Dayan had adopted a strategy of attacking Arab territory with the "surprise preemptive blow, the hard-driving, even reckless, offensive aimed at breaking the enemy's morale."[20]

Egyptian President Gamal Abdel Nasser then visited the Gaza Strip and increased Egyptian forces both there and in the Sinai. He declared the Israeli February attack in Gaza to be "the turning point. . . . This disaster was the alarm bell. We at once started to examine the significance of peace and the balance of power in the area." Egypt began to train Palestinian agitators and by April 1955 had created the first Fedayeen ("sacrificer") terrorists for raids into Israel.[21]

In May, Israel threatened Egypt with a major military operation which Nasser understood to mean capture of the Egyptian Sinai.[22] Hostilities increased and UN appeals were ignored by both sides. In July, Nasser signed a Czech arms deal. In August, Fedayeen terrorist attacks resulted in the murder of seventeen Israelis. Israel responded by boldly entering the Gaza Strip, blowing up an Egyptian police station at Khan Yunis and killing more than forty. Egyptian and Israeli aircraft sometimes tangled.

In October 1955, Israeli and Egyptian armies clashed at al-Auja in the demilitarized zone (DMZ).[23] Israel had illegally established a military force there disguised as a kibbutz.[24] When Egypt then established a checkpoint in the DMZ and Israel demanded its removal, Egypt refused. The IDF went south, wiped out an Egyptian army post at al-Quntilla in the Sinai and then attacked Egyptian forces at al-Auja, killing fifty. The UN Security Council censured Israel but Ben-Gurion, now (November 1955) both prime minister and defense minister, ordered the IDF to remain in place.

In April of 1956, Egyptian artillery shelled several Israeli settlements (casualties unknown). In retaliation, Israel shelled the city of Gaza (59 dead, 152 wounded) and attacked Fedayeen bases in Jordan.[25] In response to the Gaza shelling, the Fedayeen entered Israel and killed over a dozen Israelis.[26]

By U. N. reports, Israel launched more than seventeen military raids in one form or another on Egyptian-held territory between 1949 and 1956, and a total of thirty-one attacks against Arab towns or military forces during these seven years. Virtually all of these were condemned by the Egypt-Israel Mixed Armistice Commission or censured by the Security Council – as, occasionally, were Arab provocations.[27]

Syria: In 1951, Israel claimed territory in a DMZ area and evicted 2,000 Syrian farmers. When the UN Security Council ordered the return of the land to the farmers, Israel blew up their villages.[28] Eventually, 350 farmers returned to the land and were again evicted in 1956.

However, the main source of contention between Syria and Israel was water, not land. In 1953, Israel had begun a project to divert water from the Jordan River to a hydroelectric plant and water reservoir from which the Negev Desert and other areas in Israel were to be watered. Because this project at Banat Yaqub, twelve miles north of the Sea of Galilee, was in a DMZ, Syria had grounds to object. Small-scale military exchanges ensued. The UN Security Council pressured Israel to abandon the project.

Then in October 1955, Syria captured five Israeli soldiers wiretapping in Syria. Israel retaliated by invading Syria, destroying a Syrian military convoy and taking five hostages for bargaining purposes. Two months later, after exchange negotiations failed, Israel again attacked Syria, killing twenty-six soldiers and twelve civilians. The UN Security Council denounced the act, as it had other Israeli adventures against Syria.[29]

> U.S. diplomats . . . watched with amazement, and reported to Washington on Israel's apparent efforts to keep the border areas in turmoil and increase the appearance of threats to its own security.[30]

Divergent strategies concerning security

UN condemnations made it evident that Israel was not winning world support for its actions. Dayan complained bitterly: "What is 'allowable' to the Arabs – and to other peoples – will not be forgiven to Jews and Israelis. Not only foreigners, but Israeli citizens and world Jewry expect from us a 'purity of arms' [reservation in use of force] greater than that normally found in any army."[31] On the other hand, Israel's ambassador to the UN, Abba Eban, was convinced that Israel was injuring itself by its own militancy: "Retaliation is just finished as a policy, and our people should become used to obeying the same rules, even under provocation, as other governments when provoked."[32]

While Eban and Sharett looked on provocative IDF adventures with fear that large-scale operations would antagonize public relations in the West, Ben-Gurion had disdain for such considerations, attacking Sharett for worrying too much about "what the Gentiles will say."[33]

"Retaliation" and "reprisal" for what Arabs might initiate were not what

Ben-Gurion and his protege Dayan had in mind, according to historian Shlaim:

> Gradually, Dayan developed the theory that the [1948] War of Independence was not yet over and that several further large-scale operations were required to bring it to a more favourable conclusion. Various proposals were floated by Dayan for the capture of the Gaza Strip, Mount Hebron, and the West Bank, all designed to stem the tide of infiltration, to round off Israel's borders, and to assert her military dominance in such a crushing manner that the Arabs would give up any hope of a second round. Instead of Israel being threatened with a second round, Dayan wanted Israel to threaten the Arabs and to constantly escalate the level of violence so as to demonstrate her superiority and to create the conditions for territorial expansion.[34]

Menachem Begin, leader of Herut (the second strongest party in 1955) also demanded a "preventative" war in which Egypt would be destroyed. The matter was continuously debated in the Knesset (parliament) during 1955-1956.[35] The argument espoused was that Israeli *weakness* required preventative war now. The United States countered that even with the Egyptian-Czech arms deal there was no real danger to Israel's survival.[36] Rather, the United States, certainly the U.S. consul general in Jerusalem, believed that Israel was "spoiling for [a] fight."[37] But there was no question that national anxiety in Israel was putting pressure on the government for war.

Sharett (prime minister during 1954) wrote in his diary:

> The conclusions [of Dayan's position] are clear: This State has no international obligations, no economic problems, the question of peace is nonexistent. . . . It must calculate its steps narrow-mindedly and live on the sword. It must see the sword as the main, if not the only, instrument with which to keep its morale high and to retain its moral tension. Toward this end it may, no – it must – invent dangers, and to do this it must adopt the method of provocation-and-revenge. . . . And above all, let us hope for a new war with the Arab countries, so that we may finally get rid of our troubles and acquire our space.[38]

But Sharett and Ben-Gurion, dove and hawk, agreed about one thing: the Palestinians should be kept out. Sharett thought that that should be accomplished through *negotiation* with Arab nations burdened with unwanted refugees. Ben-Gurion preferred *force*. Even if force did stimulate Palestinian terrorism or Arab nation involvement, that would, according to Benny Morris, serve to justify even greater Israeli "retaliations" which would prove fatal to those nations.

Paradoxically, from some point in 1954, the retaliatory strikes were also designed with a directly contrary purpose, at least as seen by the new IDF CGS [Chief of the General Staff] Dayan – and that was to help prod this or that Arab state into a premature war with Israel. Dayan wanted war, and, periodically, he hoped that a given retaliatory strike would embarass or provoke the Arab state attacked into itself retaliating, giving Israel cause to escalate the shooting until war resulted – a war in which Israel could realize such major strategic objectives as the conquest of the West Bank or Sinai, or the destruction of the Egyptian army. Such, certainly, was the main motive behind the IDF strikes against Egypt . . . and Syria . . . in 1955.[39]

In a year's time, in October 1956, Israel would have its war with Egypt for the Sinai, the Suez War, the confrontation that Dayan and Begin had sought.

Notes

1. David Ben-Gurion, *War Diary: The War of Independence, 1948-1949* [(in Hebrew) [November 27, 1948], G. Rivlin and E. Orren, eds. (Tel Aviv: Ministry of Defence, 1982), cited in Avi Shlaim, *Collusion across the Jordan* (New York: Columbia University Press, 1988), 343. Mustafa Kemal was the leader who transformed Turkey into a modern state.

2. Shlaim, *Collusion,* 570.

3. Jonathan Shimshoni, *Israel and Conventional Deterrence: Border Warfare between 1953 and 1970* (Ithaca: Cornell University Press, 1988), 49.

4. It was in the summer of 1953 that so-called innocent infiltration became more politically motivated and involved instances of murder and sabotage. Jordanian military leader Pasha Glubb similarly dates the turning point in the amount and nature of infiltration from innocent to malevolent. Shimshoni, *Conventional Deterrence,* 34-44, 46.

5. Shimshoni, *Conventional Deterrence,* 43 (Table 4).

6. Howard Sachar, *A History of Israel: From the Rise of Zionism to Our Time,* Vol. I (New York: Knopf, 1986), 443-4.

7. Benny Morris, *Israel's Border Wars, 1949-1956* (New York: Oxford University Press, 1993), 138.

8. Morris, *Border Wars,* 137.

9. Morris concludes that 200 to 250 Israeli civilians were killed by 1956, with another 500 to 1,000 wounded. *Border Wars,* 415. According to Sachar, 1,300 were killed or wounded. *History,* Vol. I, 450.

10. Shimshoni, *Conventional Deterrence*, 86.

11. Sachar, *History*, Vol. I, 442-3. "What was unsalvageble was not their existence but their morale."

12. Shimshoni, *Conventional Deterrence*, 74. "Through August of 1953 there is no evidence that either Israel or Egypt was unduly concerned with these events [incidents of infiltration]. . . . In all of 1953 we record three incidents of serious infiltration involving mining or sabotage."

13. The raid had no discernible deterrent or retaliatory function and has been explained by one scholar as having possibly been a "unit building" exercise. Shimshoni, *Conventional Deterrence*, 76.

14. Ben-Gurion was prime minister *and* defense minister from 1947 to 1963, except for periods between November 1953 and February 1955 (not defense minister) and between November 1953 and November 1955 (not prime minister). During those interim times Sharett was prime minister and Lavon was defense minister. In February 1955, Ben-Gurion replaced Lavon as defense minister – Lavon had quit because of Sharett's failure to act against Shimon Peres for Peres's role in framing Lavon in the "Lavon affair." Sharett was foreign minister after November 1955, but Ben-Gurion removed him in June 1956. Sachar, *History*, Vol. I, 480-1.

15. Donald Neff, *Warriors at Suez* (Brattleboro, Vt.: Amana Books, 1988), 420.

16. It may have been that the Sharon commandos superficially searched the ground floor only of houses before blowing them up. Yet UN observers stated: "Bullet-riddled bodies near the doorways and multiple bullet hits on the doors of the demolished houses indicated that the inhabitants had been forced to remain inside until their homes were blown up over them." Elmo H. Hutchison, (an American UN observer), *Violent Truce: A Military Observer Looks at the Arab-Israeli Conflict, 1951–1955* (New York: Devin-Adair, 1956), 44.

17. Shimshoni, *Conventional Deterrence*, 81.

18. Shimshoni, *Conventional Deterrence*, 79.

19. Shimshoni, *Conventional Deterrence*, 82-3.

20. Sachar, *History*, Vol. I, 479.

21. According to Dayan, the Fedayeen movement began in April 1955. Shimshoni, *Conventional Deterrence*, 82. Other historians have dated the start of the movement later (August 1955), e.g., Walter Lehn, "The Development of Palestinian Resistance," Information Paper No. 14. (North Dartmouth, Mass.: Association of Arab-American University Graduates, June 1974).

22. Shimshoni, *Conventional Deterrence*, 83.

23. See Sachar, *History*, Vol. I, 449, for description.

24. Six thousand Bedouins had been evicted from the area, others were deprived of water and crops, and thirteen were killed for resisting.

25. Sachar, *History*, Vol. I, 482.

26. Shimshoni, *Conventional Deterrence*, 84. The Egyptian army and Fedayeen lost 182 between September 1955 and 1956 (Table 3, 39).

27. Sachar, *History*, Vol. I, 449-50.

28. Donald Neff, *Warriors for Jerusalem* (Brattleboro, Vt.: Amana Books,

1988), 54-5.

29. One year before (December 12, 1954), in response to Syrian capture of Israeli spies, Israeli warplanes hijacked a Syrian civilian airliner – the first case of international skyjacking.

30. Edward Tivnan, *The Lobby: Jewish Political Power and American Foreign Policy* (New York: Simon and Schuster, 1987), 42-3. Sharett observed: "[The U.S.] State Department [has] the conviction that an Israeli plan of retaliations, to be realized according to a pre-fixed timetable, exists, and that the goal is that of a steady escalation of the tension in the area in order to bring about a war." Livia Rokach, *Israel's Sacred Terrorism* (Belmont, Mass.: Association of Arab-American University Graduates Press, 1986), 31.

31. Shimshoni, *Conventional Deterrence,* 49, quoting Moshe Dayan, *Story of My Life* (London: Weidenfeld and Nicolson, 1976), 115.

32. Sachar, *History,* Vol. I, 450.

33. Tivnan, *The Lobby,* 47.

34. Shlaim, *Collusion,* 571.

35. Shimshoni, *Conventional Deterrence,* 101.

36. Shimshoni, *Conventional Deterrence,* 97.

37. Tivnan, *The Lobby,* 43.

38. Sharett's diary entry on March 26, 1955, concerning Dayan's refusal to accept a military pact with the United States in exchange for no further expansion of borders by force, reported to Sharett by Ya'acob Herzog. Rokach, *Sacred Terrorism,* 41.

39. Morris, *Border Wars,* 178-9.

Chapter 11

International Cold War Politics and the Suez War (1956)

Chapter 10 described the local situation in Palestine from 1948 to 1955, one of Israeli militancy against Palestinian refugees and the surrounding Arab nations. The shooting of returning refugees and attacks on refugee camps galvanized Palestinian terrorism after five years of destitute living. Egypt, in particular, increasingly met these Israeli attacks in Gaza with counterattack. Israel was prodding Egypt and Jordan into a "second round" of the 1948 war, predictably fatal to these countries. While hostilities headed toward war, the Cold War was a critical contributing factor to the Suez War in that it polarized Israel and the Arab countries even further.

Cold War alignments: the United States with Israel; the U.S.S.R. with Egypt
    The single most important international factor governing Middle East events in the 1950s was the Cold War. The United States devoutly pursued a policy of "containment" of the Soviet Union and its ideological influence through creation of small NATO-like defense organizations around the perimeter of the U.S.S.R. The United States and Britain fashioned one such "defense" organization out of Islamic countries south and west of the U.S.S.R. – Turkey, Iran, Pakistan and Iraq. The United States made bilateral treaties with Turkey and Pakistan, and the Central Intelligence Agency installed the pro-West Shah of Iran, while Britain made progress in Iraq. By 1955, Turkey, Pakistan, Iran, Iraq and Britain comprised a single defense organization called the *Baghdad Pact.* U.S. membership remained unofficial.

The Baghdad Pact concerned Israel because Iraq, its putative enemy, would be in line to receive broad Western military assistance. The United States, Britain and France had assured Israel that they would intervene if Arab countries were to violate armistice agreements with Israel (Tripartite Declaration, 1950). Israel treated those assurances as insufficient. Israel wanted a *direct* military alliance with the United States – something that would clearly have spoiled U.S.-Arab relations.

The United States demonstrated its commitment to Israel by making significant direct loans, grants and tax-free gift provisions. Yet Israel's commitment to the United States was equivocal – a stance of "non-identification" with the Western allies and the Eastern bloc in hopes of military and economic assistance from both sides. But the Korean War altered that. Israel was obliged to align with the United States when the the latter sought UN condemnation of North Korean aggression in 1952. Israel's support of the U.S. position on Korea precipitated a strong anti-Jewish reaction in the Soviet and communist bloc countries (e.g., Prague show trials).[1]

Egypt was also critical of the Baghdad Pact but for different reasons. The pact seemed to be the backdoor route through which the West would further what Egypt saw as Western imperialism: control of Arab oil and exploitation of Arab nations for cold war purposes. Initially, Egypt, like Israel, assumed a stance of non-identification with West and East for the sake of aid from either or both sides. But Egypt's fundamental stance was increasingly anti-Western. In 1952, Gamal Abdel Nasser, Anwar Sadat and others had successfully dethroned the British-controlled King Farouk in a bloodless coup. Nasser's new popularity was based on his anti-West, anti-imperialist, pro-Arab-nationalist stand. Nasser rejected British imperialism, U.S.-supported Jewish colonization of Palestine, the Baghdad Pact and the French colonization of Algeria. To say the least, he was profoundly unpopular in the West.[2]

Eisenhower versus Truman

Another important factor in polarizing the Middle East in the 1950s was the election of Eisenhower in 1952. The new president was a different man in a different time. Truman, while not unprincipled, was certainly a political pragmatist: "Gentlemen, I have no Arabs in my constituency." Whereas Eisenhower seemed, or could afford to be, above the political fray. A war hero, not a politician, Eisenhower was convinced of his own principledness, his immunity to popular sentiment and the virtue of disregarding special pleadings. His attentive, consistent, global-minded style was less improvisational than Truman's. He intended to be impartial yet sympathetic toward both Arabs and Jews in order to gain Middle East cooperation in thwarting Soviet aggression.[3] What he managed to achieve, as we shall see, was further polarization of Arabs and Jews.

Eisenhower's policies and attitudes toward Israel

Eisenhower thought it should be possible to reduce tensions between Arabs and Israelis and, in doing so, support both Israel and the Arab countries as an effective way to counter and contain the U.S.S.R. To this end he sought further cooperation between Israel, Jordan and Syria. For example, the United States proposed a Jordan Valley Authority water distribution project in 1953 to reclaim arid land in all three countries and, at the same time, create employment for Palestinians still languishing in refugee camps.[4] The project failed, even in its negotiation phase. The United States made other attempts to negotiate friendship between Egypt and Israel through the backdoor diplomacy of Robert Anderson (future American treasury secretary). These, including negotiations regarding border adjustments, linkage of Egypt and Jordan through the Negev, compensation for refugees and the end of the Arab boycott/blockade, also failed.

Eisenhower was prepared to maintain financial support for Israel, acknowledging Israel's "strong position in the heart and emotions of the Western world because of the tragic suffering of the Jews throughout twenty-five hundred years of history."[5] At the same time, he did not want to impair Arab relations by creating a unique U.S.-Israeli defense treaty or supply of weapons. In fact, he judged that the existing balance of military power favored Israel and he knew that Israel was receiving arms from France.[6]

Eisenhower was displeased with Israel's diversion of water from the Sea of Galilee and was very critical of Israel's aggressive raids into Syria, Jordan, Egypt and Gaza in the name of preventing Palestinian refugee infiltration. He was also disturbed that Israel would neither repatriate nor compensate Palestinian refugees for expropriated land and property in Israel. That issue had heated up in 1952 when West Germany agreed to pay reparations to Israel and to pay restitution to Jewish refugees and their families who had fled German-occupied countries.[7] In June of 1953, Secretary of State Dulles called for Israeli parallel restitutions to Palestinian refugees – to no effect.[8]

The United States also considered Israeli attacks on Arab countries to be not "retaliatory" but rather tension-making in the service of Israeli expansion of borders through war. In fact, Eisenhower suspended aid to Israel in October 1953 at the request of the UN, which was critical of Israel's mode of "defense." The president believed that Israel would "profit immeasurably" were it to limit its violence and show concern for the "self respect and interests of the Arabs."[9] Dulles pressed Israel to take "a more moderate stand" and to agree to territorial adjustments. In January 1955, the United States tried to make a deal as hostilities heated up between Egypt and Israel: the United States would defend Israel in case of attack, if Israel would commit to no further extension of its borders by force.[10] Israel rejected the offer. Dayan explained to Israeli ambassadors in Washington, Paris and London that "it would put handcuffs on our military freedom of action," preventing "reprisal" attacks into Syria, Jordan and Egypt.[11] Dayan claimed, further, that increases in tension were necessary to keep the Israeli public combative.[12]

Eisenhower's policies and attitudes toward Egypt

If Eisenhower was not sympathetic to Israel, neither was he sympathetic to Egypt. Because he viewed the Arab world as monolithic, he was surprised and displeased when Egypt criticized the Baghdad Pact and when Egypt and Iraq exhibited conflictive relations. And he was disturbed by the intensity of Egyptian anti-imperialist attitudes toward the West.

Eisenhower and Dulles imagined that Egypt would come into the Western fold were the *general* level of tension between Arab countries and Israel reduced. But Egypt needed *specific* help – financing for the Aswan High Dam and arms to achieve parity with Israel. Initially, the United States offered to finance the dam and implied that it would sell arms, only to renege later on both assurances. Pressure came from the Israeli lobby in Washington and from U.S. cotton-state senators fearful that the Aswan Dam would, by increasing arable land, compete with the U.S. cotton crop. Nasser was balking anyhow, fearing that the United States would control the Egyptian economy and limit his freedom to buy arms.[13]

Five months after Israel's major February 1955 attack on Egyptian facilities in the Gaza Strip, Egypt turned to the Soviet bloc. In July, a large arms deal was arranged with the Czechs through the Soviets, who additionally financed the Aswan Dam. Played off against the Soviets, Eisenhower was miffed. But it was Nasser's recognition of Communist China that year that assured his persona non grata status. Secretary of State Dulles now depicted Nasser as "an extremely dangerous fanatic."

Middle East weapons, the means of war

With tense relations between Israel and Egypt, access to the latest weapons was always a major issue. Ben-Gurion and Dayan counted on superior Israeli striking power and demonstration of Israeli prowess to intimidate the Arab world.[14] So the Egyptian-Czech arms deal announced in October of 1955 called for a reevaluation of Israel's normal military advantage. While this arms deal "revolutionized the Middle East system by destroying the control of relative power so long enjoyed by the West,"[15] Israel was not thereby placed in jeopardy. Eisenhower judged that "even with the Czech arms deal, there was no real danger to Israeli survival."[16] Nor was Eisenhower inclined to supplement Israel's arsenal after Israel had conducted harsh raids in Gaza (November 1955) that killed 386 Palestinians over several days (at Khan Yunis and Rafah) and thirty-eight Syrians in December.

Dulles insisted that Israel's security did not reside in more arms, but it was France, not the United States, on whom Israel really counted. Ben-Gurion accepted Shimon Peres's contention that France was the proper and most likely source of arms.[17] France had, after all, been aligned with the Jews since the mid-1940s, providing weapons, recruitment, ports, asylum for Jewish terrorists and financial support during the 1948 war. Politically, the French Left took a pro-Jewish attitude toward "socialist" Israel; the French Right shared Israel's hostility toward Arab nationalism (e.g., in Algeria).

Then Eisenhower changed his mind. It was probably *not* the cooperation between France and Israel on nuclear weapons since the 1950s – a nuclear capacity no longer to be doubted by 1960 – that convinced Eisenhower to provide conventional weapons to Israel. It was the fact that the United States was unable to control France. The United States knew that Israel was receiving, over U.S. protest, huge quantities of heavy French weaponry beyond that officially reported.[18] From this source Israel had "access to all the modern weaponry it needed to crush the Egyptian army before it could absorb its new Czech arms."[19] So Eisenhower gave in, lifting U.S. prohibitions on the sale to Israel of armaments then earmarked for NATO. The United States even asked Canada to provide Israel with a squadron of jets.[20] Israel was freely purchasing weapons in quantity and quality on a level with Egypt's recent acquisitions.[21]

With this continuing massive build-up of modern arms, Israel was ready to win a war. UN observers speculated that Israel was preparing a major preemptive strike before the Egyptian army could assimilate its own large quantity of Soviet/Czech arms.[22]

The Suez Crisis, 1956

It will be recalled that Egypt had barred Israeli ships from the Suez Canal since the 1948 war.[23] While Israel had no real shipping industry, the blockade was, in principle, illegal and a politically hostile act.[24] Eisenhower had dismissed Israel's protests because the matter was of little economic importance and because Egypt needed some sort of domestic face-saver after the 1948 debacle. But also at issue was the Strait of Tiran, an alternative route to the Red Sea and the East. Egypt had denied Israel free passage through the strait on ground that it was Egyptian territorial waters. The legal-territorial issue had never been tested in international court, yet political tensions existed.[25] Again, Eisenhower was no more sympathetic to Israel over the strait than over the Suez Canal.

It was not until Nasser, in an effort to finance the Aswan Dam, *nationalized* the Suez Canal Company (July 1956) that all hell broke loose. While he compensated fully and on schedule the British and French holders of bonds and shares, Britain and France were immediately concerned about the public and political consequences at home.[26] They "passionately" wanted to go to war.[27] There were as well large economic issues: loss of Canal revenue, loss of control over transport of oil and other vital supplies, and spreading Arab nationalism cutting into colonial riches (Britain's loss of Egypt, a major colony and military base, and France's impending loss of Algeria, a rich source of oil, minerals and cheap labor). After Nasser nationalized the canal, British Foreign Secretary Anthony Eden and French Prime Minister Guy Mollet sold him to the world as "the Hitler of the Nile."

Eisenhower cautioned Britain and France, seeing no legal grounds for attacking Egypt. For one thing, Nasser's agreement to compensate European investors seemed to make the nationalization legal. Secondly, the canal was due to revert to Egypt in 1968 anyhow. Thirdly, Egypt kept the canal open to European shipping.[28]

Eisenhower's warnings only served to drive Britain and France underground. They staged a charade, an international conference on the future of the canal, in order to gain six weeks to prepare for attack. Diplomatic wrangling dragged on and Dulles proposed that a Suez Canal Users Association be formed. But as time passed with the canal running smoothly, the whole notion of an international shipping crisis was undercut. Moreover, when Britain and France took the matter of Canal nationalization to the UN Security Council, Egypt unexpectedly *accepted* the Europeans' own compromise proposal. Thus, Britain and France were forced to do a diplomatic turnabout and sabotage their own proposal.

Grounds for an Anglo-French military adventure all but evaporated.

The Europeans shifted strategy, adopted the idea that a casus belli could be found in Egypt-Israeli tensions. European military intervention in Egypt would seem justified were *Israel* to attack Egypt. The Europeans could then invade in a pretense to be "saving the Canal" by "separating the combatants." Britain and France both wanted the Canal revenues back, France wanted to stop Nasser's support of Algerian independence and Britain wanted to regain control in Egypt. These interests dovetailed with Ben-Gurion's and the Israeli public's desire to wage war against a country perceived as an enemy – a war that would finally gain for Israel the long-coveted Sinai Peninsula.

Relations between Israel, France and Britain: The feasibility of collaboration

By September of 1956, France and Israel enjoyed a virtual military alliance.[29] Shimon Peres assured Mollet that Israel would attack Egypt if France would.[30] Ben-Gurion wanted Britain also to be involved, but British and Israeli relations were problematic. Mutual bitterness over Jewish terrorism during the mandate remained, and as late as October 1956, Britain threatened to defend Jordan against Israel's harsh raids on Jordanian-based Fedayeen camps.[31] A further complication was that Jordan had a mutual defense pact with *Egypt.* Any British attack on Egypt would require, technically, Jordan to fight its own ally, Britain.

Given these strains and complications, the French were reluctant to reveal to the British the extent of their growing collaboration with the Israelis – a needless worry since Foreign Secretary Eden "could not resist the opportunity to unseat Nasser, even if it meant collusion with the Israelis."[32] Eden wanted to collaborate with Israel. Preliminary assassination attempts on Nasser's life by both Britain and France did not succeed.[33]

Nasser's intentions

In the spring of 1956, Nasser tried to reassure the Israelis that he had absolutely no plans for war, pointing out that his troops in the Sinai were in defensive positions and that few forces were deployed along the Gaza border.[34] Furthermore, after the nationalization of the Suez Canal in late July, Nasser had withdrawn half his forces from the Sinai, away from Israel. At the same time, he was making belligerent speeches for popular consumption: "We must be strong in order to gain the rights of the Palestinians by force." His army commander in chief informed the troops: "The hour is approaching when [we] . . . will stand in the front ranks of the battle against imperialism and its Zionist ally." [35]

Nasser's intentions were a product of conflicting pressures. Necessary to his popularity and power base was support of Palestinian culture and statehood. Yet he could not risk provoking a war with Israel. He needed belligerency short of official challenge to Israel.[36] His notion of such a middle ground seemed to be support of Fedayeen activity with reduced Egyptian army involvement.

Ben-Gurion made claims that Nasser's intention was war. Nasser and the international community believed that Ben-Gurion was spoiling for war – the only question was where: Egypt, Jordan or Syria? The fact remained, Israel was preparing with Britain and France for war against Egypt.

Secret plan: Israel to attack Egypt; Britain and France to "save the Canal"

In order not to damage relations with the United States or Arab countries, the British sought to avoid all appearance of *direct* attack on Egypt. To this end the British foreign secretary proposed that Israel invade the Suez Canal area, followed by a British attack on *Israeli* forces to create an impression that Britain was acting to separate the Egyptian and Israeli combatants and protect the canal.[37] Understandably, the Israelis refused this invitation to be attacked. Israel eventually agreed to invade the Sinai and land paratroopers near the canal, after which Britain and French would demand that both Israel and Egypt withdraw from the canal area. Clearly, Egypt would refuse to withdraw from its own territory under attack, so Britain and France would seem to have an excuse to invade.

The United States was kept in the dark because of Eisenhower's opposition to any European or Israeli invasion of Egypt – despite Nasser's persona non grata status. The last thing the United States wanted, in its effort to court young independent nations and combat communism through anti-imperialist policies, was to have World War II allies war on Egypt, champion of national independence movements.[38] The United States had suspicions, of course, about the European plan to invade – the preparations for invasion (Operation Musketeer) were simply too massive to escape notice.[39] Britain's contribution was to be 50,000 troops, bombers, fighter planes and 100 warships; France's, 30,000 men, several fighter squadrons, 30 ships and hundreds of landing craft; Israel's, 32,000 troops. Seven aircraft carriers and 20,000 vehicles were also to be involved. Eisenhower issued stern warnings to Britain about intervention in Egypt and warned Ben-Gurion about the use of force in *Jordan* – Israel had been accelerating attacks on Jordan as a diversionary tactic to disguise the true target.[40]

Specific military strategy of the Suez War

The specific invasion plan called for an Israeli invasion of the Egyptian Sinai on the night of October 29, 1956, with a battalion of paratroopers landing near the canal. Several other Israeli battalions would advance southeast through the Sinai and then meet up near the canal. The RAF and French air force would destroy Egyptian planes on the ground, thereby eliminating any danger to European troops preparing to invade Alexandria. Anglo-French forces would advance on the main Egyptian army and capture Cairo. In the event that some Egyptian planes happened to survive the blitz and attempt retaliation, the French air force would protect Israeli cities while French warships would guard the Israeli coast. If things happened to go badly for the Israelis in the initial Sinai invasion, the whole brigade would be pulled back and the operation passed off as just another retaliatory raid for Egyptian aggression.[41]

If successful, the plan would: (1) yield Israel the whole Sinai Peninsula, including the Gaza Strip, (2) restore shipping through the Strait of Tiran, and (3) topple Nasser. Ironically, this plan was identical to the one Ben-Gurion had proposed to Britain in 1951. Now Britain was ready to cooperate.

The outcome

The Israeli attack proceeded largely as planned. Ariel Sharon led the southeast-bound forces over the Sinai and then joined a batallion of paratroopers dropped at Mitla near the canal. The Egyptians first thought the paratroopers were on a sabotage raid. But once Sharon's forces joined up, Egypt had reason to mobilize its army. Ben-Gurion advanced a deception by issuing an announcement to the world that Israel had "engaged Fedayeen units . . . this action follows the Egyptian assaults on Israeli transport on land and sea destined to cause destruction and the denial of peaceful life to Israel's citizens."[42]

On schedule the British and French issued their ultimatum: invasion, unless Egypt and Israel both withdrew ten miles from either side of the canal – in effect "ordering the victim (Egypt) to withdraw from the Sinai to the west of the Canal, and allowing the invader (Israel) to advance to a distance 10 miles east of the Canal."[43] Dulles declared the Anglo-French ultimatum to be a device "about as crude and brutal as anything he has ever seen."[44] As expected, Egypt refused. Nasser took the British and French threats to invade as a ruse to draw Egyptian troops away from the Sinai and permit an easy Israeli victory. Hence, he deployed more troops to the Sinai.

On October 31, an armada of 200 British and French fighter-bombers destroyed 95 percent of the Egyptian air force on the ground. Neither the U.S.S.R., Jordan nor Syria aided the Egyptians. Eisenhower considered intervening militarily in conformity with existing U.S. treaty obligations (the Tripartitite Declaration of 1950) to defend *any* nation attacked in violation of the Arab-Israeli armistice. He was livid. He declared the Anglo-French intercession to be a betrayal of the Atlantic relationship and expressed shock when the British and French vetoed a UN Security Council resolution calling for withdrawal of Israel and all other states.

Eisenhower threatened Israel: "You ought not to forget that the strength of Israel and her future are bound up with the United States. I expect a prompt reply."[45] Israeli ambassador Abba Eban replied that, thanks to Israel's occupation of the Sinai, "Nasser is going to lose all his credit. A more moderate government will replace his."[46] Dulles rebutted that he was not prepared to violate the UN Charter and international law for the sake of beating up someone he disliked. Eisenhower and Dulles were worried that the Soviets would gain influence in the Arab world if the Israelis were not forced to withdraw.

Once the British and French had destroyed the Egyptian air force, Nasser withdrew his soldiers from the Sinai to concentrate on the defense of Alexandria and Cairo against a likely Anglo-French land invasion. This enabled Israel to capture the *whole* of the Sinai (the Gaza Strip had already been captured after heavy artillery duels and naval bombardments at Rafah). For the next several days, the IDF advanced southward over difficult land on the west and east coasts of the Sinai. These advances included systematic destruction of Fedayeen bases, round up of Fedayeen from prepared lists and executions on the spot.[47]

On November 2, the UN General Assembly voted 64 to 5 for an immediate cease-fire and withdrawal of all occupying forces from Egypt. At this point, the Israelis had not completed their sweep of Egypt's Sinai so they rejected the UN resolution. The Anglo-French armies were still aboard their 100 ships steaming toward Egypt, still 500 miles away. The international atmosphere was one of great crisis. At the time, Soviet tanks were rolling into Budapest to quash the Hungarian revolution. The Soviets sent a scorching note to the Israelis and an ominous nuclear warning to the British and French.[48] The world seemed to be teetering on the brink of an atomic cataclysm.[49]

Israel ignored the UN resolution of November 2 and completed the capture of the southern tip of the Sinai Peninsula and the Strait of Tiran on November 4.

That day the UN voted overwhelmingly to create a UN Emergency Force to prevent the imminent Anglo-French invasion. Israel still intended to capture al-Qantara on the canal to clear an area for French paratroopers to land. Britain vetoed this idea since it would give the lie to the notion that European forces were landing to "separate the combatants."

Israel accepted a cease-fire after completing its capture of the Sinai. This enraged the British and French. Israel had gotten what it wanted but now, by *accepting the cease-fire,* had destroyed the Anglo-French rationale for their invasion, i.e., to separate the combatants. Israel had thereby prevented the Europeans from getting what they wanted: control of the Suez Canal. Obligingly, the Israelis *undid* their acceptance of the cease-fire by adding some impossible conditions.

On November 5, Anglo-French paratroopers finally descended on Port Said (not Alexandria, as originally planned) and on November 6, ships shelled the city at the mouth of the canal. Commandos landed and after surrender of the city, armored forces went south, approaching the other end of the canal at Suez City. Only then did the British accept the UN demand for a cease-fire.

Chill of the Cold War

The Suez War was a failure for the British and French. They ended up neither toppling Nasser nor gaining control of the Suez Canal. Cover for their invasion of Egypt was blown once the combatants had accepted a cease-fire. The UN branded Israel, Britain and France as aggressors and concentrated its efforts on evicting Britain and France from Egypt. France delayed withdrawal in order to give Israel time to carry off the booty of Czech and Soviet trucks and weapons left in the Sinai by Egypt. By December 22, all British and French troops had left Egypt.

Britain had been sobered by the Soviet military threat and the U.S. economic threat to deny it $1 billion in IMF loans (necessary to prop up the sagging pound). Israel, too, was disappointed. One of its "most devoutly cherished hopes . . . the fall of Nasser himself . . . would remain unrealized."[50] Yet Ben-Gurion's long-cherished goal of capturing the Sinai was accomplished. Moreover, the Strait of Tiran was cleared for shipping. Israel seemed to be the sole victor. Ben-Gurion intimated to the Knesset that he would annex the Sinai Peninsula. Within days, geographers, geologists, archeologists, prehistorians, philologists and scholars of the Bible were descending on the new territory.[51]

Israel resists withdrawal

Despite arrival of UN Emergency Forces, Israel refused to vacate the Sinai. Eisenhower's anger unnerved the Israelis to a degree. He alluded to a possible cessation of "friendly cooperation" with Israel and warned that Israel should not count on U.S. help in the event of a Soviet or Soviet-assisted attack. Britain and France were also concerned about both Soviet and U.S. threats and advised Israel to withdraw from the Sinai. Dag Hammarskjold, the UN general secretary, adamantly opposed Israel's recalcitrance on both moral and legal grounds. The Afro-Asian bloc, too, was outraged by what it considered a show of British, French and Israeli imperialism. The Europeans again pressed Israel to withdraw since their economies were crippled by Nasser's refusal to clear the blocked Canal until Israel withdrew.

When the UN demanded (74 to 2) an Israeli withdrawal, grudgingly Israel pulled back in stages, though neither from the Gaza Strip nor the southern tip of the Sinai.[52] Further negotiations were attempted: The United States agreed to recognize the right of all nations to free travel through the Strait of Tiran; the UN offered to provide forces to buffer the Gaza Strip. Israel rejected both proposals. It wanted a *UN* (not U.S.) guarantee of passage through the strait and insisted that the United States and the UN send their own flagships to test the strait. Israel further demanded that a UN regime replace the Egyptian administration in Gaza. Hammarskjold refused to allow UN test ships to be used as agent provocateurs through the strait. Nor, he argued, should the UN provide a sovereign government for Gaza.

Eisenhower considered Israel's flaunting to be brazen and unconscionable.[53] While he hoped to rely on the UN, he also implied that the United States would impose sanctions on Israel. In a nationwide speech, he posed the question of whether a nation that had used force could demand guarantees as a condition for its withdrawal. The speech was badly received by American Jewish leaders. Opposed to Eisenhower were the congressional friends of Israel, especially Lyndon Johnson (Democratic leader of the Senate at the time). Johnson threatened to halt congressional passage of a White House domestic program. Why, he argued, should Israel, given its security concerns, be punished when the Soviet Union was not punished for invading Hungary? This argument (for the equality of immoralities) was not convincing, but it did focus effectively on Israel's security concerns. Johnson insinuated that Israel's security concerns were those of an innocent party under foreign threat, not a case in which Israel had threatened the security of another nation.

Eventually, final settlement came through semiofficial arrangements. The major maritime nations recognized Israel's right of free travel through the strait (under Article 51 of the UN Charter) and UN forces informally established headquarters within Gaza and at Sharm el-Sheikh at the tip of the Sinai next to the Strait of Tiran. Israel then withdrew on March 16, 1956. Grateful for an end to the impasse, the United States rewarded Israel with a generous loan from the World Bank. Other loans soon followed.[54] The body count: Israel lost 160 to 180 soldiers; Egypt lost 2,000 and nearly 1,000 civilians were killed in Port Said. Together, Britain and France lost thirty-three soldiers.[55]

The new Israel

For Israel, the Suez War represented a quantum leap change in political image and character. The alliance with Britain and France placed Israel on center stage as a major hardball player in a Cold War moving precariously toward nuclear war. Israel had aligned itself with its former mortal enemy, Britain, alleged suppressor of Jewish self-determination, and formed a virtual military alliance with France, suppressor of Algerian self-determination. No longer was Israel an underdog.

Though condemned as an aggressor by the UN and the United States, Israel ended up with lavish U.S. financial support and virtual moral carte blanche from the American public. In America, Israel was a victim defending itself against Arab aggression. Its actions against Egypt, Jordan and Syria were seen by the U.S. public as defensive and retaliatory in nature – Holocaust victims fighting back – rather than aimed at overthrowing a foreign government or grabbing territory. What, from the viewpoint of Islamic nations, was unmitigated European colonial aggression toward Egypt, Israeli expansionism into the Sinai and Israeli state terrorism against Palestinian refugees was, from the viewpoint of the American public, an understandable mischievousness – perhaps a bit of over-reaction on the part of the traumatized little nation.

From the international perspective, Israel emerged as both a formidable military power in its own right and a willing cooperator with the superpowers. Moreover, Israel suddenly attained that "hands off" status of truly powerful nations. The issue of human rights for Arab-Israeli citizens was now relegated to an *internal* matter, no longer appropriately addressed by other nations. And the issue of the right of Palestinian refugees to repatriation or compensation lapsed into a polite conspiratorial silence. Similarly, the U.S. and British governments made no further issue over Israel's boundaries, previously judged by them to be unfair to the Palestinian people. Legitimacy, an offshoot of power, conferred on Israel the right of self-regulation. Freed of scrutiny, no longer a ward of the UN, Israel was the new international player whose conflicts with Palestinians passed into the shadows.

In terms of territory, the Suez War resolved little. It was, in fact, the preliminary round of the main event a decade later, the 1967 "Six-Day" War. The Sinai would again be taken, and much more. Politically, the war was important – even the ousted prime minister, Moshe Sharett, acknowledged that in his diary:

> I go on repeating to myself: nowadays admit that you are the loser! They showed much more daring and dynamism . . . .they played with fire, and they won. Admit that the balance sheet of the Sinai war is positive. Moral evaluations apart, Israel's importance in the world has grown enormously.[56]

Notes

1. Of the top fourteen communist officials accused of disloyalty in Prague, eleven were Jews. In the 1952 trials of "economic criminals" in the Soviet Union, most were Jews – so, too, in the 1953 "conspiracy of doctors" accused of planning to liquidate Soviet and political leaders. Howard Sachar, *Diaspora: An Inquiry into the Contemporary Jewish World* (New York: Harper and Row, 1985), 385-6.

2. There were many U.S. State Department bureaucrats, as well as the head of CIA operations in the Middle East, who favored support of Egypt.

3. Steven L. Spiegel, *The Other Arab-Israeli Conflict* (Chicago: University of Chicago Press, 1985), 55.

4. Through the UN, the United States provided food rations for Palestinians in shantytowns in surrounding Arab countries. The aim to reduce unemployment failed completely.

5. Spiegel, *Other Conflict,* 55.

6. Spiegel, *Other Conflict,* 64.

7. The Germans paid $715 million to Israel and $1.7 billion to Jewish individuals, most of whom had left Germany before the war for racial, religious or political reasons and subsequently settled in Israel. Additional monies went to individuals or their heirs who left for the United States and elsewhere during or before the war. Howard Sachar, *A History of Israel: From the Rise of Zionism to Our Time,* Vol. I (New York: Knopf, 1986), 469.

8. Sachar, *History,* Vol. I, 475.

9. Spiegel, *Other Conflict,* 55.

10. Moshe Sharett, *Yoman Ishi* [Personal Diary] (in Hebrew) Yaqov Sharett, ed.

(Tel Aviv: Ma'a, 1979). Selections translated in Livia Rokach, *Israel's Sacred Terrorism* (Belmont, Mass.: Association of Arab-American University Graduates Press, 1986), 38.

11. "We do not need (Dayan said) a security pact with the U.S.: such a pact will only constitute an obstacle for us. We face no danger at all of an Arab advantage of force for the next 8-10 years. Even if they receive massive military aid from the West, we shall maintain our military superiority thanks to our infinitely greater capacity to assimilate new armaments. The security pact will only handcuff us and deny us the freedom of action which we need in the coming years. Reprisal actions which we couldn't carry out if we were tied to a security pact are our vital lymph . . . they make it possible for us to maintain a high level of tension among our population and in the army. Without these actions we would have ceased to be a combative people and without the discipline of a combative people we are lost. We have to cry out that the Negev is in danger, so that young men will go there." Sharett, *Yoman Ishi*, 41.

12. Spiegel, *Other Conflict*, 64.

13. Initially, the United States thought that financing the dam would, by strengthening Nasser's position in Egypt, make it easier for him negotiate peace with Israel. Spiegel, *Other Conflict*, 68.

14. Ben-Gurion intended "to quash any enemy or belligerent till he riseth not, as we did in the Yoav Campaign and the Gaza Raid." Quoted in *Ha'aretz*, April 1, 1956. Cited by Jonathan Shimshoni, *Israel and Conventional Deterrence: Border Warfare from 1953 to 1970* (Ithaca: Cornell University Press, 1988), 87.

15. Shimshoni, *Conventional Deterrence*, 86.

16. Shimshoni, *Conventional Deterrence*, 97.

17. "Peres was revolutionizing the defense ministry, bringing under its jurisdiction Israel's armaments industry, expanding the production of local weapons, fostering nuclear research and development." French and Israeli scientists covertly cooperated in 1953 in the development of nuclear installations and in 1954 Dayan was honored in Paris with the sale of thirty jet fighters. Sachar, *History*, Vol. I, 483.

18. Donald Neff, *Warriors at Suez* (Brattleboro, Vt.: Amana Books, 1988), 238.

19. "In addition to the weapons and jet planes already on order, the Israeli requirements included 100 medium tanks, 300 half-tracks, 50 tank transporters, 300 trucks, 1,000 recoilless rifles, and a squadron of Nord-Atlas transport planes." Sachar, *History*, Vol. I, 490.

20. Sachar, *History*, Vol. I, 485.

21. Shimshoni, *Conventional Deterrence*, 88.

22. Sachar, *History*, Vol. I, 482.

23. The UN ordered Egypt to end its blockade of the Suez Canal in 1951 but was unable to stop the resumption of that blockade when Britain evacuated the canal zone in 1954.

24. By the Constantinople Convention of 1880, free passage for all countries was to be provided through the Suez Canal. It was, as well, assumed by UN negotiators during the Arab-Israeli war armistice talks that the Egyptian blockade of Israeli ships

would be lifted. Sachar, *History,* Vol. I, 455.

25. Sachar, *History,*Vol. I, 456.

26. Stephen Green, *Taking Sides: America's Secret Relations with a Militant Israel* (Brattleboro, VT: Amana Books, 1988), 133.

27. Spiegel, *Other Conflict,* 71.

28. Two ships under charter to Israel were allowed to pass after nationalization. Hugh Thomas, *Suez,* (London: Weidenfeld and Nicolson, 1967), 64.

29. Spiegel, *Other Conflict,* 73.

30. Sachar, *History,* Vol. I, 489.

31. Spiegel, *Other Conflict,* 73. In late 1955, additional Israeli-British ill will was generated when Israel refused to make territorial concessions on the Jordanian border, as requested by Britain.

32. White House Memorandum of Conference with the President, October 30, 1956, 4. Cited in Spiegel, *Other Conflict,* 73.

33. According to Foreign Office minister Anthony Nutting, Eden declared "I want Nasser murdered." A poisoning was attempted. According to Mohammed Heikal, editor and Nasser spokesman, the French tried an attack by frogmen on Nasser's headquarters. Nasser sought personal protection from the Soviets.

34. Shimshoni, *Conventional Deterrence,* 90.

35. Sachar, *History,* Vol. I, 488.

36. Shimshoni, *Conventional Deterrence,* 90.

37. Spiegel, *Other Conflict,* 74.

38. Secretary of State Dulles had "worried for two or three years about our identification with countries pursuing colonial policies." Spiegel, *Other Conflict,* 71.

39. Sachar, *History,* Vol. I, 487, 496.

40. Jordan seemed to be the target of increasing Israeli warfare, for example, the attack on the Jordanian police fortress at Qalqilia in a battle involving tanks, artillery and planes. This approached full-scale war. Forty-eight Jordanians were killed as well as 118 Fedayeen in Jordan just prior to the Suez War. Israel also withdrew from the UN (Israeli-Jordan) Mixed Armistice Commission while Israeli intelligence was circulating rumors about impending war against Jordan. Sachar, *History,* Vol. I, 490, 493.

41. Sachar, *History,* Vol. I, 492-5.

42. Sachar, *History,* Vol. I, 497.

43. Sachar, *History,* Vol. I, 498.

44. Spiegel, *Other Conflict,* 75.

45. Sachar, *History,* Vol. I, 503.

46. Sachar, *History,* Vol. I, 503.

47. Sachar, *History,* Vol. I, 500.

48. Israel was accused of "playing with the fate of the whole world, with the fate of its own people. It is sowing hatred of the State of Israel among the peoples of the East." The British and French were warned by the U.S.S.R. that it was prepared to

crush the "warmongers" by using "every kind of modern destructive weapon."
Sachar, *History,* Vol. I, 505.

49. Sachar, *History,* Vol. I, *505.*
50. Sachar, *History,* Vol. I, 513.
51. Sachar, *History,* Vol. I, 506.
52. Sachar, *History,* Vol. I, 508.
53. Sachar, *History,* Vol. I, 508.
54. Sachar, *History,* Vol. I, 512-3.
55. Sachar, *History,* Vol. I, 501.
56. Sharett, *Yoman Ishi,*49.

Chapter 12

External and Internal Stresses on Israel (1956-1967)

In the period between the 1956 Suez War and the 1967 Six Day War, Israel was subject to a variety of stresses, some coming from outside, others from within. Pressures from the outside related, firstly, to Israel's political isolation from African and Asian Third World emerging nations that denounced Israel's brutalization of the Palestinian population and collusion with European imperial powers in the Suez War. Secondly, there was the stress of growing Palestinian-Arab terrorism.

Internal stresses related more to the collapse of a bubble economy; class conflict between Ashkenazim, Sephardim and Palestinian-Israeli citizens; and self-doubts about actions against Arabs and moral questions concerning Zionist behavior during World War II.

External stress: Isolation from Third World nations

Israel's alliance with Britain and France in the Suez War garnered international prestige but predictably elicited scorn from African and Asian developing nations, who saw Israel as a colonialist intruder in Palestine and as a collaborator with European imperialist powers.

To combat this disapproval and political isolation, Israel adopted a policy of courting emerging Third World nations. By softening its imperialist image through aid and investment, Israel hoped to gain African and Asian political support at the UN on matters relating to the Arab countries. No secret was made of the pragmatic reason for aid and investment in the these new nations.[1] Assistance was given in diverse areas: technical and medical training, agricultural and irrigation methods, rural planning and capital investment.

To a large extent Israel merely passed along U.S. resources, while engaging in its own entrepreneurial projects. Still, the policy met with eventual success. Israel gained diplomatic recognition from many Third World countries and leverage enough at the UN to block demands for withdrawal in the forthcoming Six Day War. Israel also benefited from secret military goals in these developing nations. It was a policy designed by Defense Minister Shimon Peres which armed and trained Ethiopia, Uganda, Zaire and Ghana to create a counterforce to Egypt.[2] Israel also reversed U.S. government disfavor over the Suez War by secretly functioning as a U.S. surrogate, providing military training to Africa's future pro-West dictators, such as Idi Amin and Joseph Mobutu.[3]

External stress: Formation of the PLO and Fatah

Palestinian refugees in surrounding Arab countries began countering Israeli attacks on their camps through terrorist incursions into Israel in 1953. The relative ineffectiveness of these actions related in part to the fact that political organization was proscribed in host countries (other than Jordan).[4] Palestinian refugees were isolated and generally held in disdain.

In Jordan, Palestinians attained a degree of political status through representation in the lower house of parliament (and eventually in the upper house). But because the pro-U.S. monarchy had the power to dismiss parliament, Palestinians gained little governmental attention to their problems. Until 1967, Palestinians within the Jordanian system created no specifically Palestinian political parties nor engaged actively in dissenting ethnic politics.[5]

Sixteen years of exile had passed before Palestinian refugees admitted that neither the Arab nations nor the United States had the desire or capacity to help them retrieve their lost land and homes. In 1965 a Palestinian refugee, Yasir Arafat, organized a militant group called Fatah, which, after 1967, absorbed another paralyzed organization called the Palestinian Liberation Organization (PLO).[6] Fatah was an organization of less than 200 that made pinprick incursions into Israel. Arafat, an engineer, had been a schoolboy in Jerusalem when made a refugee by the 1948 war. Like most angry and restless Palestinians, he grew tired of Arab posturing about the Palestinian cause.

The idea of fighting *directly and locally* for national liberation had been popularized internationally in 1962 by the successful Algerian rebellion, as well as by the Vietnamese rebellion against French and U.S. domination. Arafat knew, of course, that Fatah was a mere mosquito with which the IDF had to deal. "Even though the damage that the Fatah could inflict remained comparatively minor and its threat as a military force was nonexistent, Fatah was a menacing challenge to Israel as a symbol of Palestinian and Arab resistance."[7] And the Israeli public was being made anxious.

More fundamentally, Arafat believed that guerrilla/sabotage actions in Israel would increase tension *between Israel and the surrounding Arab countries.* Eschewing all intra- and inter-Arab disputes and alliances – rejecting even Nasser's rhetoric about pan-Arab unity, Arafat favored direct attack on Israeli soil for the purpose of *causing* the unity of Arab nations needed, he thought, to defeat Israel. Perhaps, too, the international community could be aroused to pay some attention to the Palestinian cause, all but ignored since the Suez War.[8]

Internal stress: Israel's faltering bubble economy

Hyperconsumption led to Israel's burgeoning trade deficit: $330 million per year between 1957 and 1960, $570 million per year by 1964, $1 billion per year following 1967, and $5.3 billion per year by 1983. This deficit spending was financed by American Jewish tax-free gifts, U.S. government direct grants, technical assistance, and German compensation for the settling of World War II Jewish refugees plus, loans on highly favorable terms. Between 1949 and 1965, 29 percent of Israel's trade deficit was paid for by German reparations, the remainder by U.S. government and citizens. Israel's income was derived from tourism, ex-Palestinian citrus groves, fur trading, diamond processing and weapon manufacturing, including missiles and Uzi machine guns.

Borrowed and foreign monies resulted in an excess money supply – an 18 percent annual inflation rate between 1962 and 1965. The Histadrut, Israel's labor organization, made matters worse by blocking efforts to limit wages or dismiss redundant employees. Strikes by government employees in the professional classes further increased the cost of living. The huge military budget grew 1,600 percent between 1952 and 1966 and progressively amounted to more than a third of the gross national product. Gifts of weapons or military sales on favorable terms from the French and Germans added nothing to the productive segment of the economy.[9] German money went for the purchase of a symbolic maritime fleet – to serve the political goal of a "tangible sovereign presence in the harbors of the world" – but contributed less than 1 percent to the national income.[10] Money spent on border settlements, while serving the political goal of occupying former Palestinian lands, provided no financial return.

In 1965-1967, the government instituted austerity measures to fight the hyper-inflation. Reduced government spending, restrictions on bank credit and freezing of some German restitution payments led to the emigration of some in the Israeli professional classes. Emigration exceeded immigration in 1966. Housing construction slumped, resulting in unemployment among unskilled construction workers. The pain of the contracting economy fell heaviest on remote development towns and rural populations, largely Sephardic and Arab populations with larger families to support. With the ending of the 1960s boom, ethnic tensions mounted.

Internal stress: Ethnic conflicts

After 1965, Sephardic (Spanish and North African) Jews outnumbered Ashkenazi (European) Jews. Zionist egalitarian principles collapsed in the face of this Sephardic majority. Sephardim were often sent to rural pioneering areas and settlement towns on the fringe of the desert, working on quarry or drilling gangs.[11] The bottom fifth of the population, largely Sephardim, earned 5 percent of the national income in 1961; the upper fifth, largely Ashkenazim, earned 40 percent, with the gap increasing.[12] The crime rate among Sephardim was eight times higher than that of the Askenazim in 1958. By 1967, 83 percent of all Jewish families living in substandard or slum housing were Sephardic.[13] Only a small fraction of college students were Sephardic. Few could afford Israeli high school tuition. Per capita, the Ashkenazim had twelve times more seats in the Knesset than the Sephardim.[14]

Class unrest was symbolized by a 1959 riot at Wadi Salib, an overcrowded Sephardic slum in Haifa. What began as a bar room brawl turned into a riot that included revenge on the police, much injury from stoning, the burning of cars and wrecking of twenty shops and cafes – a mass protest with implications "far deeper than a barroom fracas."[15] At the commission investigation, the response of a Sephardic witness who had served in the army was typical: "You ask if there is prejudice in this country. A North African is always down at the bottom of the list wherever he applies – whether in the development authority, the city administration, the welfare organization for the aged, or the Jewish Agency. It's always the European immigrants who get the most favored treatment."[16] Other witnesses spoke about the shanties they had to live in because the Jewish Agency allotted better homes to European Jews. Some spoke about the priority in school admissions given "the enlightened, true" Jews. The Sephardim encountered "an almost complete apartheid," first in immigrant camps and later discovered "a similar wall in the nation at large."[17] Housing, food and employment were increasingly secured through patronage and political connections. "The Ashkenazim possessed those connections. The Orientals did not."[18]

In addition to this two-class system, a third class was comprised of Arab-Israeli citizens, 12.6 percent of the population by late 1967.[19] Traditionally farmers, 75 percent lived in rural areas. But with confiscation of their land, 65 percent had to commute to cities to work at the less-remunerative jobs and suffer discrimination in wages and social benefits compared with Jews. Those who chose to rent rooms to save commuting time generally found themselves confined to the slum areas of town.[20] Until 1959, the Histadrut excluded Arab-Israelis from membership and rarely was industry located in or near Arab villages in Israel. The government refused to employ Arab-Israeli citizens (even university graduates) and discouraged construction of worker's flats in cities in order to keep Arabs in distant villages.[21]

The Israeli political system also excluded Arab-Israeli citizens. In the late 1950s and 1960s, the one attempt to organize a specifically Arab-Israeli political party (the Ard or "land" movement) was declared illegal by the Israel Supreme Court.[22] "The truth was that for nearly twenty years the Israelis, consciously or unconsciously, had sought to isolate their Arab population from the Middle East, and in their first decade of statehood even to isolate the Arabs from Israeli society at large."[23]

A stark example of the indifference of the Israeli authorities to Arab-Israeli citizens was the 1956 massacre of forty-seven citizens from the village of Kafr Qasim (outside of Tel Aviv). After the villagers had left for work, the military placed the village under a 5 p.m. to 6 a.m. curfew. The Israeli Patrol knew the villagers had no way of knowing about the curfew. Nonetheless, they executed the unsuspecting villagers, men, women and children without warning as they straggled home from work.[24] Hardly a common event, the massacre nevertheless came to symbolize the violations being inflicted upon Arab-Israeli citizens.[25]

The fabric of Jewish idealism was torn by Israeli treatment of its Sephardic and Arab citizens. Historically, Jewish idealism was socialist, egalitarian, utopian and nonpolitical. But under the pressure of Polish and Russian persecutions, that idealism increasingly narrowed to a political goal – a Jewish state as haven for European Jews. The egalitarianism frayed when Arabs remained as citizens and when Oriental Jews, steeped in Arab culture, emigrated to Israel. The European Jewish belief in the utopian state came into question once Sephardim and Arab citizens became neighbors. To the extent that a shadow of idealism remained, it took the form of seeking to reclaim their lesser

Jewish brethren – a movement to "reform the primitives," those needing to be "purified of the cross of Orientalism."[26]

Internal stress: Self-doubt and voices of conscience

In the 1950s and 1960s some Israeli intellectuals and writers were disturbed by the "apartheid" character of their society. Some weighed their questions of conscience in novels and essays that depicted the sorry condition of their Sephardic brethren and the destitute and stateless Palestinian refugees, whose plight was reminiscent of their own Jewish history. Others, more ethnocentric, were concerned about what the oppression of Palestinian Arabs was doing to the Jews. "How many wars will our boys fight before they will become animals?" asked an Israeli paratrooper-hero from World War II.[27]

Naturally, Israelis were preoccupied with their safety and survival, having as they did a perception of living in a land containing and surrounded by Arabs who hated them. Without considering the consequences of their own actions and contempt, there was a Jewish sense of being vulnerable to Arab hatred about which little could be done. It may have been self-justifying, but Israelis seemed to think of Arab hatred as ineradicable, almost characterological, a quasi-racist notion about a naturally violent creature, a kind of Arab wolf, held by the ears, that could neither be destroyed nor safely let go.[28] Most Israelis wanted peace along with the land, yet were frustrated.[29] Their government had not achieved nor seriously attempted to bring about a political conciliation with either the Arab countries or the Palestinians and their refugees.[30]

Some writers who were second and third-generation native-born Israelis – the *sabras* (cactus, native to the desert) – differed with the pioneering fathers' focus on Zionism at all costs. In a sense they reverted to the position of the early, religious, apolitical Jews who rejected Zionism as a corruption of the idea of world redemption through spiritual repair. These young Israelis, less taken with their forebears' self-righteous glorification of war and romantic mystique about the Jewish tribe and in-gathering of the Diaspora, were unclear about who, exactly, the enemy was. Their idealism, more flexible, practical and self-doubting, included concern about those who had been crushed. The idea surfaced that the Palestinian Arabs, like the American Indians, had a case after all. And the popular idea that the Jews were the victims of Arabs – like the popular idea that the American colonialists were the victims of Indians – came under direct examination. The notion of the *conqueror as victim* was being questioned by some young writers in the 1960s. While no "moral malaise" was sweeping

Israel, certainly these writer were read and the public was disturbed.[31]

In 1963, Avraham B. Yehoshua wrote a popular novella, *Facing the Forests*, in which the forests symbolized the new Israel built upon the ruins of the Palestinian people.[32] It described a subversive cooperation between an old mute Palestinian caretaker-arsonist and an Israeli history student on watch against forest fires. The forest, bearing plaques in honor of contributors ("Louis Schwartz of Chicago," "The King of Burundi and his People"), grows on top of a flattened Arab village bulldozed during the 1948 war. The old Arab conveys to the student how the Israelis hid everything and buried the village, including his murdered wives, under the forest. The student, trying to torch the forest, is exhilarated when the old Arab succeeds. The student stumbles through the smoldering remains in the "sad nakedness of lost wars and vainly shed blood." The work was criticized as masochistically identifying with the enemy.[33]

In his novel *Michael Mine*, Amos Oz describes how a young Israeli woman, living a monotonous bourgeoise existence in Jerusalem, is haunted in her dreams by Arab twins with whom she played as a child. The twins storm her house in revenge for her intrusion into their former home. The cathartic resolution comes through a fantasy of destruction. Another Oz novel, *Crusade*, takes place during the Christian Crusades – an allusion to the Six Day War. The Crusaders, preoccupied with infidels hidden among them, kill their way to Jerusalem in a holy war against Moslems. Spilling blood by day, praying by night, the Crusaders are overtaken with disease and deprivation and stripped of everything, including a sense of identity, until they suffer enough to be human.

Notable liberal voices heard in the early 1970s were those of Arieh Eliav, (*Land of the Deer*) and Ya'akov Talmon ("Is Force an Answer to Everything?"). Asserted was that the rights of Arabs were no less compelling than those of the Jews and that predatory expansionist policies, fortified by ideas of a Jewish "special mission," ignored the fact that other peoples lived in the coveted areas. Liberalism of this political variety was not popular with the Israeli government, press censorship attempted, and imprisonment of several editors, as a deterrent to others, only increased public unrest.[34]

Internal stress: Doubts about Zionist morality; the Kastner-Eichmann affair

In 1955, moral questions about Zionist complicity with Nazi Adolf Eichmann during World War II spread through Israel. An Israeli official, Rudolf Kastner, the public relations director of the Ministry of Commerce and Industry in 1953, had been chairman of the Jewish Rescue Committee in Budapest during

World War II. He was accused by Malchiel Gruenwald of being a collaborator with Eichmann – of having arranged in 1944 to save his own family and village in exchange for misleading 450,000 Hungarian Jews who, had they known, might have resisted deportation to death camps. The Israeli government, to its regret, decided to make an example of Gruenwald by prosecuting him for libel against an Israeli government official.

Gruenwald was cleared of all libel charges and the court concluded that Kastner, in cooperation with Eichmann, had in fact failed to warn the Jewish community to go into hiding and, by allowing tranquilizing rumors to be circulated, had crucially contributed to the murder of 450,000 Jews. Kastner had selected, besides his family and friends, certain prominent Jews and others he deemed the best material to fulfill Zionist goals.

The Israeli government appealed the court decision, causing a split between the Mapai and Herut parties, the latter of which submitted a motion of nonconfidence in the government and demanded Kastner's arrest as a Nazi collaborator. Prime Minister Sharett resigned and was replaced by Ben-Gurion. Kastner was assassinated by a right-wing Jewish terrorist group in 1957 before the Supreme Court decision. In 1958, the court judged that Kastner had perjured himself in defense of a Nazi war criminal, but, in a 3 to 2 split, concluded that what Kastner had done could not legitimately be considered collaboration. Much of the Israeli public refused to accept that verdict.[35]

Partly on trial was Zionist indifference to Jews not serving Zionist ends. In Kastner's words, "The Hungarian Jew was a branch which long ago dried up on the tree."[36] Other Zionists also considered that the Hungarian Jewish community was without any ideological Jewish background.[37] While some judges felt that Kastner was forced to choose between informing the whole community, and perhaps losing them all, or keeping quiet and saving several thousand, Kastner's view about the paramount goal of a Jewish state and selection for life of those Jews best able to contribute to it, was too close to Nazi death camp selection not to inflame the Israeli community. At the 1960 Eichmann trial, the collaboration between Kastner and Eichmann again threatened to resurface.[38]

Notes

1. Howard Sachar, *A History of Israel: From the Rise of Zionism to Our Time,* Vol. I (New York: Knopf, 1986), 575.

2. Sachar, *History,* Vol. I, 577.

3. Sachar, *History,* Vol. I, 576-7.

4. Edward Said and Christopher Hitchens, eds. *Blaming the Victims* (London: Verso, 1988), 250. A very limited number of Palestinians did participate in movements of a Pan-Arab, reformist, anti-imperialist and liberationist character. But labor, teacher and writer unions were generally proscribed.

5. Said and Hitchens, *Blaming,* 250.

6. The PLO had taken shape in 1964 at an Arab summit meeting. Syria raised the idea of a Palestine Liberation Organization made up of Palestinians authorized "to carry out their role in liberating their homeland and determining their destiny." Nasser reluctantly agreed. Some Palestinian refugees, mainly from Gaza, were recruited as troops. Cognizant of the fatal consequences of being drawn into armed conflict with Israel, Nasser kept these troops on tight rein in and away from actions in Israel. When the leader of the PLO, Ahmed Shukeiry, was wounded, the movement foundered. The PLO remained a rhetorical entity, condemning Israel and seeking a secular, democratic state over all of Palestine until later merged with Fatah.

7. In May 1966, Israel's ambassador to the UN noted: "Although boastful and exaggerated, these [Fatah] communiques are reasonably accurate about times and places [of attack] . . . The raids follow fairly standard procedures. They are usually carried out by a squad of three armed men who have crossed the border under cover of darkness and have returned before dawn. Demolition charges of a uniform type, with time fuses, are attached to village dwelling houses, water installations and other civilian targets, or different roadways are mined in the same fashion." Donald Neff, *Warriors for Jerusalem* (Brattleboro, Vt.: Amana Books, 1988), 34-5.

8. Neff, *Jerusalem,* 33-4.

9. Sachar, *History,* Vol. I, 562.

10. Sachar, *History,* Vol. I, 469.

11. Sachar, *History,* Vol. I, 524.

12. Sachar, *History,* Vol. I, 531. "It was found in 1957-58 that the bottom tenth of Jewish urban families, virtually all of them Oriental, received a meager 1.6 percent of the nation's total personal income. The upper tenth, nearly all Europeans, received 24.2 percent" (420).

13. Sachar, *History,* Vol. I, 540.

14. Sachar, *History,* Vol. I, 541.

15. Sachar, *History,* Vol. I, 422.

16. Sachar, *History,* Vol. I, 423.

17. Sachar, *History,* Vol. I, 423.

18. Sachar, *History,* Vol. I, 423.

19. The Jewish population of Israel was 2,384,000, the Arab population under 300,000 – a virtual reversal of the 1948 ratio.

20. Sachar, *History,* Vol. I, 534.

21. Sachar, *History,* Vol. I, 538. By 1975, 2 percent of university students were Arab-Israelis (580, 583).

22. Said and Hitchens, *Blaming*, 250.

23. Sachar, *History*, Vol. I, 538.

24. Two Israeli officers and six men were convicted. Token prison time was served.

25. Three years later, some restrictions on the military government were instituted, e.g., the end of the requirement for Arab citizens to get permission to travel to work in Jewish areas. By 1963, Arab-Israeli citizens could freely move around Israel unless considered security risks or living near borders.

26. Reported in *Davar* (September 1950). Cited by Sachar, *History*, Vol. I, 423. Golda Meir: "Shall we be able to elevate these immigrants to a suitable level of civilization?" Mark Tessler, *A History of the Israeli-Palestinian Conflict* (Bloomington: Indiana University Press, 1994), 822, n 91."The belief that Western culture and civilization are . . . .superior to the 'lethargic' and 'drowsy' civilizations of the East . . . is still accepted by many thinking Israelis." Sachar, *History*, Vol. I, 424.

27. Amos Elon, *The Israelis, Founders and Sons* (New York: Penguin Books, 1984), 231.

28. Said by Thomas Jefferson about slaves in America. Elon, *The Israelis*, 255.

29. In 1965 a frustrated Israeli citizen shut down his business and flew a private plane to Egypt in order to try to negotiate a peace with Nasser.

30. In the early 1950s Prime Minister Sharett did make secret attempts at peaceful negotiation with Nasser but was undermined by militarists Lavon and Dayan. See, Stephen Green, *Taking Sides* (Brattleboro,VT: Amana Books, 1988), 104.

31. Elon, *The Israelis*, 261.

32. Elon, *The Israelis*, 268-71.

33. Elon, *The Israelis*, 268.

34. *Encyclopaedia Britannica – Book of the Year* (1968), 450.

35. Lenni Brenner, *Zionism in the Age of the Dictators* (Westport, Conn.: Lawrence Hill, 1983), 262.

36. Brenner, *Zionism*, 262.

37. Brenner, *Zionism*, 262.

38. Eichmann on Kastner: "I believe that Kastner would have sacrificed a thousand or a hundred thousand of his blood to achieve his political goal. He was not interested in old Jews or those who had become assimilated into Hungarian society. But he was incredibly persistent in trying to save biologically valuable Jewish blood – that is, human material that was capable of reproduction and hard work. 'You can have the others,' he would say, 'but let me have this group here'" Eichmann, 1955 interview in *Life* magazine, 1960. Cited in Brenner, *Zionism*, 257. Potential witness Andre Biss worked with Kastner and corroborated Eichmann's statement about Kastner. When prosecutor Gideon Hauser asked Bliss not to mention anything about the Kastner affair, Bliss refused and was dropped as a witness. Brenner concludes: "Israel had gained great prestige from Eichmann's capture and the government did not want the focus of the trial to shift away from Eichmann towards a re-examination of the Zionist record during the Holocaust"(263).

Chapter 13

Cold War Polarization of the Arab-Israeli Conflict (1957-1966)

Between 1957 and 1967, Presidents Eisenhower, Kennedy and Johnson contributed to a worsening of Arab-Israeli relations by their common preoccupation with containment policies directed at the Soviet Union. Each president sought political and military alliances with Arab nations that encircled the Soviet Union. Naturally, the Soviet Union attempted to counter this by championing Arab causes. As a result, these nations, traditionally divided by rivalries (e.g., Saudi vs. Hashemite, nationalist vs. monarchist), were further polarized by alignments with either the United States or the Soviets. The superpowers, each aiming to extend its own influence and limit the other's, effectively split and destabilized the Arab world.

Not only did adversarial relations between the Arab countries intensify, Arab nations were also destabilized from within. Usually through the secret services of the Central Intelligence Agency, the United States sought to undermine any Arab government or faction that was suspected of communist sympathies and to support pro-Western Arab regimes, however undemocratic. This interstate polarization (dividing) and intrastate destabilization (weakening) of Arab countries suited Israel's interests. The Arab response was mainly forceful tirades against Western imperialism and Israel.But most lethal for Arab-Israeli relations was the *arming* of the whole Middle East by superpowers courting political allegiance through weaponry.

Eisenhower's efforts to enlarge U.S. influence in the Arab world (1957-1960)

The Eisenhower Doctrine was the U.S. policy of coming to the aid of any country subject to outside communist aggression (direct or indirect) by means of military and economic alliance. The policy not only backfired but increased tensions in the Middle East. In the early 1950s, Eisenhower hoped to keep the Soviets out of the Middle East by mitigating Arab-Israeli conflicts. Failing, he turned in the late 1950s toward strengthening U.S. alliances with Lebanon, Jordan and Saudi Arabia. Turkey, Pakistan, Iran and Iraq were already safely tucked into the pro-Western Baghdad Pact (see chapter 11). Intensely nationalistic, nonaligned countries such as Egypt and Syria created special obstacles for the president. A few of his misadventures in the Middle East bear review.

Jordan: Jordan was the single Arab nation which Eisenhower successfully wooed, largely through U.S. financial support of the monarchy. But the rule of King Hussein (grandson of Abdullah, assassinated in 1951) was being threatened by Jordan's Palestinian factions opposed to Hussein's alliance with Britain and the United States. The Palestinians pressed for union of Jordanian, Syrian and Egyptian armed forces. As Eisenhower saw it, this last was a communist plot (because of the Soviet connection to Egypt). King Hussein obligingly denounced communism and dismissed his own parliament, which contained many Palestinians. The United States warned the world against interference in Jordan and sent the Sixth Fleet to the eastern Mediterranean. Eisenhower had brought Jordan solidly into the American camp, but at a cost of alienating Jordan's Palestinian population on its east and west banks.

Syria: Freed from French and British domination after World War II,[1] Syria seemed to Eisenhower to be succumbing to communism. There were, in fact, some reports of Soviet arms being brought in. According to the domino theory, if Syria fell to communism, so might other Arab nations.[2] To combat this, some historians believe that U.S., British and Iraqi intelligence groups planned a military coup that failed.[3] Eisenhower again resorted to display of the Sixth Fleet off the coast of Syria and sought assistance from U.S. allies Iraq, Jordan, Lebanon and Turkey for a "preemptive" strike against Syria for its "anticipated" (that is, communist) aggression. Only Turkey considered attack, backing off when the Soviet Union warned Turkey against moves against Syria. Egypt's Nasser sent two battalions to defend Syria.[4] The crisis did not subside until November 1958. Eisenhower's efforts to detach Syria from Soviet and Nasserian communist influences failed badly. Indeed, his actions inspired a new merger of Syria and Egypt, called the United Arab Republic (UAR).[5]

Lebanon: Torn by many internal rivalries and sects, this country was another land mine for the American president. When Lebanon's pro-West president Camille Chamoun tried to extend his term of office by amending the constitution, anti-Chamoun Arab nationalist factions rioted, inspired in part by Nasser's recent success in keeping the United States out of Syria. Eisenhower and Secretary of State Dulles saw the rioting as communist agitation. This was at a time when Iraq was facing a communist military coup (July 1958), leading Eisenhower to think that a generalized Middle East revolution was in progress.[6]

To justify U.S. intervention in Lebanon, Dulles reinterpreted the Eisenhower Doctrine (concerned with outside aggression) to include *internal* aggression within a country if aid was "requested" by the ruling regime. Eisenhower succeeded in obtaining such a request from Chamoun. When the U.S. marines landed on the beaches at Beirut, they were greeted by sunbathers and soft-drink peddlers, with no one to fight.[7] Britain conjointly landed paratroopers in Jordan, presumably to save the king from the "revolutionary tide" coming from Lebanon and Iraq. The United States also sent forces to Jordan, Saudi Arabia and Kuwait.

The Soviets thundered against Western "imperialist piracy" in Lebanon and warned against any move on Iraq.[8] Eisenhower was clearly overextended and, facing congressional criticism, needed a way to back down. He was saved when the UN demanded that all foreign troops in Lebanon and Jordan be withdrawn. Lebanon reverted to its traditional factional balance, no longer pro-West. Iraq, no longer pro-West, withdrew from the pro-West Baghdad Pact.[9]

The consequences of Eisenhower's meddling in Middle Eastern affairs

Eisenhower's injudicious adventures in the Middle East bear comparison with the British/French/Israeli debacle of the 1956 Suez War in that they were imperialistic, dismissive of the UN and unsuccessful. The effort to strengthen or create new alliances with Arab countries only resulted in a deterioration in relations with Lebanon, Syria and Iraq. Eisenhower's fixation on global communism led him to dismiss the idea that Arab nationalists might legitimately wish to be aligned with *neither* the United States *nor* the Soviets. By placing himself at odds with the Arab nationalist movement, he created a polar split between Arab "revolutionary" nationalists and Arab "conservative" monarchists. Certainly he foreclosed the possibility that Arab nations might *unite* under an American umbrella – the initial goal of his Soviet containment policy. The thought that U.S. interests might be advanced by *fostering* Arab nationalism awaited the next president, John Kennedy.

Kennedy seeks rapprochement with Nasser and Arab nationalism (1961-1963)

Many Jewish-American leaders and lobbyist organizations considered Eisenhower to be "anti-Israel" – not simply because he had insisted that Israel return the spoils of its Suez war, but because he was not "pro-Israel." His announced policy of "friendly impartiality" towards Arabs and Israelis was viewed by Jewish leaders as covertly hostile to Israel and, what is more, a barrier to Jewish influence in the White House.[10] That changed in November 1960 with Kennedy's election.

Kennedy had defeated Henry Cabot Lodge for a Senate seat in 1952 with the help of eminent Massachusetts Jews, and he was grateful and always sensitive about Jewish approval or criticism. Kennedy was also defensive about the "anti-Semitic" label attached to his father by Jewish leaders and sought to detach himself by drawing parallels between the struggles of Jewish and Irish-Catholic minorities. Like other politicians, he dreaded the "anti-Israel" ("anti-Semitic") label.[11]

Jewish leaders had an effective lobby both in Congress and in the Kennedy administration. And yet they were disturbed by two imponderables: (1) the young president was not automatically opposed to Arab nationalism and (2) he was personally concerned about the repatriation of, or compensation for, a million Palestinian refugees squatting in camps outside Israel. Jewish leaders criticized Kennedy for questioning the notion that Arab nationalist movements were necessarily communist-inspired or antithetical to U.S. Cold War interests. Kennedy thought that such movements could be legitimate internal movements and took a "decidedly more positive stance towards states seeking an independent path between East or West."[12] He even made overtures to Nasser, exchanging informal letters and increasing aid to Egypt – much to the despair of the Pentagon and Congress.[13] Kennedy seemed too friendly to Israel's "enemies," despite his assurances to Golda Meir about their "special relationship . . . comparable to that . . . with Britain."[14] He was perceived as insufficiently *for* Israel.

Kennedy's interest in the matter of repatriation of Palestinian refugees, an interest predating his presidency,[15] resulted in his appointment in 1961 of Joseph Johnson of the Carnegie Foundation as the American representative on a UN commission studying the problem.[16] Johnson's proposal was that Palestinian refugees be offered a choice of repatriation or compensation. Resettlement was to be gradual and all governments would have the right to end the plan at any time. Israel feared that the refugees would choose to return home. Arab nations, burdened with Palestinians, feared the opposite, that refugees would *not* want to return to Israel to live under oppressive Israeli Emergency Regulations. Israel responded with "continuing skepticism" about the Johnson plan.[17] Nasser was non-committal, which the U.S. State Department took as tacit acceptance.[18] Lebanon and Jordan also gave indefinite replies. The fact was, *both* Israel and the host Arab countries wanted to be rid of Palestinian Arabs and both hesitated, uncertain of what the Palestinians might choose. The United States argued that most refugees would accept compensation rather than repatriate.

After Syria and Israel rejected the plan, Kennedy tried a bribe. He sent a secret envoy to Ben-Gurion with an implicit quid pro quo: The United States would give Hawk missiles to Israel with the expectation that Israel would accept the Johnson plan.[19] When Israel took the missiles but rejected the Johnson plan, the State Department was embittered.[20] Johnson considered Israel to be largely responsible for the breakdown, yet Arab countries were just as glad, fearing they would be saddled with refugees creating economic and political problems.

If Kennedy was disappointed by Israel, he was also soured by Egypt's military involvement in the Yemen civil war. Nasser had taken sides with the progressive army officers whose anti-monarchist coup took the form of blocking succession by the prince upon the king's death. The officers enlisted Egyptian help; the prince enlisted pro-West Arab monarchies such as Saudi Arabia and Jordan.[21] The civil war devolved into a protracted Egyptian-Saudi international war (Nasser's "Vietnam").

Kennedy's dilemma: either support the nationalist-republican officers against despotic rule, as Egypt was doing, or support monarchist rule, as oil-rich Saudi Arabia was doing. Soviet intervention was another worry. Kennedy tried to negotiate a Saudi withdrawal from Yemen, but, failing, gained for himself a reputation as a protector of the Saudi conservative monarchy and opponent of Arab/Egyptian nationalism.[22] This was the very image Kennedy had sought to avoid.[23]

Nasser had himself to blame for the Yemen/Saudi imbroglio, but Kennedy's interest in Saudi oil effectively isolated and weakened Egypt. As Nasser's international and domestic image eroded, he intensified his condemnation of Western imperialism and its favoritism toward Israel – further isolating himself. Israel was the beneficiary, strengthening its military with Hawk missiles and firming its "special relationship" with the United States.

President Johnson and the Soviets arm the Middle East (1963-1968)

Lyndon Johnson unabashedly favored Israel. He had, it will be remembered, opposed Eisenhower's demand that Israel roll back gains from the 1956 Suez War. Now as president, he surrounded himself with Jewish leaders sympathetic to Israel.[24] His administration contained many pro-Israeli "believers."[25] And through his biblical mentality, Johnson seemed to see in Israel the Judaic well-source of his Christianity – not a political struggle between Jews and Arabs.[26]

Of course, Johnson, like his predecessors, pursued a policy of containment of the Soviet Union. He was more ready even than Eisenhower or Kennedy for grand, global interventions (e.g., Vietnam) in the "pax Americana" tradition.[27] Flatly opposing Kennedy's pluralist efforts to make friends with neutral countries or independence movements unwilling to huddle under America's wing, Johnson opposed any nationalistic rebellion even minimally tinged by communist influence. He was even more hair-trigger than Eisenhower. For example, he directly intervened in a Dominican Republic rebellion (1965) in support of a right-wing government (Juan Bosch) and had the CIA pay Israel to supply weapons and training for a rightist government army in the Belgian Congo (Zaire). In fact, the president regularly used Israel as a surrogate for illegal or unacceptable subversions of foreign governments.[28]

Seeking influence in the Arab Middle East, Johnson continued the polarization of the Arab world by bestowing arms and money on the conservative pro-West regimes in Saudi Arabia, Lebanon, Jordan, Morocco, Tunisia and Libya.[29] The Soviet Union armed the more nationalistic Arab countries, Egypt, Syria and Iraq. The Arab world was politically split by the Cold War, as well as armed because of the Cold War.

Johnson also arms Israel

Naturally, Israel objected to changes in the Israeli-Arab balance of weapons. Though superiority still remained with Israel in 1964, Johnson agreed to sell it more weapons.[30] And, for the first time, he supplied *offensive* weapons (tanks). He overruled his advisors who sought a commitment from Israel not to continue the development of missiles or nuclear bombs (a known program in 1960).[31] Johnson needed Jewish support for the Vietnam War and the forthcoming election in 1966. He embarked on an explicit strategy of economic and military aid to Israel in record amounts.[32]

Arms transfers to Israel were complicated by the fact that Israel wanted *West German*, not U.S., tanks. Israel had, for more than five years, been secretly receiving large quantities of weapons near-gratis from West Germany.[33] The German weapons had to be smuggled into Israel lest discovery by Arab countries lead to boycott of German goods or retaliatory recognition of East Germany. Further shipments of German tanks might blow the secrecy of these transfers. Complicating the issue, too, was Israeli terrorism against German scientists in Egypt working on rudimentary missiles.[34] After several Israeli agents were discovered and convicted of assassinations in June of 1963, Ben-Gurion canceled the terrorism program out of fear that Israel's violent anti-German campaign might endanger the secret arms deal.[35] As it turned out, the German arms transfers were uncovered anyhow (October 1964), raising a furor in Germany and in the Arab nations. Nearly all Arab nations severed relations with West Germany. The shipments stopped.

President Johnson then agreed to supply U.S. tanks and submarines – for which Germany would pay the bill.[36] The United States delivered 210 tanks in 1965 and agreed to sell forty-eight Skyhawk bombers the next year. These arms marked the turning point in Johnson's readiness to supply Israel with large numbers of offensive weapons.[37] It seemed a matter of prudence to Johnson to provide conventional offensive weapons rather than face the prospect of Israeli use of nuclear weapons.[38] It was the United States, Britain, France and Germany that supplied the arsenal which Israel needed for its 1967 blitzkreig war.[39]

Both Israel and the Arab countries were heavily armed by the superpower Cold War rivals.[40] In fact, the Arab countries, taken all together, had about 50 percent more troops than did Israel and double the number of tanks and planes.[41] But they were not, of course, a unit. More often they were enemies with each other: Egypt and Saudi Arabia were enemies over the Yemen war and oppositely aligned with the U.S.S.R. and United States, respectively. Syria and Egypt went their own ways (dissolving their UAR merger) but both were enemies of Jordan's pro-West monarchy. The Arab world, whatever its weapons, was polarized and nowhere in possession of quality military leadership or trained men able to use those weapons. For this reason, Johnson was able to assure Abba Eban in 1967 that if Egypt or Syria attacked, "you would whip the hell out of them."[42] It followed, too, that if there was to be war, now was the time for Israel to initiate it – while the enemy was incompetent.

Notes

1. Syria and Lebanon had become a French mandate after France marched on Damascus in 1920 and banished King Feisal, head of a fiercely nationalistic Syria. King Feisal's brother, Abdullah, intended to remove the French from Syria and reinstate his brother, as well as to rule Iraq himself. But Britain had other plans. To keep Abdullah from disrupting Anglo-French agreements regarding Syria, Britain gave to Abdullah rule over part of mandated Palestine (Transjordan) as compensation for not interfering in Syria. Britain made Feisal a puppet king in Iraq. Then in 1941, Britain invaded Syria after the French Vichy government allowed German planes to land there. Britain did grant Syria and Lebanon independence in 1941, however, and all French and British forces withdrew after World War II. Syria's governments proved highly unstable for decades, averaging one coup d'état per year.

2. Steven L. Spiegel, *The Other Arab-Israeli Conflict* (Chicago: University of Chicago Press, 1985), 86.

3. There is some speculation about this. Nadav Safran, *Israel: The Embattled Ally* (Cambridge, Mass.: Belnap Press, 1978), 362.

4. Safran, *Embattled,* 363.

5. Syria began moving toward an alignment with oil-rich Iraq and away from Egypt, resulting in a September 1961 military coup and breakup of the UAR. Another coup in Syria in 1962 brought to power the Ba'ath (Renaissance) party that did have a distinct Leninist, anti-Western, anti-Israeli orientation.

6. Safran, *Embattled,* 364.

7. Spiegel, *Other Conflict,* 88.

8. Safran, *Embattled,* 364.

9. After the 1958 military coup, Iraq drew closer to the Soviet Union. Ba'athist and Istiqual nationalists in Iraq had favored merger with the United Arab Republic, while Iraqi communists opposed the merger. After heavy armed struggle the communists under General Kassem gained control of Iraq. Relations between Iraq and the United Arab Republic degenerated into a cold war. In the earlier 1950s, when Iraq sought military and economic aid, relations with Britain were more friendly. Traditionally, however, relations were strained. The British had suppressed an Iraqi nationalist revolution and taken mandate control in 1920. After formal independence in 1932 and a military coup in 1936, the Iraqi government was still dominated by Britain, e.g., Britain suppressed a pro-Axis faction in 1941.

10. Edward Tivnan, *The Lobby: Jewish Political Power and American Foreign Policy* (New York: Simon and Schuster, 1987), 36.

11. Kennedy to Ben-Gurion, 1961: "I know I was elected because of the votes of American Jews. I owe them my election. Tell me, is there something I can do for the Jewish people?" according to Michel Bar-Zohar, Ben-Gurion's biographer, cited in Tivnan, *The Lobby,* 56.

12. Spiegel, *Other Conflict,* 96-8; Tivnan, *The Lobby,* 53. Kennedy was always nervous about Jewish opinion. For example, he feared that Jews would blame him, not

UN Ambassador Adlai Stevenson, for U.S. condemnation of an Israeli raid on Syria in 1962. He felt a need to redeem himself with American Jews critical of his being "soft" on Joseph McCarthy and supporting, as did Nasser, the Algerian cause against the French. Kennedy positioned in his administration a number of pro-Israeli Jews, such as Myer Feldman, deputy special counsel, as conduits for Jewish leaders' attitudes.

13. The Pentagon feared that Nasser's pan-Arab nationalism might someday threaten U.S. domination of oil-producing Arab countries such as Saudi Arabia.

14. Presidential conversation with Israeli Foreign Minister Meir, December 27, 1962. Cited in Spiegel, *Other Conflict*, 106.

15. "Let those refugees be repatriated to Israel at the earliest practical date who are sincerely willing to live at peace with their neighbors, to accept the Israeli Government with an attitude of *civitatus filia*. Those who would prefer to remain in Arab jurisdiction should be resettled in areas under control of governments willing to help their Arab brothers, if assisted and enabled to earn their own living, make permanent homes, and live in peace and dignity. The refugee camps should be closed." Kennedy speech in 1957. Spiegel, *Other Conflict*, 111.

16. Spiegel, *Other Conflict*, 111.

17. Spiegel, *Other Conflict*, 113.

18. Spiegel, *Other Conflict*, 114.

19. Spiegel, *Other Conflict*, 113. Kennedy also wanted Israel's word that it had no plans to make nuclear weapons – the nuclear reactor at Dimona had been uncovered by the CIA in 1960. Israel gave its word about nuclear weapons, but did not accept the Johnson plan. The missiles were delivered.

20. Spiegel, *Other Conflict*, 117.

21. Chaim Herzog, *The Arab-Israeli Wars* (New York: Vintage Books, 1984), 148.

22. The United States promised Saudi Crown Prince Faisal political and military support, yet recognized diplomatically the progressive regime in Yemen. The war dragged on until December 1967, years after Kennedy's assassination and well into Lyndon Johnson's second term.

23. Spiegel, *Other Conflict*, 105.

24. Spiegel, *Other Conflict*, 128. In the national security apparatus were pro-Israeli officials such as Arthur Goldberg, ambassador to the United Nations, and Eugene Rostow, undersecretary of state for political affairs.

25. Spiegel, *Other Conflict*, 129.

26. Spiegel, *Other Conflict*, 129. Johnson referred to his "very deep ties with the land and people of Israel . . . for my Christian faith sprang from yours. Bible stories are woven into my childhood memories as the gallant struggle of modern Jews to be free of persecution is also woven into our souls."

27. He even envisioned creating a Tennesee Valley Authority for the Mekong Delta, bringing his "Great Society" to Vietnam.

28. In the 1960s the United States subsidized newly independent African countries emerging from colonialism, to prevent Soviet influence – or true

independence. Israel was equally interested in winning the allegiance of Black and Moslem African countries and turning them against the Soviet Union and Egypt. Israel played a military role in rightist governments in Ghana, Ethiopia, Bokassa's Central African Republic, Nyerere's Tanzania, Dahomey, Cameroon, Senegal, Togo and the Ivory Coast. Joseph Mobutu and Idi Amin, later presidents of the Congo (Zaire) and Uganda, were trained in Israel. See Howard Sachar, *A History of Israel: From the Rise of Zionism to Our Time*, Vol. I (New York: Knopf, 1986), 577-8; Noam Chomsky, *Towards a New Cold War* (New York: Pantheon, 1973), 315.

29. Kennedy supported these conservative governments only reluctantly.

30. Spiegel, *Other Conflict*, 131.

31. Spiegel, *Other Conflict*, 131.

32. Johnson was frustrated by American Jewish neutrality about Vietnam. "Dammit, they want me to protect Israel, but don't want me to do anything in Vietnam." Johnson liked to parallel Israel and South Vietnam as small countries facing hostile forces. Spiegel, *Other Conflict*, 129-30. To win Jewish support for Johnson's Vietnam policies and re-election, loans to Israel were strategically spaced out throughout the campaign period. Donald Neff, *Warriors for Jerusalem* (Brattleboro, Vt.: Amana Books, 1988), 83.

33. German ends were served by supplying weapons to Israel: providing a Middle East bulwark against the Soviets. Moreover, Defense Minister Franz-Joseph Strauss needed to stay on good terms with Israel in order to bolster a liberal political image. Sachar, *History*, Vol. I, 562.

34. The Mossad exaggerated the danger of Egyptian missiles. Neff, *Jerusalem*, 102 It attempted in July 1962 to assassinate an Egyptian-Swiss engineer, killing only his wife. The secretary of another engineer was mutilated by a mail bomb. Israel was in possession of missiles and rockets through joint development with the French beginning in 1959. Sachar, *History*, Vol.I, 564-5, 569.

35. Sachar, *History*, Vol. I, 565.

36. And in subsequent years Germany made easy-term loans to Israel. Sachar, *History*, Vol. I, 567.

37. Spiegel, *Other Conflict*, 134.

38. Spiegel, *Other Conflict*, 135.

39. Tanks to mount the blitzkrieg, fighter planes to cover those tanks in open country and bombers for "anticipatory" first strikes.

40. Spiegel, *Other Conflict*, 132.

41. Neff, *Jerusalem*, 193-4, citing Trevor Dupuy, *Elusive Victory: The Arab-Israeli Wars, 1947-1974* (New York: Harper and Row, 1978).

42. Spiegel, *Other Conflict*, 141

Chapter 14

Precipitation of the Six Day War (1967)

The high probability of war in 1967 had much to do with attitudes common to both the Israeli and Arab governments: *(a)* the desire to show resolve, neither appeasing nor negotiating when threatened; *(b)* the need for prestige in national affairs, to "prove" something to the enemy and the public back home; and *(c)* an impetuousness, if not arrogant miscalculation, of the other's threshold of tolerance, as shown by Nasser's intolerance for passivity in the face of Israeli threats against Syria and Israel's intolerance of challenge without unleashing full military might. It was a war importantly about international image. But it was also Israel's war of destruction against its purported future enemies.[1] And it was a war about acquisition of land and water.

Controversy still rages about which side bears more responsibility. Certainly both Egypt and Israel, in order to mask domestic economic and internal political stresses, were free with their war-talk. Certainly Syria and Israel had grievances about political and physical injury at the hands of the other. But at heart, the issue had to do with a choice facing Israel: whether to use international and diplomatic channels in its dealings with Egypt and Syria or to destroy the military forces (still developing) in those nations as yet another proof of its might and political resolve to "go it alone" despite international restraints.

Provocations at the Israeli-Syrian border

Since the 1956 Suez War, the United Nations Emergency Force (UNEF) had maintained relative quiet at the Gaza and Sinai borders, as well as the Strait of Tiran, border tension along the Syrian border had been festering since 1948.

Israeli security was the alleged reason for military action in Syria's Golan Heights, but conflict over water resources and farmland were important issues in themselves. According to Moshe Dayan, Israeli kibbutz leaders pressed Prime Minister Levi Eshkol in 1967 to take the Heights for its coveted farmland, more than for security reasons. Israel intentionally precipitated hostile exchanges with Syrian farmers in order to justify larger military adventures in the Heights: "I know how at least 80 percent of the clashes there started. It went this way: We would send a tractor to plow some . . . demilitarized [off-limits] area, and knew in advance that the Syrians would start to shoot. If they didn't shoot, we would tell the tractor to advance further, until in the end the Syrians would get annoyed and shoot. And then we would use artillery and later the air force also, and that's how it was."[2]

Conflict about the water-rich Golan Heights dated back to 1953 when Eisenhower sent Eric Johnson to work out a water-sharing plan between Lebanon, Syria, Jordan and Israel. Israel demanded 60 percent of the Jordan River and its headwaters, Syria to get 10 percent. Johnson hinted to Arab countries that unless they agreed, the UN (primarily the United States) would stop funding Palestinian refugee camps and Israel would undertake its own water initiatives. Israel eventually agreed to take 40 percent but Syria still objected, with Egyptian support. The Johnson plan was shelved. Arab countries were not ready to cooperate on a project that would imply recognition of the Jewish state and convert the Negev into a vast industrial and agricultural area for further Jewish immigration. The atmosphere at this time (August 1953), it will be recalled, was one of deteriorating Arab-Israeli relations because of Ariel Sharon's attacks on refugee camps in the Gaza Strip.

In 1956 Israel began work on a construction project *within* Israel, a pump station and conduit that would remove water from the Sea of Galilee, which it shared with Syria. Nearing completion in 1963, the project was opposed by Syria and other Arab nations who planned to limit Israel's ability to pump out the Sea of Galilee by damming Syrian headwaters that supplied the Jordan River and sea. The Hasani and Banyas Rivers were to be diverted south to the Yarmouk River in Jordan, bypassing the Sea of Galilee. When Israel began pumping from the Galilee in the summer of 1964, Syria went ahead with its damming projects. Israel shelled, bombed and strafed these projects in 1964 and 1965. Mutual artillery shelling made the border a tinderbox.

Tension between Syria and Israel further increased in 1965 when Syria hanged an Israeli spy (Eliahu Cohen) who had penetrated the top echelons of the

Syrian government. Israel called for revenge. In Syria, the scandal of a government so incompetent as to have allowed this breach led to a military coup in 1966.[3] The new government took on a distinctly pro-Palestinian cast, increasingly permitting Fatah to maintain bases in Syria for small-scale sabotage runs into Israel.[4]

Further escalation occurred when, on April 7, 1967, Israel responded to some artillery exchanges at the Golan Heights by sending fighter planes against Syrian gunner positions and several Syrian villages. Six defending Syrian planes were shot down in all-out dogfights without Israeli loss. Other Syrian planes were chased back to Damascus. The Israeli planes buzzed the Syrian capital in a show designed to undermining the authority of a humiliated government. Politically and militarily too weak to mount a serious counter-response, the Syrian military leader, Col. Salah Jadid, appealed to the Soviet Union for support, while delivering fire-breathing diatribes against U.S. support of Israel.[5] Nasser threw cold water on hotheaded Syrian demands for a war of liberation against Israel by pointing out the reality of Israeli power and the sorry condition of the Syrian army.[6]

Syria seriously feared that Israel would invade and topple the government. Eshkol had been advertising this intent, threatening to mount a large armed thrust into Syria with heavy air attacks on Syrian gun positions in the Golan Heights. This would end Fatah incursions into Israel and simply remove the Syrian regime in Damascus.[7] IDF Chief Yitzhak Rabin publicly alluded to the same plan. The April 7 air action certainly "seemed an omen of even graver retaliatory moves."[8] The *New York Times* reported that Israeli leaders had already decided that use of force against Syria "may be the only way to curtail increasing terrorism" – that is, security, not water or land was being taken as the issue.

Conflict at the Jordanian border

It will be recalled from chapter 10 that Israel's massive strike on Qalqilia in Jordan led to virtual all-out warfare in 1956. After that time the Jordanian border had been relatively quiet. King Hussein made great efforts to police the 392-mile border against Palestinian guerrilla runs into Israel, though neither Jordan nor Israel was capable of effectively doing so. In April 1966 three Israeli houses were blown up. A few days later an Israeli army truck was damaged by a mine. Perhaps Fatah was involved. Israel took revenge, blowing up the Jordanian villages of Rafat and Tel Arabain, killing eleven civilians. The UN Mixed

Armistice Commission condemned the attack, calling on Israel "in the strongest terms to desist from their aggressions against Jordan."[9]

On November 12, 1966, Arab sabotage in Jerusalem injured four civilians and a land mine exploded near Hebron (in Jordan's West Bank) under a military vehicle, killing three and wounding four Israeli soldiers. The next day a large force of Israeli tanks entered the West Bank under air cover and descended on the village of Samu. Five thousand villagers were routed from their homes and 125 homes as well as the village clinic and school were blown up.[10] Another twenty-eight houses and the mosque were damaged. Jordanian troops rushed to the scene but were ambushed. A Jordanian plane was shot down. Fifteen Jordanian soldiers were killed, thirty-seven wounded, in addition to the villagers killed and wounded. Other villages and police posts were heavily damaged. The UN Security Council censured Israel for violation of the UN Charter and Armistice Agreements with Jordan (Resolution 228 of November 24, 1966).

"The boldness and destructiveness of the Israeli raid on Samu outraged the Arab world and nearly brought about the fall of King Hussein's monarchy in Jordan. Riots swept the nation."[11] Palestinians resented Hussein's inability to protect Palestinian West Bankers from overkill Israeli raids. King Hussein both feared for his monarchy and feared an Israeli invasion of the West Bank – though President Johnson assured Hussein that in such event the "gravest consequences" would arise for Israel.[12] Nevertheless, the world was wondering whether it was Syria or Jordan that would be invaded first.

Israel debates strategy

Debate intensified concerning the wisdom of violent and massive Israeli attacks on Syrian and Jordanian towns. Most Israeli analysts argued in favor of militancy – that Israel could not remain idle in the face of Fatah actions and that indecisive action would only encourage further attacks. Moreover, Israeli attacks had the advantage of demonstrating and encouraging Arab disunity, as, for example, when Nasser came to the aid of neither Syria in April nor Jordan at Samu in November.

On the side of moderation, some Israeli officials pointed out that massive attacks on Jordan had only served to destabilize the sole Arab leader, King Hussein, who sought no confrontation with Israel. Nor did it seem to be in Israel's interests to "humiliate Nasser and create a situation in which the Egyptian leader might be goaded into action [in defense of Syria], perhaps removing UNEF troops from Sinai and Gaza"[13] (as in fact happened). Finally, this minority opinion pointed out that Israel was handing Fatah an important propaganda victory by treating as major assaults actions that were in fact no more than minor incidents, creating an impression of serious injury that would only embolden guerillas and enlist new recruits.[14] More preferable would be "static" defense measures: electrified fences, increased border patrol and special detection equipment which the United States was offering to supply.

With Ben-Gurion out of office since 1963 and Dayan no longer IDF chief, these former hawks, once advocates of a policy in which Arab countries should be provoked into wars they could only lose, now espoused a more cautious, less militant stance. Dayan considered IDF attacks on Syrian and Jordanian villages to be provocative and berated IDF Chief Rabin and second-in-command Gen. Ezer Weizman for overkill military operations. According to Rabin, it was Dayan's view was that Israel erred in placing Nasser's leadership of the Arab world in jeopardy:

> The nature and scale of our reprisal actions against Syria and Jordan had left Nasser with no choice but to defend his image and prestige in his own country and throughout the Arab world, thereby setting off a train of escalation in the entire region.[15]

The Soviets prod Nasser to respond to Israeli threats against Syria

The Soviet Union was looking for a client state in the Middle East. Socialist regimes in Algeria, Indonesia and Ghana had been toppled. The United States had sponsored rightist regimes in the Congo and Greece. So in February 1966, when the Jidid faction of the socialist Ba'ath party in Syria included some communists, the Soviets found their way to gain a client state.

Nasser was critical of Syria for allowing this subordination, yet was himself indebted to the Soviets after the United States cut off loans and wheat sales to Egypt. Trying to further consolidate their role in the Middle East, the Soviets fostered a partial reconciliation between Syria and Egypt, estranged since the 1961 UAR breakup. Egypt reluctantly agreed in November 1966 to Foreign Minister Andrei Kosygin's proposal for a Syria-Egypt mutual defense treaty. Nasser's interest in this military coupling was largely that of inhibiting Syria's foolhardy impulse to counterattack Israel. Egypt wanted to prevent a Syrian-Israeli war because Egypt could easily get drawn in – a war that could be fatal to both Syria and Egypt.[16] Nasser was fully aware of the danger of war with Israel, a danger not only because of Israel's military superiority and Syria's deplorable army but because Jordan would be of no military help – given Jordan's pro-West, anti-Nasser, anti-Syria orientation.[17] Nasser repeatedly warned not only Syria but all Arab nations about the danger of taking actions that might set in motion an uncontrollable drift toward war.[18]

Nasser's treaty-strategy backfired. He could neither control the Syrian military nor prevent Syrian-Israeli border hostilities.[19] Consequently, *Syria controlled Egypt* by obligating Egypt to respond to Syrian military entanglements with Israel. Nasser sought to minimize this obligation by claiming that the Syrian-Egyptian defense treaty applied only to cases of "all-out" war.

The Soviets were both dissatisfied with Nasser's "passivity" toward Israel and wanted to show their willingness to defend Syria against Israeli attack. Jacob Malik, deputy foreign minister of the Soviet Union, bluntly warned Israel after its April 1966 attack that further aggression toward Syria would endanger "the very fate of their state."[20] Israel responded with notice to the UN Security Council that it regarded itself as "fully entitled to act in self-defense" against Syria.[21] The following day, on May 12, 1967, the Soviets informed *Egypt* about a "massing of Israeli troops on the northern frontier for a surprise attack on Syria" and prodded the reluctant Nasser to take the "necessary steps."[22] At this point, Nasser's continued inaction was unsupportable, not only because of the defense treaty with Syria, but because of Nasser's increasing military dependency on the Soviet Union. The Soviets seemed to be encouraging war to show their importance to Arab countries.

The Arab nations taunt Nasser

Nasser was forced to make some concrete gesture of support for Syria.[23] If Israel were truly massing for war as the Soviets indicated, then the gesture would need to be limited enough to give Israel no *excuse* for attack of either Syria or Egypt. On the other hand, if the Soviet report was exaggerated, then Nasser had some room for stronger gestural display. The latter would please the Soviets and counteract accusations of passivity coming from the other Arab nations.

Nasser's image with Arabs was suffering. Iraq, Jordan and Saudi Arabia were taunting him about his "cowardice" in letting Israel get away with aggressive attacks. And he had permitted foreign (UNEF) troops on Egyptian soil after the Suez war whereas Israel had permitted none.[24] Even more shameful politically, he had permitted Israel to force open the Strait of Tiran, considered throughout the Arab world to be Egyptian territory. Nasser's domestic image was also suffering. His unsuccessful bout with Western "imperialism" in the Suez War was one thing, but high unemployment, food shortages and the desperate financial drain of the Yemen war were another.[25] The U.S. ambassador to Egypt surmised that Nasser "needed a diversion and something to cover this internal difficulty."[26]

Nasser did make some military gestures in response to Israel's reported intention to attack Syria. He paraded two armored divisions through the streets of Cairo, over the Suez Canal and onto the Egyptian Sinai Desert under maximum military alert – yet in defensive positions. He warned Israel that he would go to battle if Israel attacked Syria. Yitzhak Rabin responded by sending a tank brigade to the Gaza Strip. This was the usual tit-for-tat pattern of Egyptian-Israeli altercations since 1960. It merely led Israelis and others to deride Nasser's maneuver as empty show. Searching to further bolster his credibility, Nasser asked the UN for a limited withdrawal of some UN forces from a few points along the Egyptian Sinai-Israeli border – but not from UN headquarters in Gaza or from Sharm al-Sheikh near the Strait of Tiran.[27] This call for partial removal of UNEF troops along the Israeli-Sinai border – presumably to enable Egypt to cross that border in case of Israeli attack on Syria – was designed to demonstrate commitment to the Syrian-Egyptian mutual defense treaty. Nasser thought that Israel might be *deterred* from attack on Syria were that attack to require a second front with Egypt.[28]

Israeli officials did not necessarily consider Nasser's call for partial UNEF withdrawal to be a serious threat. Some viewed it as little more than another rhetorical expression of symbolic support for Syria.[29] Nevertheless, by May 18, 1967, the UN peacekeeping role in the Middle East was somewhat uncertain. Britain, the United States and Canada suggested that the UNEF be shifted from the Egyptian to the Israeli side of the Sinai border.[30] Nasser agreed, but Israel refused. Then the United States urged that UN forces be employed along *both* sides of the Israeli-Egyptian border. The argument: If Israel is *truly* concerned about Egyptian attack, then it should agree to UN forces on its own side of the border.

UN secretary-general U Thant and his deputy, Ralph Bunche, were well aware that Nasser had no wish that the UNEF be withdrawn from the *whole* Sinai border – since that would expose *Egypt* to *Israeli* invasion by the same route Israel had taken in the Suez War. Consequently, Bunche assumed that Nasser would withdraw his request for partial withdrawal if forced to an all-or-nothing choice. Accordingly, the UN rejected partial withdrawal and insisted on withdrawal along the whole length of the Sinai border *as well as* in Gaza and

Sharm al-Sheikh – a bluffing tactic enduringly regretted by U Thant.[31] However, Nasser was unable to reverse himself, having already made public his request for partial withdrawal.[32] Once UNEF troops were withdrawn, including from Sharm al-Sheikh, Nasser "could hardly refrain from imposing a blockade on Israel at a time when Jerusalem was thought to be planning an attack on his Syrian allies."[33]

Closing of the strait and response of the international community

President Johnson, deeply mired in Vietnam, was resolved not to get involved militarily in the Middle East. But Israel became "impatient with the low-key American response to Nasser's moves . . . and complain[ed] that the American approach actually invited Nasser to interfere with free passage in the Strait of Tiran."[34] Johnson acquiesced to the pressure and sent the Sixth Fleet to the eastern Mediterranean on May 22. Later that day, Nasser formally announced the closing of the Strait of Tiran to Israeli ships or other ships carrying military materials to Israel. Nasser added, belligerently, that "the Jews threaten war; we tell them: Welcome. We're ready for war."[35] The next day Israel mobilized all its forces and adopted a complete civil defense war footing. Israel declared the closing of the strait to be a violation of international law and an act of aggression against Israel.

Israel may fairly have viewed the closing of the Strait of Tiran as a casus belli. Either through war or international diplomacy, Israel would reopen them. Foreign Minister Abba Eban and, surprisingly, IDF Chief Rabin favored the use of diplomatic and international pressure. The United States and France appealed to Israel not to react to the closing of the strait or to attempt to send ships through. The British proposed a plan whereby a group of nations would affirm the right of free passage through the strait and, if unsuccessful, mount a naval task force to challenge the Egyptian blockade. The United States also wanted the major maritime nations to declare the strait to be international waters and, failing that, mount an international flotilla ("Red Sea Regatta") to sail through the strait.[36] This, it was thought, would head off any unilateral Israeli military action, a major concern of the West.

Most Israeli military leaders argued that it was not just the strait that mattered. As in 1956, the Strait of Tiran was a political symbol more than an economic or navigational matter – Israel rarely used the strait when it was open to them in the 1950s and 1960s.[37] But challenge was being made to Israel's ability and determination to defend itself. "For the deterrent power of Israel's military strength to remain credible . . . it was necessary that the Jewish state *itself* [not the international community] reopen the Strait of Tiran."[38] In fact, the issue was largely symbolic for *both* Israel and Egypt – a symbol of determination not to be subject to challenge or aggression by the other.

Aharon Yariv, the chief of Israeli military intelligence, summed up Israel's position: "It's no longer just a matter of freedom of navigation. If Israel takes no action in response to the blockade of the straits, she will lose her credibility and the IDF its deterrent capacity."[39] Not all Israeli officials disagreed.[40] But for the military hard-liners who dominated Israel's policies, credibility was the issue. They argued that diplomatic negotiation or political pressure on Egypt, were it exerted by the international community rather than Israel itself, would *diminish* Israel's deterrent potential by raising doubt about Israel's resolve to act militantly and alone. Nadav Safran explains: "Unless Israel *itself* nullified Nasser's action, his challenge [to Israel's deterrent power] would prove successful . . . and would be a signal for further encroachments and harassments that would sooner or later lead to war but under more unfavorable conditions [for Israel]."[41]

The Arab perspective equally required confrontation: "The opening of the narrow straits as a result of the 1956 Suez war rankled in the Arab world as yet another Israeli victory over the Arabs, another humiliation of Egypt and Nasser" – an Israeli imposition on Egyptian territorial waters.[42]

Legal questions about the Strait of Tiran as international waters

Johnson declared Egypt's blockade to be illegal and "potentially disastrous to the cause of peace." At the same time, he did not declare overt support for Israel. The United States supported Israel's contention that the Strait of Tiran was in international waters but the legal issue was not so clear. The strait, at the mouth of the Gulf of Aqaba, did lie within Egyptian territorial waters. Yet farther up the gulf, where the gulf widens, waters existed which lay *beyond* Egypt's territorial limit – and thus were international. Dispute centered on whether the *entrance* to the gulf (i.e. the strait) must be considered international in order to provide other nations access to international waters farther up the widening gulf.

Unclear, too, was whether the UN or the International Court of Justice had jurisdiction over the issue.[43] Diplomat Charles Yost cabled President Johnson: "While this [closing of the straits] may appear in U.S. as 'aggression,' it is seen here [in the Arab world] as [an] entirely legitimate restoration [of the] 1956 status quo which was upset by Israeli aggression. . . . Moreover, [the] legal case is at least open to doubt."[44] French officials also expressed some doubts about

Israel's legal right to use the strait.[45] Nasser told U Thant that he would consider going to international arbitration or the International Court of Justice to determine the legality of his position, an alternative Israel rejected since demonstration of resolve, not legality, was seen as the issue.

Johnson maintains that Israel has no grounds for attack

On May 25-26, three days after the closing of the Strait of Tiran, Israeli Foreign Minister Abba Eban met with President Johnson, conveying to him an alarmist and exaggerated cable from Prime Minister Eshkol's office (authored by Rabin) that expressed belief in an "imminent" Egyptian attack. It stated that Israel might have to decide on war or peace as early as two days hence (Sunday, May 28).[46] This scare-tactic contradicted U.S. intelligence reports. Johnson and his aides became "annoyed about the Israeli alarm over what they considered an improbable Egyptian attack," suspecting Israel of "undue nervousness or deviousness."[47] Secretary of State Dean Rusk surmised that Israel was seeking to justify a first strike and warned Eban, "I do not wish to assume that your information is meant to give us advance notice of a planned Israeli preemptive strike. This would be a horrendous error."[48]

No official in Washington believed that Egypt was going to attack.[49] Johnson judged that Nasser had neither the intention nor the strength to attack Israel.[50] The president's concern was that *Israel* would precipitate some event which would draw Nasser into war and trigger the blitzkrieg which Syria, Jordan, Egypt and the Soviet Union had been expecting. Believing that the strait could be opened through diplomacy, Johnson and his secretaries of defense and state concurred that it was preferable for the United States to assume some responsibility rather than "unleash" the Israelis.[51] By addressing the specifics of the conflict, however, Johnson failed to appreciate either the intensity of the *prestige-humiliation-credibility* struggle raging between Israel and Egypt or the strength of Israel's intent to demolish Nasser and his military while it was still incompetent.

Repeatedly pointing out that Israel was in no danger from Egypt, Johnson, Defense Secretary Robert McNamara and CIA Director Richard Helms were preaching to the converted.[52] If Egypt were to attack Israel *first*, "You will whip the hell out of them," Johnson assured Eban. Joint Chiefs Chairman Earle Wheeler told Johnson that "if there were a war, the Israelis would win it in five to seven days. . . . There's just no question."[53] The estimates were unequivocal, whether made by Israel, the U.S. Defense Intelligence Agency, the CIA or armed forces intelligence agencies.[54] "Israel could defeat any combination of Arab states or all of them at the same time and do it within a week."[55] Of course these estimates were not news to the Israeli generals or Eshkol.[56]

Johnson may have sensed his own foolishness: these estimates of certain, quick victory could only *encourage* Israel attack by confirming Egyptian incompetence. After a meeting with Eban, the president declared: "I failed. They're going to go. . . . Yes, they're going to hit. There's nothing we can do about it."[57]

Israel has questions about "going it alone"

Johnson had addressed Eban as though Eban were seeking U.S. help in *defending* itself against Egyptian attack. In fact, Israel had been feeling out Johnson's attitude about Israel attacking Egypt – wishing not to repeat the Suez debacle in which an attack on Egypt without prior U.S. approval resulted in a U.S. demand for withdrawal and return of the spoils of war. Would the United States, through the UN, immediately *stop* a war because of UN obligations to stop *all* violations of the 1948 armistice, as Nasser assumed? Or would the United States take the position that Israel was a *victim* of aggression and allow Israel to both conduct the war and keep the predictable territorial gains? And what about the Soviet card? The Soviets had warned: "If Israel starts military action the Soviet Union will extend help to the attacked party." Might the United States dissociate itself from Israel in order to avoid tangling with the Soviet Union?[58] Was Johnson's warning that "Israel will not be alone unless it decides to go alone" a condemnation of Israel for eschewing international diplomacy (or collective action) or did Johnson secretly *prefer* Israel to go it alone so that the United States would not to have to confront the Soviet Union or get bogged down in another Vietnam? These were ambiguities in U.S. policy and Israel needed answers before attacking Egypt.

Israel delays attack until June 5, 1967

Upon returning to Israel on May 27, 1967, Eban discovered that Rabin's scare cables about imminent Egyptian attack were fabrications.[59] And yet at an Israeli cabinet meeting that night, Eban found that Eshkol was caving into Rabin, Weizman and the whole military establishment.[60] However, the cabinet decided to delay attack on Egypt for two weeks in order to take full measure of Johnson's true attitude about an Israeli first strike. It was not a question of *whether* to attack but one of "political timing."[61] Playing for time, Eshkol made a fumbling speech to the nation on the eve of May 28, making reference to *international* measures to open the Strait of Tiran rather than direct Israeli action. An anxious Israeli public and military were appalled by Eshkol's "shilly-shallying" and "begging protection from Paris and Washington."[62]

On May 29, in a long press conference, Nasser again made clear that he had no plans to go to war – he had, after all, achieved what he sought, that is, opening the strait and parity with Israel regarding placement of UNEF forces. He condemned the United States, Britain and Canada for their pro-Israeli stance and insensitivity to Arab rights and explained that the crisis had developed because "Eshkol had threatened to march on Damascus, occupy Syria and overthrow the national Syrian regime. It was our duty to come to the rescue of our Arab brother." Provocatively, he added:

> The existence of Israel in itself is an aggression . . . what happened in 1948 was an aggression – an aggression against the Palestine people. Israel expelled the Palestinians from their country and robbed them of their property. Today there are one million homeless Palestinians. . . . Where are the rights of Arabs? There is no one who is talking about the rights of Arabs . . . [only] the rights of Israel.[63]

That Nasser turned the crisis away from the narrower issue of the strait and toward Palestinian Arab grievances seemed to Israelis to be an *escalation* that raised questions about the very legitimacy of the Jewish state. For were Palestinian grievances to be redressed, the integrity of the Jewish state might be in doubt. Nasser's focus on Palestinian grievances equally alarmed Jordan's King Hussein, since half his subjects were restive Palestinian refugees who welcomed Nasser's championing of them. To protect his throne from a possible Palestinian coup,[64] Hussein flew to Cairo and signed a mutual defense treaty with Nasser (his traditional enemy) on May 30.[65] He thereby became an instant hero with Palestinians, but aroused great anxiety in Israel.

While the United States and France[66] tried to restrain Israel, the Soviet Union, by threatening to intervene if Egypt or Syria was attacked, created in Nasser a false sense of confidence. He believed in concrete Soviet assurances of assistance in case of war.[67] On the other hand, Eshkol correctly judged that the Soviet threat could be ignored as long as the United States stood by Israel. It became imperative, thus, to determine the *true* U.S. attitude about an Israeli first strike.

Eshkol sent General Meir Amit, head of the Mossad, to Washington to ferret out White House attitudes. By June 1 Amit had reported: "There is a growing chance for American political backing if we act on our own."[68] Israeli Embassy Minister Ephraim Evron performed the same sort of reconnaissance. He approached Walt Rostow at the National Security Council about possible U.S. attitudes if Israel should by itself force open the Straits blockade, be fired on, and then attack the Sinai. Would the United States consider that a legitimate act of self-defense? If, as reports suggested, the United States was decreasingly enchanted with the prospect of pushing warships through the strait (and running a risk of engaging the Soviets), could the United States really *justify* restraining Israel from acting on its own?[69] Evron got the idea from Rostow that the United States might actually *prefer* (for the sake of relations with the Soviet Union) that Israel act on its own and leave the United States uninvolved.[70] Partly this was related to Johnson's unpopular Vietnam war. One advisor urged him not to interfere with Israel but rather to seek political profit from the Middle East crisis: "Many of the Vietnam doves are hawks on Aqaba."[71] Indeed, virtually all U.S. religious, political and public figures were full of pro-Israel sentiment – Nasser remained "Hitler of the Nile" – and Johnson could profit from support of Israel's "defense."

Israel now worried about further delay of attack, fearful that the United States might find some *compromise* solution. It was worrisome that U.S. representatives such as Robert Anderson, a former cabinet official, were privately obtaining assurances from Nasser that he was not going to start a war and would take the issue of the strait to the International Court of Justice – something Israel rejected.[72] While Nasser complained that all he heard from Washington was a public declaration of support for Israel,[73] he agreed to send his vice president to Washington on June 7 to discuss with Johnson new ways to resolve the dispute with Israel.

Whatever restraints Eban previously had exercised on the military he now removed. From Israel's viewpoint, a diplomatic compromise or rapprochement between Egypt and the United States could mean that Israel might lose some part of its gains from the Suez war (opening of the strait) and lose a chance to destroy Nasser and his military. Nasser could only gain in prestige from the talks in Washington.[74] And were Egypt and the United States to actually arrive at some modus operandi after years of enmity, Israel would be a major loser.[75] Eban noted: "It was probable that this [Washington] initative would aim at a face-saving compromise – and that the face to be saved would be Nasser's, not Israel's. For us the importance of denying Nasser political and psychological victory had become no less important than the concrete interest involved in the issue of navigation."[76]

Militants attack Eshkol and infiltrate the cabinet

Eshkol was not "shilly-shallying" as the public thought. He was getting his ducks in a row – determining if he had U.S. support, or at least acquiescence, to an Israeli first strike. Without that, Israel was in danger of both Soviet military intervention and subsequent international demands for return of the territorial gains Israel expected to reap in the Sinai, the West Bank, Gaza, the Golan Heights and Jerusalem.

Though Egyptian troops were in defensive positions, the Israeli public perceived the situation as "dire" and "live or perish." A fierce Israeli military and even Prime Minister Eshkol's own Mapai party successfully demanded on June 1 that the Defense Ministry portfolio – also held by Eshkol – be relinquished to retired former IDF chief Moshe Dayan. Further, ex-terrorist Menachem Begin was made a cabinet minister to share in the duties of preparation for war.[77] Begin's entry into government represented "a revolutionary change in Israeli political history."[78] Not only did it give him mainstream political legitimacy, it set the militarist course for this and future governments.

The blitzkrieg was launched on June 5, two days before the scheduled Egyptian talks in Washington.

Summary: Arab and Israeli motivations and the causes of war

Nasser explained to U Thant that his purpose was to return to the conditions established by the armistice of the 1948 war – that is, to reverse Israeli gains garnered from the 1956 Suez War.[79] He wanted to regain control of the Strait of Tiran and achieve parity with Israel regarding UN troop placement on his soil – a past source of intra-Arab ridicule. But it was obligations arising from Eshkol's threatened overthrow of Syria that vaulted the ambitious leader of the Arab world into imprudent gestures under the erroneous expectation that the Soviet Union would protect Egypt.

Concerning Israeli motivations, journalist/historian Donald Neff concluded:

> It was not fear of Egypt or the closure of the Straits of Tiran that motivated the Cabinet's decision. It was the generals' confidence that victory would be theirs and the need to prove to the Arabs that Israel could not be intimidated.[80]

Neither Eban, Ben-Gurion nor Rabin thought that Nasser intended to attack.[81] Indeed, it was Nasser's unwillingness to attack Israel that created an obstacle to those Israeli ministers seeking war as means to topple Nasser and expand Israeli territory. Was Nasser's closing of the strait designed to intimidate Israel and require war? Or was it the reverse, that Israel's massive border assaults on surrounding Arab nations in 1966-1967 were designed to intimidate and provoke belligerence from the Arabs? Did these assaults on Arab nations force them to act, at least for domestic consumption, *as if* they were *not* intimidated – that is, force them to sound strong without intending to actually go to war? Was it not Soviet influence-peddling that forced Nasser from his passivity into gestural displays which Israel could use to justify a war to topple him – destroying him politically, destroying his developing military capability and gaining territory to boot? A supportable case can be made that Israel *sought* or welcomed belligerent Arab postures to justify war against a weak Arab world as *prophylaxis* against possible future war. Rabin outlined this very need for Arab belligerence in his 1964 address to the Knesset (summarized by Sachar):

> Any future war would have to be won in four days. It could not take substantially longer for economic reasons. The implications were that Israel should attack preemptively. Yet, to avoid alienating world opinion, the nation was left with no recourse but to allow the enemy to mobilize, gather on Israel's borders, proclaim to the world that this time the Jews would be liquidated – then strike out at the enemy with an "anticipatory counteroffensive" at the last possible moment.[82]

While war could gain for Israel the Sinai, the West Bank, Gaza, Jerusalem and the water-rich Golan Heights, just as important, it could eliminate the leader of the Arab world, politically and psychologically and militarily. Israel's "pre-emptive strike," not against impending attack, seemed to be against the one leader who could in the future have sufficient military power to enable him to demand of Israel meaningful negotiations.

Notes

1. Nasser had a need to show strength but did not deliberately seek military confrontation with Israel. "All the evidence runs against such a supposition and everyone, including Nasser and the Israelis, as well as interested and neutral

observers, rightly rejected it." Nadav Safran, *Israel: The Embattled Ally* (Cambridge, Mass.: Belnap Press, 1978), 391.

2. Interview with Dayan in 1976 by reporter Rami Tal, as described by Serge Schmemannn, "General's Words Shed a New Light on the Golan," *New York Times,* May 11, 1997, 3.

3. Syria was roundly condemned by many Arabs for this breach in security and governmental inefficiency and corruption.

4. Before the coup, Syria had severely limited Fatah use of its territory for fear of Israeli reprisal. Donald Neff, *Warriors for Jerusalem* (Brattleboro, Vt.: Amana Books, 1988), 37.

5. The ruling Leninist, anti-West Ba'athist Party, led by Colonel Hafez (a Sunni Moslem), was overthrown by Col. Salah Jadid (an Alawite Moslem) in a February 1966 coup. However, Jadid was unpopular with the Sunni majority and barely survived armed revolts in September 1966 and February 1967.

6. The Syrian army was in disarray because multiple coups had liquidated many officers. Syria was averaging one coup per year. For the politics of this period, see Howard Sachar, *A History of Israel: From the Rise of Zionism to Our Time,* Vol. I, (New York: Knopf, 1986), 618-23.

7. *Washington Post,* February 4, 1967.

8. Sachar, *History,* Vol. I, 622.

9. UN S/7325, Annex, May 16, 1966. Cited in Neff, *Jerusalem,* 36.

10. All details from Neff, *Jerusalem,* 40.

11. Neff, *Jerusalem,* 42.

12. Neff, *Jerusalem,* 49-50.

13. Mark Tessler, *A History of the Israeli-Palestinian Conflict* (Bloomington: Indiana University Press, 1994), 380.

14. Tessler, *History of Conflict,* 380.

15. Yitzhak Rabin, *The Rabin Memoirs* (Boston: Little, Brown and Co., 1979). Cited in Neff, *Jerusalem,* 116.

16. Tessler, *History of Conflict,* 378.

17. Neff, *Jerusalem,* 166. Syrian and Jordanian hostile relations worsened when in early June 1967 a Syrian bomb killed many Jordanian villagers.

18. Safran, *Embattled,* 387.

19. Because Syria would not allow Egyptian troops on its soil, Egyptian military control of Syria was limited.

20. Sachar, *History,* Vol. I, 621.

21. Sachar, *History,* Vol. I, 622.

22. Sachar, *History,* Vol. I, 622.

23. Sachar, *History,* Vol. I, 623.

24. Sachar, *History,* Vol. I, 623. "Israel had always adamantly opposed a UN

force on their side of the border because they distrusted UN personnel and argued that it was the Egyptians and not they who allowed terrorists to cross the border." Steven L. Spiegel, *The Other Arab-Israeli Conflict* (Chicago: University of Chicago, 1985), 140.

25. Western bank and IMF loans were cutoff during the Yemen war.

26. Spiegel, *Other Conflict*, 136.

27. Safran, *Embattled*, 394; Sachar, *History*, Vol. I, 623.

28. Tessler, *History of Conflict*, 390.

29. Tessler, *History of Conflict*, 388.

30. Spiegel, *Other Conflict*, 137. Sachar, *History*, Vol. I, 625. Egypt was legally entitled to remove the UN forces only because Israel refused UN forces on its side.

31. Sachar, *History*, Vol. I, 624.

32. Safran, *Embattled*, 395.

33. Tessler, *History of Conflict*, 392. An Egyptian commander stated, "[Were we] to abstain from exercising Egypt's legal right to control its territorial waters and close the Gulf of Aqaba to Israeli navigation . . . our attitude would be characterized as weak and would be subject to political and propaganda attacks by some of the Arab states." Richard B. Parker, *The Politics of Miscalculation in the Middle East* (Bloomington: Indiana University Press, 1993), 74.

34. Spiegel, *Other Conflict*, 137.

35. Safran, *Embattled,*388.

36. An international flotilla would take time, but delays would be to Israel's advantage since the cost of keeping forces was relatively greater for an overextended Egypt (in the assessment of Johnson's Joint Chiefs of Staff chairman). Moreover, the United States agreed to underwrite Israel's interim mobilization costs. Spiegel, *Other Conflict*, 139-40.

37. No Israeli ship had used the Strait of Tiran for nearly two years prior to Nasser's announced closing of it on May 22, 1967. Neff, *Jerusalem*, 87.

38. Tessler, *History of Conflict*, 395.

39. Neff, *Jerusalem*, 92.

40. Interior Minister Moshe Chaim Shapira argued against the security argument as justification for fighting over the strait: "In 1950 and 1951 the straits were closed; did Israel [under Dayan and Ben-Gurion] rush into a war? The straits remained closed up to 1956; did that endanger Israel's security?" Neff, *Jerusalem*, 116.

41. Safran, *Embattled*, 409.

42. Neff, *Jerusalem*, 87.

43. Tessler, *History of Conflict*, 334-5.

44. Neff, *Jerusalem*, 188.

45. Neff, *Jerusalem*, 119.

46. This cable, suggesting the danger of an imminent attack, was not taken seriously by Israeli intelligence. It was fabricated by Rabin to get Eban, unaware of the exaggerations, to press the Americans harder. The goal: to either gain U.S. support or test the U.S. attitude about Israel going it alone. Spiegel, *Other Conflict*, 138; Neff, *Jerusalem*, 133.

47. Spiegel, *Other Conflict*, 138-9.

48. Neff, *Jerusalem*, 134

49. Spiegel, *Other Conflict*, 139.

50. Sachar, *History*, Vol. I, 629.

51. Spiegel, *Other Conflict*, 139, 141.

52. Spiegel, *Other Conflict*, 139.

53. Earle G. Wheeler, *Lyndon Baines Johnson Oral History Interviews* (Austin, Texas), May 7, 1970, tape 2, 22-23. Cited in Spiegel, *Other Conflict*, 141. "The only question in U.S. intelligence circles was whether the war – the 'turkey shoot,' as Walt Rostow called it – would be over in six days or seven." Edward Tivnan, *The Lobby: Jewish Political Power and American Foreign Policy* (New York, Somon and Schuster, 1987), 64. Rostow (NSC Chief) referred to the war as a "turkey shoot" in a secret memo to Johnson on June 5, 1967. National Security File, NSC History – Middle East Crisis, May 12-June 19, 1967, Vol. 4, tabs. 111-127, Lyndon Baines Johnson Library. Cited by Stephen Green, *Taking Sides* (Brattleboro, Vt.: Amana Books, 1988), 203.

54. Spiegel, *Other Conflict*, 141.

55. Neff, *Jerusalem*, 140, summarizing the Board of National Estimates report.

56. Neff, *Jerusalem*, 91-2, 162.

57. Eugene Rostow, December 2, 1968, 18; and John P. Roche, July 16, 1970, tape 2, 68, in *Johnson Oral History Interviews* (Austin, Texas). Cited in Spiegel, *Other Conflict*, 142.

58. "If we ignored [Johnson] and war broke out, we would find ourselves alone in the international arena. And without the United States to keep the Soviet involvement in check, Israel would be in a tough predicament." Rabin, *Rabin Memoirs*. Cited in Neff, *Jerusalem*, 92.

59. Neff, *Jerusalem*, 161.

60. Second in the Israeli military after Rabin, Ezer Weizman represented the new breed of Israeli *sabra* generals – bold and disdainful of caution, diplomacy or dependence on outside help or opinion. Weizman had pressed for the conspicuous, day-time massive raid on Samu, spoke unabashedly about capture of the West Bank, and now pressed Eshkol to attack Egypt.

61. Abba Eban, *An Autobiography* (New York: Random House, 1977), cited in Neff, *Jerusalem*, 161.

62. Verbal accusations to Eshkol's face by military commanders. Neff, *Jerusalem*,

167.

63. Neff, *Jerusalem,* 163.

64. "The King has maneuvered carefully . . . but no one is offering bets on how long these efforts will succeed in holding up his throne. If there is war and Jordan is not aggressive enough for Palestinian taste he will be in trouble." Flora Lewis, "Jordan Still Is Cautious Under Pact" *Washington Post,* June 5, 1967, A10.

65. Egypt (like Syria) held Jordan in contempt for its alignment with the United States and Britain. Hostilities between Egypt and Jordan (enemies even before the 1948 Israeli-Jordanian collusion) were polarized by the U.S.-Soviet rivalry. Radio Cairo depicted King Hussein as a "Hashemite whore," a "British agent" and a "moral chameleon." Nasser criticized Hussein for passivity in the face of Israeli attacks (e.g., Samu). Hussein taunted Nasser for hiding behind the UNEF.

66. De Gaulle warned that he would cut off France's massive supplies of arms if Israel fired the first shot.

67. Nasser's defense minister had misinterpreted the words concerning the commitment of the Soviet defense minister. Neff, *Jerusalem,* 174-5.

68. Michael Brecher, *Decisions in Israel's Foreign Policy* (New Haven: Yale University Press, 1975) 417 f.

69. Neff, *Jerusalem,* 182.

70. Neff, *Jerusalem,* 186.

71. The memorandum continues, "As your position in the Middle East has been firm and resolute, you stand to be cheered now by those who were jeering last week. To some extent . . . the Mideast crisis can turn around the 'other war' – the domestic dissatisfaction about Vietnam." Ben Wattenberg to Johnson, May 31, 1967. Cited in Neff, *Jerusalem,* 69.

72. Parker, *Politics of Miscalculation,* 49.

73. Neff, *Jerusalem,* 125. Anderson, treasury secretary under Eisenhower, was meeting with Nasser behind the scenes. He reported that Nasser would consult his lawyers about the strait issue and did not completely rule out the possibility of a speedy World Court review (179).

74. Neff, *Jerusalem,* 179.

75. Vilification of Nasser in the United States was "spurred by Nasser's own open criticism of the United States and by Israel's effective propaganda aimed at keeping his relations with America in a constant state of animosity." Neff, *Jerusalem,* 103.

76. Eban, *Autobiography,* cited in Neff, *Jerusalem,* 181.

77. Tessler, *History of Conflict,* 397. Begin's Herut party (now merged into the Gahal Bloc) traced its origins to Jabotinsky and the Irgun and demanded that Israel encompass the whole of Palestine and Jordan (historic Palestine). Sachar, *History* Vol. I, 371-2. Begin patched up past hatreds with Ben-Gurion and unsuccessfully

demanded Eshkol's replacement by Ben-Gurion, but successfully demanded return of admired militarists Moshe Dayan and Shimon Peres to the defense ministry.

78. Yoram Peri, *Between Battles and Ballots: Israeli Military in Politics* (Cambridge: Cambridge University Press, 1983), 250.

79. Neff, *Jerusalem,* 158.

80. Neff, *Jerusalem,* 194.

81. "Nasser did not want war, he wanted victory without war." Eban, *Autobiography,* cited in Neff, *Jerusalem,* 147. "Ben-Gurion later admitted that he never thought Nasser wanted war." Rabin said the same. "Rabin: Nasser Wanted Gains without War," *New Outlook* (June/July 1977), translated in *Yediot Ahronot* and cited in Tivnan, *The Lobby,* 64.

82. Sachar, *History,* Vol. I, 635.

Chapter 15

The Six Day War and Its Consequences

The three-hour war

At 7:45 a.m., Monday, June 5, repeated waves of Israeli bombers skimmed over the Mediterranean Sea under clear skies and destroyed the Egyptian Air Force sitting on the ground:

> One hundred eighty-three Israeli planes took part in the first attack. Flights of four planes each roared in low over the airfields and radar stations using their cannons for devastating runs against the parked Egyptian planes and their bombs to crater runways so the Egyptians could not fly up to challenge them. The flights stayed over their targets for about seven minutes, enough time for a bombing run and three or four strafing passes, and then minutes later were replaced by other attackers. The initial assault lasted eighty minutes and accounted for 189 planes destroyed on the ground, sixteen radar stations smashed, and six airfields rendered inoperable, four in the Sinai and two west of the Suez Canal. Almost immediately afterward, a second wave of 164 planes, some of which had already taken part in the first strike, hit Egyptian targets with crushing ferocity for another eighty minutes of hellish bombings and cannon fire. Before 11 a.m. Israeli time, 5 a.m. in Washington, the war was essentially won.[1]

This precision plan was the work of Gen. Mordechai Hod and his predecessor, Gen. Ezer Weizman: "For five years I had been talking of this operation, explaining it, hatching it, dreaming of it, manufacturing it link by link, training men to carry it out."[2] This was the critical and decisive operation of the war; it *was* the war. The Egyptians no longer had an air force to counter Israeli air power raining bombs and napalm down on their land forces. Thus, Egyptian troops and tanks in the Sinai were unable to advance or even protect themselves against Israeli air attack. At 10 a.m., even before the Egyptian air force was completely destroyed, Weizman called his wife: "We've won the war!"[3]

The Egyptian wreckage was formidable. "In the main attack, nineteen Egyptian air bases in the Sinai, in the Nile delta, the Nile valley and Cairo area were attacked in some 500 sorties, destroying 309 out of 340 serviceable combat aircraft including all 30 long-range Tu-16 bombers."[4]

Defense Minister Moshe Dayan shrewdly forbade communications about Israel's total victory over Egypt. He assumed that Egypt would be unable to admit complete defeat to its allies (Jordan, Syria and Iraq) and that these other nations would thus be drawn into the war, providing grounds for similar devastations there: "Arab vanity and extravagance now served us well."[5] Indeed, Radio Cairo initially spoke of unprecedented *Egyptian* breakthroughs, very likely misleading Jordan.[6] In truth, Nasser did not know the facts until 4:00 that afternoon.[7]

The air war continued:

> Some three hours after Israel struck . . . Syrian planes made some forays against Megiddo, Acre-Haifa Bay, and Tiberias, and Jordanian planes attacked Natanya and an air base near Kfar Sirkin. The attackers caused some slight damage and suffered considerable losses before the Israeli air force was free to turn on them. . . . In a series of raids on Jordanian and Syrian airfields, the entire Jordanian air force of some twenty fighters was destroyed and two-thirds of the Syrian air force was put out of action. An Iraqi medium bomber was able to penetrate Israeli air space on the second day of the war and to drop some bombs on Natanya. It was shot down on its way back to base and elicited an Israeli attack on the base itself in which most of the Iraqi expeditionary air contingent was destroyed.[8]

This completed the Israeli air victory. No plane from any Arab country penetrated Israeli air space without being shot down and for all practical purposes Israel had eliminated the air force of each Arab state in the first day of fighting.[9] Nearly all Egyptian combat planes were destroyed, along with all of Jordan's jets and two-thirds of the Syrian air force.[10] Of 416 Arab aircraft, 393 were destroyed on the ground.[11] With virtually all Arab planes destroyed and Arab land forces trapped without air protection, Israel's overland blitzkreig proceeded largely unopposed.

Back in Washington

By the time President Johnson was awakened with the news that the war had begun, Weizman had declared victory to his wife. "How did it start? Who fired first?" Johnson asked Rostow.

The Israeli Defense Ministry lied to Washington, cabling: "Egyptian armored and aerial forces . . . moved against Israel and our forces . . . went into action to check them."[12] Then a second cable arrived: "Egyptian armored forces advanced at dawn toward the Negev. Our own forces advanced to repel them. At the same time a large number of radar tracks of Egyptian jets were observed on the screen. The tracks were directed towards the Israeli shoreline. . . . IDF air force craft took to the air against enemy aircraft."

Israeli Foreign Minister Abba Eban personally misinformed the U.S. ambassador to Israel: "Early this morning Israelis observed Egyptian units moving in large numbers toward Israel and in fact considerable force penetrated Israeli territory and clashed with Israeli ground forces."[13]

In Washington a Middle East expert from the U.S. National Security Council was assigned to determine who began the fighting, though nearly every official assumed it was Israel.[14] The question was moot since Johnson and the American public were so committed to Israel that the circumstances of war did not matter – or were better left unknown.

The State Department reiterated its official U.S. policy of "neutrality" – a policy dating back to 1948 when the United States committed itself to upholding the Arab-Israeli armistice agreements. This neutrality announcement caused an uproar in the American Jewish community. Johnson was livid with the State Department and struggled to distance himself.[15] He had no desire to be seen as neutral – a stance widely considered to be an abandonment of Israel. At the same time, Johnson wished to avoid taking any corrective military actions such as defending the attacked party – as the United States was committed to do. He decided to take the position that the United States was not sure who started the hostilities. He chose to ride the popular presumption that Egypt had started the war by its provocations. Congressmen rushed to pledge unswerving support for Israel.

The land war on three fronts

It took the remainder of Monday, Tuesday and Wednesday (June 5, 6, 7) – days one, two and three – to capture East (Arab) Jerusalem, Egypt's Sinai Desert and Jordan's West Bank. Capture of Syria's Golan Heights was delayed a few days, completed on Saturday, June 10 – the sixth day of the war.

The primary goal was to gain territory as fast as possible before a cease-fire could be imposed. A second goal was to assess the U.S. attitude about Israeli *retention* of captured territory. Johnson and Soviet Foreign Minister Andrei Kosygin were constantly on the hot line over both matters – cease-fire and withdrawal. The Soviets became so angered by the fifth day of the war that they threatened military intervention. The two superpowers were on a collision course as the U.S. Sixth Fleet steamed toward the Soviet fleet on the last (sixth) day of war.

The Sinai front: The IDF rush over the Sinai was made possible by highly detailed knowledge of the major Egyptian defense facilities – "the Israelis could have found their way blindfolded."[16] On day one, June 5, Israeli ground divisions, led by Generals Tal, Yoffe and Sharon, made their way through the Gaza Strip, along the coast to al-Arish and southward, some thirty miles, to the perimeter of Abu Egeila, without air cover – the air force being otherwise occupied.[17] On day two, the absence of an Egyptian air force meant that the land forces could advance at will. One goal of the advance was to destroy Egyptian second-line defenses and block Egyptian escape routes from the Sinai. Egyptian troops and tanks, unprotected from the air and in panicky retreat, were at the mercy of the Israeli air force.[18] Their retreat was possible only in the utter confusion of night since the Israeli air force was incinerating them with napalm by day.[19] The Soviets angrily condemned the Israelis, accusing them of "marching in the bloody footsteps of Hitler's executioners."[20] The desert was an inferno of burning tanks, with thousands of desperate Egyptian soldiers, stunned, shelterless, often shoeless, fleeing across the hot sands toward the safety of the Suez Canal, while advancing Israeli armored units raced toward the canal to trap these remnants of the Egyptian army.[21]

The Sinai campaign had gone exactly as planned and as the CIA had predicted. On day three, the Strait of Tiran was captured and the Egyptian air and ground forces there were completely destroyed. The Egyptian army lost 80 percent of its equipment, including 700 tanks; Israel lost 61 tanks. About 11,500 Egyptian officers and men were killed and several times that number were wounded. Egyptians taken prisoner numbered 5, 000 to 6,000. Israel lost 275 to 300 officers and men plus 800 to 1,000 wounded.[22]

The Jordanian (West Bank) front: Within an hour of Israel's attack on Egypt, the highest UN military official in Jerusalem (Lt. Gen. Odd Bull) was told by the deputy director-general of the Israeli Foreign Ministry that Egypt had started the war. Bull was asked to convey this to Jordan and to say that Israel would not attack Jordan unless Jordan initiated hostilities, in which case Israel would "react with all our might"[23] – what Bull called a "threat, pure and simple." King Hussein knew that Bull was misinformed about Egypt attacking Israel and, given his mutual defense obligation to Egypt, knew he could not just stand aside. Hussein, as custodian of the Moslem shrines in Jerusalem and leader of an inflamed Palestinian population, was not free to try to appease Israel. Wrongly believing that Egypt had put up some kind of adequate defense, he also thought that the Israeli threat might be a deception or delaying device to avoid engagement on two fronts (Sinai and West Bank).

The Jordanian army opened an artillery barrage against West Jerusalem and many other points along the border, seizing the strategically located UN Headquarters in Jerusalem on the first day. But by afternoon the Israelis were on the advance in the West Bank and soon recaptured the UN Headquarters. Without an air force – destroyed that afternoon – Hussein saw how vulnerable his West Bank ground forces were to air attack. He sought a cease-fire at 8 a.m. on day two (June 6). Israel ignored Hussein's cease-fire efforts despite U.S. State Department pleas.[24] Israel made unsupportable claims that Jordan's cease-fire effort was a deception.[25] By noon of day two, a U.S. Embassy cable from Jordan described the situation as follows:

> Most Jordanian units fighting isolated battles without central control. Jordanian Air Force destroyed; all runways out of commission along with . . . radar . . . losing tanks at rate of one every ten minutes. IDF Air Force yesterday and again today hit many civilian targets on West Bank where there are absolutely no military emplacements. . . . Street fighting continues in Old Jerusalem. . . . [Jordanian] Army casualties "unbearably high." . . . Syrians have done bare minimum to help out since beginning of conflict.[26]

Jordan had some ten brigades and auxiliaries distributed over the West Bank in a basically defensive stance, entrenched in mountainous terrain not readily attackable by large motorized Israeli forces.[27] Yet without the protection of a Jordanian air force, these troops were at the mercy of the Israeli air force, which dropped liberal amounts of napalm, incinerating great numbers of Jordanians and Palestinians.[28]

The UN adopted cease-fire Resolution 233 on the evening of day two (early morning of day three, Israeli time) and Jordan immediately accepted. The

Soviets caved in to U.S. demands that withdrawal from territorial gains *not* be included in the cease-fire resolution.

Foreign Minister Eban made a speech at the UN heard by many millions and winning important support for Israel:

> Israel, by its independent effort and sacrifice, has passed from serious danger to successful and glorious resistance . . . and is now willing to demonstrate its instinct for peace.

Yet Israel continued its military advance and Kosygin, on the hot line to Washington, objected to Israeli violations of the cease-fire. He directly warned Israel that the U.S.S.R. might break off diplomatic relations and was considering other "necessary steps." Israel accepted the cease-fire (late night of June 7, day three), conditional upon Arab acceptance, once it completed its capture of East Jerusalem that morning and the whole of the West Bank later that day.[29]

As in the Sinai, the actual course of operations went according to plan, almost without hitch. The IDF did have to fight harder, pay a heavier price in casualties and depend more on support of the air force than expected. Yet in less than three days, it had totally routed the Jordanian army and captured all of the West Bank, including Jerusalem.[30]

Israel had long-range *political* objectives in Egypt, Jordan and Syria according to a CIA report:

> Immediate and primary GOI [government of Israel] war aim is destruction of the center of power of the radical Socialist movement, i.e., the Nasser regime. . . . If the arms of the radical Arabs can be destroyed, the GOI assumes [that] Turkey, Iran and Israel [U.S. client-states at the time] will represent an overwhelming balance of military power in the area. . . . Israel will attempt to destroy the Syrian regime and to eliminate both Syria and Jordan as modern states.[31]

The Syrian (Golan Heights) front: When Israel attacked Egypt, Syria attempted a few air attacks but made no major offensive into Israel. Adopting a wait-and-see attitude, Syria preferred simply to shell the Galilee town of Rosh Pina and its neighboring settlements.[32] Israel responded with a vigorous artillery and air force attack on day one. Syria's air force effectively gone, Syrian troops continued with some hostilities at the local level.

Israel delayed its planned major offense in Syria for several days in order to finish operations in the West Bank and Jerusalem. Then, on June 8 (day four) at 10 a.m., UN observers reported to the United States that the Israelis, in violation of their agreement to a cease-fire of the night before, "have just launched intensive air and artillery bombardment of Syrian positions opposite central demilitarized zone as apparent prelude to large-scale attack to seize heights overlooking border kibbutzim." Because of grave U.S. warnings about this cease-fire violation, Israel decided to delay the massive *land* invasion of the Golan Heights that was to follow this air and artillery attack.

Israel was stymied by U.S. disapproval of its pursuit of war in Syria. The U.S. warning had stressed complete cessation of Israeli military action except in self-defense. Since Syria had made no major move throughout the war, Israel lacked grounds for attack.[33] Moreover, Egypt had accepted the UN cease-fire injunction on the evening of day four and Syria had followed suit.

Not that there was question whether Israel was going to invade Syria. It was merely a question of timing, according to General Weizman: "With almost our whole air force available, and the Egyptian, Jordanian and Syrian air forces practically eliminated, our strength was enormous. . . . For years we have awaited such an opportunity for settling accounts with our most bitter foes."[34] Not only were the senior officers in favor of more conquest, but the mood in the country was one of jubilation and revenge – Israelis and Syrians hated each other the most. Syria having provided bases for the Fatah, the cabinet ministers demanded an assault on Syria.[35]

Israel attacks the USS Liberty *in preparation for assault in Syria*

Israel was concerned that U.S. foreknowledge of Israeli plans for a land invasion of Syria might elicit ultimatums and withdrawal of support from the United States – if not direct Soviet intervention in defense of its client state.[36] The United States was monitoring Israeli military communications from an intelligence-gathering ship, the USS *Liberty,* floating off the coast of Gaza. The *Liberty* could be expected to discover and transmit to Washington Israel's plan for a combined air and ground attack on Syria set for the morning of June 8 (day four)[37] – the air phase having already been unleashed.

At 2 p.m. on June 8, Israel bombed and torpedoed the USS *Liberty.* Miraculously, despite persistent attacks, the ship did not sink. Israel jammed the *Liberty*'s transmissions, torpedoed the section of the hull in which the electronic gear was housed and destroyed all antennae (to prevent the crew from calling for help or transmitting communications already intercepted that morning). Three delta-winged Israeli planes attacked again and again with rockets and 30mm armor-piercing shells:

Then came more planes, Mysteres with rockets, cannon and, most dreaded of
all, napalm. The jets . . . .released their silvery canisters of jellied gasoline that
exploded into flames on contact, slopping along the decks and through the
doors and the large holes gouged out by the rockets and cannon fire. The
Liberty was now a floating hell of flames and screaming men. The wounded
and dead were everywhere.[38]

When it first seemed that the ship would have to be abandoned, Israeli forces
destroyed several life rafts. A majority of the crew were killed (34) or wounded
(171). Initially, the United States thought the Soviets were responsible.
President Johnson felt out the Soviets on the hot line and informed them he was
sending U.S. planes to the rescue with orders to "use force including
destruction" against *whoever* was responsible. Then Johnson confronted Israel.
Israel admitted the attack, claiming it to be an "accident" – at first claiming that
the ship had been misidentified as an Egyptian freighter. Johnson recalled the
U.S. attack planes but informed Israel that he knew Israel had identified the ship
as American. The *Liberty* had been conspicuously marked with huge American
flags, distinctive antennae and microwave communication dishes, and had been
closely and repeatedly reconnoitered by the planes for six hours before the attack.
Israel then agreed but claimed that this information had simply not reached the
field.[39] Nevertheless, senior U.S. officials were convinced that the attack was
deliberate.[40] The CIA reported that the Israelis knew it was a U.S. ship and one
report identified Dayan as the person who personally ordered the attack.[41]

Johnson brushed the attack under the carpet. The deputy secretary of defense
ordered that no news releases be made by either the survivors or any navy
source. Government officials were ordered to remain silent. The White House
concluded that the Israeli explanation was acceptable. The public was not
informed. Johnson knew that criticism of Israel was politically unwise while the
American public was jubilant over Israel's capacity to "end Arab aggression." It
was also deemed unwise to confront Israel openly at a time when the United
States was seeking to persuade Israel not to invade Syria.

On Friday morning, June 9 (day five), Israel was free to pursue its final
objective, the capture of Syria's Golan Heights, without fear of U.S.
eavesdropping.[42] Israel made the claim that Syria had shelled sixteen Israeli
villages and with that justification launched a powerful five-prong land assault on
the Golan Heights. Syrian fortifications in the Heights were well-known from the
work of Israeli spy Eli Cohen. The Heights contained, in addition to the

TransArabian Pipeline, the highly valuable headwaters of the Jordan River, which had for a decade been a source of bitter hostilities.

The UN Security Council demanded another cease-fire that day to which both Syria and Israel agreed. Syria insisted that Israel was violating the cease-fire, which Israel vigorously denied while continuing its attack – the thrust was just gathering momentum.[43] The UN was unsure of what was happening without the *Liberty* monitoring the fighting. Early the next day, Saturday, June 10 (sixth and last day of the war), Israeli forces pressed simultaneously from all directions after very heavy artillery bombardment and with massive support from the air.[44] UN observers reported Israeli bombing of the Damascus suburbs. Syria was in panic, fearing that the Israeli military machine was going to keep moving until the government in Damascus was overthrown – a well-advertised Israeli threat.[45] Israel's ambassador to the UN denied the air attacks on Damascus and claimed that Israel was abiding by the cease-fire.[46]

The Russians were incensed. They severed diplomatic ties with Israel, threatened sanctions and warned Johnson on the hot line about "grave consequences" and "necessary actions, including military." Johnson, not wanting the Soviets in the Middle East, sent the Sixth Fleet steaming toward Russia's fleet of twenty warships, eight submarines and supporting vessels. A collision course was averted only when Israel agreed to end hostilities on Saturday evening, having completed its invasion of the Golan Heights.

The war was over: Israel lost 766 men; the Arabs, 20,000.[47] The amount of land under Israeli control more than tripled.

Destruction and eviction in Jerusalem, the West Bank and Golan Heights

Israeli occupation troops destroyed Arab homes in the cities, bulldozed Arab villages in the West Bank and forced expulsion of Palestinian residents. These operations were undertaken largely after the fighting had ended on June 10.

The day following the war (June 11), the homes of 135 Palestinian families in the Moghrabi (Moslem) Quarter of Old Jerusalem were bulldozed and 650 religious Moslems were evicted before the international community could object.[48] Two weeks later Israel passed laws that gave Israel complete control over all of Jerusalem. The city was enlarged to incorporate Palestinian-Jordanian West Bank land.[49] City utilities in the east and west (electricity, water, telephones) were later integrated, taxes collected from Jordanian Palestinians, Jordanian banks replaced with Israeli banks and Palestinians issued religious identification cards. Abba Eban declared that this fusion of Arab and Israeli

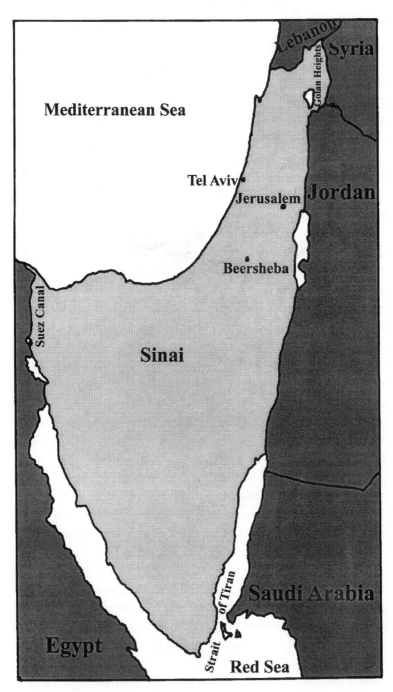

Cease-fire Lines after the Six Day War (1967)

182

Jerusalem was a legal formality, not an annexation. The United States and most other nations deplored the rapid fait accompli manner of "creating facts." The White House declared that "the United States has never recognized such unilateral action by any state in the area as governing the international status of Jerusalem."[50]

Still, the United States abstained from a UN vote declaring Israel's claim to Jerusalem invalid. Ignoring world protest, Israel took Jerusalem as its capital – it had been earmarked for incorporation as Israel's capital even before the war.[51] Arab land surrounding Jerusalem was subsequently confiscated and large housing projects for Jews only were built in East Jerusalem – a violation of the Fourth Geneva Convention of 1949.[52]

During the war, in the predawn darkness of June 6, three villages in the West Bank were leveled with dynamite and bulldozers because they obstructed a direct route between Jerusalem and Tel Aviv. According to Arab sources, 10,000 residents were turned out without possessions, food or water, to wander aimlessly.[53] In the Palestinian village of Qalqilia, 14,000 residents who had fled during the fighting returned to find 850 of their homes destroyed in an Israeli punitive action for some Palestinian sniping. On June 11, 2,500 villagers from Beit Awa were ordered out and a week later found that 360 of their homes were completely destroyed, others damaged and groves burned. Many such villages were systematically destroyed, allegedly for security or safety reasons.

Israeli agents prodded Palestinians to flee into Jordan, Lebanon or Egypt. In Bethlehem soldiers drove around with loudspeakers announcing that residents had two hours to leave before their homes would be shelled. Israeli buses and trucks were made available to tens of thousands of frightened Palestinians who were warned to vacate their homes and flee or remain to find they had no home. Many took to living in the hills under trees in the chill night, hungry and thirsty, descending on neighborhoods uninvited and helpless.[54] Those taken to the Jordanian border waded through the muddy banks of the Jordan River in chaos and misery – the Allenby Bridge having been destroyed – in hope of reaching refugee camps in Jordan.[55] Less than 8 percent were ever allowed to return to the West Bank.[56] About 100,000 refugees, men, women and children, crowded into Amman, sleeping in public buildings and doorways and foraging through garbage pails. In Syria's Golan Heights, nearly all the 115,000 residents became refugees.

Those who remained in the West Bank often found their homes, if still standing, looted – a widespread practice, especially in Jerusalem.[57] Israeli soldiers also looted all UN vehicles and office equipment in the Gazan UN headquarters. Kuneitra, the provincial capital of the Golan Heights, having fallen without a fight, was, according to UN reports, stripped by Israeli soldiers.[58]

Israeli officials denied that any Arabs had been displaced by deliberate destruction of their houses. Almost nothing of the looting and destruction was reported in the press, at first, since reporters were prohibited from traveling in the West Bank without Israeli escort. Yet the destruction and dispersal of populations was indisputable. By UN estimate, the war created 323,000 new refugees.[59] Of these, 178,000 came from the West Bank, 102,000 from Syria's Golan Heights and 38,000 from the Sinai. The Palestinian Arab diaspora was about one million by 1967, not including children born in refugee camps.

Conflict over Israeli withdrawal

That November following the June Six Day War, the UN passed Resolution 242 concerning the withdrawal of Israeli forces from conquered Arab territory and declaring that acquisition of land through war was contrary to UN principles. Earlier, Israel had stated a willingness to give back most but not all of the territory in exchange for political considerations. The United States had been lulled by the soothing assurances of Abba Eban that Israel sought no territory. In October, however, when Dean Rusk asked Eban about prime minister Eshkol's June assurances to Johnson that Israel had no "colonial" aspirations, Eban replied, "That was before Syria and Jordan entered the war."[60] The political consideration that Israel now expected, while retaining the Gaza Strip, was return of the Sinai to Egypt in exchange for a peace treaty. This divide and conquer strategy was not acceptable to either Nasser or King Hussein. For "[a] separate peace [with Egypt] would leave Israel free to deal with the other Arab nations as it wished... [leave Israel] in such a commanding position that it would probably not give up the West Bank."[61] The Arab position, thus, was "total peace for total withdrawal." The appearance of a solution to the impass came in the form of a vague UN Resolution 242 that hedged on how much territory Israel was obliged to return in exchange for peace (see chapter 16).

This issue of what to return for peace was a matter of diverse opinion within the Israeli government in the following years. In 1971, deputy prime minister Yigal Allon, while advocating an Israeli security border in the West Bank along the Jordan River (Allon Plan), opposed defense minister Dayan's "creeping annexation" policies in the territories. On the other hand, Ben-Gurion, past advocate of Israeli militancy, out of office in 1973, advoated the return of the

Sinai and the West Bank. The public response: "The old lion has finally gone soft."[62]

Perspectives

For readers under 45 years of age, it may be impossible to appreciate how irrelevant to the American public in 1967 were the specific reasons, causal analyses or proper assignment of responsibilities for the "Six Day" War. Few cared who started it or why it was occurring. The dominating specter was that of the Holocaust, the central and oppressive tragedy of World War II, which seemed somehow reversed in a burst of jubilation when the Jewish state fashioned a spectacular victory against the Arab enemy popularly viewed as intent on a second Holocaust. This reading of the times and circumstances of 1967 through analogy with events in Europe in the 1940s misled by distorting the facts and imposed political and emotional justifications belonging to another time. This "Holocaust syndrome," by which Arab became Nazi and the Jew became a near-victim rising up with sword in hand, created a powerful emotional reaction that cast historical fact and the plight of the "enemy" into deep shadow. Historian and journalist Donald Neff made some observations along these lines:

> With only a few notable exceptions, stories coming out of Israel and printed in the major U.S. dailies during this period were almost invariably focused on the glory of Israel's achievements and the humanity of its occupation policies. They were mute about the plight of a people suddenly rendered captive or homeless in their own land, silent now that victims of the past had suddenly become oppressors of the present. This blindness to a whole people's suffering and the unrestrained glorification of Israel was widely shared and partly explained by the lingering Holocaust guilt of the West. The Christian West experienced a sense of relief, of expiation, with Israel's triumph. There was in the West an undercurrent of feeling that finally its guilt over the Nazi atrocities was at last exculpated.[63]

Notes

1. Donald Neff, *Warriors for Jerusalem* (Brattleboro, Vt.: Amana Books, 1988), 203.
2. Ezer Weizman, *On Eagles' Wings: The Personal Story of the Israeli Air Force* (London: Weidenfeld and Nicolson, 1976), 221.
3. Neff, *Jerusalem*, 204.

4. Chaim Herzog, *The Arab-Israeli Wars* (New York: Vintage Books, 1984), 152.

5. Neff, *Jerusalem*, 205.

6. Howard Sachar, *A History of Israel:From the Rise of Zionism to Our Time*, Vol. I (New York: Knopf, 1986), 642-3.

7. "None of his [Nasser's] commanders gave him the actual facts. It was only at 4:00 p.m. that a headquarters officer arrived with straight information." Sachar, *History*, Vol. I, 645.

8. Nadav Safran, *Israel: The Embattled Ally* (Cambridge, Mass.: Belnap Press, 1978), 242.

9. Neff, *Jerusalem*, 204.

10. Sachar, *History*, Vol. I, 640

11. Herzog, *Arab-Israeli Wars*, 153.

12. Neff, *Jerusalem*, 210.

13. Neff, *Jerusalem*, 210.

14. Neff, *Jerusalem*, 211.

15. Steven L. Spiegel, *The Other Arab-Israeli Conflict* (Chicago: University of Chicago Press, 1985), 152.

16. Sachar, *History*, Vol. I, 636.

17. Safran, *Embattled*, 245.

18. Safran, *Embattled*, 245.

19. Neff, *Jerusalem*, 209.

20. Neff, *Jerusalem*, 238.

21. Neff, *Jerusalem*, 240.

22. Mark Tessler, in *A History of the Israeli-Palestinian Conflict* (Bloomington: Indiana University Press, 1994), 397, reports that 11,500 Egyptians (according to Nasser) and 345 Israelis were killed on the Egyptian front. See Safran, *Embattled*, 246, and Neff, *Jerusalem*, 262.

23. Neff, *Jerusalem*, 205.

24. Neff, *Jerusalem*, 228. In order that Hussein not be overthrown by his Palestinian population, the United States suggested that the cease-fire be kept secret.

25. Unsupportable according to the U.S. ambassador in Jordan. Neff, *Jerusalem*, 238.

26. Amman Embassy to SecState, Secret flash cable 4098A, 2:33 p.m., June 6, 1967. Cited in Neff, *Jerusalem*, 228-9.

27. Safran, *Embattled*, 246-8.

28. Neff, *Jerusalem*, 228.

29. "As with the Sinai offensive, the Israeli offensive against Jordan was planned in two continuous phases. The first was intended to secure certain minimal objectives before any possible interruption of the fighting [cease-fire], while the second was designed to capitalize on the achievements of the first phase to secure the maximal objectives if time and circumstances permitted . . . capturing the entire West Bank and routing or destroying the Jordanian army." Safran, *Embattled*, 250.

30. Israeli casualties ran relatively high – an indication of the intensity with which the West Bank was defended. About 550 were killed and 2,400 wounded. About 306 Israelis were killed on the Jordanian front and 115 on the Syrian front, according to Tessler, *History of Conflict*, 397. The number of Jordanians killed has been estimated to be many times that of the Israelis but could have been as few as 696. Neff, *Jerusalem*, 247. Another historian reported that about 300 Israelis were killed and 1,500 wounded, the bulk in the fight for Jerusalem. Safran, *Embattled*, 250.

31. Richard Helms to Walt Rostow, CIA secret study, "Israeli Objectives In The Current Crisis – Soviet Policy And Miscalculation," June 6, 1967. Cited by Neff, *Jerusalem*, 230.

32. Sachar, *History*, Vol. I, 643.

33. Neff, *Jerusalem*, 254. Because Israel enjoyed total air superiority, Syria was reduced to firing artillery attacks against Israeli troop concentrations and fortified kibbutzim. Dayan later admitted: "The Syrians carried out two unsuccessful attacks on a northern kibbutz and a military post on June 6. Thereafter, they confined themselves to shelling our kibbutzim and a few of our army camps." Moshe Dayan, *Moshe Dayan: Story of My Life* (New York: William Morrow and Co., 1976)., cited in Neff, *Jerusalem*, 265.

34. Neff, *Jerusalem*, 253.

35. Sachar, *History*, Vol. I, 655.

36. Neff, *Jerusalem*, 253.

37. Neff, *Jerusalem*, 254.

38. Neff, *Jerusalem*, 255.

39. James M. Ennes, *Assault on the Liberty* (New York: Random House, 1979), 154.

40. Dean Rusk wrote in 1981 to survivor James Ennes: "I still do not know at what level in the Israel government the attacks were launched, but I am convinced that it was not trigger-happy local commanders." Neff, *Jerusalem*, 356.

41. CIA Information Report, "Attack on USS *Liberty* Ordered by Dayan," November 7, 1967. Another CIA Information Report, "Comment on Known Identity of USS *Liberty* ," July 27, 1967, stated that "He [the source] was emphatic in stating . . . that they [Israel] knew what kind of ship USS Liberty was and what it was doing offshore." Both CIA reports cited in Neff, *Jerusalem*, 265n.

42. Neff, *Jerusalem*, 263.

43. Sachar, *History*, Vol. I, 657-8; also Neff, *Jerusalem*, 267.

44. Safran, *Embattled*, 255.

45. Tessler, *History of Conflict*, 386; Neff, *Jerusalem*, 276.

46. Neff, *Jerusalem*, 277.

47. Sachar, *History*, Vol. I, 658, reports 759 Israelis killed and up to 30,000 Arab casualties. Tessler, *History*, 397, cites 766 Israelis killed and 20,000 Arabs killed.

48. Jerusalem Mayor Teddy Kolleck wrote, "My overwhelming feeling was: do it now; it may be impossible to do it later, and it *must* be done." Neff, *Jerusalem*, 290.

49. Deputy Mayor Meron Benvenisti: "When the city's boundaries were marked

out, Arab-populated neighborhoods were excluded in order to ensure an overwhelming Jewish majority." Neff, *Jerusalem*, 312.

50. In 1948, Israel and Jordan jointly took control of Jerusalem for themselves, East and West, respectively, contrary to the UN call for international jurisdiction.

51. Neff, *Jerusalem*, 195.

52. Israel was a signatory to this convention. Article 49(6) states: "The Occupying Power shall not deport or transfer parts of its own civilian population into the territory it occupies."

53. Israeli sources put the figure at 4,000. Neff, *Jerusalem*, 291-2.

54. Neff, *Jerusalem*, 293.

55. Neff, *Jerusalem*, 293-4.

56. Of 178,000 Palestinians made refugees, 14,000 were allowed, after bitter negotiations, to return to the West Bank. Neff, *Jerusalem*, 320.

57. Neff, *Jerusalem*, 294.

58. Neff, *Jerusalem*, 295.

59. UNWRA report (UN A/6797) on the mission of the special representative to the occupied territories, September 15, 1967. Cited by Neff, *Jerusalem*, 320.

60. Neff, *Jerusalem*, 337.

61. Neff, *Jerusalem*, 339.

62. Sachar, *History*, Vol. I, 713.

63. Neff, *Jerusalem*, 297.

Chapter 16

The Yom Kippur War (1973) and Its Antecedents

UN peace efforts – Resolution 242

International diplomatic efforts to bring peace to the Middle East following the 1967 war focused on the idea that Israel would return occupied Arab lands in exchange for peace treaties with Arab countries. UN Resolution 242, adopted by the Security Council in November of 1967, was the central document expressing this exchange and, while largely ineffectual, constituted the dominant Middle East political document for the next several decades. UN Resolution 242 states:

The Security Council . . . emphasizing the inadmissibility of the acquisition of territory by war and the need to work for a just and lasting peace in which every State in the area can live in security . . .

1) Affirms . . . the following principles:

(a) Withdrawal of Israeli armed forces from territories occupied in the recent conflict;

(b) Termination of all claims or states of belligerency and respect for and acknowledgment of the sovereignty, territorial integrity and political independence of every State in the area and their right to live in peace within secure and recognized boundaries free from threats or acts of force;

2) Affirms further the necessity

(a) For guaranteeing freedom of navigation through international waterways in the area;

(b) For achieving a just settlement of the refugee problem;

(c) For guaranteeing the territorial inviolability and political independence of every State in the area, through measures including the establishment of demilitarized zones.

Responses to Resolution 242

The central stipulation that Israel withdraw from captured Arab lands in exchange for peace treaties with Arab countries – the "land for peace" concept – was questioned by both Israel and the Arabs.

In the case of Israel, the dominant military power in the Middle East, there existed no need for peace treaties. According to Abba Eban, Israel was in no mood to withdraw from occupied Arab lands which had tripled Israel's size. Zionism and Israeli attitudes had changed after 1967:

> We interpreted the war not just as a victory, but as a kind of providential messianic event that changed history permanently and gave Israel the power to dictate the future. . . . [The new Zionism] says that we will not give any territory back; if the Arabs don't like it here they can get the hell out, and if they stay we will not give them all their human rights, and being Jewish is more important than being democratic.[1]

At the same time, Israel knew that it could not simply annex occupied Arab territory without acquiring massive numbers of Arabs, mostly Palestinians. If those Arabs were given equal rights then they would threaten a state explicitly established for the benefit of Jews. On the other hand, depriving Arabs of political rights would turn Israel into an explicitly undemocratic, conceivably apartheid nation. Israel preferred a third alternative, the status quo – continued occupation, expansion of Jewish settlements in Gaza and the West Bank, diversion of West Bank water to Israel and possible withdrawal from some land if and when it proved necessary.

Whereas Israel objected to Resolution 242 because Israel wanted to retain territory, supposedly for security reasons,[2] Syria, Jordan and Egypt had misgivings about it because it did not clearly state that *all* lands occupied in 1967 should be returned – the wording ambiguous regarding extent of withdrawal. The initial draft of Resolution 242 did explicitly call for "withdrawal from *all* the territories," but the United States and Britain subsequently watered the language down. "All territories" became "territories" (without a definite article) implying that *partial withdrawal* might satisfy the resolution. While the Arab countries and Israel eventually accepted Resolution 242, the ambiguities clearly served Israeli, not Arab, interests.

Palestinians, on the other hand, objected to Resolution 242 because it said nothing about their fate, their right to self-determination or their right of refugee return. It addressed itself to "every State in the area" (a recognition of Israel and the established Arab states) but made no reference to Palestinians or their statelessness. That is, Resolution 242 was concerned with *interstate* relations (the Arab states and Israel), not with Palestinians. Palestinians thus felt abandoned by the resolution, as well as by the United States, U.S.S.R. and surrounding Arab nations, none of whom had done anything to end Israeli military occupation of the West Bank and Gaza. The plight of some one million Palestinians living under martial law, curfews, deportations and collective punishments aroused little interest in the international community. In destitute refugee camps in the West Bank, Gaza, Lebanon, Syria and Jordan, they were, according to Resolution 242, merely displaced persons in need of relief and rehabilitation, not a people entitled to statehood. Palestinian statehood was further jeopardized by Israel's incorporation of East Jerusalem (in the West Bank) and growing confiscation of land and water throughout the West Bank and Gaza.

The PLO proposes a single, secular, democratic state over all of Palestine

Discouraged Palestinians had three alternatives available to them: the militant route, the community infrastructure improvement route and the ideological route.

The militant route, proposed by extremist Palestinian groups critical of an ineffectual Fatah, foundered. Israel had a tough and effective security apparatus in the West Bank and Gaza. Consequently, Fatah leader Yasir Arafat focused on social programs and community infrastructure. With monies solicited in various Arab capitals, he set up Palestinian vocational training centers, literacy programs, clinics, workers' bureaus and military training for women at the community level and in refugee camps. Arafat revitalized the old 1964 conservative Palestinian Liberation Organization (PLO), making it a comprehensive political front that sought to represent all Palestinians and all forms of resistance.[3] He was made chairman of the new PLO, which nevertheless retained its original constitution affirming armed struggle as the only way to liberate Palestine.

The ideological approach emerged from a developing Palestinian national consciousness. New political objectives led the PLO to propose in January of 1969 that *all* of Palestine (mandated Palestine) become a *single, democratic, secular* state – "an indivisible territorial unit" granting both Jews and Palestinians equal political and civil rights. The PLO was suggesting a political formula that articulated the rights of Palestinians and offered a possible solution to the conflict with Israeli Jews.

This ideological change in PLO thinking had origins in a larger Arab self-criticism about Moslem religious conservatism. Sadeq al Azm, a Syrian intellectual, was criticizing the fatalism, passivity and conservativism of Moslem codes as well as Arab failure to adopt modern, scientific, socialist and secular thinking. The PLO took up these notions in the concept of a secular state in which Jews, Christians and Moslems could enjoy citizenship without preference or discrimination.

Clearly, the PLO was rejecting a Zionist theocracy by proposing that Jews "agree to live with us" in a democratic state over all of Palestine in which no Jew would be pushed into the sea and no Arab into the desert. This was not a rejection of Judaism but an acceptance of Judaism without Zionism.[4] It represented a shift, or attempted shift, away from Arab anti-Semitism. PLO leaders, touring the West Bank, condemned the anti-Jewish character of some Arab propagandists.[5]

By favoring a single, secular state over all of Palestine, the PLO was, of course, attempting to cure the statelessness of Palestinians through the democratic model. This constituted a rejection of both the UN partition (two-state) solution of 1947 and UN Resolution 242, which aimed at restoring the pre-1967 status quo between Israel and the Arab states whereby the West Bank would return to Jordanian control.

Israeli reactions were profoundly negative, treating the idea of a single secular state as an insincere propaganda ploy for Western benefit – a charge virtually impossible to disprove.[6] Yehoshafat Harkabi, an articulate critic for Israel, made some cogent rebuttal points.[7] He drew attention to ambiguities in the PLO National Charter (ambiguities needed to bridge factional differences within the PLO). Yet Palestinian leaders were flexible in discussion. Careful scholars have concluded that Israel's disregard of the PLO proposal was "premature and intellectually unfounded."[8] There was something "constructive, positive and sincere in the Palestinian ideology"[9] – if only in that the PLO denounced Arab anti-Semitism and seriously called for cooperation between Arabs and Jews.

These PLO proposals effected no change in Israeli policy. The superpowers, too, largely ignored Palestinian political and ideological efforts. Yet these efforts served to heighten international perceptions of the Middle East conflict and of the Palestinians as a people with a legitimate political agenda.[10]

The war of attrition (fall 1968 to 1970)

If Resolution 242 ignored the plight of Palestinians, it also failed to bring peace in exchange for land to Arab nations and Israel. Egypt in particular was unwilling to passively accept Israel's continuing occupation of the Egyptian Sinai and hostilities accelerated in 1968. Israeli forces were situated on the east bank of the Suez Canal while Egyptian forces were posted on the west side, a separation of a mere 200 yards. Mutual shelling was continuous and at first, Israel was outgunned. Then Israel took to retaliatory raids on electric plants and bridges over the Nile River in the fall of 1968. Egypt and Israel became locked in battles aimed at inflicting unacceptable costs on and defying each other.

In December of 1969, Presient Richard Nixon's secretary of state, William Rogers, proposed that Israel return to its pre-1967 borders in exchange for binding peace commitments with Egypt and Jordan – largely a call for fulfillment of Resolution 242.[11] Egypt, Jordan and moderate Arab countries praised the proposal but Israel rejected it.[12] The following month, Israel made bombing raids deep into Egyptian territory, dropping bombs a few miles from Cairo. In June 1970, Israel dropped more than 4,000 bombs on Egyptian positions. During this "war of attrition" some 1,500,000 Egyptians fled their homes.[13] Neither Gunnar Jarring of the UN nor the Big Four were able to negotiate a peace. However, the unremitting violence resulted in increased Egyptian military strength because Nasser was forced to invite Soviet military advisors to Egypt, complete with SAM-3 missiles and even pilots to fly in defense of Egypt.

Eventually, in the summer of 1970, the war came to a halt when U.S. diplomacy brought about a cease-fire agreement. Israel's 1967 war gains remained intact: occupation of the Golan Heights, the Gaza Strip, the West Bank and the Sinai Peninsula. Syria, Jordan and Egypt continued to be the humiliated losers of the 1967 war. The potential for further war was increased by the fact that Egypt and Israel were increasingly armed during the war of attrition. President Nixon assured Prime Minister Golda Meir in 1969 that the "special relationship" between the United States and Israel was such that Israel would never be without U.S. military support while Egypt and Syria were being armed and trained by the Soviets.[14]

So superpower rivalry had fueled Middle East instability and Resolution 242 had resolved nothing. Moreover, Arab contempt for the uncritical support of Israel by the United States and continuing Israeli occupation was opening doors to Soviet influence.[15]

The Middle East players in 1970

The United States and Kissinger: Nixon took control of U.S. Middle East policy away from Secretary of State Rogers and gave it to his national security advisor, Henry Kissinger. Rogers had seen settlement of the Middle East conflict as a local matter of Israel returning land in exchange for peace treaties with Arab countries. Kissinger, on the other hand, saw the Middle East conflict as a *global* matter between the conflicting Cold War superpowers. Rather than settlement, Kissinger sought *stalemate* in the Middle East (inaction on Resolution 242 and continued Israeli retention of occupied Arab territory) on the theory that stalemate would diminish Soviet influence in the Middle East by frustrating Arab nations with the Soviet Union expected to restore lost Arab land. Nixon was torn between Rogers' wish to advance the 242 blueprint for settlement and Kissinger's wish for the status quo to Israel's advantage and the Soviet's disadvantage.[16] Nixon gave Kissinger control of Middle East policy not because he was so pro-Israeli but in order to concentrate on the Vietnam war.[17] Nevertheless, U.S. policy effectively became pro-Israeli in the sense that Kissinger supported Israel's retention of Arab land and ignored the plight of Palestinians living under an oppressive Israeli occupation.

Egypt and Sadat: Nasser died of a heart attack in 1970. While he had led Egypt into two disasters (the Suez and Six Day Wars), he was nevertheless beloved by the Arab multitudes as a defender of Arab independence against European and Zionist imperialism. At death his powers legally fell to his widely ridiculed vice-president, Anwar Sadat. Considered to be "incredibly incompetent" by the West, Sadat was regarded in Egypt as a weak and clownish sycophant of Nasser. He faced open political challenge in Egypt.[18]

Syria and Assad: One month after Sadat's precarious assumption of power, Hafez Assad, Syria's minister of defense, staged a bloodless coup against a Ba'athist government. Syria was known for its yearly coups but Assad's government proved more durable. Assad was militantly opposed to Meir's intention to keep the Golan Heights and, in addition, was a formidable competitor of Sadat for leadership of the Arab world.

Jordan and Hussein: King Hussein of Jordan was a lesser player.[19] He was a recipient of CIA money and considered by Palestinians to be a pro-Western conservative who, like his grandfather Abdullah, was too friendly with Israel. Hussein's monarchical rule was under challenge from Palestinian nationalist revolutionaries in Jordan (Jordan's population was 40 percent Palestinian). Palestinians were increasingly critical of the king after his army failed to protect them in the battle of Karameh (a Fatah command center) during massive Israeli air attacks in which 270 Palestinians and Jordanians were killed in 1968.[20]

A showdown occurred in 1970 when the Popular Front for the Liberation of Palestine (PFLP), a radical offshoot of Arafat's Fatah lead by George Habash, hijacked four European airplanes and took hostages to Amman in hopes of a prisoner exchange. When Palestinian revolutionaries sought to remove King Hussein, the monarch declared martial law, suppressed all political expression and embarked on a bloody civil war against Palestinians in Jordan. Jordanian troops and tanks entered Palestinian refugee camps, killing at least 3,500 Palestinians – some say as many as 30,000.[21] Syria sent some tanks toward Jordan to protect the Palestinians but Israeli planes, at U.S. request, threatened attack and the tanks hightailed home. The Palestinian nationalist movement in Jordan collapsed after this "Black September" civil war. The fragmented PLO leadership and some 4,000 PLO relocated to Lebanon. In terms of identity, Hussein seemed to be regarded as neither an Arab nor a Jew.

Israel and Meir: Israel's chief player was Golda Meir, head of a conservative Labor government that had replaced that of the more moderate Levi Eshkol in 1969.[22] She repeatedly and publicly declared her intention of retaining Jerusalem, Gaza, the Golan Heights, part of the West Bank (as called for in the Allon Plan)[23] and a demilitarized Sinai, including Sharm el-Sheikh and access roads at the southern tip. Meir's opponent on her political right was ultra-nationalist Menachem Begin, a popular cabinet member since his role in war preparations in 1967. Begin, destined to become prime minister in 1977, argued for Israeli retention of *all* occupied Arab land. There were, thus, policy differences within the Israeli establishment.

Sadat peace offering ignored in 1971; Nixon courts Israel at election time

The war of attrition was a disaster and a humiliation for the Egyptian public and a threat to Sadat's political authority. Sadat publicly declared that 1971 was his "year of decision" for resolving the conflict with Israel, either by diplomacy or war. Accordingly, on February 4, 1971, he offered to sign a peace agreement with Israel and open the Suez Canal (closed since 1967) to international and Israeli shipping if Israeli would withdraw its forces a few miles from the canal. The offer was largely ignored by both Israel and the United States

Days later, Gunnar Jarring, the UN special envoy, offered his own more comprehensive resolution: Israel to withdraw to pre-1967 borders (subject to practical security arrangements) in exchange for Egyptian agreement to respect

Israel's independence, its right to live within secure borders and its right of passage through the Suez Canal and the Strait of Tiran. Sadat liked Jarring's proposal and agreed to sign a peace treaty with additional conditions attached. Israel was bluntly negative, declaring that there would be no withdrawal to the pre-1967 lines – a missed opportunity to avoid the 1973 Yom Kippur war.

Nixon turned actively pro-Israeli as he faced the coming 1972 presidential election. Continued Israeli retention of Arab territory – Kissinger's successful status quo policy[24] – could only help Nixon to garner Jewish votes and money. Nixon additionally used Yitzhak Rabin, Israeli ambassador to the United States, and Kissinger to advertise this policy to the voters.[25] The president also began a massive transfer of technology in November 1971 which gave Israel a new capability to produce many of its own weapons.[26] In February 1972, Nixon further pledged a huge shipment of forty-two F-4 and ninety A-4 warplanes. He promised Meir that he would not seek return of Arab territory and promised not even to *talk* with Arab countries without Israel's approval. Taken literally, "the United States had tied itself almost completely to the Israeli position."[27]

Because Sadat's peace offer was rebuffed and Nixon was solidly behind Israel, Egypt's situation looked bleak. Students were rioting in January 1972 over Sadat's failure to make good on his promised 1971 "decision year." He was mocked not only by the Egyptian public but by the Israeli public as well for brave talk and weak excuses.

Sharon and Palestinian terror increase tensions

Gen. Ariel Sharon, commander-in chief of the Southern Command, was flaunting IDF power in the Sinai, Gaza and Lebanon. For example, in January 1971, Sharon removed the mayor and Municipal Council in Gaza, placed the refugee camps under round-the-clock curfew, searched houses and rounded up men (forcing some to stand for hours in the winter Mediterranean Sea). Following these raids, some 12,000 family members of suspected Palestinian commandos were deported to detention camps in the Sinai. Sharon "thinned out" refugee camps further in July 1971 – 13,000 more Palestinians were sent to the Sinai. Many Palestinian guerrillas were killed in gun battles during these operations.[28] In early 1972, Sharon's operations drove off some 10,000 farmers and Bedouins from northeast Sinai, destroying crops and wells in order to build Jewish settlements and a resort (Yamit).[29] In February 1972, when three Israelis were killed by Palestinian terrorists coming from southern Lebanon, the IDF was sent into Lebanon, killing sixty and wounding 100. In September 1972, when two Israeli soldiers were killed in the Golan Heights, Israel again went into Lebanon, killing twenty-three Lebanese civilians, eighteen Lebanese soldiers and thirty Palestinian guerrillas.

Dissident Palestinian terror groups grew bold and criticized the Fatah for its passivity. In September 1972, the Fatah attempted to restore its reputation through a dramatic act expected to gain worldwide attention for the Palestinian cause.[30] This was the infamous, bungled hostage-taking of Israeli athletes at the Munich Olympics. It resulted in the deaths of eleven Israelis and five Fatah terrorists.[31] Israel retaliated two days later, killing 200 to 500 Lebanese, Syrians and Palestinians. When three of the captured Munich terrorists were later released from a German jail in a skyjacking hostage exchange, Israel raided Syria (which was supportive of the PLO), killing sixty civilians and fifteen guerrillas and wounding seventy others.

These kinds of hostilities seemed to be leading toward war and were costing lives – in 1972, somewhere between 700 and 1,000 Arabs were killed, as were thirty-six Israelis (including the Munich athletes).[32] In January 1973, an Israeli air attack on Syria downed many defending planes and destroyed the entire Syrian village of Dail – 500 killed, by Syrian count.[33] In February, Israel shot down a Cairo-bound Libyan civilian airliner that strayed over the Sinai.

The UN General Assembly voiced concern in 1972 about Israel's military actions in Arab territories and, over U.S. objection, passed three resolutions: (1) condemnation of Israel's razing of 15,855 Palestinian homes in Gaza; (2) recommendation that Israel accept the return of the 1967 Palestinian refugees; and (3) declaration that the Palestinians have a right of self-determination. These kinds of favorable resolutions concerning Palestinians were of no practical help to Sadat or Assad.

Sadat breaks with Russia

Nixon, fearing a major outbreak of war in the Middle East and a possible U.S.-U.S.S.R. military clash, sent Kissinger to a summit in Moscow in May of 1972. Soviet Premier Leonid Brezhnev acceded to Kissinger's status quo Middle East policy[34] in exchange for U.S. credits and technology. Sadat and Assad saw that the humiliating and politically threatening Israeli military occupation of Arab soil was of no importance to the Russians.[35] Frustrated by this and by Brezhnev's failure to deliver arms as promised, Sadat ousted thousands of Soviet advisors from Egypt in July 1972. This unilateral action was a major surprise to both the United States and the U.S.S.R. Kissinger hailed the ouster as the "triumph" of his anti-Soviet Middle East policy. Yet the actual effect was that *(a)* the Soviets suddenly and heavily armed Syria in order to forestall a similar ouster there, and *(b)* the moderating effect of the Soviets on Sadat's sense of the inevitability war was removed. Kissinger's "triumph" ended up increasing the potential for war in the Middle East and strengthening Soviet influence in Syria.[36]

The last straw for Sadat was a February 1973 summit in Washington in which Meir fixedly refused to return the Sinai. She was full of mistaken confidence that Sadat had no military option. In fact, by courting Saudi Arabia's King Faisal, Sadat had obtained the necessary monies to make large purchases of Soviet arms.[37]

The October 6, 1973, Yom Kippur War – against the odds

Sadat and Assad agreed that the loss of sovereign territory in 1967 was intolerable. Egyptians were again rioting over Israel's continued occupation of the Egyptian Sinai. The two leaders secretly agreed that they would force Israel to engage in a two-front (Egyptian and Syrian) war.

Assad's goal was explicitly military – to push Israel out of Syria's Golan Heights. Sadat's goal was more political and diplomatic. He intended a limited military operation – seeking "only enough territory to show the Israelis that their forces were not invincible and, accordingly, that the Jewish state's security lay not in maintaining a territorial buffer [the Sinai] but in seeking good relations with its neighbors."[38] Sadat sought to end the stalemate and to shock the major powers and Israel into a realization that occupation of Arab territory was unacceptable and restoration of Arab dignity was paramount.[39]

Militarily, Egypt was clearly vulnerable to Israel's superior air power (faster planes and experienced pilots). Moreover, for Egypt to cross the Suez Canal to establish a beachhead on the east bank was considered impossible by all military observers. It would require building bridges under Israeli artillery fire on a canal that Israel would set aflame with oil. Even if successful in crossing, Egyptian soldiers and tanks would have to scale a seventy-foot hill of sand, stone and steel topped with artillery and fortresses along its 100-mile length. This formidable "Bar Lev Line" defense gave Meir confidence about Egyptian powerlessness.

Yet Egypt had some advantages – military, psychological and political. One military advantage was Egypt's air defense system, designed to protect Cairo, but equally able to protect soldiers and equipment from Israeli air attack if they stayed within 10 miles of the canal (the range of Egypt's defensive anti-aircraft missiles). Egyptian engineers thought, too, that they had solved the problem of penetrating the Bar Lev mountain of sand on the east bank by use of high-pressure water hoses! And the flaming oil? Egyptian frogmen believed that they could block Israeli discharge pipes on the east side of the canal. Because penetration seemed impossible, Israel posted only 451 frontline troops in the twenty forts along the top of the Bar Lev Line, another Egyptian advantage. While these IDF troops were backed up by an army of 18,000 men and 290 tanks sitting in the Sinai, these forces were not *immediately* at the canal. Israel and Egypt both had a total of 1,700 tanks, but Egyptian tanks were being surreptitiously moved within range of the west bank of the canal.[40] Syria, too, in the Golan Heights, had a greater number of tanks than did Israel.[41] Israeli intelligence was asleep.

Egypt's *psychological* advantage had to do with Israel's complacency about its invincibility and a certain racist assumption about the inferiority of Arab soldiers.[42] Ten days before the war, IDF Chief of Staff David Elazar expressed his contempt for Syrian forces, quipping, "We'll have one hundred tanks against their eight hundred. . . . That ought to be enough."[43]

Egypt's *political* advantage turned on Israeli politics. The governing Labor party was campaigning for re-election on claim that the Arabs were no military threat. The Egyptians reasoned that this Labor government, in the event of an Egyptian attack, would be hesitant to admit error and call up military reserves.

But Egypt's greatest advantage had to be *surprise* – a rapid crossing to a beachhead on the east bank of the canal on an unexpected day (Yom Kippur). Secrecy and deception were key. Egypt broadcast elaborately misleading military and diplomatic signals acknowledging the impossibility of crossing the canal.

The attack

The surprise worked, as did the pressure hoses and the plugging of the underwater oil-discharge pipes. In twenty-four hours Egypt successfully crossed half its army over the canal and established a beachhead on the east side. That alone seemed to make Egypt's symbolic point: that Israel was not invincible.

The Egyptians inflicted horrendous losses on the IDF for two days, as did the Syrians in the Golan Heights. Moshe Dayan told Meir on the second day of fighting, "We are heading towards a catastrophe. We shall have to withdraw on the Golan Heights to the edge of the escarpment overlooking the valley and in the south in Sinai to the passes and hold on to the last bullet."[44] After two and a half days, Israel had lost 49 airplanes and 500 tanks. Essentially, Egypt and Syria had succeeded in a massive ambush of an unprepared and overconfident IDF. While Egypt had planned and fought exceedingly well, a success turning on surprise, failed Israeli intelligence and a disorganized and disbelieving Israeli military command could not last indefinitely.[45] It took several more days for Israel to get its footing – to mobilize and transport men and tank reinforcements to both the Golan Heights and Sinai fronts – and turn the tide.

Rearming by the United States and the Soviet Union

Israeli officials flew to Washington to get an immediate airlift of military supplies. Washington hesitated. Saudi Arabia's King Faisal warned Nixon that a massive U.S. resupply of Israel could lead to an oil embargo against the United States. The CIA and the State and Defense Departments were not convinced that Israel needed more weapons. Problematic, too, was the politics of image. There was a principled difference between 1967 and 1973 – between helping Israel to (presumably) *protect* its borders in 1967 and helping Israel to retain its 1967 *conquests* in 1973. However, pro-Israeli Sen. Henry Jackson demanded immediate resupply of Israel. Israeli ambassador Simcha Dinitz threatened to "go public" if Nixon denied Israel arms. Moreover, the U.S. knew that Israel had and might use nuclear weapons. Nixon obliged with a U.S. airlift of conventional weapons – jets, tanks, electronics and missiles, "one of the largest airlifts ever undertaken" – and promised to replace all the arms lost in the war.[46] "We would risk confrontation with the Soviets," Kissinger admitted, putting at risk not only the détente with the Soviets but also Saudi oil.

For their part, the Soviets supplied Syria and Egypt with eighty-four more planes. Iraq moved 300 tanks toward the Syrian border. Libya pledged weapons and oil. Jordan's gesture was 150 old Centurion tanks.[47] King Faisal pledged $200 million and praised Sadat: "You have made us all proud."[48]

Israel regains its strength and fortunes turn

After days of bitter fighting on the Golan Heights, Israel turned the tide with tank reinforcements and announced publicly that it would advance on Damascus. An alarmed Assad asked Sadat to draw off the IDF from Syria by advancing Egyptian forces eastward into the Sinai. Sadat was reluctant to move forces beyond Egypt's protective air defense umbrella (beyond its secure beachhead on the east bank). Nevertheless, he felt bound to respond to Assad's needs for both political and military reasons. Not only was Assad an ally, but if Sadat refused

Assad's request, then Assad might fold and leave *Egypt* exposed to the full force of the IDF. Together, Syria and Egypt had a tiger by the tail and neither could let go.

The Soviets were pressing the United States to support a UN cease-fire and threatened to intervene militarily if Israel advanced on Damascus. Kissinger threatened U.S. military engagement if the Soviets intervened.[49] His intent was to block the Russian demand for a cease-fire in order to permit Israel to secure its rapid gains.[50] To stop the war before Israel had achieved victory would be, in his view, handing the Soviets a victory and weakening Israel's future negotiating power. As it turned out, Syria deflected Israel's advance on Damascus after a week of intense fighting.[51] But the Egyptian forces, advancing beyond their 10-mile defense umbrella, were devastated by Israeli air power.[52]

General Sharon was itching to cross the Suez Canal and advance to the Nile and Africa. The government's need of a symbolic victory overwhelmed military and political doubts. But military progress was slow. Rivalries between commanders, poor communications and disobedience afflicted the Israeli effort.[53] Moreover, the desert roads to the Suez Canal were completely jammed with Israeli armaments, including a barely portable (400-ton) bridge for crossing the canal. After days of traffic jam, Israel managed to get seventy tanks across the canal.

The Kremlin again pressed for a cease-fire and Kissinger again stalled, "to gain a little more time for Israel's offensive."[54] When Nixon, wounded by Vice President Spiro Agnew's resignation and Watergate, gave another $2.2 billion in emergency aid to Israel, Sadat admitted to himself that he could not fight both Israel and the United States.

Oil embargo

The Arab countries were furious about the $2.2 billion gift to Israel. OPEC imposed an oil embargo on the United States, an economic jihad that created chaos around the world. To lift the embargo, Nixon instructed Kissinger to discuss a joint, comprehensive Middle East plan with Brezhnev – the president ready to pressure the Israelis "regardless of the domestic political consequences." Kissinger ignored Nixon's instructions and arranged with Brezhnev a UN cease-fire to Israel's advantage.[55] While Meir objected, on October 22, 1973, UN Resolution 338 directed all parties to stop fighting and negotiate a "just and durable peace."[56] Meir had to accept, as did Sadat.[57]

Nuclear alert, cooling down and shuttle diplomacy

Kissinger appears to have given Meir his private approval for violation of the Resolution 338 cease-fire.[58] The Russians were furious when, over the next three days, Israel repeatedly violated the cease-fire. They saw the United States as reneging on its promise to control Israel and were embarrassed in front of the Arab states by their failure to make the United States and Israel keep their word. After the Russians proposed a second UN cease-fire resolution, Meir sent a "blistering" note to Kissinger accusing him of cooperating with the Soviets. She refused a new cease-fire, claiming that Egypt was the violator.[59] When the UN Security Council passed Resolution 339, reaffirming Resolution 338, Israel continued massive air and land attacks on the Egyptian city of Suez – presumably to prove continuing military prowess. However, an overconfident IDF was beaten back by local Egyptian defense forces.

Brezhnev again scolded Nixon about Israeli violations, ordered a fleet of transport ships to the Mediterranean and supported Sadat's request for a UN peacekeeping force to police the cease-fire. Kissinger saw this last as an unacceptable imposition on Israel and a Soviet ploy to get Soviet troops onto Middle East soil under UN auspices. He informed Brezhnev that the United States would veto UN peacekeeping forces in the Sinai. Brezhnev threatened unilateral action. U.S. military forces and nuclear units were put on world-wide alert.[60] U.S. aircraft carriers and bombers headed to the Mediterranean. The crisis was finally resolved when the United States and the U.S.S.R. agreed to install peacekeeping *observers* (not troops) to monitor (not enforce) the cease-fire in Egypt. Heavy U.S. pressure forced Israel to end cease-fire violations.

UN Resolution 440 demanded that all sides *return* to their former military positions at the time of the first cease-fire (October 22). Israel refused. Using "step-by-step" diplomacy, Kissinger treated Israel like a fragile and traumatized nation that would experience a "psychological collapse." were an overall settlement along the lines of Resolution 242 be imposed.[61] Over the next two years, he got some agreements: Israel and Syria made some military reductions in the Golan Heights and accepted a UN peace-keeping force separating their armies. In the Sinai, Israeli forces withdrew fifteen miles to the east of the Suez Canal with a UN peace-keeping force immediately east of the canal. These concessions from Israel came with a massive U.S. loan forgiveness of $1.5 billion in June 1975. Kissinger had averted any significant Israeli withdrawal from its 1967 territorial gains.

Consequences and costs of the Yom Kippur War

There was no decisive victor in the Yom Kippur War. Israel did push Syrian forces back from the Golan Heights, yet Syria had many remaining forces with which to fight. In the Sinai, Egypt did cross the Suez Canal to the east, but so did Israel to the west. And all armies suffered major losses. In nineteen days of combat, Egypt had 7,000 killed or wounded, Israel 11,600, Syria 9,100. In terms of equipment, Egypt lost 1,100 tanks, Israel 840, Syria 1,200; Egypt lost 223 aircraft, Israel 103, Syria 118.

Six months after the war, under mounting public pressure, Meir resigned, replaced by Yitzhak Rabin in June 1974.[62] Eight months after the war, Nixon also resigned, replaced by Gerald Ford. Kissinger, dubbed a "miracle man," appeared on the cover of *Newsweek* as a bespectacled Superman.

Kissinger blamed Israeli intransigence for his failure to get serious Israeli territorial withdrawals in exchange for Sadat's March 1975 pledge of "no use of force."[63] Israel did agree in September 1975 to another twenty to forty mile withdrawal east of the canal, a concession requiring a Ford/Kissinger promise "to be fully responsive on an on-going and long-term basis to Israel's military equipment and other defense requirements, to its energy requirements and to its economic needs"[64] – additionally, a promised "not to recognize or negotiate with the PLO as long as the PLO does not recognize Israel's right to exist."[65]

Notes

1. Abba Eban. Reported by Thomas L. Friedman, "Eban in '87 on Fringe of Politics" *New York Times,* June 14, 1987, 3.

2. A Palestinian state, it was argued, would become a launching pad for Arab missiles and armies – though Arab countries were already adjacent to Israel.

3. Most guerrilla groups were members: Fatah, George Habash's Marxist Popular Front for the Liberation of Palestine, the Syrian-sponsored Saiqa and the Iraqi-sponsored Arab Liberation Front. Combined, these groups had 15,000 to 30,000 members in 1970. Mark Tessler, *A History of the Israeli-Palestinian Conflict* (Bloomington: Indiana University Press, 1994), 430.

4. Alain Gresh, *The PLO: The Struggle Within, Toward an Independent Palestinian State* (London: Zed Books, 1985), 44.

5. Tessler, *History of Conflict,* 440.

6. Israel and its supporters vigorously denounced the secular state proposal and rejected the concept of Palestinian nationalism. Meir claimed in 1969 that there was no such thing as a separate Palestinian people or nation. Thus, the PLO's political

claims were artificial and no way comparable to the ancient and historical national rights of the Jews.

7. Harkabi pointed out that the PLO was vague about whether *all* Jews in Israel were to be included as citizens in the new Palestinian state. In 1969 and 1970, Palestinians increasingly *did* assert that all Jews presently in Palestine would be entitled to full citizenship in the proposed democratic state. Arafat stated in February 1970 that "every Jew who will give up the Zionist ideology" will be welcome (Gresh, *The PLO*, 44) and that Palestinians "would not insist on having an Arab majority" (*Time*, December 21, 1970). Harkabi also noted that the PLO criticized Israel as an undemocratic, theocratic state yet side-stepped the undemocratic and theocratic character of Arab nations. Yet revolutionary Palestinians *did* frequently assert the universality of their vision of secular, democratic states throughout the Arab world, and, in the case of George Habash of the PFLP, overtly condemned these reactionary Arab states. Tessler, *History of Conflict*, 441.

8. William Quandt, Fuad Jabber, and Ann Mosely Lesch, *The Politics of Palestinian Nationalism* (Berkeley: University of California Press, 1977), 107.

9. Tessler, *History*, 443. "Even though some critical analyses of the PLO's ideology may be persuasive, it does not follow that the Palestinians' proposals were put forward with duplicity and cynicism" (442).

10. Tessler, *History of Conflict*, 444.

11. The Rogers Plan was a *variation* on Resolution 242: *(a)* Israel should withdraw from *all* Arab lands captured in 1967 in exchange for binding peace treaties with Arab countries; *(b)* Israel would be guaranteed freedom of passage through international waterways; *(c)* the Palestinian refugees would be allowed to choose between repatriation and compensation; and *(d)* Jordan and Israel should seek direct agreement on the future of Jerusalem. The reasoning behind the Rogers Plan was based on Israel's claim that its initiation of the 1967 Six Day War had only been for *defensive* purposes necessary for security. If true, Resolution 242 peace treaties with Arab countries would have satisfied Israel's concerns, which they clearly didn't.

12. Israel affirmed that "Israel will not be sacrificed by any power or interpower policy and will reject any attempt to impose a forced solution on her." William B. Quandt, *Decade of Decisions: American Policy toward the Arab-Israeli Conflict* (Berkeley: University of California Press, 1977), 91.

13. Chief of Staff Mordechai Gur, interview, summarized by Ze'ev Schiff (*Ha'aretz*, May 15, 1978).

14. The Soviets had previously financed the Aswan Dam and other projects as a counterweight to U.S. financial and military aid to Israel.

15. Arab alienation from the United States was expressed by "rupture of diplomatic relations with Washington by six Arab countries, reduction in economic interchange, expulsions of Western residents in the area, closing and sequestering of American schools, universities and libraries, temporary oil embargoes, suspension of overflight rights, boycotts of Western shipping, trade and banking, total or partial

nationalization of certain enterprises, and threats of drastic action against the oil companies. It was this alienation that the Soviet Union exploited to its own advantage by trying to substitute itself for the diminishing Western presence in the area." George Lenczowski, *Soviet Advances in the Middle East* (Washington,: American Enterprise Institute, 1971), 162-3.

By 1970, the Soviets had make some significant Middle East gains, e.g., naval bases off the Egyptian Mediterranean coast rivaling those of the United States CIA, *Mediterranean Strategy and Force Structure Study* (extract), August 19, 1970, 3. Cited in Neff, *Israel*, 61.

16. Kissinger: "Nixon probably spent as much time mediating between Rogers and me as between the Arabs and Israelis." Cited in Seymour M. Hersch, *The Price of Power: Kissinger in the Nixon White House* (New York: Summit Books, 1983), 349.

17. Nixon: "One of the main problems I faced . . . was the unyielding and shortsighted pro-Israel attitude in large and influential segments of the American Jewish community, Congress, the media and in intellectual and cultural circles. In the quarter-century since the end of World War II this attitude had become so deeply ingrained that many saw the corollary of not being pro-Israel as being anti-Israel, or even anti-Semitic. I tried unsuccessfully to convince them that this was not the case." Richard M. Nixon, *The Memoirs of Richard Nixon* (New York: Grosset and Dunlap, 1978), 481. On Nixon's disagreement with Kissinger, see Henry Kissinger, *White House Years* (New York: Little, Brown and Co., 1979), 564.

18. Especially from Ali Sabri, a former prime minister and the second strongest political power in Egypt after Nasser.

19. Tessler, *History of Conflict*, 458.

20. Palestinian guerrillas were based in Jordan. The IDF entered the Jordanian village of Karameh and killed 170. The IDF lost 28. One hundred other Jordanians were killed. Tessler, *History of Conflict*, 425.

21. Tessler, *History of Conflict*, 463.

22. Meir was "incapable either by temperament or by age of modifying her views of the Arabs as perennial enemies with whom one dealt not in trust but out of strength." Howard Sachar, *A History of Israel*, Vol. I (New York: Knopf, 1986), 711.

23. The Allon Plan, drafted shortly after the 1967 war, called for a division of the West Bank. About half, on the west side, was to be returned to Jordan, the east side retained by Israel. The Jordanian half was to be further divided into north and south pieces connected by a single road passing through Israeli territory. The northwestern piece was also to be connected to Jordan through a narrow eastward corridor.

24. "By the end of 1971, the divisions within our government . . . had produced the stalemate for which I had striven by design." Kissinger, *White House Years*, 1289.

25. George McGovern, the Democratic presidential candidate, also felt the need to propose that the U.S. Embassy be moved from Tel Aviv to Jerusalem, which virtually

no country recognized as Israel's capital.

26. The United States would also sell jet engines which Israel put in Mirage III fighters manufactured in Israel from stolen Swiss blueprints. Neff, *Israel*, 69.

27. Quandt, *Decade of Decisions*, 147. Quandt was an NSC analyst.

28. Tessler, *History of Conflict*, 472.

29. Sharon was reprimanded by an Israeli military commission. Yoram Peri, *Between Ballots and Bullets: Israeli Military in Politics* (Cambridge: Cambridge University Press, 1983), 97.

30. The "Black September" group (named for the 1970 civil war in Jordan) and the PFLP were upstaging Arafat's less-effective Fatah. The Fatah, dating from the mid 1960s, was not as radical, ideological or aggressive in its attacks on Israeli property, facilities or persons as the PFLP. The PFLP was highly ideological, intensely anti-imperialist, pro-Marxist and anti-Arab-monarchist. PFLP founder George Habash, radicalized by the 1967 war, declared: "We do not want peace. Peace would be the end of all our hopes. . . . We had to shock both an indifferent world and a demoralized Palestine nation. The world has forgotten Palestine." Neff, *Israel*, 74.

31. It appears that the intent of the action was to take Israeli athletes for a hostage exchange for 200 Palestinian guerrillas in Israeli jails. The Germans wanted to negotiate, but the Israelis refused, insisting on surrender or death. Setting a trap of pretended negotiations, Israeli agents opened fire along with 600 German sharpshooters. Neff, *Israel*, 94-6.

32. Neff, *Israel*, 103. Arab totals taken from battles described in Neff and Tessler.

33. UN investigators confirmed at least 125 through eyewitness accounts.

34. "I got the blandest possible Middle East formulation . . . acceptance of the status quo . . . bound to be taken ill not only in Cairo but elsewhere in the Arab world. As far as we were concerned, our objectives were served if the status quo was maintained until the Soviets modified their stand or moderate Arab states turned to us for a solution." Kissinger, *White House Years*, 1247.

35. The Moscow summit was frustrating to Assad who had, until then, been signaling the United States a new willingness to make peace with Israel in exchange for an end to the occupation, i.e., an acceptance of Resolution 242.

36. Neff, *Israel*, 89, 90.

37. Sadat was able to win over King Faisal by distancing himself from Nasser's antimonarchistic, communistic sympathies. For Faisal, Zionism and communism were the two evils of the world. Hence, he looked favorably on Sadat's ouster of the Soviets. Faisal's oil money was to be used to regain occupied Arab lands and Jerusalem, the third most holy city in Islam. Faisal also threatened an embargo on oil to the United States: "America's complete support of Zionism against the Arabs makes it extremely difficult for us to continue to supply U.S. petroleum needs and even to maintain friendly relations with America." Neff, *Israel*, 113. Faisal became king in 1964, replacing his deposed brother, King Saud.

38. Tessler, *History*, 479-80.

39. Fred J. Khouri, *The Arab-Israeli Dilemma* (Syracuse, N.Y.: Syracuse

University Press, 1985), 370.

40. Khouri, *Dilemma*, 140, 144.

41. Syrian troops and tanks numbered 60,000 and 1,300, respectively, compared to Israeli troops and tanks of 12,000 and 177, respectively. Neff, *Israel*, 146.

42. A U.S. House of Representatives subcommittee study later concluded that U.S. and Israeli intelligence underestimated the Arabs because of a belief that the Arab soldier "lacks the necessary physical and cultural qualities for performing effective military services." Neff, *Israel*, 130.

43. Neff, *Israel*, 130.

44. Chaim Herzog, *The War of Atonement* (Tel Aviv: Steimatzky's Agency, 1975), 116.

45. "The highly efficient execution of carefully prepared plans resulted in one of the most memorable water crossings in the annals of warfare. . . . No other army could have done better." Trevor N. Dupuy, *Elusive Victory: The Arab-Israeli Wars, 1947-1974* (New York: Harper and Row, 1978), 417.

46. Neff, *Israel*, 221, 231. Neff reports that Kissinger ordered a United States airlift that exceeded the Soviet resupply of the Arabs by twenty-five percent, comprising 22,300 tons of equipment and 88 planes, citing *Aviation Week and Space Technology*, December 10, 1973, 16-9.

47. Under Arab pressure, King Hussein had to make a token contribution. Hussein wanted Israel to assure him that it would not counterattack. Israel refused but was relieved not to have to engage on a third front. Neff, *Israel*, 213.

48. Neff, *Israel*, 211.

49. Henry Kissinger, *Years of Upheaval* (Boston: Little, Brown and Co., 1982), 501-2.

50. Kissinger acknowledged, "We had been stalling the Soviets for twenty-four hours on a ceasefire in place," and complained to the Israelis that their announced advance on Damascus would cause the Soviets to see in his stall a collusion with Israel. Kissinger, *Years of Upheaval*, 504.

51. Syrian success was partly due to the assistance, however uncoordinated, of some Iraqi tanks and token forces from Jordan, Kuwait and Saudi Arabia.

52. Golda Meir ascribed this victory to the U.S. weapons resupply: Golda Meir, *My Life* (New York: G. P. Putnam's Sons, 1975), 431.

53. Neff, *Israel*, 195-6. The southern commander, Shmuel Goren, wanted to relieve Sharon of his command for disobeying orders. Many suspected that Sharon, running for office with Begin, was seeking to be an instant hero in order to enhance his political fortunes. His tank division was dubbed the "Likud Party Division."

54. Kissinger, *Years of Upheaval*, 538-41.

55. Neff, *Israel*, 262. Kissinger knew that a UN-sponsored cease-fire would involve delays that would provide Israel time for last-minute gains. The *in place* cease-fire would permit Israel's retention of those gains.

56. The Arabs considered that UN 338 undermined Resolution 242 because the latter called for the return of land *before* peace negotiations were undertaken.

57. Syria delayed acceptance for two days.

58. Kissinger told the Israelis he would understand if there was a few hours' "slippage" in the cease-fire deadline. He cabled the Israeli ambassador, "We would understand if Israelis felt they required some additional time." Department of State, Flash Top Secret Moscow #13148, "Eyes Only for [Brent] Scowcroft from Kissinger," October 21, 1973. Cited in Neff, *Israel*, 271.

59. Kissinger admitted that Meir's claim was "imposing on my credulity."

60. DefCon III, state of readiness just short of a determination that war was likely.

61. Kissinger, *Years of Upheaval*, 615.

62. Rabin replaced Defense Minister Dayan with his political rival Shimon Peres.

63. Steven L. Spiegel, *The Other Arab-Israeli Conflict* (Chicago: University of Chicago Press, 1985), 292. President Ford was "mad as hell" at the Israelis, declaring: "Again the Egyptians bent over backward. Again the Israelis resisted" (295).

64. Edward R. E. Sheehan, *The Arabs, Israelis, and Kissinger: A Secret History of American Diplomacy in the Middle East* (New York: Reader's Digest Press, 1976), 190. Included were guarantees of all domestic oil needs; contingency planning for emergency arms transport; annual military and economic aid packages from Congress; advanced equipment (F-16s); a study of transfer of Pershing missiles (usually for atomic warheads); and support against threats by a "world power" (i.e., the Soviet Union).

65. The PLO idea of a democratic state of Arabs and Jews in Palestine was taken as a denial of an exclusively Jewish state's (Israel's) right to exist.

Chapter 17

The PLO, the West Bank and the Lebanon Wars (1982)

Though guerrilla/terrorists remained within the organization, the Palestine Liberation Organization reduced military operations after 1973 and made public efforts to find long-term political solutions to the Palestinian-Israeli conflict. The PLO revised its 1969 proposal for a unitary, secular state over all of Palestine and advanced a more practical proposal in 1974: *partition* of Palestine into Israel and a small Palestinian state consisting of Gaza and the West Bank. The PLO was looking for a comprehensive Middle East solution that might satisfy both Jewish and Palestinian national aspirations.

This two-state idea won considerable international attention and support. In November of 1974, Arafat was permitted to address the United Nations. In 1975 the General Assembly granted observer status to the PLO and acknowledged the Palestinian people's "right to national independence and sovereignty."[1] The UN also called for Israeli withdrawal from all territories occupied in 1967 and member states were instructed to refrain from economic and military aid to Israel until this was accomplished. According to Abba Eban, the PLO "leaped forward to broad international recognition" despite the fact that the United States rejected the notion of Palestinian rights and vetoed UN affirmation of those rights.[2] However, storm clouds in Lebanon obscured the trajectory of the PLO's star.

Civil war in Lebanon 1975-1976 – Christian minority (and Israel) versus Moslem majority (and PLO)

A civil war in Lebanon had a major effect on Palestinian refugees residing in camps in southern Lebanon. In 1975 there were some 250,000 to 300,000 such refugees who had fled the 1948 and 1967 wars (330,000 by 1982). The PLO was active in the administration of these camps and headquartered in Lebanon after its ranks had been depleted and routed during the Jordanian civil war of 1970-1971.

The Lebanese factions at war with each other were many and complex. Their differences related to sect, class, money, political power and attitudes about the presence of Palestinians, Syrians and Israelis in Lebanon. In a country composed of strong factional differences in diverse local communities, national unity was virtually nonexistent – fertile ground for civil war.

The official Lebanese government was traditionally dominated by an elite group of Maronite Christians, who made up some 2 to 3 percent of the population, while the working-class majority was Moslem.[3] The presence of the PLO in Lebanon was an additional provocative factor in the civil war in that the Maronite Christians largely opposed the PLO while the Moslem majority largely accepted the PLO and Palestinian refugees in their country.[4] The Maronite Christian government had traditional "rightist" links with the West and increasingly with Israel.[5] Its military force was also loosely aligned with various independent Christian militia groups which clashed with the more-populist Moslem and Druze militias comprising the Lebanese National Movement (LNM). The PLO entered the civil war after Maronite Christian forces attacked a Palestinian refugee camp, Tal al-Zaatar, in early 1976.[6]

The opponents in this civil war were not simply the Christian right and the Moslem left. Rivalrous Christian militias battled each other. For example, Christian *Phalangist* fought Christian *non-Phalangists*. And these opposing Christian groups sought support from opposing foreign countries, e.g., Israel and Syria.[7] Even *within* Pierre Gemayel's Christian Phalangist party, his two sons led competing militias. Bashir Gemayel hoped to oust the PLO and the Syrians from Lebanon and, to that end, received $150 million in arms from Israel during the three-year Rabin administration.[8] On the other hand, Bashir's brother, Amin, blamed Israel for forcing Palestinians to flee into Lebanon and sought support from Israel's enemy, Syria. Bashir Gemayel's Christian Phalangist militia, in alignment with Israel, finally dominated during the civil war and figured in Israel's invasion of Lebanon in 1982.

Israel was not only a player through support of Bashir Gemayel's Christian Phalangist militia but additionally maintained its own surrogate militia in southern Lebanon, called the South Lebanese Army (SLA). Led by Saad Haddad, the SLA continually clashed with PLO guerrillas.

Syria, the other major player, had 35,000 troops and 200 tanks in Lebanon.[9] Initially supportive of the LNM and the PLO, Syria gradually shifted toward neutrality in an effort to preserve a military balance and political stability in Lebanon.[10] This tangled civil war between diverse Lebanese factions was, in fact, a kind of proxy war between Israel and the PLO and Israel and Syria.

The civil war will not be described beyond this inventory of participants relevant to the later 1982 Israeli invasion. But when this devastatingly brutal and complex civil war ended in late 1976, the lives of some 60,000 to 80,000 Lebanese had been lost, with perhaps three times that number wounded.[11] Syria was assigned a peace-keeping role by agreement between the antagonists. But nothing was resolved, indeed, Lebanon's sectarian and class antagonisms only deepened.

Palestinian refugees suffered greatly during the civil war, yet their national identity strengthened. After the war, the influence of the PLO in Lebanon was enhanced because the PLO filled a social-service vacuum left by wartime disruption of normal UN and Lebanese government services in the camps. Using financial aid from oil-producing Arab states, the PLO maintained electric and telephone services and opened workshops, factories, eight new hospitals (for the Palestine Red Crescent Society) and twelve new clinics for Lebanese and Palestinians alike. The PLO constituted a virtual state within Lebanon and had roughly 15,000 fighters in southern Lebanon along coastal areas (from Tyre to Beirut) and inland (south of the Beirut-Damascus Highway).[12] Less felicitous were some Fatah factions of the PLO that acted improperly toward Lebanese villagers. Despite Arafat's efforts to control his men, commanders sometimes intimidated Lebanese villagers, extracted taxes, extorted money from the wealthy.[13] However, the PLO presence in Lebanon was relatively secure after the war until Israel made peace with Egypt and turned north to destroy the PLO.

Sadat's olive branch and the Camp David Accords (1977)

Shocking to the PLO in 1977 were two major events. Firstly, Anwar Sadat extended an olive branch to Israel, effectively separating Egyptian interests from those of the Palestinians. Secondly, Menachem Begin, former guerrilla/terrorist and Greater Israel hawk, was elected prime minister of Israel. Begin was intent on retaining the West Bank and Gaza[14] and crushing the Palestinians' PLO leadership ensconced in Lebanon.

The Sadat peace initiative was partly a response to poor economic conditions in Egypt. The Yom Kippur War had drained the government of funds. Reduced government food subsidies resulted in riots in January 1977. The increased cost of food sparked attacks on police stations, shops and hotels. In Cairo alone, army intervention resulted in seventy-seven civilian deaths. The new U.S. president, Jimmy Carter, offered aid to Sadat as a reward for peace with Israel. Carter was fond of Sadat and encouraged him to think in terms of future economic, military and political ties with the United States similar to those enjoyed by Israel.

In contrast to Henry Kissinger's focus on global communism, Carter focused on Third World human rights issues. The Palestinian cause and comprehensive settlement of the Middle East conflict were central issues in his administration. He was, thus, unpopular with American Jews and from the very first made statements such as: "There has to be a homeland provided for the Palestinian refugees"[15] and "For many years [Assad] has been a strong supporter in the search for peace."[16] Carter's unpopularity also related to his desire to curb arms sales to Israel and to encourage Soviet and Saudi pressure on Israel and the Arabs to come to the negotiating table.[17] Carter had no sympathy for Begin's declared intention to retain and build Jewish settlements in the West Bank, Gaza and the Sinai.[18] He bluntly declared the settlements to be both a "serious obstacle to peace" and "illegal." (The 1907 Hague International Convention prohibits an occupying power from confiscating land, property, food and water resources – Israel pipes 80 percent of West Bank water to Israel and Jewish settlers – and the Fourth Geneva Convention prohibits an occupier from establishing any settlements for its population in occupied territory.)

It was, however, Sadat, not Carter, who advanced negotiations otherwise locked in tension and stalemate. Sadat artfully circumvented conflicts between Carter and Begin, bracketed Syria's conflict with Israel, ignored the Saudis and startled the world by addressing the Knesset on November 19, 1977. Sadat's bold proposal was for a *bilateral* peace agreement between Egypt and Israel.

Sadat's unilateral action suggested to Arab states that he might be seeking a *separate* "land for peace" deal with Israel in order to get back the Sinai, leaving his Jordanian, Syrian and Palestinian brothers to fend for themselves. His words suggested otherwise. Sadat insisted that Israel's withdrawal from *all* Arab territories captured in 1967 was a fundamental necessity for peace and would be the only basis for Israel's security. He promised to accept all international guarantees demanded by Israel and included the Palestinian issue as essential to any durable and just peace. "It is no use to refrain from recognizing the Palestinian people and their right to statehood as their right of return."[19]

The response was one of skepticism. The Arab states and Palestinians feared that Sadat's solo overture to Israel might unwittingly result in a piecemeal Middle East solution. The United States, Jordan and Saudi Arabia were skeptical because Egypt and Israel were so far apart on major issues (notably Begin's intention to retain the West Bank and the Golan Heights at all cost).

It was Begin's hope to counter Sadat's dramatic visit. In consultation with Washington, he made a counterproposal: a *partial* withdrawal from the Sinai in exchange for (*a*) a peace treaty with Egypt and (*b*) negotiations concerning limited administrative autonomy for the West Bank and Gaza. Carter believed, naively it proved, that the autonomy idea was offered in good faith. The offer of only partial withdrawal displeased Sadat. Then Begin underscored his position by defiantly and provocatively beginning new construction of Sinai settlements two months after Sadat's visit to Israel. He also affronted the Palestinians with a vastly expanded network of Jewish settlements in the West Bank and Gaza. Clearly he intended to "create facts on the ground" that would reduce the chance of any future Israeli withdrawal from the Sinai or the West Bank. Moreover, Begin was stepping up support of Christian militia operations against the Palestinians' PLO leadership in Lebanon.[20] Secretary of State Cyrus Vance insisted in vain that a comprehensive settlement in the Middle East had to include the Palestinians, not simply a bilateral agreement between Egypt and Israel.

Carter invited Sadat and Begin to Camp David in September 1978 to reconcile their differences. Begin absolutely rejected withdrawal from the West Bank and Gaza. He reiterated his proposal for partial withdrawal from the Sinai in exchange for a peace treaty – insisting on keeping an airfield and new Jewish settlements in the Sinai. After Carter offered a $3 billion loan to move the airfield to the Negev, Begin agreed and gave up the settlements.

The Egyptian-Israeli peace treaty (concluded in March 1979) specified that Israeli withdrawal from the Sinai would occur within *three* years. Egypt assured Israel free passage through the Suez Canal and Gulf of Aqaba. Also agreed upon in vague language was that the status of the West Bank and Gaza would be negotiated on the basis of UN 242 and in recognition of the legitimate rights of the Palestinians (final status to be negotiated within five years). Until then, autonomy in the West Bank and Gaza would proceed through Palestinian elections aimed at creating a self-governing authority. IDF occupation forces would be withdrawn. (Note: This plan for autonomy without sovereignty, with nearly all matters to be negotiated, was the forerunner of the Shamir autonomy plan of 1989 and the Oslo Peace Accords of 1993.)

Normalization of Egyptian-Israeli relations (business, education, tourism and diplomacy) proceeded on schedule. In this respect, Camp David proved to be a significant breakthrough. Negotiations over autonomy in the West Bank and Gaza foundered. Begin claimed to a frustrated Carter that at Camp David he had promised only to *negotiate,* not to *agree* to any particular outcome concerning autonomy. Then Begin began construction of even more settlements in the West Bank and Gaza, deepening rather than reducing the Israeli presence which Carter understood Begin to have promised. Jordan gave up hope that these autonomy negotiations would come to anything, particularly since Israel and Egypt could not agree about which Palestinians should be allowed to vote, what autonomies were to be included and in what locations.[21]

Palestinian leaders, as well as some members of Begin's own cabinet, saw "autonomy" as Begin's way of disguising his intent to legitimatize Israel's occupation.[22] Certainly, autonomy was a nonstarter. There were no Palestinian elections, no self-governing authority and no withdrawal of any Israeli forces. Begin's opposition to Palestinian self-rule and Israeli withdrawal was evident upon his return from Camp David when he openly declared his opposition to any division of Palestine.[23] Yosef Burg, the minister of the interior, head of the National Religious Party and head of the Israeli delegation for autonomy talks, expressed Begin's position that autonomy was dangerous and could lead to a Palestinian state: "My task [is] to prevent that possibility absolutely."[24]

Consequences of the Camp David Accords

The Egyptian-Israeli separate peace impaired chances for a comprehensive settlement of Palestinian and Syrian conflicts with Israel. The Camp David Accords, freeing Israel of military entanglements with Egypt, enabled the IDF to go north to crush the PLO in Lebanon.[25] The return of the Sinai also gave Begin some room to argue that UN 242 was now satisfied – that return of the Golan Heights, the West Bank and Gaza was not required. And nothing in the accords precluded a creeping annexation of the West Bank and Gaza through settlement expansion.[26]

Over the next several years, Begin doubled the number of West Bank settlements, tripled the Jewish population in the West Bank and increased five-fold the number of Jewish settlers inserted, provocatively, into densely packed, traditional Palestinian centers. Begin also sought to change the *legal status* of the territories by imposing Israeli law[27] – though it was illegal to do so under the Hague International Conventions and the Fourth Geneva Convention. After 1979, legal restrictions on Jewish land acquisition in the West Bank were effectively removed, giving the government the authority to seize virtually any area it considered desirable for settlement.[28]

(Note: Begin set a precedent for future prime ministers. Israel gained exclusive control of 35 percent of the West Bank by 1983;[29] 50 percent by 1988;[30] and 64 percent to 70 percent by 1994,[31] with 80 percent of West Bank water going to Israel or Jewish settlements.[32])

A Begin-Shamir-Sharon hard-line government; Sadat assassinated

Defense Minister Ezer Weizman and Foreign Minister Moshe Dayan were highly critical of Begin for his intransigence concerning implicit Camp David promises about Palestinian autonomy. Both men resigned over the issue, on May 1980 and October 1979, respectively. Begin replaced Dayan with Yitzhak Shamir on March 1980.

When Begin faced re-election in June 1981, he barely won. His coalition of ultranationalist, religious parties raised doubts and fears among the Israeli public, the Labor party and liberal groups such as Peace Now.[33] Yet Begin profited from class warfare in Israel as well as from the divisiveness within the Labor party caused by enmity between Yitzhak Rabin and Shimon Peres.[34] The more frustrated, more chauvinist working-class Sephardim in Israel, an ever-increasing portion of the population, favored Begin ("the King of Israel") over the traditional ruling elite, the monied European-bred Ashkenazim.[35] Moreover, a few days before the election, Begin ordered the bombing of Iraq's nuclear reactor – an action unnecessary at that time that elicited harsh international and U.S. criticism, but which enhanced the prime minister's standing with the public.[36]

The new government, a kind of Begin-Shamir-Sharon triumvirate (Ariel Sharon became defense minister) marked the definitive *end* of the long domination of government by the Labor party (1948 to 1977). It was a triumvirate that easily dismissed the views of others in the cabinet and created a solid front aimed at the destruction of the PLO and maximal retention of occupied territory.

Four months after Begin's re-election, Sadat was assassinated by Moslem fundamentalists.[37] Begin's militance went unchecked by Egypt's new president, Hosni Mubarak, who acquiesced to the collapse of the autonomy negotiations in order not to jeopardize a promised Israeli withdrawal from the Sinai, due in April 1982 and still six months away.

Begin's hard-line policies in the territories were not, however, completely unopposed. International bodies increasingly recognized the legitimacy of the Palestinian cause and the PLO. After Yasir Arafat and other PLO leaders consulted with the heads of many European nations, formal recognition of the PLO was granted by Italy and Austria. And a nine-member European Council had already in 1980 affirmed the Palestinians' right to self-determination and recommended a two-state solution in Palestine in the Venice Declaration (supported by Egypt and Morocco). This declaration called for the halt of illegal Jewish settlement, end of the occupation and inclusion of the PLO in future negotiations. This support of the PLO had little effect on Begin. While PLO officials had repeatedly indicated to Begin in the early 1980s their "readiness for a political settlement based on compromise" and Arafat indicated in private that he would recognize Israel in return for a Palestinian state in the West Bank and Gaza, Begin continued to insist "that the PLO was a terrorist organization dedicated to the destruction of the Jewish state."[38]

Sharon expands settlements and tightens control over Palestinians

Able to control the army and dominate Begin's cabinet from his position as defense minister, Ariel Sharon sought to undermine Palestinian nationalism and create irreversible "facts on the ground" that would assure Israel *de facto* sovereignty over the West Bank and Gaza. His approach was three-pronged: (1) change of the demographic character of the West Bank and Gaza through Jewish settlement; (2) undermining of Palestinian nationalism by establishing an Israeli-controlled alternative leadership to the PLO; and (3) intensifying military operations in order to halt Palestinian resistance to occupation.

Moreover, demographic change in the occupied territories was no longer to depend on religious, ultranationalist Jewish settlers. The government built and subsidized housing for ordinary Israelis in Gaza and the West Bank. Many Israelis were lured to bedroom communities within commuting distance of Jerusalem and Tel Aviv. In the fall of 1982 there were some 20,000 to 25,000 Jews in 103 Jewish settlements in the West Bank, but Sharon's goal was 300,000 by the end of the decade. The government was spending roughly 8 percent of its total annual budget on settlement building.

President Carter, still in office in the fall of 1980, had little power or energy to halt the expansion. He was preoccupied with the Iranian hostage crisis, the Iran-Iraq war, the Soviet invasion of Afghanistan and a re-election struggle with Ronald Reagan. Having stressed the illegality[39] of Jewish settlements, where his election opponent saw mere "obstacles to peace," Carter had weakened his image with the American public and efficacy in Middle East affairs.[40]

Sharon, Begin and Menachem Milson (a university professor appointed by Sharon to be head of the Civilian Administration in the West Bank) believed that Palestinian nationalism could be curbed by an imposition of an *alternative leadership* in the occupied territories. Because they believed that Palestinian nationalism and resistance to occupation was a *creation of the PLO*, not an ambition independently shared by the people,[41] Milson reasoned that were the PLO leadership removed, Palestinians would welcome an alternative leadership, even one controlled by Israel. Accordingly, Milson dismissed many Palestinian mayors and municipal councils elected in 1976 and replaced them with Israelis and/or collaborating Palestinians in "village leagues" (new local administrations).[42] The plan failed badly and finally was abandoned.

Other methods were adopted to undermine Palestinian nationalism. Sharon periodically shut down West Bank universities in an attempt to silence nationalist sentiment. The army sometimes controlled the selection of faculty, students and textbooks; censored newspapers; arrested publishers; and banned all newspapers and books coming into the West Bank and Gaza from outside.[43]

Sharon's attempt to end resistance to occupation through increased intimidation led him to sanction the use of live ammunition by the army at demonstrations, to arrest and jail demonstrators without bringing charges and to impose collective punishments on the Palestinian population (curfews, demolitions of homes of suspected terrorists, land expropriations, etc.). Jewish settlers were permitted, sometimes encouraged, to take the law into their own hands and were rarely held accountable for murders. The Karp Report of May 1982 documented settler crimes and the government's complicity.[44]

Intimidation of Syrians in the Golan Heights was also intended to end their resistance to occupation. But when Israel annexed the Golan Heights in December 1981 (by the claim that Israeli law, jurisdiction and administration had application there),[45] the Druze community in the Heights was angered. This fiercely independent sect of Arabs, ordinarily friendly to and favorably treated by Israel, cut off relations with the IDF and called a strike. The IDF resorted to brutal coercion and collective punishments.[46]

Israeli doves and some Labor party leaders objected in vain to Sharon's harsh policies in the occupied territories. Some reservists publicized accounts of military orders to beat, humiliate and intimidate Palestinian inhabitants, and public opinion polls showed that at least half of Israeli citizens had reservations about the government's settlement policies. Favored was a return of occupied land in exchange for peace. But when Palestinians in the West Bank and Gaza and the Druze in the Golan Heights refused to be intimidated by the IDF, mounting demonstrations, calling strikes and throwing stones (and even some grenades), the cycle of mutual violence simply escalated.

Reagan, Haig and Sharon in 1981

Israel was relieved to be rid of Carter and welcomed Reagan's November 1980 victory. Secretary of State Alexander Haig was even more taken with the idea that Israel was a "strategic asset" than was his boss. The old Cold-War warrior, like Kissinger before him, ignored the Israeli-Palestinian conflict in favor of U.S. and Soviet "global" issues. Haig wanted to fashion a "strategic consensus" in Israel, Egypt, Jordan and Saudi Arabia in opposition to the Soviet Union (and, implicitly, its presumed surrogates, Syria and the PLO).[47] He was far off the mark. Jordan and Saudi Arabia informed Haig that the chief Middle East problem was the conflict between Israel and the *Palestinians* – that the Soviets could play the Middle East card only because there *already* existed a problem, that problem being Israel's insistence on retaining the occupied territories and ending Palestinian resistance to occupation.

Haig took a rather passive if not permissive stance toward the Begin-Shamir-Sharon intent to crush the PLO leadership in Lebanon, oust the Syrians and control the Christian government of Lebanon. This last idea, Lebanon allied with Israel, was an old and popular idea which David Ben-Gurion and protégé Moshe Dayan had insistently advanced during the mid-1950s and before.[48] Now, with the PLO in Lebanon in 1981, the idea was again actively advanced by Sharon and IDF Chief of Staff Rafael Eitan. In fact, as soon as he was made defense minister by Begin, Sharon made preparations for an invasion of Lebanon to destroy the PLO and set up a puppet Lebanese government.[49] This invasion was to be the first step in Sharon's grand design for the whole Middle East. It was a design premised on Israeli military might[50] in which destruction of the PLO and control of the Lebanese government were to be simultaneously solved in a single military adventure – an initial, massive "clean-up" step in a larger geopolitical design. Historian Howard Sachar describes that design:

> He intended first to crush the PLO as a military-political factor in Lebanon, then in Palestine, and subsequently to complete the annexation of the West Bank and Gaza. With these goals achieved, Sharon would proceed to unseat King Hussein and give Jordan over in its entirety to the Palestinians, who already comprised two-thirds of the population there. Syria and Iraq were to

be destabilized . . . and [Lebanon to retain] a Maronite-dominated regime under the presidency of Bashir Gemayel [who was loyal to Israel]. . . . The implications of this master plan were clear, and they far transcended the destruction of Palestinian guerrilla concentrations along Israel's northern frontier ["Peace in Galilee"], or even of PLO influence in the West Bank.[51]

Lebanon as the key to control of the West Bank

Sharon's intention to control the West Bank and Gaza through IDF intimidation and imposition of an Israeli-controlled leadership had failed. Destruction of the PLO, the Palestinian leadership headquartered in Lebanon, was now seen as the key to the pacification of Palestinians in the occupied territories. Presumably, a leaderless demoralized people would submit to Israeli control. Sharon believed, "Following the elimination of the PLO in Beirut, the road will be open for real negotiations with the Arabs of Eretz Israel."[52] The war in Lebanon against the PLO was not primarily about terrorism in Galilee but was premised on an Israeli belief that the PLO was the root *cause* of Palestinian nationalism and resistance to Israeli rule in the territories.[53] As one U.S. State Department official put it: "The Israeli government believes it has a Palestinian problem because of the PLO; not that it has a PLO problem because of Palestinians."[54]

Background on hostilities leading to war in Lebanon

It will be recalled that Israel was active in Lebanon during the 1975-1976 civil war, pursuing the destruction of the PLO through support of Christian and SLA militias. Begin had initiated a large-scale air, land and sea invasion (Operation Litani) in March 1978, seizing all of southern Lebanon up to the Litani River. Over 1,000 civilian Palestinians and Lebanese were killed in that operation and 100,000 to 200,000 fled their homes.[55] Carter condemned the attack as a "terrible overreaction"[56] and condemned Israel's use of American weapons, including cluster bombs, in violation of U.S.-Israeli agreements. In the UN, the United States sponsored a resolution calling for Israeli withdrawal from Lebanon and establishment of an interim UN peace-keeping force. Israel reluctantly withdrew but refused to allow the UN to replace Israel's surrogate militia (the SLA) on the southern Lebanon border.

Once Reagan had replaced Carter, Begin and Sharon had freedom to mount major attacks in Lebanon designed to destroy Syrian forces and the PLO and set up an accommodative Christian government. Reagan assured Begin that the United States would not openly criticize military intervention in Lebanon, handing Israel a "new flexibility" for "air strikes and ground assaults against Palestinian bases" and support for Christian militias.[57]

Begin implemented his pledge to Bashir Gemayel of direct military intervention in April of 1981.[58] Gemayel's Christian militia had provocatively shelled Syrian military headquarters outside of Zahle and infiltrated the Lebanese city.[59] In response, Syria placed Zahle under a brutal and paralyzing siege to be continued until the Phalangists departed.[60] Syria also dug some missile sites without warheads near Zahle and informed the Israelis that it had no fight with them. Begin declared that Gemayel was defending a persecuted Christian minority and that another "Holocaust" had to be prevented.[61] When Israel shot down some Syrian helicopters, Syria installed warheads on the missiles, which Israel pledged to destroy. This was the preliminary round in the Begin/Sharon war against the PLO and Syrian influence in Lebanon.[62]

In May 1981, Israel turned to bombing PLO concentrations in southern Lebanon. Attacks continued for five days between May 28 and June 3. The Palestinians feared a crushing Israeli ground invasion and responded gingerly.[63] For another five days Israel bombed PLO strongholds (July 5-10). On the fifth day, the PLO fought back, shelling an Israeli resort town on the Mediterranean (casualty figures unknown). Eitan received cabinet approval for further escalation and bombed Fatah and DFLP headquarters in a heavily populated Palestinian area in West Beirut. Some 100 to 150 people were killed and 600 wounded.[64] The PLO responded in the Galilee[65] with a rocket attack that killed six and wounded fifty-nine, disrupting settlement life.[66]

A cease-fire between the PLO and Israel, July 24, 1981

The United States, Western Europe and the UN Security Council condemned Israel's West Beirut bombing. The United States deferred delivery of F-16 fighters to Israel. American mediator Philip Habib pressed for a cease-fire amidst the escalating violence (sometimes called the Two-Week War). This proved to be a watershed event – a cease-fire, signed by both Begin and the PLO, that lasted *nearly a year*.

As weeks passed, some Israeli officials began to have second thoughts about the cease-fire because the PLO was scrupulously abiding by it. Fear was growing that the United States might begin to view the PLO as a respectable organization that kept its word. For the PLO to be seen as an "orderly political body" was "more terrifying to the government of Israel than the powerful terrorist PLO."[67] A respectable PLO could not easily be excluded from possible future negotiations about occupied territory.

Israel's loose cannon, Ariel Sharon, was a critic of the cease-fire and falsely suggested to the United States that the PLO was violating the cease-fire.[68] In a meeting with Habib on December 5, 1981, he insisted, "If the terrorists *continue* to violate the cease-fire, we will have no choice but to wipe them out completely in Lebanon, destroy the PLO's infrastructure there . . . [and] we will eradicate the PLO in Lebanon."[69] Sharon was searching for a pretext for war since Israeli provocations had been unsuccessful.[70] Now he was asking for U.S. approval for a war against the PLO. Yet the Reagan administration didn't know its mind. Haig called for closer ties with Israel while Defense Secretary Casper Weinberger insisted that the United States was being held "hostage to Israeli policy."[71]

Begin wanted U.S. permission to destroy the PLO but he was in diplomatic trouble. The week following the Sharon-Habib meeting, Begin faced protests from the United States, the UN Security Council and Syria for his annexation of the Golan Heights.[72] So Begin moved cautiously, trying out a semantic ploy. He sent IDF Chief of Military Intelligence Yehoshua Saguy to convince Haig that the cease-fire (covering the Lebanese-Israeli border) could be considered violated and warrant Israeli military intervention if *any* Palestinian terrorism occurred *anywhere*. Haig, believing that an Israeli invasion of Lebanon might benefit U.S. anti-Soviet policy (removal of Soviet clients), made no objection. He knew that "anywhere" was a pretext for invasion.[73] Haig did say, however, that the terrorist activity would have to be "significant" (undefined) and directed by the PLO from Beirut.[74] This the Israelis took as green light for war. That was February 1982. What Israel did not know was that Bashir Gemayel was losing his desire to fight alongside Israel against the PLO and Syria.[75]

War in the air: Israel seeks to provoke the PLO to gain pretext

The U.S. intelligence community, and soon the world, was aware in early April 1982 that Israel was going to invade Lebanon. NBC reporter John Chancellor described the probable plan in detail: 1,200 tanks to advance in separate spearheads north to block the Syrians, southwest to attack Palestinian camps on the coast and northwest to Beirut to attack PLO headquarters.[76]

On April 21, 1982, four days before Israel's scheduled (Camp David) withdrawal from the Egyptian Sinai, Israel broke the July 1981 cease-fire with major air strikes against PLO bases. Two Syrian MiG fighters attempted to deter the Israeli bombers but were shot down. On the ground, twenty-three were killed and many wounded.[77] The PLO deliberately did not respond. On May 9, Israeli planes again attacked, killing sixteen, wounding fifty-four.[78] This time the PLO fired eight volleys of artillery fire into northern Israel, away from towns and settlements – a simultaneous show of capacity to inflict punishment but reluctance for war.[79] Arafat issued a declaration that the PLO would continue to abide by the cease-fire, as it had for nearly a year.[80] Syria, also looking to avoid war, advised PLO restraint lest Israel find genuine pretext for a ground assault.[81] Sharon immediately authorized a major troop concentration along the Lebanese border and in the Golan Heights.[82]

Major war was less than a month away. It would be dubbed Operation "Peace for Galilee" even though no attacks or Israeli deaths had occurred in the Galilee for a year.[83] Historian Mark Tessler notes:

> It was not the case that PLO aggressiveness left the Jewish state no choice but to go to war. On the contrary, the PLO had shown considerable restraint during eleven months between June 1982 and the ceasefire agreement signed the preceding July; and it was Israel's determination to clean out PLO strongholds in southern Lebanon, rather than any recent aggression by Arafat's guerrillas, that provided the impetus for the invasion.[84]

Israel invades Lebanon in a war against the PLO and Syria, June 6, 1982

The immediate catalyst for the June 6 invasion was an attack in London on June 3rd by Palestinian extremists *hostile* to the PLO in which the Israeli ambassador to Britain was wounded. The PLO denounced the attack and truthfully denied responsibility. Begin knew at the time that the attack was likely the work of Abu Nidal, an arch-enemy of Arafat and the PLO.[85] However, Begin preferred to wave this complication away, declaring, "They're all PLO," and "We will not stand for them attacking an Israeli ambassador." On June 4 Begin authorized major "retaliatory" air strikes against PLO positions in southern Lebanon and Beirut, causing at least forty-five Palestinian and Lebanese deaths (210 by Lebanese police count) and 150 to 250 wounded.[86] The PLO responded with sporadic shelling of some settlements that wounded eight Israelis.[87]

The UN Security Council ordered an immediate cease-fire. Nevertheless, Israel attacked. The June 6 blitzkreig (Operation Big Pines) involved some 80,000 Israeli troops, 1,240 tanks and 1,520 armored personnel carriers that sweptswept across the Lebanese border and pushed past 7,000 to 8,000 PLO fighters unable or unwilling to offer a futile resistance.[88] The UN Security Council again demanded withdrawal of all Israeli forces (Resolution 509). Acting

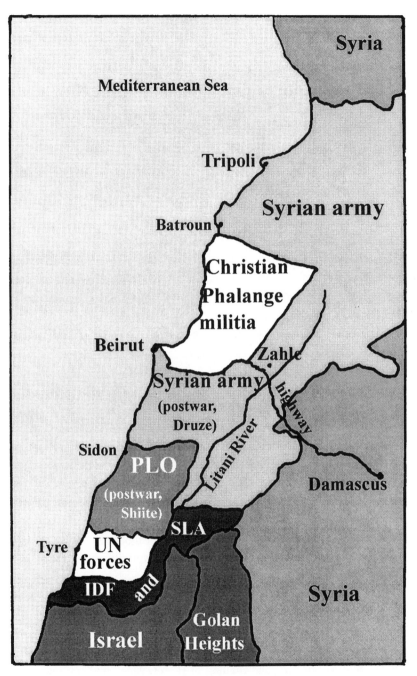

Zones of Control in Lebanon before the 1982 Israeli Invasion

on his own,[89] Sharon pushed beyond the cabinet-approved forty-kilometer limit (the range at which PLO artillery could not reach Israel), and, on the second day (June 7), drew the reluctant Syrians into battle. On June 9, Israeli planes bombed the Syrian missile site near Żahle and downed as many as ninety Syrian jets sent to defend the site – effectively ending all Syrian resistance. The IDF now controlled the Beirut-Damascus highway and on June 11, the chief target, the PLO in Beirut, was within sight.[90]

The Israeli advance resulted in many casualties, mainly Palestinians in refugee camps near major highways. IDF tanks trampled Shi'ite Lebanese villages on the way to destroying Palestinian camps. Home-guard forces in the camps often defended to the death, but Israeli ground assaults with tanks and heavy air bombardments with napalm were devastating. Some camps were completely leveled. Thousands of civilian Lebanese and Palestinian deaths occurred. The head of the American Red Cross judged that by the sixth day of the Israeli invasion there were already 10,000 deaths – others thought fewer.[91] Some 100,000 were made homeless.

Reagan was angered by the extent of the advance and degree of destruction. On June 11, Haig pressured Israel and arranged a fragile cease-fire between Israel and Syria. The Soviets threatened that further Israeli attack on Syrian forces would have "global implications."[92] Arafat offered to include the PLO in this cease-fire but Israel ignored the offer. On June 14, the IDF cut off West Beirut and surrounded PLO headquarters. Heavy civilian casualties were inflicted with cluster and concussion bombs. The UN Security Council again demanded a cease-fire and an end to the blockade of West Beirut. With the PLO headquarters in a noose, Sharon asked Gemayel to use his Christian Phalangist militia to go in and "clean out" the PLO. Begin also pressed the reluctant Gemayel to fight, insisting to his cabinet that the Christian Phalange must "capture the part of Beirut inhabited by the terrorists and . . . must get rid of them."[93] But Gemayel refused, fearing that fighting alongside the IDF would hurt his chances in a presidential election scheduled for August.[94]

Reagan "deplored" the outbursts of violence yet vetoed those Security Council resolutions which condemned Israel. He considered the Palestinians and Syrians to be "pro-Soviet" and wanted Israel to drive them out and set up a pro-West puppet government in Lebanon.[95] At the same time, Reagan criticized Israel's saturation bombing and shelling of Beirut, which was causing massive loss of life, all seen on American television. A single raid in early July killed 209 people, almost all of them civilians.[96] The European nations were unequivocally and deeply upset by what they branded as Israel's "flagrant violation of international law."

Reagan wished to hold the Israelis back from directly descending on the PLO in the center of West Beirut, where the collateral death and destruction would be monumental. He halted shipment of U.S.-made cluster bombs and threatened to cut off U.S. aid if Israel didn't withdraw from Beirut.[97] U.S. negotiator Philip Habib pressured Israel to allow the PLO *safe evacuation* out of West Beirut to foreign soils.[98] Sharon's objections were overruled by the Israeli cabinet. Furious, Sharon ordered his fiercest-yet saturation and artillery attack on Beirut, from dawn to dusk. This violence, which Reagan called "unfathomable and senseless," killed 300 that day, August 12.[99]

Concerning the Habib proposal for evacuation, the PLO feared that once it left Beirut, the IDF or Christian Phalangist militias would likely take revenge on noncombatant Palestinians living in West Beirut refugee camps. Habib, after consultation with Jerusalem and the Lebanese government, offered the PLO a written U.S. guarantee for the safety of "law-abiding non-combatant Palestinians left behind in Beirut, including the families of those who have departed."[100] The PLO then agreed to leave Beirut and Israel agreed not to enter West Beirut after the PLO had departed. In late August, the PLO, as well as some Syrian fighters, were evacuated under the supervision of U.S., French and Italian peace-keeping troops. By September 13, the peace-keeping troops themselves had departed. The war seemed to be over.

Coda: The Sabra and Shatilla massacres

On September 14, 1982, Bashir Gemayel, president-elect of Lebanon, was killed by a bomb attack – the work of a fanatical Syrian nationalist. The next morning the IDF invaded West Beirut in violation of U.S.-Israeli agreements. Samuel Lewis, U.S. ambassador to Israel, and Morris Draper, assistant to Philip Habib, vehemently protested this violation to Sharon and Eitan. Sharon made the improbable claim that there were still, after the PLO evacuation, 2,000 to 3,000 armed terrorists hiding in two West Beirut refugee camps (Sabra and Shatilla) and that they would have to be eliminated.[101] Lewis challenged Sharon's claim, but unbeknownst to Lewis, wheels were already turning.[102]

Within hours of Gemayel's death, Sharon and Eitan were overheard making the final decision to send the Christian Phalangists (rather than IDF) into the Sabra and Shatilla refugee camps to clean out PLO allegedly remaining there.[103] Sharon's decision to use the Phalangists was influenced by Begin's and the

Israeli public's anger that the Phalangists had been strengthened by the war without doing any fighting. For months Begin and his cabinet had been coaxing Gemayel to fight. Now, after his assassination, Christian Phalangist militiamen thirsted for revenge.[104]

On September 15, the day the IDF entered West Beirut, Sharon and Eitan concluded last-minute details at Phalange headquarters for "Operation Iron Mind." The plan: the Israelis were to encircle and seal off the Palestinian camps while their Phalangist allies entered. Initially, Begin did not know that the Phalangist militia was to be used.[105] Yet when Begin and his cabinet did learn the next day that the Phalange were in the refugee camps, they did nothing to stop what Eitan and the Mossad had previously told them would be a "convulsion" and a "rampage." Perhaps they did nothing because Eitan had implied that the Phalange would be under firm IDF control.[106]

The IDF command did in fact expect the Phalange militia to pursue a course of revenge. It was not a matter of "*should* have known."[107] Nor was it a matter of faulty intelligence. It was a matter of setting in motion a military action that they knew with high probability would be a bloody revenge on Palestinians. "Israeli officials were fully aware that sending [in] Phalange troops . . . could well have disastrous consequences."[108]

Three groups of Christian Phalangist soldiers (fifty each) entered the Sabra and Shatilla Palestinian refugee camps at 6:00 p.m., September 16, and began a three-day massacre.[109] The IDF provided flare-lights. During the first few hours, the chief intelligence officer of the Phalangists, Elie Hobeika, watched from a rooftop observation post. One soldier, having rounded up fifty women and children, radioed questions up to Hobeika about what he should do with them. "This is the last time you're going to ask me a question like that, you know exactly what to do," responded Hobeika, surrounded by the raucous laughter of Phalangist personnel.[110] "As reports began to arrive about the actions of the Phalangists in the camps, no proper heed was taken of these reports . . . and no energetic and immediate actions were taken to restrain the Phalangists and put a stop to their actions."[111] Different accounts have been given but according to one historian, IDF troops surrounding the camps and besieged by screaming women, prevented their escape.[112]

On September 17, IDF officers met with Phalangist leaders. At that time "Eitan, Drori, Levi, Yaron and other officers knew that Phalangists would be in the camps [again] all night and that they were using bulldozers [to dispose of corpses]; they also knew about the flight of panic-stricken civilians."[113] Not only did the IDF officers not take steps "to hasten departure of the Lebanese [Phalangist] Forces or put an end to the wanton bloodletting," they authorized *continuation* of Phalange operations in the camps for another day. What Eitan had not told Begin was that the IDF would *not* exercise control over the Phalangists – that is, would not call a halt to bloodshed.[114] Two different Israeli journalists separately approached Shamir and Sharon on September 17 with descriptions of the bloodletting, to no effect.[115] "There is no doubt that Israeli military and political leaders learned of the massacre while it was still taking place."[116]

The "butchery" of about 3,000 Palestinian civilians[117] was later reported by two on-the-spot Israeli journalists, Ze'ev Schiff and Ehud Ya'ari:

In addition to the wholesale slaughter of families, the Phalangists indulged in such sadistic horrors as hanging live grenades around their victims' necks. In one particularly vicious act of barbarity, an infant was trampled to death by a man wearing spiked shoes. The entire Phalangist action in Sabra and Shatilla seemed to be directed against civilians.[118]

We have had many accounts of women raped, pregnant women, their fetuses cut out afterward, women with hands chopped off, earrings pulled.[119]

The Israeli public is outraged by their government's actions

On September 29, an estimated 400,000 Israelis gathered in a mass rally in Tel Aviv to demand that those responsible be identified and punished. Sharon refused to resign his Defense Ministry post and Begin refused to remove him, declaring to the cabinet: "The goyim kill the goyim and they accuse the Jews!" One cabinet minister did resign. The Israeli cabinet issued a laundering statement, advertised worldwide, asserting that all claims that the IDF bore any blame were baseless and a product of anti-Semitic "blood libel" against the Jewish state.

Yet public criticism mounted. The newspaper *Ha'aretz* referred to "War Crime in Beirut" and *Davar* asserted, "What has been perpetrated by those who carried out the Deir Yassin massacre [Begin], the commander of the Qibya raid [Sharon] and the one who commuted Daniel Pinto's sentence [Eitan], defames the entire nation today."[120] Under great pressure, Sharon finally relinquished his Defense Ministry post but remained in the cabinet – became national infrastructures minister and later, Benyamin Netanyahu's foreign minister.

Israeli President Yitzhak Navon recommended that the whole affair be submitted to formal judicial scrutiny. This would have exposed top Israeli political as well as military leaders.[121] Begin strenuously objected and chose rather to appoint the Kahan Commission to inquire into the tragedy. Liberal Israelis condemned the commission's minimalist conclusions.[122]

An international commission, looking into violations of international law, harshly condemned Israel's "grave breach" of the Geneva Conventions related to protection of civilians and called attention to the "dehumanization" of Palestinians by Israel's political and military leaders that created conditions conducive to massacre.[123] Israeli journalists Schiff and Ya'ari concluded: "If there is a moral to the painful episode of Sabra and Shatilla, it has yet to be acknowledged [by the government of Israel]."[124]

Many Israelis expressed outrage, demonstrating again a general diversity in public attitude toward government policies and actions. That diversity arises from within the strata of Israeli society itself, whether with regard to differences among European, Russian and Oriental Jews, between Labor and Likud policies, between secular and religious Jews or between liberal peace groups and conservative ultranationalist groups. Public outcry against the Lebanon tragedy reflected this diversity, as have the voices of respected figures protesting government policies. For example, Nahum Goldmann, president in 1977 of the World Jewish Congress, once expressed frustration about Israeli government obstructionism in the Middle East:

> In 30 years Israel has never presented the Arabs with a single peace plan. She has rejected every settlement plan devised by her friends and by her enemies, she has seemingly no other object than to preserve the status quo while adding territory piece by piece.[125]

Goldmann was observing that government policy over many years had remained surprisingly monolithic in its militant, hard-line policies toward Palestinians and surrounding Arab nations.

Why has this kind of dissenting voice and criticism of the Israeli government after the Lebanon war *not* had more effect on government policy and action? Public attitudes toward the Lebanon invasion *prior* to its tragic consequences offer some clues. In June 1982, the majority of Israelis favored the war. Thirteen percent were opposed. Even during the siege of Beirut, the popularity of Begin and Sharon was rising and 93 percent thought that the invasion was justified.[126] It was after viewing the actual *consequences* of that invasion that the public changed its opinion.

This is a familiar phenomenon. Moreover, it seems generally true that a public rallies behind a government's military adventures. Patriotism, aided by governmental creation of consent (often through propaganda), dominates opinion until a shameful brutality is witnessed, as many considered happened in the case of America's own Vietnam War. Israeli public opinion is diverse, like that of other nations, yet that diversity faded at the prospect of military adventure.

The consequences of the Lebanon war included the deaths of some 360 Israeli soldiers by mid-September 1982, with another 240 killed before eventual retreat in 1985.[127] Abba Eban observed bitterly that the "Peace in Galilee" operation against the PLO in Lebanon had taken the lives of more Israeli soldiers "than all the world's terrorists had been able to inflict on Israelis in all the decades."[128] If Eban is right that fewer than 600 Israeli civilians were killed by terrorists between 1948 and 1982, then the bitter irony is not the comparable IDF loses but the cost to Palestinian and Lebanese civilians of some 33,000 dead from that single operation, with 100,000 seriously wounded and half a million made homeless.[129]

It was, by the way, IDF devastation of Lebanese (Shi'ite Moslem) villages, which took no action against Israelis and stood aloof from Arab nationalists, that gave rise to the Party of God (Hizb'allah). Supported by Iran, the Party of God retaliated against Israeli troops and took hostages (British and American) for the next decade.[130]

On the politics of terrorism

Terrorism is violence, usually against a civilian population, used to achieve political, not military ends. It may be committed by a powerless and alienated group or by a state. Typically, the group or state claims that the other is the true terrorist, that the other in some overt or hidden way "started it," and that one's own "retaliatory" terrorism is meant to be a deterrent – a war *against* terrorism.

Advertising the terrorism of the opponent serves the political goal of discrediting him. Moreover, the other's terrorism may be needed (and in its absence, provoked or falsified) in order to arouse public outrage and seeming justification for attack. Israel faced this problem in 1981 when the PLO honored the U.S. cease-fire and deprived Israel of a pretext for attack. It was an *absence* of terrorism (and the growing political respectability of the PLO) that was, as one Israeli scholar put it, "a veritable catastrophe in the eyes of the Israeli government."[131]

So the politics of terrorism is not only that of calling attention to a political cause or of depicting an enemy, rightly or wrongly, as a monster and then destroying him. Focus on the other's terrorism may disguise or displace attention from one's own political agenda. In 1998, Prime Minister Benyamin Netanyahu's claim that Palestinian terrorism (Israel's security) was the reason for continued occupation of the West Bank appeared to be part of a larger rejectionist policy resisting withdrawal from the West Bank. Similarly, in 1982, Begin's Lebanon "war on PLO terrorism" provided camouflage for an intent to depict the PLO as a "group of thugs" in order to deprive West Bank Palestinians of serious political leadership. "Peace in Galilee" was more about political control of the West Bank than about PLO terrorism in Galilee:

> The [Israeli] government's hope is that the stricken PLO, lacking a logistic and territorial base, will return to its earlier terrorism . . . will lose part of the political legitimacy that it has gained . . . [thereby] undercutting the danger that . . . Palestinians might become a legitimate negotiating partner for future political accommodations.[132]

State terrorism usually escapes the opprobrium of small group terrorism because, by definition, the state is not an "alienated" group lacking military means. Yet state terrorism may be terroristic just because the state's military means *are* available and are used for *disproportional* massive destruction. Issues about who "started it" then have little relevance. When the anti-terrorist "deterrent" response is overwhelmingly destructive, that is disproportional state terrorism.[133]

Notes

1. Most Palestinians recognized the PLO as their legitimate representative. Even groups such as the Palestine National Front (PNF) and the Palestine Communist Organization (PCO) accepted this and supported PLO ideas about the division of Palestine into Israel and a Palestinian state. In 1976 the PLO filled 75 percent of the municipal council seats in a West Bank election. Mark Tessler, *A History of the Israeli-Palestinian Conflict* (Bloomington: Indiana University Press, 1994), 493.

2. Fred Khouri, *The Arab-Israeli Dilemma* (Syracuse, N.Y.: Syracuse University Press, 1985), 381-2. When the UN declared Zionism to be "a form of racism or racial discrimination" in 1975, stern U.S. warnings spared Israel loss of UN membership.

3. Most Arabs are Moslem but about 10 percent are Christian (Greek Orthodox

and Roman Catholic in roughly equal parts). Roman Catholics divide further between members of the Latin church, the Melkites and the Maronites. Another Arab group, the Druze, who follow Ismali theology, are independent, having split off from the Shi'ite Moslems in the 11th century.

4. While the civil war reflected Lebanese political, sectarian and class differences, some observers have seen the PLO as disruptive of a delicate political balance and thus a *contributor* to the civil war. Others have seen the PLO influence in Lebanon as the *result* of a pre-existing flawed political system collapsing under the pressure of sectarian rivalries. Tessler, *History of Conflict*, 493.

5. Camille Chamoun, ex-president and Maronite Christian, was complicitous with Eisenhower in 1958.

6. In this refugee camp, besieged by Christian militias, at least 2,200 inhabitants were killed, many children and babies dying from dehydration, until the camp surrendered in August 1976.

7. One non-Phalangist militia, led by Suleiman Frangieh, was allied with the Syrians. Another non-Phalangist militia was led by Danny Chamoun (son of former president Camille Chamoun). Chamoun's militia was liquidated by Bashir Gemayel's Phalangist militia, which was allied with Israel.

8. Ze'ev Schiff and Ehud Ya'ari, *Israel's Lebanon War* (New York: Simon and Schuster, 1984), 18-25, 28. This book, written by two well-known Israeli journalists, one the military editor for *Ha'aretz*, has been cleared by Israeli military censors and is used extensively in this chapter.

9. Schiff and Ya'ari, *Lebanon War*, 24.

10. Syria wished to avoid domination in Lebanon by either the Moslems or Christians in order that Lebanon not come to be partitioned along sectarian lines. A partitioning would have had repercussions in Syria, which was also religiously divided. Domination by Moslems would also have caused Israel to intervene in Lebanon, ending Lebanon's buffer function against Israeli expansion. Syria had deep historical ties to Lebanon, which was part of Syria until France divided them in 1926. Khouri, *Dilemma*, 387.

11. Tessler, *History of Conflict*, 495n.

12. Tessler, *History of Conflict*, 497.

13. Schiff and Ya'ari, *Lebanon War*, 79-80. Some of the lower ranks were suspected of rape and robbery. However, journalists for the *Jerusalem Post* investigating stories of PLO terror in Lebanon reported that they "could find little or no substantial proof for many of the atrocity stories making the rounds." See Noam Chomsky, *The Fateful Triangle* (Boston: South End Press, 1983), 186-8.

14. Begin declared in the Knesset: "We do not even dream of the possibility . . . of abandoning these areas [West Bank and Gaza] to the control of the murderous organization that is called the PLO. . . . We have a right and a demand for [Israeli] sovereignty over these areas of Eretz Israel. This is our land and it belongs to the Jewish nation rightfully." Walter Laqueur and Barry Rubin, eds., *The Israel-Arab Reader; A Documentary History of the Middle East Conflict* (New York: Penguin

Books, 1984), 607. Begin netted much support from Sephardic and religious Jews for his Greater Israel policies. The National Religious Party and the Gush Emunim (Bloc of the Faithful) religious settlers saw Jewish occupation of all of Palestine as ushering in the Messianic era.

15. Steven L. Spiegel, *The Other Arab-Israeli Conflict* (Chicago: University of Chicago Press, 1985), 332.

16. Ibid., 333.

17. Carter was not successful in curbing arms sales to Israel except for the sale of concussion bombs. When he allowed the sale of air-to-ground missiles to Saudi Arabia, Israel objected. He was forced by Congress and Vice President Walter Mondale to reinstate Israel as a favored arms recipient. Carter and his National Security Advisor, Zbigniew Brzezinski, rejected the notion that Israeli security depended on the possession and continuing occupation of Arab land taken in 1967. They favored Israeli withdrawal from the occupied territories, as well as recognition of the "legitimate rights of the Palestinian people." Some comprehensive Middle East settlement was, of course, essential to maintaining U.S. oil supplies and to this end, Saudi Arabia was offered a role in negotiations. Spiegel, *Other Conflict*, 322-30.

18. The tensions between Begin and Carter related to other differences as well. Carter made clear his willingness to deal directly with Begin's declared enemy, the PLO, if the PLO accepted Israel's "right to exist" or UN 242 (which recognized Israel). Carter argued with Foreign Minister Moshe Dayan about future Israeli withdrawals and found him inflexible. He also blamed Jewish terrorism (including the actions of Begin and Shamir) for the creation of the 1948 Palestinian refugee problem.

19. "Transcripts of Sadat and Begin Addresses" *New York Times,* November 21, 1977, 17-8.

20. This support for anti-PLO Christian militias and for Israel's Haddad-led SLA militias in southern Lebanon was accompanied by a threatening display of Israeli warplanes over PLO headquarters in Beirut in July 1978.

21. Israel would not permit East Jerusalem (West Bank) Palestinians to vote because Israel considered all of Jerusalem to be Israeli. Nor would Israel permit Palestinians in exile to vote. Israel refused to include the power to draft laws in its autonomy idea. No agreement was found concerning areas in which autonomy should exist. Tessler, *History of Conflict,* 518-9.

22. Begin's defense minister, Ezer Weizman, charged that "Begin saw it [autonomy] as a way to prevent Israeli withdrawal . . . [and he] backed away from implementing the autonomy agreements because his desire for annexation under the old Herut dream ultimately overcame the vision in him that would strive for peace." Ezer Weizman, *The Battle for Peace* (New York: Bantam Books, 1981), 119ff, 122, 191. Foreign Minister Dayan told Carter that Begin "was firmly committed to retaining maximum control over the West Bank in spite of the Camp David commitments." Jimmy Carter, *Keeping Faith: Memoirs of a President* (New York: Bantam, 1982), 494.

23. Begin's drive to incorporate the West Bank and Gaza was formally stated in an agreement with his coalition parties that "under no conditions will a Palestinian

state emerge . . . [that] the autonomy agreed upon at Camp David means neither sovereignty nor self-determination . . . [and] at the end of the transition period, set down in the Camp David agreements, Israel will raise its claim, and act to realize its right of sovereignty over Judea, Samaria [the West Bank] and the Gaza Strip." Tessler, *History of Conflict*, 546-7.

24. Tessler, *History of Conflict*, 519.

25. This was the view of military intelligence chief Shlomo Gazit. *Yediot Ahronot*, June, 18, 1982. Cited in Chomsky, *Triangle*, 202. Ariel Sharon, then minister of agriculture, was critical of Begin for giving up the Sinai but finally backed him. A treaty with Egypt eliminated a potential southern front, freeing Israel to go north for war against the PLO in Lebanon.

26. Secretary of State Vance held that "Israel's retreat from autonomy . . . [and its] unwillingness to declare a moratorium on the creation of new settlements . . . had struck an almost fatal blow to the hopes for success [in negotiations concerning Palestinians]." Cyrus Vance, *Hard Choices: Critical Years in America's Foreign Policy* (New York: Simon and Schuster, 1983), 254.

27. For example, Israel applied Jewish law to settlers in occupied land; incorporated settlements into regional councils based on Israeli municipal law; opened Israeli courts in settlements; and effectively annexed East Jerusalem (in the West Bank) by making Jerusalem Israel's capital. Tessler, *History of Conflict*, 521.

28. When in 1979 the Israeli Supreme Court ruled *against* expropriation of private lands for settlement purposes, Agriculture Minister Ariel Sharon and IDF Chief of Staff Rafael Eitan circumvented the Supreme Court by simply claiming areas closed for "security" reasons. Don Peretz, *The West Bank: History, Politics, Society and Economy* (Boulder, Colo.: Westview Press, 1986), 62-6. The Jewish National Fund raised money for land purchases in the West Bank and other occupied territories. Tessler, *History of Conflict*, 523.

29. Howard Sachar, *A History of Israel: From the Aftermath of the Yom Kippur War*, Vol II (New York: Oxford University Press, 1987), 153.

30. Edward Said and Christopher Hitchens, eds., *Blaming the Victim*(London: Verso, 1988), 252.

31. According to Israel Shahak, president of the Israeli League for Human and Civil Rights, Israel has expropriated nearly 70 percent of the West Bank and more than a third of the Gaza Strip for Jewish settlements and military "security" zones. (*Ha'aretz*, March 26, 1993). Reports and maps of the West Bank prepared by the CIA are available on the Internet (www.odci.gov/cia/publications/factbook), showing the breakdown of Israeli land use into categories and areas and showing how and where Palestinians are effectively barred from use of the land Also see Perry-Castenada Library Map Collection, University of Texas, Austin.

32. Edward Said, "The Mourning After," *London Review of Books* (21 October 1993);Douglas Jehl, "Water Divides Haves From Have-Nots in West Bank," *New York Times*, August, 15, 1998, A3.

33. Labor's position was that Begin was undermining the peace process and

creating serious security problems by seeking to permanently control all occupied territory (Greater Israel): Greater Israel would dilute with Arabs the Jewish character of Israel. At the same time, Labor did not advocate an independent Palestinian state – rather, it desired a merger of part of the West Bank with Jordan. Peace Now was a liberal organization born in 1979 upon Sadat's visit to Jerusalem.

34. Rabin attacked Peres's integrity, e.g., Peres was implicated in the framing of Lavon in the 1954 "Lavon affair." Sachar, *History*, Vol. I, 543-6.

35. Begin took an unyielding position toward the PLO in Lebanon and on retention of the occupied territories. He called Assad a "chicken," Peres a "saboteur" and the Ashkenazic-dominated Labor Alignment "kibbutz millionairs with their swimming pools and beauty parlors." Peres called the Sephardim "chakchakim" – a derogatory reference to the Moroccan "riffraff." Sachar, *History* Vol. II, 130.

36. Sachar, *History* Vol. II, 128.

37. Moslem fundamentalists were critical of Sadat's open (Western-style) government that was, in fact, infected by elitism, corruption and inflation due to U.S. money pouring into the upper classes. When Sadat instituted a sweeping political crackdown on fundamentalist critics, he was assassinated.

38. Tessler, *History of Conflict*, 536.

39. By decision of the High Court of Justice, Israel is required to observe the Hague Conventions.Sachar, *History*, Vol II, 96.

40. In March 1980, the United States voted for a Security Council resolution that strongly *condemned* Israel's settlement policy. But facing an election and pro-Israel protests, Carter *repudiated* that vote, ascribing it to a "communication breakdown." Reagan went further, promising not to talk with the PLO and supporting Israeli sovereignty over Jerusalem (even though East Jerusalem was in the occupied West Bank).

41. Palestinian nationalism had strong roots: 98 percent of Palestinians favored a Palestinian state and 86 percent favored governance solely by the PLO – though not necessarily headed by Arafat. Survey by Pori Institute of Tel Aviv and Israeli sociologists from Hebrew University described in. *Time*, May 17, 1982.

42. "Quislings" was the word used for Israel's Palestinian collaborators by the Israeli Defense Ministry coordinator for the occupied territories, General Benyamin Ben Eliezer. *Ha'aretz* March 12, 1984. These collaborators were given administrative powers by Israel that often forced Palestinians to bypass their own elected officials. Israel had cancelled Palestinian elections, due in 1980, out of fear that PLO-backed candidates would win. Khouri, *Dilemma*, 417.

43. Tessler, *History of Conflict*, 550-1.

44. The Karp Report "bears out the initial suspicion that a systematic miscarriage of justice is being perpetrated in the West Bank. Jewish settlers, wishing to assert their rights to the area, take the law into their own hands . . . the files are closed without anyone being booked." Editorial: "Twenty-month coverup," *Jerusalem Post*, February 9. 1984, 8. The Karp Commission chairperson resigned in protest over Israeli government indifference.

45. The Knesset gave its approval and Labor (Rabin, Peres and Allon) made no objection.

46. *Ha'aretz*, March 15, 1982, Editorial. Retired Israeli Supreme Court Justice Chaim Cohn referred to IDF "barbarism." The IDF invoked martial law and imposed a state of siege on the Druze by imprisoning them "in their villages without food supplies (excepting foodstuffs sold by the IDF), without regular medical services, medicines and other vital commodities." Cited in Tessler, *History of Conflict,* 560.

47. William Quandt, "Reagan's Lebanon Policy: Trial and Error," *Middle East Journal* (Spring 1984): 238.

48. Ben-Gurion and Dayan hoped in 1954 to mount a coup that would create a Christian government allied with Israel – a "pet scheme" since 1948. Avi Shlaim, *Collusion across the Jordan* (New York: Columbia University Press, 1988), 392. Prime Minister Moshe Sharett summarized Dayan's urgent request in his diary: "All that is needed is to find a [Christian Lebanese] officer, even a captain. We should win his heart or buy him, to get him to agree to declare himself the savior of the Maronite population. Then the Israeli army would enter Lebanon, occupy the necessary territory and set up a Christian regime allied to Israel. The territory from the Litani southward will be totally annexed by Israel." Sachar, *History,* Vol. II, 168. See also David Lamb, "Politics Upset a Blitz Timetable," *International Herald Tribune,* July 17-18, 1982, 4.

49. Khouri, *Dilemma*, 428, citing Amnon Kapeliuk.

50. Sachar, *History,* Vol II, 172. Sharon estimated that Israel was the world's fourth-largest military power – presumably, after the United States, U.S.S.R. and China. Experts agreed with Sharon's estimate, according to Chomsky, *Triangle,* 213.

51. Sachar, *History,* Vol. II, 172. Sharon claimed that the Palestinians already had their state (Jordan) to which Palestinians in Lebanon and the West Bank could be transferred. The idea that "Jordan *is* Palestine" was well-advertised in Israel. Khouri, *Dilemma,* 429, n.23. An additional motive for war in Lebanon was removal of the large community of Palestinian refugees sitting, unacceptably, along the Lebanon-Israeli border. This community, in flight from wars in 1948 and 1967, constituted a quasi-state within Lebanon and numbered some 330,000 in 1982.

52. Shai Feldman and Heda Rechnitz-Kijner, "Deception, Consensus and War: Israel in Lebanon," in *Jaffee Center for Strategic Studies of Tel Aviv University, Paper No. 27* (October, 1984), 19. Cited in Tessler, *History of Conflict,* 579. "I believe Palestinians will come forward prepared to negotiate with Israel on the autonomy plan proposed by Prime Minister Menachem Begin." Ariel Sharon, "Gains from the War in Lebanon" *New York Times,* August 29, 1982, E19.

53. Tessler, *History of Conflict,* 569.

54. Quoted in M. Thomas Davis, *40 Km into Lebanon: Israel's 1982 Invasion* (Washington: National Defense University Press, 1987), 68, cited in Tessler, *History of Conflict,* 829, n.64. The notion that, but for the PLO, Palestinians in the West Bank and Gaza would accept Israeli rule bears comparison with the notion of

American Southerners that, but for northern civil rights agitators, blacks in the south would not press for their rights.

55. Khouri, *Dilemma*, 405; *Amnesty International Country Report*, July 1996. (Index MDE 15/42/96). Chomsky, in *Triangle*, 99, reports 2,000 dead and 250,000 made refugees.

56. The rationale for the attack was as retaliation for a beach landing in Israel by a small band of Fatah commandos who seized a bus with intent to trade the passengers for release of Palestinian prisoners in Israel. When the IDF stormed the bus, thirty-six Israelis and eight commandos were killed.

57. David Shipler, "Israeli Raids on Lebanon: A Change in U.U. Position" *New York Times*, April 18, 1981, 3. Haig made it clear on his April trip to Israel that the interests of the United States and Israel virtually coincided. Schiff and Ya'ari, *Lebanon War*, 31-2, 43.

58. Schiff and Ya'ari, *Lebanon War*, 28-9; Sachar, *History*, Vol. II, 122.

59. Zahle was a largely Greek-Christian Lebanese city close to the Beirut-Damascus highway, considered by Syria vital to the defense of Damascus.

60. Schiff and Ya'ari, *Lebanon War*, 32-3.

61. The army chief of intelligence, Yehoshua Saguy, and the head of Mossad, Yitzhak Hofi, suspected that the Christian Phalangists had provoked Syria in order to assure Israel military involvement (possibly with IDF Chief of Staff Eitan's agreement – although denied by him).

62. Sharon's plan to crush the PLO, drive out the Syrians and install Bashir Gemayel as president through manipulation of the August 1982 Lebanese elections became urgent because he thought that Syria intended a similar a puppet government through Suleiman Frangieh, a Syrian ally and long-time rival of Bashir. Schiff and Ya'ari, *Lebanon War*, 31-2, 43.

63. Schiff and Ya'ari, *Lebanon War*, 35.

64. Estimates vary. See Schiff and Ya'ari, *Lebanon War*, 36; Khouri, *Dilemma*, 424.

65. Schiff and Ya'ari, *Lebanon War*, 36. The Galilee was a Palestinian area which the government began appropriating for Jewish settlements in 1959-1960 in order to counter future demand for its return – known as the "Project for the Judaization of Galilee." Sabri Jiryis, *The Arabs in Israel* (London: Monthly Review Press, 1976), 104; Ian Lustick, *Arabs in the Jewish State* (Austin: University of Texas Press, 1980), 129-30.

66. Khouri, *Dilemma*, 424. The PLO stopped attacks on northern Israel once Israel stopped attacking the PLO in Lebanon. "PLO shelling had been in response to an escalation initiated by Jerusalem," according to Tessler, *History of Conflict*, 569.

67. Danny Rubinstein, "A Political PLO Is More Dangerous Than a Powerful PLO." *Davar*, September 6, 1982. A version of this article appeared in Danny Rubinstein, "PLO's Future" *New York Times*, September 14, 1982, A27.

68. For more on the PLO abiding by the cease-fire, see Tessler, *History of*

Conflict, 571-2.

69. Habib was appalled: "General Sharon, this is the twentieth century. . . . You can't go around invading countries just like that, spreading destruction and killing civilians. In the end, your invasion will grow into a war with Syria, and the entire region will be engulfed in flames." Schiff and Ya'ari, *Lebanon War,* 66. Sharon quote: my emphasis.

70. Between August 1981 and May 1982 (the cease-fire period) *Israel* violated Lebanese airspace 2,125 times. The UN reported that the Israeli-supported SLA engaged in military maneuvers in southern Lebanon that were "intensive, excessive and provocative." Robin Wright, "Israeli 'provocations' in southern Lebanon fail to goad PLO – so far." Robin Wright, "Israeli 'Provocations' in Southern Lebanon Fail to Goad PLO – so far," *Christian Science Monitor,* March 18, 1982;12. Alexander. Cockburn and James.Ridgeway, "War in Lebanon," *Village Voice,* June 22, 1982, 20., citing UN records.

71. Spiegel, *Other Conflict,* 403. Also see Bernard Gwertzman, "Reagan Aides at Odds" *New York Times* February 15, 1982. In August 1981, Reagan sought to fulfill Carter's promise of AWACS (intelligence-gathering planes) to Saudi Arabia and Sharon threatened to shoot them down. Schiff and Ya'ari, *Lebanon War,* 67.

72. The annexation was a violation of UN 242 and the Camp David Accords. UN 242 obligated Israel to negotiate a peace with Syria based on withdrawal from the Golan Heights – a commitment reaffirmed by a 1974 Israeli-Syrian disengagement agreement. Sachar, *History,* Vol. II, 150. Nevertheless, the United States vetoed full condemnation at the UN Security Council.

73. Khouri, *Dilemma,* 428.

74. Schiff and Ya'ari, *Lebanon War,* 68. Some State Department professionals thought that Sharon wanted war immediately, before April 25, 1982, the date for withdrawal from the Sinai, in order to sabotage the peace treaty between Israel and Egypt.

75. While Saguy was meeting with Haig, the PLO and Bashir Gemayel were engaged in secret talks to work out a deal to *prevent* an Israeli invasion of Lebanon. Schiff and Ya'ari, *Lebanon War,* 88. Gemayel thought that his association with the Israelis would be a disadvantage in the upcoming Lebanese presidential elections and would impair his ability to rule over a largely Moslem country bitterly opposed to Israel. Oppositely, Sharon thought that Gemayel could never be elected "as long as the terrorists control southern Lebanon and two-thirds of the city of Beirut, and as long as the Syrians control whole sections of Lebanon." Sachar, *History,* Vol. II, 172.

76. "The Americans knew more about the probable course of events in Lebanon than about any previous war in the Middle East . . . leaks became inevitable." Schiff and Ya'ari, *Lebanon War,* 69.

77. Tessler, *History of Conflict,* 570; Khouri, *Dilemma,* 429. The Israeli pretext was that an Israeli soldier was killed when his vehicle hit a mine in a Haddad-controlled enclave. Schiff and Ya'ari, *Lebanon War,* 55.

78. The Israeli pretext: discovery of unfired explosive devices in Ashkelon and

Jerusalem, sources untraced.

79. Tessler, *History of Conflict*, 572.

80. Bernard Gwertzman, "Haig Says Truce Break in Mideast Worries U.S." *New York Times*, May 11, 1982, A10. Edward Cody, "Israeli Jets Strike PLO in Lebanon" *Washington Post*, April 22, 1982, 1. Arafat sent a letter to Begin making explicit his desire to avoid war. Tessler, *History of Conflict*, 572.

81. Schiff and Ya'ari, *Lebanon War*, 69.

82. Sachar, *History*, Vol. II, 172.

83. From a letter about the loss of an Israeli's son in Lebanon: "With unabashed effrontery, Menachem Begin, Ariel Sharon, Rafael Eitan and the ministers who voted for the war in Lebanon sloganized 'Peace in Galilee' when there had been no shots in Galilee for over a year." Jacobo Timerman, *The Longest War* (New York: Knopf, 1982), 101. The total number of Israeli deaths from terrorism *anywhere* in Israel in all of 1982 was two – in 1981, five. Source: *Peace Watch* and news reports, cited by IRIS (Information Regarding Israel's Security, an independent information organization in Israel). In the Galilee area, Israel sustained an average of seven deaths per year (1978 to 1982). David Shipler, "Israel's Longest Year" *New York Times*, June 7, 1983, A2.

84. Tessler, *History of Conflict*, 571.

85. Arafat and Nidal were sworn enemies. Nidal made repeated attempts on Arafat's life and Arafat pronounced a death sentence on Nidal. Nidal had placed a bomb in PLO offices in Sidon and attacked PLO figures considered accommodative to Israel. He may have been seeking to provoke an Israeli offensive against the PLO. As a recipient of Iraqi support, Nidal may also have been an agent of revenge for Israel's destruction of Iraq's nuclear reactor. Schiff and Ya'ari, *Lebanon War*, 98-9.

86. Tessler, *History of Conflict*, 571, 830, no. 68.

87. Some investigators report five wounded. One Israeli died of a heart attack.

88. Tessler, *History of Conflict*, 574-6. The PLO lost its command structure within hours and did not fight well. David Lamb, "Politics Upset a Blitz Timetable," *Jerusalem Post*, July 17-18, 1984, p. 4.

89. Sharon often acted without Israeli cabinet approval and sometimes without the knowledge of the prime minister. Spiegel, *Other Conflict*, 415.

90. Sharon manipulated the cabinet into believing that the goal was limited to ending PLO capacity to shell northern Israel, as though "Peace in Galilee" was the main issue. He insisted that the operation would take twenty-four hours, that neither Beirut nor the Syrian forces garrisoned in the Bekaa Valley (east) would be involved. Begin cited the forty-kilometer figure to both Reagan and the Labor party.

91. The London *Guardian* reported only about 3,000. See Tessler, *History of Conflict*, 576.

92. Khouri, *Dilemma*, 430.

93. Schiff and Ya'ari, *Lebanon War*, 199.

94. Sachar, *History*, Vol. II, 172.

95. Khouri, *Dilemma*, 431.

96. Robert Fisk, *Times* [London], July 13, 1982.

97. Reagan acceded to a Congressional *increase* in aid to Israel in early 1983.

99. Most were to depart on ships to Cyprus, some overland to Syria.

99. Schiff and Ya'ari, *Lebanon War*, 225-6.

100. Khouri, *Dilemma*, 432.

101. The number of armed Palestinians remaining in the camps after evacuation is not precisely known but observers on the scene put the number at a few dozen. The figure could be as high as 200 if part-time members of the camps' self-defense militias were to be included. Schiff and Ya'ari, *Lebanon War*, 257. Also Rashid Khalidi, *Under Siege: PLO Decision-making during the 1982 War* (New York: Columbia University Press, 1986), 179. That only 150 soldiers were sent in to round up an alleged 2,000 to 3,000 armed PLO fighters indicates that Sharon knew otherwise.

102. Sharon and Eitan had strategized entry into the refugee camps in coordination with the Phalangist militia weeks *before* Bashir Gemayel's assassination and *before* the completion of the PLO evacuation. Thus, the claim that the PLO remained in the camps *after* evacuation was either mere assumption or an excuse to enter for darker purposes. Tessler, *History of Conflict*, 594.

103. Tessler, *History of Conflict*, 594. On September 14, Sharon told senior IDF commanders that Phalange forces would go into the camps.

104. *The Beirut Massacre: The Complete Kahan Commission Report* (New York: Karz-Cohl, 1983), 54 (Referred to as Kahan Report). The Phalange were known for their hatred of Palestinians.

105. Initially, Begin approved IDF entry into West Beirut, violating an agreement with the United States, but not Phalange entry. Sharon told Begin that the IDF was needed to *prevent* the Phalange from unleashing vengeance but made no mention that the Phalangists were going into the camps.

106. Schiff and Ya'ari, *Lebanon War*, 263; Tessler, *History of Conflict*, 595.

107. General Saguy, director of military intelligence: "The Phalangists will find a way to get them [PLO fighters] and settle old scores. . . . Murders . . . will just go on and on without end." Schiff and Ya'ari, *Lebanon War*, 250. Eitan stated, after Bashir Gemayel's assassination but before the massacre, that the Phalangists were "thirsting for revenge and there could be torrents of blood" (258). Even *before* Gemayel's assassination, Phalangist officers bragged about the slaughter they would visit upon Palestinians. Already, low-keyed "liquidation campaigns" to "take out" PLO and purported Syrian agents had occurred in Sidon and Tyre – areas under IDF control (252).

108. Tessler, *History of Conflict*, 595.

109. Israeli-sponsored SLA militiamen may also have accompanied the Phalangists. Thomas Friedman provides extensive evidence for SLA involvement in "The Beirut Massacre: The Four Days" *New York Times*, September 26, 1982, 19-22.

110. *Kahan Report*, 22. Hobeika's instructions and those of others, including such remarks as "Do God's will," were overheard by an IDF officer on the rooftop, who reported them to his commanding officer.

111. *Kahan Report*, 63.

112. Tessler, *History of Conflict*, 591. Schiff and Ya'ari, on the other hand, reported, surprisingly, that fleeing Palestinians said *nothing* to the IDF about a massacre.

113. Schiff and Ya'ari, *Lebanon War*, 274-5.

114. Some IDF warned Phalange leaders that civilians should not be harmed. That was the extent of control.

115. Schiff and Ya'ari, *Lebanon War*, 274-5. On the morning after the first evening of bloodshed (September 17), Ze'ev Schiff, military affairs editor of *Ha'aretz*, informed Shamir about reports of killings. Shamir failed to investigate. Another Israeli military correspondent, Ron Ben-Yishai, informed Sharon of details of the murders on the 17th – and was again ignored. Tessler, *History of Conflict*, 597.

116. Tessler, *History of Conflict*, 596.

117. In an authoritative study, Amnon Kapeliouk states: "Between 3,000-3,500 men, women and children were massacred within 48 hours between September 16 and 18, 1982." He further notes: "The Kahan Report follows official Israeli statistics in minimizing the number of victims, placed at 700-800 deaths. The exact number will never be determined. However, according to official Lebanese sources quoted on October 14, 1982 in *L'Orient le Jour*, 762 corpses were buried by different organizations. The same sources indicate that 1,200 bodies were recovered and buried by their relatives. To this, one must add the hundreds of bodies dumped in mass graves [using bulldozers] by the assailants, those permanently buried under the rubble of their leveled homes, and finally the hundreds of missing persons never accounted for." Amnon Kapeliouk, *Sabra and Shatilla* (Belmont, Mass.: Association of Arab-American University Graduates Press, 1984), 63, 89.

118. Schiff and Ya'ari, *Lebanon War*, 264.

119. Franklin Lamb, ed., *Reason Not the Need: Eyewitness Chronicles of Israel's War in Lebanon* (Nottingham, England: Bertrand Russell Peace Foundation, 1984), 541.

120. Kapeliouk, *Sabra and Shatilla*, 73-4. Begin was responsible for the massacre of 254 Palestinian civilians at Deir Yassin in 1948, Sharon for the killing of sixty-nine at Qibya in 1953 and Eitan for commuting the sentence of Daniel Pinto, an IDF officer found guilty of the murder of civilians in Lebanon in 1978.

121. Were the military to plead that they were simply following orders, the government would be implicated.

122. The Kahan Commission's recommendations: (1) Saguy, the director of military intelligence, to be dismissed; (2) Yaron to no longer serve as IDF field commander; (3) Eitan, whose "acts and omissions" led to "grave conclusions" and who likely warranted dismissal, to be allowed to retire; (4) Sharon, found to bear "personal responsibility," to be considered for removal from the cabinet by Begin if he did not voluntarily resign; and (5) Begin, who knew about the Phalangists in the camps on September 16 yet "showed absolutely no interest in their actions," to be assigned "a certain degree of responsibility." Shamir was also found to have "erred"

in not taking any measures when he learned of the continuing slaughter.

123. The commission, chaired by a former secretary-general of the UN, noted the pejorative and inciting language commonly used with reference to Palestinians by Israeli leaders such as Begin, e.g., "extermination," "purification," "two-legged animals." Such language persisted with other leaders: "cut off their testicles" (Sharon); "drugged roaches in a bottle" (Eitan); "grasshoppers" (Shamir); and "kill the mosquito" (Foreign Minister Ehud Barak). *Yediot Ahronot,* December 29, 1982; David Shipler, "Most West Bank Arabs Blaming U.S. for Impasse" *New York Times,* April 14, 1983, A3;Muhammad Ali Khalidi, "Israeli Discourse Still Reflects Hatred" *New York Times,* May 24, 1996, A22.

124. Schiff and Ya'ari, *Lebanon War,* 285.

125. Editorial, "Israel's dreadful dilemma," *MEI,* January 10, 1997.

126. Tessler, *History of Conflict,* 577, 599.

127. More than 300 by August 1982 (Tessler, *History of Conflict,* 584); 383 by late September (Sachar, *History,* Vol. II, 205); and finally, over 600 (Tessler, 584).

128. Quoted in Ehud Ya'ari "Israel's Dilemma in Lebanon," in *Middle East Insight 3* (April-May, 1984), 18-23. Cited in Tessler, *History of Conflict,* 584. Civilian losses to terrorism anywhere in Israel between 1967 and 1986 have numbered between fifteen and eighteen per year. B. Michael, *Ha'aretz,* June 22, 1982; Shulmit Har-Even, *Ha'aretz,* June 30, 1982; Amnon Kapeliouk, "The liquidation of the Palestinian obstacle," *Le monde diplomatique,* July 1982; B. Michael, *Ha'aretz,* July 16, 1982 (citing Israeli police statistics). *Peace Watch* statistics and news reports compiled by IRIS (Information Regarding Israel's Security).

129. Between 1967 and 1982, Palestinian and Lebanese civilian losses were 1,000 (1967-1975), plus 1,000 to 2,000 (1978, "Operation Litani"), plus some 30,000 in 1982 ("Peace in Galilee"). Figures are necessarily imprecise because of the large number of persons missing, buried by relatives on the spot, never taken to hospitals, buried under rubble in Beirut or under leveled refugee camps, or bulldozed into mass pits. Lebanese government figures for late August,, *prior* to Sabra and Shatilla, cite 19,000 killed (90 percent civilians) and over 30,000 wounded, based on police records, which in turn are based on hospital, clinic and civil defense center reports but which "do not include people buried in mass graves in areas where Lebanese authorities were not informed." Robert Fisk, *Times* [London], July 13, 1982). Said and Hitchens, estimating the *uncounted,* concluded that "as many as 40,000" Palestinian and Lebanese were killed, over 100,000 "seriously injured" (amputations, serious burns, etc.) and over 500,000 "left homeless" – a range of 20,000 to 40,000 killed being "not unreasonable." Said and Hitchens, *Blaming,* 257, 273. The Red Cross estimated that 15,000 were taken prisoners by the IDF. The UN estimated 13,500 severely damaged homes in West Beirut alone – countless homes in towns and camps in southern Lebanon not included.

130. Israel locked as many Shi'ite Lebanese in its southern detention center at Ansar as it did Palestinians. Iran provided support for Hizb'allah. Hostage taking began after Israel's client Christian militia kidnapped four Iranians and apparently

murdered them. Hizb'allah murdered eight Western hostages during the hostage-taking period (1982-1991).

131. Yehoshua Porath, *Ha'aretz*, June 25, 1982. Cited in Chomsky, *Triangle*, 200.

132. Ibid.

133. In the Galilee-Lebanon area during a fifteen-year period (1967-1982), the ratio of Palestinian and Lebanese deaths to Israeli deaths was about 300:1.

Chapter 18

Likud's Greater-Israel Dream and the Intifada (1988)

Since the 1967 war, Begin had contemptuously rejected a description of the occupied West Bank areas as either "occupied" or "administered," and had insisted that they be identified by their biblical titles of Judea and Samaria. . . . It bespoke his lifelong commitment to a wholly redeemed Land of Israel.[1]

Reagan seeks a solution for Palestinians under occupation

President Reagan offered a proposal for a Middle East settlement on September 1, 1982. While he had no love for the PLO, he hoped to address the problem of Palestinian homelessness and considered that Jewish settlements in the territories were an "obstacle to peace." His plan called for (1) "full autonomy" for Palestinians in the West Bank and Gaza during a transitional period, at the end of which a self-governing Palestinian entity (but not a state) would be associated with Jordan; (2) a freeze on *new* Israeli settlements in the occupied territories; and (3) negotiations on the status of Jerusalem.

What was new was that Palestinians were importantly considered. Rather than viewing the Israeli-Arab conflict as one only between Israel and its neighboring Arab states (an *interstate* conflict), Reagan and his new secretary of state, George Shultz, saw the underlying conflict to be that between Israel and the Palestinians.[2] Menachem Begin, on the other hand, thought of the Palestinians as an *internal* Israeli issue – as though the West Bank and Gaza were already parts of Greater Israel.

Reagan maintained that Israeli settlements in occupied territories were "in no way necessary" for the defense or security of Israel. He also rejected Begin's earlier notion of autonomy that gave Palestinians control over only certain *services* (e.g., schools and tax collection) without control over the land itself. He favored for Palestinians "real authority over themselves, the land and its resources" and thought that such authority, in association with Jordan, would satisfy moderate (Laborite) Israelis.

Whereas Shimon Peres and the Labor party saw the Reagan Plan as a "basis for dialogue,"[3] Begin and the Israeli Knesset rejected it outright. Indeed, regarding the central issue – that Palestinians should control the West Bank and Gaza – Begin immediately "answered" Reagan by announcing the establishment of new settlements in the occupied territories as part of his plan to settle 1.4 million Israelis in Judea and Samaria over the next three decades.

Yasir Arafat saw merit in the Reagan Plan, as well as some flaws: (1) Syria's conflict with Israel over the Golan Heights annexation was not addressed; (2) an independent Palestinian state was precluded; and (3) extant Israeli settlements were accepted. Arafat stated his willingness to accept the Reagan Plan were it to include a reference to the national rights of the Palestinians. Syria's Hafez Assad was upset by Reagan's snub of Syria and accused the United States of having concern only for Israel's security.[4] The Soviets characterized the Reagan Plan as a "farce" – seemingly out of fear that the plan would lock them out of the Middle East.

The week after the Reagan Plan was announced, twenty Arab League governments convened in Fez, Morocco, and proposed their own ("Fez") plan: (1) complete Israeli withdrawal from *all* occupied territories, including East Jerusalem (as Arabs interpreted UN 242); (2) dismantling of all Israeli settlements in the territories; (3) establishment of a Palestinian (West Bank and Gaza) state under leadership of the PLO; (4) compensation to unrepatriated Palestinian refugees; and (5) UN Security Council guarantees for the peace and security of all states in the region. This *two-state* plan was essentially a return to the original 1947 UN partition proposal (with half as much land for the Arab state) and implied Arab recognition of Israel.[5] Too radical, it nevertheless reflected a consensus in Arab nations about seeking peace with Israel.[6]

The condition of the PLO after Lebanon: popular support but internal conflict

Israel's political goal of destroying the PLO in order to destroy Palestinian nationalism had failed. "Despite Israeli attempts to suppress expressions of nationalism, inhabitants of the West Bank and Gaza continued to articulate both their identification with the PLO in general and their preference for the political line espoused by Arafat and Fatah in particular."[7] The Lebanon war "increased tension and opposition to Israeli rule . . . and increased support for the PLO not only in the West Bank and Gaza, but among the Israeli Arabs."[8] What the Israeli government had overlooked, according to Yehoshafat Harkabi of Hebrew University, was the fact that Palestinian nationalism, like Jewish nationalism, was an *idea* that would not diminish as a result of war or oppression.

After the Lebanon war, the *diplomatic* orientation of Arab nations and the PLO intensified. In early 1983, the Arab League states sought to convince the United States that differences between the Reagan and Fez Plans could be bridged.[9] Moroccan King Hassan announced that "the Arab nations will recognize Israel if it returns to its pre-1967 borders." These diplomatic efforts failed, however, partly because Reagan, despite his own proposals, was unwilling to press Israel to freeze settlements or to withdraw from Lebanon. Arafat and Hussein saw bad faith in this reluctance.[10] Accordingly, Arafat rejected the Reagan plan in early 1983.

Extremist factions within the PLO split with Arafat over his failed reliance on diplomacy.[11] Whether that of the PLO or the Arab states, diplomacy had produced nothing and violence now seemed to them the only way.[12] For example, the Arab states (notably Syria) had not aided the Palestinians militarily even during the devastations of the Lebanon war.[13] Israel might consider Arafat a fanatical terrorist enemy but PLO extremists considered him a pro-West (Hussein/Reagan) compromiser who favored recognition of Israel and abandonment of the fight for all of Palestine.

In May of 1983, Arafat faced a mutiny led by Abu Musa and some other Fatah commanders.[14] Fatah dissidents, with the assistance of Syria, engaged in armed clashes with Arafat loyalists in Lebanon. Arafat traveled to Lebanon to mediate the conflict. There, he and his followers were cornered by these dissident forces in the northern Lebanese city of Tripoli in September 1983. Armed conflict did not end until December when Saudi Arabia intervened diplomatically. Arafat and 4,000 of his men were, for a *second* time in little more than a year, forced out of Lebanon, not this time by the IDF but by dissident Fatah.

The United States and Israel mired in Lebanon – more civil war (1983-1984)

After the Sabra and Shatilla massacre of September 1982, Reagan had rushed U.S. Marines to Beirut as part of an international peace-keeping force that included France, Britain and Italy. The IDF had remained in Lebanon because Begin hoped to conclude a peace treaty with the new president of Lebanon,

Amin Gemayel, brother of assassinated Bashir. Begin hoped to obtain security and political concessions favorable to Israel and to salvage an appearance of accomplishment from the Lebanon war. Reagan, too, wanted this treaty signed so that the IDF would withdraw and U.S. forces could return home.

The Israeli public clamored for IDF withdrawal as casualties mounted.[15] Yet IDF withdrawal meant leaving the Christian Phalangists to fend for themselves against Druze factions supported by Syria. When the IDF tried to withdrew from one area in the Shouf Mountains, a violent civil war erupted in which the Druze defeated the Christians.[16] Some 1,000 lives were lost with 50,000 made homeless.

After this defeat of Gemayel's forces and after the bombing of the U.S. embassy in Beirut in April 1983 (sixty killed), the United States dropped all prior pretense of peace-keeping.[17] Reagan became an uncritical ally of Gamayel's pro-West government and attacked Gamayel's enemies (Druze, Syrians and Lebanese Shiite extremists). Massive U.S. naval bombardments and air attacks on the Druze in the Souf area precipitated suicide bombings – of the U.S. Marine barracks in October 1983, killing 241; of French forces, killing fifty-nine; of Israeli forces, killing sixty. With Israel fighting in Lebanon, necessitating a Syrian presence,[18] the United States bogged down in a hopeless war.

A compelling symbol of the futility of U.S. policy was the unleashing of the huge sixteen-inch guns of the battleship *New Jersey* on Druze positions in February 1984. This "fantastically destructive" display, demonstrating "unconscionable disregard for civilian casualties," accomplished nothing.[19] Reagan saw himself engaged in a U.S. "credibility struggle on a global scale." He saw his task as that of preventing the entire Middle East from being "incorporated into the Soviet bloc." His logic: because Syria, a Soviet client, has supplied the Druze with weapons, the Druze must be clients of the Soviets.[20]

The United States failed completely. The Druze and Shi'ite militias made additional gains in the Beirut area, Gamayel's army was routed and Beirut faced chaos. Reagan withdrew the marines anyhow. A desperate Gemayal, facing military and political collapse, turned not to Israel but to *Syria*. Gemayal and Syria then called for removal of the IDF from southern Lebanon (partly accomplished in June 1985). It was Syria which attained what Begin and Sharon had wanted: dominance in Lebanon.

Begin retires in despair; a Shamir-Peres government continues the hard line

Begin suddenly retired in September 1983, a year and a half before the expiration of his term – his wife's death a factor. Military losses (600) in Lebanon had polarized the nation. Inflation was soaring (400 percent) due to war expenses in Lebanon and accelerated settlement-building in the occupied territories.[21] Foreign Minister Yitzhak Shamir was selected by the Likud coalition's dominant party, Herut, to replace Begin. Moshe Arens remained defense minister. Shamir and Arens were both committed to the retention of the West Bank and Gaza with continued construction of Jewish settlements. Arens has been described as "a Sharon hawk with polish," Shamir as "not a bargainer . . . a two-dimensional man . . . one dimension [being] the length of the Land of Israel, the second, its width."[22]

However, when Shamir introduced unpopular economic austerity measures (currency devaluation, new taxes and increased prices for state-subsidized goods), a small religious party broke rank and Shamir faced an electoral challenge after only six months in office. He managed to retain leadership of Likud despite a formidable challenge from the popular Ariel Sharon. Peres headed the Labor Alignment. The election in July 1984 ended in a standoff. Likud and Labor came to an agreement to share a *national unity* government with *alternating* prime ministers: Peres was to be prime minister for two years, with Shamir as his foreign minister, then they were to exchange roles for the next two years. Yitzhak Rabin would remain defense minister throughout.

Ironically, Shamir had failed to win decisively because he lost votes to Israel's most extreme ultranationalists (10 percent of parliament). New "crypto-fascist" parties were embracing ideas about the expulsion of Palestinians, much like those of the Jewish settler-vigilantes.[23] In fact, two months before Shamir's election, twenty-seven settlers had been arrested, convicted and given light sentences for terror against Palestinians, a terrorism well-tolerated by both the Israeli government and public.[24] However, Peace Now objected:

> The Jewish terrorist movement is not a deviation or a coincidence. It is the price of Greater Israel, it is the bitter fruit of fanatical nationalist ideology, an ideology of power. The settlements – the seeds of expropriation – become the hothouse of terror.[25]

The PLO and Jordan propose confederation of Jordan with a Palestinian state

While Reagan was bogged down in Lebanon and Peres was settling into the Israeli premiership, Arafat was establishing relationships with Egypt[26] and Jordan, relations he considered essential to any PLO role in future Middle East settlement talks. Arafat and King Hussein gradually fashioned an agreement calling for an international conference to be sponsored by the UN Security Council. Announced in November 1984, the agreement supported: (1) the PLO as the sole legitimate representative of the Palestinian people and their inalienable right to self-determination; (2) the UN Resolution 242 land-for-peace principle; and (3) a *confederation* of Jordan and a Palestinian state. Here, Arafat was giving up the idea of a completely *independent* Palestinian state. The Palestinian National Council (PNC) supported this agreement, as did most Palestinians.

Peres made some conciliatory moves, including a temporary freeze on new settlements and an agreement to negotiate with King Hussein and Palestinians (but not with the PLO) on the basis of UN 242.[27] These concessions by Peres frustrated Israeli ultranationalists committed to Greater Israel just as Arafat frustrated Fatah extremists committed to Greater Palestine.[28]

It was, however, Peres's refusal to negotiate with the PLO that doomed the new Arafat-Hussein confederation plan. His refusal was allegedly based on PLO failure to officially accept UN 242 (which recognized Israel).[29] But the problem for the PLO was *not* recognition of Israel (nor the principle of exchanging land for peace, which the PLO supported). It was the failure of UN 242 to recognize a *Palestinian right to self-determination.*[30] Acceptance of UN Resolution 242 would have meant acceptance that the UN was ignoring Palestinian rights.[31] Otherwise, as Hussein made clear, the PLO accepted UN 242.[32]

Nevertheless, Peres refused to negotiate with the PLO and underscored his resolve on October 1, 1985, by ordering the bombing of PLO headquarters in Tunisia.[33] Killing sixty people, wounding many more, this act elicited world condemnation and an outpouring of anger and mass protest against "Israeli state terrorism" in much of the Arab world. Six days later, four members of the PLF (Palestine Liberation Front) hijacked an Italian cruise ship, the *Achille Lauro,* and demanded the release of a number of Palestinian prisoners held in Israeli jails. A Jewish-American tourist, Klinghoffer, was shot and thrown overboard. The world was revolted. The PLO condemned the act.

The United States and Israel pressured Hussein to break relations with the PLO and make a separate peace with Israel.[34] Instead, Hussein gained Arafat's agreement to *accept* UN Resolution 242 if the United States would permit PLO participation in peace conferences as well as recognize a Palestinian right to self-determination (January 1986). The United States waffled, even though it "fully understood that the Palestinian position did not reflect a refusal to recognize Israel's right to exist or to accept the principle of land for peace."[35] Two years of diplomacy collapsed around these evasions by the United States and Israel, obviously because a Palestinian state, even in confederation with Jordan, was considered unacceptable.

Conditions prior to the intifada

Shamir's turn to be prime minister came in October 1986. He continued with the settlements and road networks that, under Peres[36] and Begin, had tripled the settler population between 1982 and 1986 and placed 50 percent of the West Bank under Israeli control.[37] The bulk of West Bank water (81.4 percent) was also being diverted to Israel and Jewish settlements (one-third of Israel's total supply) so that Palestinians were seriously deprived of water for personal use and crop irrigation.[38] Strategically placed Jewish settlements and interconnecting road networks under Israeli military control cut off Palestinian towns and villages from each other – a plan designed by Matityahu Drobles of the Jewish Agency and World Zionist Organization and approved by Begin. The Drobles Plan ("Master Plan for the Development of Settlement in Judea and Samaria") aimed to achieve the "demographic transformation" of the West Bank by separating Palestinians into decreasing pockets (cantons) surrounded by steadily increasing Jewish settlements.[39] The result, by 1986: some 1.5 to 1.6 million Palestinians, without hope of help from the PLO, found themselves politically and geographically isolated on decreasing islands of land and with decreasing supplies of essential water.

The whole concept of "land for peace" was becoming irrelevant. Because Israel was taking land and water up front, the Palestinians could expect little in exchange for peace.[40] Israel's concept of security seemed to turn not on peace negotiations but on keeping Palestinians under tight military control on the islands of land remaining to them. This tight control, approved by the Israeli cabinet and enforced by Defense Minister Rabin, was making life miserable for Palestinians under occupation. Deportations, press censorship, school closings, curfews, demolition of homes and other collective punishments marked an occupation "more oppressive than that of [Rabin's] predecessors from Likud, including Sharon as well as Arens, and was itself a cause of heightened tension among Palestinians in the West Bank and Gaza."[41] Jewish vigilante-settler groups (notably Gush Emunim) "assisted" the IDF and spread terror with impunity, being free of all military code restraints. According to the *Jerusalem Post*, settler attacks on Palestinians had an ulterior purpose "to coerce the military authorities . . . into putting the screws on the local Arab population so painfully that they would either meekly subject themselves to Israel's rule forever – or get out."[42]

In sum, the background of the intifada was loss of land and water, an oppressive military occupation, settler terrorism, the impotence of the PLO and the indifference of the surrounding Arab states:[43]

> Palestinians felt that they had reached a dead end: they were not living as free human beings and they had no hope for the future. The PLO was too fragmented and distant, the Arab states had lost interest. Europe and the Soviet Union lacked leverage and the U.S. was too committed to Israel to comprehend the Palestinian situation, much less broker a satisfactory accord.[44]

> [Gaza resembles a] pressure-cooker ready to explode. . . . In this "forgotten corner of Palestine" one witnesses overcrowding, poverty, hatred, violence, oppression, poor sanitation, anger, frustration, drugs and crime. The military occupation responds by becoming more insecure and oppressive.[45]

The intifada

The *intifada* ("shaking off") was sparked on December 8, 1987, when an Israeli tank carrier crashed into a line of cars and vans filled with Gazan workers returning from Israel. The crash, killing four and seriously injuring seven, was rumored to be an intentional retaliation for the stabbing of an Israeli businessman. Mass demonstrations resulted in more death and injury when the IDF fired live ammunition into Palestinian crowds. Feelings were already running high from prior clashes with the IDF.[46] A week after the carrier crash, Sharon provocatively threw a party in his new home in the Arab quarter of East Jerusalem, in which 300 guests, including Shamir and various Knesset members, reportedly attended under conspicuous police protection. While Likud was congratulating Sharon on the "setting up of a new home in such a crucial location . . . best proof that the people of Israel have come to remain in the land for all eternity," Palestinian protests were mounting.

The intifada was unquestionably a *grass-roots* movement that surprised the Israeli government and PLO alike – the PLO having neither encouraged nor financed it. Shamir and Sharon seemed to believe, given a weakened PLO, that Palestinian docility under occupation would continue indefinitely.[47] In fact, PLO weakness only added to popular desperation, fostering a new activism and self-reliance at the local level.

Palestinian youth, having little to lose and even less of a future, turned militant. All their lives they had lived under an occupation in which might had made right. Older teenagers threw stones at cars and soldiers; younger teenagers barricaded roads with large stones; children set tires ablaze with gasoline; adults boycotted Israeli goods and refused to pay Israeli taxes or work in Israel.

At first, local communities acted separately. Later, a broad leadership comprising many factions emerged, called the United National Leadership of the Uprising (UNLU). The traditional elite of Palestinian nationalism (professionals, journalists and academics) were not involved initially.[48] Operating underground, the UNLU communicated through leaflets secretly printed and distributed at night. A spontaneous, fragmented resistance to occupation began to acquire a unified voice through UNLU announcements of commercial and transportation strikes, mass demonstrations, protests and solidarity drives such as flag-raisings, prayer, fasting, work projects, marches and donation activities. Israel and the United States were roundly condemned, though without focus on Jewish people. The UNLU did not encourage violence, yet stone-throwing and petrol-bombing were inevitable.

The intifada centered primarily on protest about the conditions of occupation. Gradually the UNLU consulted the PLO about how to remedy local Israeli occupation abuses – how to gain release of political prisoners, stop settlement activity and land confiscation, avoid various Israeli taxes and remove restrictions on industrial and agricultural products exported from the territories.[49] Islamic groups such as the social-service Moslem Brotherhood and Islamic Jihad were also consulted.[50] A breakaway group from within the Moslem Brotherhood, Hamas, took an early, militant interest in the intifada.[51]

Israel's response to the intifada

Shamir sought to suppress Palestinian resistance with increased force. Defense Minister Rabin claimed that he would end the intifada in a few weeks through an "iron fist" policy – a policy he characterized as "force, might and beatings . . . to instill fear of the IDF."[52] In the first few months, 160 protesters, most under age twenty, were killed. The legs and hands of young Palestinians were broken to prevent their running or throwing stones.[53] Some instances of wrongful violence by the IDF were notable, including the burying alive of four Palestinians (who survived). The Israeli secret service assassinated a close aide of Arafat.[54]

The usual methods of collective punishment were intensified by Rabin:

closing of schools, universities and charitable societies; blowing up hundreds of homes; and placing whole communities under curfew, on occasion without access to food. Tens of thousands were detained and held in administrative detention or prison during the first year. Suspected activists were deported – a violation of the Fourth Geneva Convention and an action condemned by the UN Security Council. After a year and a half, some 574 Palestinians had been shot or beaten to death, with seventeen Israelis also killed.[55]

Two years into the intifada, Rabin acknowledged that he had failed to crush the resistance to occupation. Some 615 to 716 Palestinians were dead and 15,000 to 20,000 injured, according to IDF records.[56] Rabin vowed to "continue with all the measures that we used for the first years. . . . We have reached a war of attrition." Arrests and imprisonments approached the 50,000 mark, and many prisoners were being tortured.[57]

Sharon, now minister of industry and trade, denounced Rabin for his timidity and misplaced moderation,[58] while Prime Minister Shamir sought cabinet approval for an "open-fire" policy – authority to shoot stone-throwers on sight. Rabin judged that an open-fire policy would only fuel the violence and blocked the proposal. The idea of deporting or "transferring" all Palestinians from the occupied territories became an accepted topic for debate in Israel.[59]

Some Israeli doubts

Some Israelis began to worry about their nation's "commitment to universal humanistic values." In a discussion in May 1989 at the Center for Holocaust Studies at Ben-Gurion University, a question posed was: "How does Israeli behavior compare with Nazi persecution of the Jews?" Many were offended by the question, though it was acknowledged that Israel's "dehumanization of the enemy . . . helps us understand the human infrastructure that made Nazism possible."[60]

Other Israelis were asking a practical question: How did the occupation serve Israel's security? Abba Eban, for example, pointed out that withdrawal from the West Bank, even were it to lead to a Palestinian state, posed no threat to Israel's security – that Israel had a mobilizable force of 540,000 with some 3,800 tanks and 682 aircraft whereas the PLO had "8,000 men in scattered places, zero tanks and aircraft, a few guns and no missiles, but a variety of hand grenades, mortars, stones and bottles."[61] Some of Israel's most respected analysts concluded that "although the territories have some strategic value, in the end they are a burden."[62] In fact, the vast majority of the General Staff of the

IDF believed that continued rule over the territories created a *risk* to Israel's security.[63] Moreover, the IDF command had no wish to fight the intifada as a war, especially when the strength of the army was being diffused by occupation duties largely expected to fail – "3.5 million Israelis cannot keep 1.5 million Palestinians under perpetual curfew."[64] Most obvious was that an oppressive occupation only incited more Palestinian anger and fueled terrorism.

Judgments suggesting that the holding of occupied territory was impairing Israel's security would have had more influence on policy had acquisition of land and control of water not historically been associated with increased security. Indeed, if rule over Palestinians might be costly and dangerous now, the longer-range goal of crushing the intifada and isolating Palestinians on less and less land was the traditional Zionist (Greater Israel) version of security favored by Shamir. So too, Israel's control of the waters of the Jordan River and the West Bank was traditionally viewed as adding to Israel's security. That it would finally cost in terms of Palestinian and Arab resentful actions seemed not to figure in the government's calculation of risk – though Rabin, later on, acknowledged that risk: "If we solve every other problem in the Middle East but do not satisfactorily resolve the water problem, our region will explode."[65]

The intifada sparks nationalism – Arafat declares a Palestinian state
During the first year of the intifada, in June 1988 at a summit in Algiers, Arab nations affirmed that the PLO was the sole representative of the Palestinian people.[66] King Hussein relinquished all claim to the West Bank, a step that seemed to open the way for an independent Palestinian state.[67] In fact, Palestinians closely tied to Arafat (Bassam Abu Sharif and Faycal Husayni) also called for an independent Palestinian state in West Bank and Gaza, with international guarantees for the security of both the Palestinian and Israeli state.

Then in November 1988, at a conference of the Palestinian National Council, two potentially significant events occurred: the PNC decided to recognize the State of Israel; and Arafat issued a "Declaration of Independence for the State of Palestine" on the West Bank and in Gaza, with East Jerusalem as its capital. He proposed an international conference at which all outstanding disputes would be resolved peacefully. This new Palestinian state was eventually recognized by over 100 countries, including the Soviet Union, China, India and Greece, but not by the United States, Western Europe nor Israel.[68]

Israel and the United States circled the wagons. President George Bush insisted that the PLO was a terrorist organization despite U.S. State Department findings to the contrary, and denied Arafat a visa to address the United Nations in New York. The General Assembly countered with a vote to move the UN meeting to Geneva where Arafat could speak. He did so in December and, acknowledging yet countering Palestinian extremists, gave the world his assurance that the PLO: (1) accepted UN 242 and 338, (2) recognized Israel's right to exist and (3) and condemned the use of terrorism. These were the three conditions which the United States had named as preconditions for U.S.-PLO talks.

The United States seemed cornered. When Israel strongly objected to any U.S.-PLO talks, the United States opposed Arafat's declaration of an independent Palestinian state and campaigned against full membership of the PLO in UN agencies. Israel's flat refusal to talk with the PLO was on grounds that the *original* Palestinian National Charter called for a *single* state over all of Palestine – a technicality since the Palestinians had embraced a two-state solution already in 1974 and again in 1982 with the Arab League.[69] In the spring of 1989, Arafat publicly declared that the twenty-five-year-old Palestinian National Charter was "null and void."

Israel seemed cornered. The PNC's recognition of Israel and Arafat's declaration of a Palestinian state had brought world focus back to the PLO and Palestinian national aspirations for a small state next to Israel in Palestine.

Shamir counters Arafat's initiatives with Begin-like talk about "autonomy"

Shamir resorted to the same kind of nonstarter autonomy device that Begin had used at Camp David a decade before. That spring of 1989, Shamir proposed a Palestinian autonomy plan. But he would negotiate only with Palestinians acceptable to him (non-PLO) and only *after* the Palestinians ended the intifada. Palestinians rejected these proposals as a cynical ploy to mask Shamir's intransigence. Autonomy seemed to be a device to legitimize and extend Israel's occupation. Since Shamir had publicly and repeatedly asserted that he would never relinquish sovereignty over Samaria and Judea, autonomy could not be understood to be a step toward sovereignty.

Shamir's invocation of Begin's 1979 autonomy proposal elicited Palestinian scorn for a number of other reasons: (1) Shamir, like Begin, insisted on determining who represented the Palestinians at the negotiating table; (2) Shamir's demand that the intifada be ended before negotiations could take place was a demand that Palestinians relinquish the only bargaining chip they possessed; (3) Shamir undoubtedly would insist, as Begin had, on a myriad of sabotaging conditions designed to prevent autonomy; and (4) Shamir was rejecting Arafat's declared Palestinian state by substituting autonomy talks for sovereignty.[70]

Palestinians did agree on one thing: they would end the intifada if Israel would include the PLO in negotiations for a comprehensive solution based on territorial *compromise* and *mutual* recognition.[71] But Shamir was not prepared to compromise any territory in exchange for peace and candidly admitted, as he left office in 1992, that his agenda was simply to expand Jewish settlements and complete the demographic revolution in the Land of Israel: "I would have carried on autonomy talks for ten years and meanwhile we would have reached half a million Jews in Judea and Samaria."[72]

While the out-of-power Labor Alignment was willing to consider some degree of territorial compromise with the Palestinians, Likud feared that Shamir might give too much away to the Palestinians.[73] This Labor/Likud split fractured the fragile "national unity" government of Peres/Shamir. As a result, Shamir formed a new Israeli government with Arens, David Levy and Sharon in June 1989, "the most right-wing government in Israel's history."[74]

Greater Israel was speeding ahead. Shamir had countered Arafat's Palestinian state and other peace initiatives with ultranationalist policy and was crushing the intifada while expanding settlements – whatever the security risk. At this point, the new Bush administration was demanding more flexibility from the Israelis about settlements in the territories and exploring its own talks with the PLO. Secretary of State James Baker angrily declared to Shamir, "The White House number is 202-456-1414 and when you are serious about peace, call us."

The Gulf War – January 1991

If the PLO was dead in the water in its attempts to negotiate with the Shamir government, it sank with the Gulf War. Many Palestinians supported Iraqi President Saddam Hussein. While they did not approve of Iraq's invasion of Kuwait – Arafat proposed a peace plan calling for Iraqi withdrawal – Saddam Hussein had been the only leader of an Arab nation to declare himself ready to fight on behalf of Palestinian rights.[75] Moreover, Hussein had depicted himself as a *populist* opponent of corrupt and authoritarian Arab monarchies, particularly those aligned with United States oil interests, such as Kuwait and Saudi Arabia. This suggested to many Palestinians that a real "bottom-up" revolution by "the Arab people" was in the making, a revolution that would wake up the United States and an entrenched Shamir government. Palestinians were disturbed, too, by what they regarded as a U.S. double standard – a swift and forceful response to Iraq's occupation of Kuwait yet complete acquiescence to Israel's occupation of Lebanon and earlier occupation of the West Bank and Gaza. Not to be discounted was simply the Palestinians "sweet taste of revenge" on the United States and Israel.

Israelis were outraged by the Palestinians' clutching for an Iraqi savior. The Gulf War simply added to Israeli disdain for Palestinians and topped off Palestinian exhaustion, impoverishment and loss of life – by now more than 1,000.[76]

Notes

1. Howard Sachar, *A History of Israel: From the Aftermat of the Yom Kippur War, Vol. II* (New York: Oxford University Press, 1987), 25.

2. Shultz replaced Alexander Haig as secretary of state in July 1982. He stated before the Senate Foreign Relations Committee on September 10, 1982, that the underlying issue had to do with Palestinian autonomy and security in the West Bank and Gaza. On the other hand, "Labor, like Likud, tended to see Israel's conflict with the Arabs as an interstate dispute." Mark Tessler, *A History of the Israeli-Palestinian Conflict* (Bloomington: Indiana University Press, 1994), 606. This interstate idea had little basis: Jordan was pro-West, Egypt tied to Israel by a peace treaty and Lebanon and Syria militarily impotent.

3. Labor differed with the Reagan plan by insisting on an undivided Jerusalem as Israel's capital and retention of half the West Bank (the Allon Plan).

4. Fred Khouri, *The Arab-Israeli Dilemma* (Syracuse, N.Y.: Syracuse University Press, 1985), 441. Assad later expressed a willingness to modify his position on the Reagan plan if the United States would support an Israeli withdrawal from the Golan Heights, West Bank and Gaza.

5. The Fez Plan harked back to 1947 and was contained in King Fahd's 1981 plan. Acceptance of UN 242 was tantamount to recognition of Israel.

6. Tessler, *History of Conflict*, 609.

7. Tessler, *History of Conflict*, 611.

8. Khouri, *Dilemma*, 434-5.

9. King Hassan of Morocco termed the Fez Plan a step toward nonbelligerency with Israel; King Hussein of Jordan stressed the compatibility of the Reagan and Fez Plans. George Shultz called the Fez Plan a genuine breakthrough. Tessler, *History of Conflict*, 613-4.

10. The United States signed a strategic cooperation agreement with Israel in November 1983 despite Begin's *rejection* of Reagan's own plan.

11. Nevertheless, it is clear from "a series of resolutions taken by the PNC that such acceptance [of Israel] cannot be doubted." Israeli Reserve Gen. Matityahu Peled,

"Talking to the PLO," *New Outlook* (March/April 1983) 29.

12. Extremist groups included the Popular Front for the Liberation of Palestine (PFLP), the Democratic Front (DFLP), the Palestine Popular Struggle Front and the pro-Syrian Saiqa. These groups comprised about 20 percent of the PLO fighting force, filled about 10 percent of the political positions and controlled about one-third of the monies provided by Arab states. Emile Sahliyeh, *The PLO after the War* (Boulder, Colo.: Westview Press, 1986), 91-2.

13. Tessler, *History of Conflict*, 612. Arafat criticized Syria for not helping the Palestinians during the Lebanon war. Syria retorted that Arafat was seeking compromise with an Israel that had annexed the Golan Heights.

14. The month before, a close confidant of Arafat had been assassinated for openly advocating recognition of the Jewish state. Responsible was the Abu Nidal faction, the group that had also been responsible for shooting and wounding the Israeli ambassador in London in June 1982.

15. By June 1983, the IDF had lost an additional 180 troops; by spring 1984, another 100; by 1985, a total of 600. Tessler, *History of Conflict*, 584, 629.

16. Israel armed *both* the Druze and Christians. Israel needed to remain on good terms with *Israeli* Druze (serving in the IDF) and to show Gemayel that Israel had other cards to play. Tessler, *History of Conflict*, 628-30. But the Druze were also armed by the Syrians in order to counter Gemayel and Israel. The United States secretly armed Gemayel's Christian government forces.

17. A Lebanese Shi'ite organization, Islamic Jihad (backed by Iran), claimed responsibility for the bombing.

18. Syria indicated that it would withdraw if Israel did. Khouri, *Dilemma*, 442.

19. George Ball, *Error and Betrayal in Lebanon: An Analysis of Israel's Invasion of Lebanon and Its Implications for U.S.-Israeli Relations* (Washington: Foundation for Middle East Peace, 1984), 80.

20. Tessler, *History of Conflict*, 838, n.65, 839, n.70.

21. The national debt soared, the stock market was convulsing, there was near-panic in the financial community and Peace Now was clashing with right-wing militants, raising the prospect of civil war.

22. Avishai Margalit, "The Violent Life of Yitzhak Shamir," *New York Review of Books* (May 14, 1992): 24.

23. Sachar, *History*, Vol. II, 222-3. Extremist settler parties such as Kach ("By Force") saw Palestinians as aliens to be expelled unless they were willing to live as unequals in Greater Israel. Praise for these ultranationalists came from government figures, including Begin, Shamir, Eitan (the IDF Chief) and Goren (Israel's chief rabbi). The third-largest party in Israel, Tehiya ("Rebirth"), advocated annexation of the West Bank and opposed Palestinian autonomy. Tessler, *History of Conflict*, 645-7.

24. Most of the terrorists were Jewish settlers, active in Gush Emunim, or IDF reserve officers. They received "surprisingly lenient" sentences, even in the opinion of supporters. Prominent Israelis in the Knesset (e.g., Sharon, Cohen-Orgad, Ben

Eliezer) and others in the political mainstream defended certain of the terrorists. Tessler, *History of Conflict*, 641-2.

25. Tessler, *History of Conflict*, 641.

26. Moreover, Egyptian support provided Arafat with a counterweight to Syrian support of Fatah extremists. Egypt needed Arafat's support because Egypt had lost its status in the Arab League over criticism that it had left behind the West Bank and Golan Heights in making a separate peace with Israel.

27. Peres rejected most of the names submitted by a Jordanian/Palestinian delegation.

28. Shaul Mishal, *The PLO under Arafat: Between Gun and Olive Branch* (New Haven: Yale University Press, 1986), 173-4.

29. The United States officially rejected talk with the PLO but repeatedly talked sub rosa.

30. A public opinion survey in the summer of 1986 found that 90.2 percent of Palestinians rejected UN 242 because it ignored Palestinian rights, not because it recognized Israel. Tessler, *History of Conflict*, 666.

31. One Arab editor observed: "King Hussein blames the PLO because it refused to commit suicide. . . . For the PLO, UN 242 means political liquidation." Interview, *al-Fair Jerusalem*, February 21, 1986. Cited in Tessler, *History of Conflict*, 666.

32. King Hussein announced, "Palestinians are willing to accept United Nations Security Council Resolutions 242 and 338, and the principles they contain, as a basis for a settlement." He stated that Palestinians officially reject UN 242 only because it makes no reference to their right of self-determination. Address to the American Enterprise Institute, Washington, D.C., June 2, 1985)

33. Israel claimed that the bombing was in retaliation for a Palestinian attack in Cyprus that killed three Israelis. Arafat condemned the act. Palestinian extremists may have been seeking to undermine diplomacy. Tessler, *History of Conflict*, 660.

34. Hussein wanted to avoid Egypt's mistake of making a separate peace without including the Palestinians.

35. Tessler, *History of Conflict*, 664-5.

36. "All forces operative on the ground since Begin . . . continued to operate with tremendous drive under Peres. We are not only talking about settlements but perhaps even more so about infrastructure." Meron Benvenisti, quoted in *Kol Ha'ir* (Jerusalem), October 24, 1986. Cited by Tessler, *History of Conflict*, 671.

37. Edward Said and Christopher Hitchens, eds., *Blaming the Victims*, (London: Verso, 1988), 252. Tessler, *History of Conflict*, 671. Meron Benvenisti, *The West Bank Handbook* (Boulder, Colo.: Westview Press, 1986), 140-1.

38. United States Agency for International Development (USAID) reports in 1997 that "[Water] allocations to Palestinians in the West Bank and Gaza [are] 70-80 million cubic meters per year less than demand. This situation represents a critical constraint to economic growth as it relates to household, industrial and agriculture uses of water." In 1998, it is estimated that "Israel controls nearly all the water resources in the West Bank . . . and provides the average Palestinian less than one-

third as much water as the average Israeli – and less than half of what Palestinian experts say the people need." Douglas Jehl, "Water Divides Haves From Have-Nots in West Bank," *New York Times*, August 15, 1998, A3.

39. Geoffrey Aronson, *Creating Facts: Israel, Palestinians and the West Bank* (Washington: Institute for Palestine Studies, 1987), 97.

40. See Aronson, *Creating Facts*, Ch. 6.

41. Comments of Knesset member Yossi Sarid in *Davar*, August 4, 1986. Cited in Tessler, *History of Conflict*, 674.

42. Don Peretz, *Intifada: The Palestinian Uprising* (Boulder, Colo.: Westview Press, 1979), 30.

43. A summit of Arab states in November 1987 turned its attention away from Israel and toward the Iran-Iraq War. Arafat was treated with disdain, "reflecting the low priority that most Arab states appeared to be assigning to the Palestinian problem." The United States, too, had closed the PLO information office in Washington to demonstrate its concern over what it took to be PLO-sponsored terrorism. Tessler, *History of Conflict*, 682-3.

44. Ann Mosley Lesch, "The Palestinian Uprising: Causes and Consequences," *United Field Staff International Reports, Asia*, No. 1 (1988-1989), 4.

45. Emile A. Nakhleh, "The West Bank and Gaza," *Middle East Journal*, 42 (Spring 1988), 210.

46. Two months before, thousands of Palestinians had massed in Jerusalem in protest of Israeli news reports that Israel would permit Jewish worship beyond the Western Wall (on the grounds of the al-Aqsa Mosque, Islam's third-holiest shrine). Israeli tear gas and Palestinian stone-throwing caused many injuries on both sides. That same month the IDF killed a student at Bethlehem University, shut the university down and banned newspapers expressing support for the PLO.

47. Uri Avnery, "The Intifada: Substance and Illusion," *New Outlook* (December 1989), 13.

48. Individual leaders included some from Islamic Jihad, the Popular Front, the Democratic Front, the Palestine Communist Party, the Fatah and others in the Islamic movement outside the PLO.

49. Tessler, *History of Conflict*, 690.

50. The PLO advocated a *secular* state in Palestine whereas Islamic groups hoped to establish a *religious* state as part of a larger Islamic movement throughout the Arab world. Islamic Jihad, a tiny group before the intifada, was said to be composed of men recruited while in Israeli prisons.

51. Israel supported the Moslem Brotherhood in the 1980s as a way to undermine the Brotherhood's secular rival, the PLO. When the Brotherhood spawned a militant wing (Hamas) during the intifada, Israel gradually realized that the PLO could be a force to enlist against Hamas – foreshadowing the Oslo Accords. See David Shipler, *Arab and Jew: Wounded Spirits in a Promised Land* (New York: Times Books, 1986), 176-7, and Peretz, *Intifada: The Palestinian Uprising*, 104.

Hamas and Islamic Jihad held the fundamentalist belief that nationalism was an integral part of religious faith. This paralleled the fundamentalist belief of Israeli religious groups such as Gush Emunim.

52. Joshua Brilliant, "Rabin: Use of Blows Instills Fear of IDF" *Jerusalem Post,* January 26, 1988. Rabin's prediction is discussed in Mordechai Bar-On, "Israeli Reactions to the Palestinian Uprising," *Journal of Palestine Studies* (Summer 1988): 49-50.

53. Tessler, *History of Conflict,* 697.

54. Tessler, *History of Conflict,* 850, n.77. Also, fifteen youths were bound, beaten until they couldn't walk, trucked away and dumped into a garbage fill by the IDF – eventually released

55. Statistics from *Country Reports on Human Rights Practices for 1988: Report Submitted to the Committee on Foreign Relations of the U.S. Senate and the Committee on Foreign Affairs of the U.S. House of Representatives* (Washington: U. S. State Department, February, 1989): 1376-87, cited in Tessler, *History of Conflict,* 698-700.

56. Joel Brinkley, "Israeli Defense Chief Sees Failure in Quelling Uprising," *New York Times,* December 5, 1989; *al-Fajr Jerusalem,* November 13, 1989; and Tessler, *History of Conflict,* 701. According to Brinkley, forty-five Israelis had lost their lives by the end of 1989.

57. Torture of Palestinian detainees was "virtually institutionalized" (Amnesty International) and "systematic and routine" (B'Tselem). Cited in Norman Finkelstein, *The Rise and Fall of Palestine* (Minneapolis: University of Minnesota Press, 1996), 68.

58. Rafael Eitan, former IDF chief of staff in Lebanon, demanded expanded use of collective punishment, and Shubert Spero, a prominent intellectual, held that stone and gasoline bottle throwers should be deported whatever their age (if minors, with their parents).

59. Transfer was *not* an official position of Likud. However, in a poll taken by the *Jerusalem Post* in August 12, 1988, half of all Israelis leaned towards this approach. Tessler, *History of Conflict,* 709.

60. Tessler, *History of Conflict,* 705.

61. Abba Eban, "Israel, Hardly the Monaco of the Middle East," *New York Times* January 2, 1989, 23. Eban cites figures from the Center for Strategic Studies at Tel Aviv University.

62. "Militant believers in non-violence Criticise Israel and the PLO," *Jerusalem Post,* October 25, 1988, 10. "The importance of territory (in this case the West Bank) for Israel's defense cannot be dismissed, but territory does not always enhance security. Under conditions like those prevailing in the West Bank and Gaza Strip, the risks posed by additional territory are greater than the benefits they accord." Ze'ev Schiff, "Israel after the War," *Foreign Affairs* 70 (Spring 1991), 29.

63. *Yediot Aharonot* informal survey, cited in Ron Ben-Yishai, "What Do the Generals Think about Territorial Compromise?" *Yediot Aharonot,* June 10, 1988, supplement, 6-7. Also, "Generals Dismiss the Security Value of the West Bank," *Ha'aretz,* May 31, 1988. Cited by Tessler, *History of Conflict,* 710.

64. Schiff, Ze'ev. *Security for Peace: Israel's Minimal Security Requirements in Negotiations with the Palestinians* (Washington: Washington Institute for Near East Policy, 1989), 15.

65. Stephen Kinzer, "Where Kurds Seek a Land, Turks Want the Water," *New York Times*, February 28, 1999, Sec. 4, 3.

66. In part, Arab nations were motivated by a fear that their past neglect of Palestinians might spark rank and file intifadas in their own countries. Authoritarian, corrupt and elitist regimes (not uncommon in oil rich Arab states) were vulnerable to popular uprisings.

67. Hussein was under U.S. pressure to cut the PLO out of any negotiating role with Israel. Had he agreed, he could have faced his own intifada in Jordan. By relinquishing all claim to the West Bank, Hussein ended the dilemma. Seemingly supporting Palestinian independence, Hussein was also cutting off Jordanian financial support of Palestinians.

68. Jerome Segal, "Does the State of Palestine Exist?" *Journal of Palestine Studies* (Autumn 1989), 30.

69. In 1974 the PLO first modified its initial, single-state PNC proposal to a partition proposal. "The mainstream of the PLO had, since the 1982 Arab [League] summit in Fez, been officially committed to mutual recognition between Israel and a Palestinian state located in the West Bank and Gaza, with East Jerusalem as its capital." Tessler, *History of Conflict*, 718.

70. Autonomy with regard to behavior, the right of Palestinians to service themselves, was contrasted with autonomy over land and its resources, i.e., sovereignty.

71. Tessler, *History of Conflict*, 728.

72. Interview with Joseph Harif in *Ma'ariv*, June 26, 1992. Cited in Shlaim, Avi, "Prelude to the Accord," *Journal of Palestine Studies* (Winter 1994), 10.

73. Likud's Central Committee (Sharon, David Levy, Yitzhak Moda'i) imposed four conditions on Shamir's proposal: no Palestinian negotiators from East Jerusalem, the intifada must end before negotiators selected, no land to be relinquished, and Jewish settlements must continue.

74. Shlaim, *Journal of Palestine Studies* (Winter 1994), 5-6. Arens became defense minister; Levy, foreign minister; Sharon, housing minister. This Shamir cabinet defended, for example, the October 1990 Temple Mount killing of seventeen Palestinians, plus 100 wounded, by Israeli border police despite court determination that the police had initiated the violence. Charles Smith, *Palestine and the Arab-Israeli Conflict* (New York: St. Martin's Press, 1992), 314.

75. Tessler, *History of Conflict*, 738.

76. By 1991, intifada deaths numbered 1,135 according to *Peace Watch* and news reports cited by *B'Tselem* (Israeli Information Center for Human Rights in the Occupied Territories), Jerusalem, 1997. Israel lost fourteen soldiers and twenty civilians in the territories during the same period. By 1994, intifada deaths numbered about 2,000. According to Finkelstein, 400,000 Palestinians were detained or

imprisoned through June 1993. *Rise and Fall*, 130n.

Chapter 19

The Oslo Accords and the Demise of the Peace Process (1998)

A Rabin government (June 1992) and the end of the Madrid talks

The Gulf War demonstrated that security lay in technological defense against missile attack from distant soils, not in acquiring more land in the immediate vicinity (i.e., the West Bank). Nevertheless, after the war, Israel continued spending billions of dollars for expropriation and settlement of the occupied territories in the name of security, infuriating President Bush and his secretary of state James Baker.[1] Prime Minister Shamir demanded $10 billion from the United States for even more settlements but Bush faced him down.

Secretary Baker attempted to control settlement expansion by sponsoring talks among Israel, the Arab states and Palestinians (a non-PLO delegation, including Hanan Ashwari, Faisal Husseini and Rashid Khalidi) dealing with interim forms of autonomy in the occupied territories. Ten international conferences (the "Madrid Conferences") were held between late 1991 and the middle of 1993. In the midst of these talks, a Rabin/Labor government was elected on a platform promising peace with the Palestinians in a year.[2]

Yet Rabin remained Israel's tough "security man" concerning the territories.[3] As he put it, "Security takes precedence over peace" – that is, control takes precedence over negotiation. In pursuit of that control over the occupied territories, Rabin devoted large sums for "strategic settlements"[4] in "security areas" comprising about one-half of the West Bank, with $600 million spent on construction of interconnecting roads in 1994. The prime minister also authorized the continued construction of 10,000 housing units for Jews only in the

Arab-East Jerusalem section of the West Bank.[5] By these actions Rabin brought the Madrid talks to a point of crisis in November 1992. The Palestinians were outraged, claiming that Israel would effectively control two-thirds of the West Bank.[6] Then, in early 1993, Rabin "illegally and brutally" deported 416 alleged Hamas activists – an act that discredited the talks and galvanized Palestinian extremists.[7] Thirteen Israelis were murdered a month later by terrorists and Rabin completely sealed off Israel from the occupied territories.

The Oslo Peace Accords (September 1993)

Initially, Rabin had little interest in some informal, secret, Jewish-Palestinian talks taking place in Oslo. But after the Madrid talks collapsed, Rabin had greater need to find a way to fulfill his campaign pledge of peace. Moreover, talks with Syria about conditions for Israeli withdrawal from the Golan Heights – a strategy proposed by Ehud Barak (IDF Chief of Staff) to draw the Arab countries together in order to isolate and weaken the bargaining power of Palestinians – had gone nowhere. There were other reasons why Rabin reconsidered the Oslo talks. Arafat, the key, was personally in a weak position. His declaration of a Palestinian state had been ignored by the West and he was persona non grata with President Bush. He had also lost the support of the collapsing Soviet Union and had provoked the anger of Saudi Arabia over his position on the Gulf War. Rabin saw that Arafat was at serious disadvantage as a negotiator and that the Palestinians, exhausted by the intifada, might now be willing to come to favorable terms. "It became clear that the PLO was bankrupt, divided and on the verge of collapse and therefore ready to settle for considerably less."[8]

Rabin threw Arafat a life line with little risk to himself and potential gain for Israeli security – Arafat's secular PLO might conceivably be able to suppress Islamic terror groups.[9] After eight months of secret talks, an agreement was reached – the *Oslo Peace Accords.*

What the United States called a "historic breakthrough," PNC member Edward Said called "a Palestinian Versailles" and Israel's Amos Oz characterized as "the second biggest victory in the history of Zionism."[10] On the surface, the Oslo Accords looked benignly helpful to the Palestinian cause regarding self-determination. Agreed upon was the "Declaration of Principles on Interim Self-Government Arrangements" (DOP). This was not so much a set of agreements as an *agenda* for negotiations. However, some things were agreed: There was to be a *transfer of power* to Palestinians for an *interim* period. Palestinians would be permitted to administer unto themselves in five spheres: health, social welfare, direct taxation, education/culture and tourism. After two months, Israel would withdraw from Gaza and Jericho, redeploying troops to surrounding areas. The PLO would train a police force for local, internal Palestinian security though Israel would remain responsible for overall security in the West Bank and Gaza. It was also agreed that within nine months, a *Palestinian Council* would be elected by Palestinians to take over administrative functions for the PLO. Within two years, discussions would begin concerning a *permanent* settlement to be enacted in five years, a settlement separate from any agreements made during the interim period.[11]

For the Palestinians, exhausted by the intifada and brutalized by the occupation, the idea of gaining even limited autonomy with partial IDF withdrawal was a cause for celebration. On the other hand, for Palestinian leaders outside the Arafat camp – for example, Dr. 'Abd al-Shafi, a Madrid negotiator, and PNC member Edward Said – the primary disappointment of the Oslo Accords was their failure to address the fundamental issue of Palestinian *sovereignty* over the West Bank and Gaza. Palestinian territorial rights were never mentioned, even as a negotiable item on the agenda. Nor did the Accords place any restrictions on the continued building of Jewish settlements and their interconnecting road networks – that is, further erosion of Palestinian territory (some 65 percent of the West Bank already under Israeli control).[12]

Clearly, the Accords were possible only because negotiations about all the difficult and important issues relating to the Israeli-Palestinian conflict were excluded. Sovereignty, Jewish settlements, Palestinian refugee return and East Jerusalem were all off-limits.[13] Rather, the central focus of the Oslo Accords was on the *security of Jewish settlements and Israel* and the requirement that the PLO suppress Islamic militants as a precondition for withdrawal of Israeli troops from certain Palestinian areas.[14]

The recognition letters

The most important feature of the Oslo Accords, for detractors and supporters alike, was not the DOP provisions for limited autonomy/self-rule, but the *preamble letters* that conferred mutual recognition on the PLO and Israel. Nabil Shaath, Arafat's close advisor and negotiator, found in these recognition letters a parity between the two sides. Said saw the opposite – no parity where Palestinians had no power from which to negotiate, where "mutual" recognition was really *unilateral* recognition.

It is true that in this exchange of letters Arafat gave away much, Rabin little. Arafat affirmed: (1) PLO recognition of Israel's right to exist in peace and security; (2) renunciation of the Palestinian Covenant; (3) acceptance of UN 242 and 338 (despite their omission of Palestinian territorial rights); (4) renunciation of the use of terrorism and other acts of violence; and (5) assumption of overall responsibility for the behavior of PLO elements and personnel. In exchange, Rabin gave to Arafat recognition that the PLO represented the Palestinian people with whom Israel would negotiate. That is, Arafat recognized both the Jewish State and its right to security while Rabin recognized Arafat as an agent for a collection of people without a state or a similar right to security. Ignored outright was the Palestinian state declared five years earlier and recognized by over 100 countries – a nullity in the Accords.

Palestinian critique of the legal consequences of Arafat's recognition of Israel

Arafat's recognition of Israel had, in the opinion of some Palestinian scholars, given away, wittingly or unwittingly, explicitly or implicitly, a number of important and fundamental Palestinian legal rights:

(1) Arafat's recognition of and agreements with Israel constituted an admission that Israel *rightfully* possessed powers in the territories which it was empowered or entitled, through the Oslo Accords, to *transfer,* at its discretion, to the Palestinians. Such right of power does conflict with accepted international opinion concerning Israel's legal status as an occupier of conquered territories – occupiers do not possess powers which they can legally transfer to the occupied. If Israel had practiced *de facto* sovereignty over the territories since 1967, Arafat now seemed to be conferring on Israel *de jure* sovereignty.[15] In this respect, Israel became the rightful possessor of powers, some of which Arafat hoped might be transferred to the Palestinians. "We have," declared 'Abd al-Shafi, "helped to confer legitimacy on what Israel has established illegally."[16]

(2) Arafat's admission of Israeli rights and powers in the territories also seemed to have the effect of undermining the Palestinians' right of appeal to international courts for protection normally afforded people under occupation. Such protections include the Fourth Geneva Conventions, the Hague Conventions and other international laws prohibiting use of life-threatening force and torture, prohibiting settlement of occupied territories, etc. – conventions and laws systematically violated in the territories before and after the Accords.[17] To cast off occupier status seemed to undermine the occupied's right to international appeal.

(3) Another criticism of the Accords was that recognition of Israel constituted

a recognition of Israel's *laws,* including martial law in the territories. These laws, still in force, have in fact led to expropriation of land and water, imposition of taxes and deportation of inhabitants.[18]

(4) The clause about Israel's "right to exist in peace and security" has also been construed as an Israeli right to remedy any situation it deems threatening to security – for example, reintroduction of troops or undercover agents into self-rule areas to handle settler-Palestinian conflicts or apprehend suspected terrorists.

(5) But the central Palestinian criticism of the Oslo Accords involved Arafat's commitment to Israel's peace and security. This commitment made him responsible for Palestinian terrorism, future intifadas or other violence directed at Israelis. Israel assumed no parallel responsibility for IDF or settler violence directed at Palestinians. Moreover, Arafat's pledge to end violence set him squarely against Hamas and Islamic Jihad, thereby creating conditions for a potential civil war within the Palestinian community. As historian Avi Shlaim noted, this was a Rabin strategy "aimed at playing the Arabs off one against the other in order to reduce the pressure on Israel to make concessions."[19]

With Arafat "on the ropes" (as Rabin appraised) and Hamas "flourishing" (as Israeli intelligence reported), it was unlikely that Arafat could accomplish what Israel had not during the previous six years – suppression of dissident Islamic terrorists.[20] Certainly, suicide bombings would be impossible to prevent. Consequently, Rabin had available to him seemingly justified grounds for halting negotiations whenever Arafat failed (predictably) to fulfill his commitment to Israeli security. Moreover, given Israel's continuing land expropriation, exclusion of Palestinian labor from Israel, collective punishment and Shin Bet (Secret Service) operations in the Palestinian police, Arafat's chance of suppressing dissident Palestinian terrorism could only worsen.

Rabin's goals

What was Rabin's ultimate goal in signing the Oslo Accords? Was he, like Shamir, toying with Palestinians in endless talk about autonomy while confiscating land in the cause of Greater Israel – maintaining the status quo? Or seeking the *appearance* of peacemaker without much risk or cost? Or was he seeking to shift responsibility for terrorism onto Arafat to discredit him? Did he actually think that Arafat could deliver on Israel's security?

Certainly Rabin was following Shamir's classic fait accompli strategy of expansion in the West Bank and, like Shamir, avoiding the issue of Palestinian sovereignty. And yet Rabin did *not* want to incorporate two million West Bank and Gazan Palestinians into Israel by annexing the occupied territories. He once favored the 1967 Allon Plan whereby Israel would annex Jewish settlement areas and the Jordan Valley (eastern side of the West Bank) but not the densely populated Palestinians areas better controlled by Jordan – the once-popular "Jordanian option." Certainly, he and the Israeli public wanted to be rid of the Gaza Strip, a sealed-off, packed prison of angry unemployed Palestinians that, in his view, might best "sink into the sea."[21] Turning responsibility for the Gaza Strip over to the PLO was certainly one of Rabin's goals. Hence, the defensible conclusion of Israeli researcher Meron Benvenisti that Oslo was a device to enable the Israelis to gradually evacuate "precisely those [dense Palestinian population areas] they were keen to get rid of."[22] In any event, Arafat accepted the Gaza offer and, needing to show Palestinians that he could bargain for a foothold and symbolic concession in the West Bank, demanded and received Jericho as well.

But Rabin's goal may finally have been one of *separation,* in which West Bank Palestinians were to end up in a dozen, small, densely populated "self-rule" enclaves militarily encircled and effectively walled off from Israel. This plan, described below, was announced in January of 1995, the year of Rabin's assassination.

In sum, Rabin accomplished through the Oslo Accords a number of goals on the main issues: (1) PLO recognition of Israel's power and ultimate security responsibilities over all the occupied territories; (2) PLO acquiescence to continued settlement-building on rapidly diminishing amounts of land;[23] (3) PLO responsibility for halting Palestinian terrorism and suicide bombings; and (4) PLO responsibility for the Gaza Strip. The rest of the Accords concerned protracted negotiations over secondary issues about the exact timing, meaning and extent of limited Palestinian autonomy.

Oslo II – September 1995

Two years after the 1993 Oslo Accords when the Palestinians were on their own (their former guardian, Jordan, had signed a peace treaty with Israel in 1994), the Palestinians and Israelis made further interim agreements. Dubbed "Oslo II," or the Taba agreements, these agreements were designed to slowly extend Palestinian self-rule to other towns and villages besides Gaza and Jericho. This plan, if and when completed, was to give administrative and police control (not sovereignty) to Palestinians over about 3 percent of the West Bank (called

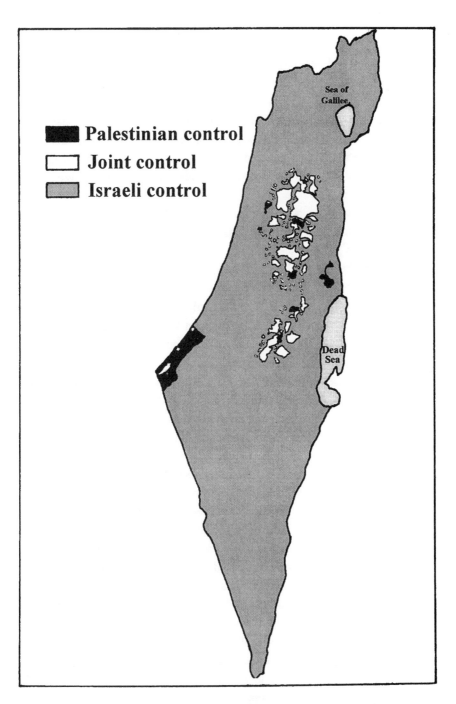

Oslo Accords Military/Security Control Zones (1997)

Area A). Another 24 percent (Area B) was to have a Palestinian administration with joint Israeli/Palestinian military control. The remaining 73 percent, comprising Israeli "public" lands, settlements, army camps and roads was to remain under exclusive Israeli control.[24] Hebron, a city of 120,000 Palestinians and 400 Israelis, posed a special case in which Israel was to retain part control of the city. The accords also allowed for construction of a system of internal roadblocks that could prevent north-south Palestinian travel in the West Bank and entry into East Jerusalem.

To summarize the agreements of Oslo I and II: *(a)* Palestinians have administrative authority to control health, social welfare, direct taxation, education/culture, tourism and policing in limited areas of the West Bank and Gaza; *(b)* Israel has responsibility for security over all the West Bank and Gaza and exclusive control of and authority for the security of all Jewish settlements and settlers even when in Palestinian self-rule (A) areas;[25] *(c)* Israel has veto power over all laws drafted by the Palestinian Council; *(d)* Israel's occupier laws remain in force throughout the West Bank and Gaza;[26] *(e)* all Palestinian administrative appointments require Israeli approval; *(f)* Israel has the exclusive power to collect customs fees and to tax locally produced Palestinian goods; *(g)* Israel controls all commercial and personal traffic between Gaza and the West Bank and between the West Bank, Israel and Jordan;[27] and *(h)* Israel controls all exits and entries to Palestinian self-rule areas and controls all roads.

Arafat's Achilles' heel and the faltering peace process

As previously described, Arafat's failure to assure Israel's security (a violation of the Oslo Accords) could be expected to threaten self-rule negotiations.[28] On the other hand, were he to successfully suppress Hamas, he would alienate Palestinians sympathetic to Hamas and jeopardize his own political base. Were Arafat more popular his dilemma would be less. But some Palestinians have seen Arafat as a dictator who has merely replaced Israel's military governor. And the PLO has been criticised as a corrupt patronage system in which members indulge in luxurious living amidst the people's poverty.[29] Arafat's strong-armed police force, charged with keeping the peace, has been accused of doing Israel's "dirty work" – torturing and killing Palestinians in pursuit of Islamic dissidents.[30] If Arafat works for Israeli and not Palestinian security, his popular support erodes.

Morerover, Hamas has enjoyed begrudging respect from more than 20 percent of Palestinians.[31] Many have rejected Hamas's terrorist acts and seen its Islamic ideology as intolerant and undemocratic. Yet Hamas has also exhibited concern for the people, delivering food, clothes, money and jobs to poor Palestinians.[32] "Many downtrodden Gazans depend on Hamas charity to feed their children – a consideration for Mr. Arafat if he were to crack down hard as Israel demands."[33] The people, in "existential crisis, demoralized, depoliticized and depressed . . . facing a cavernous void," admire the fact that Hamas and Islamic Jihad have at least *acted* against IDF and settler violence.[34]

Arafat's dilemma: he gains a degree of popular support by making progress on Israeli withdrawal, but if that requires open civil war with Hamas and Islamic Jihad, he also loses some support. Hanan Ashrawi believes that, "The more the PLO shows it can deliver on the Israelis' principle demand – security – the less it is accepted by its own people." Israel and Hamas both understand Arafat's bind – they know that it is not as simple as Israel alleges, that Arafat is a terrorist sympathizer, nor as simple as Hamas alleges, that Arafat is an Israeli collaborator.

Rabin's assassination, Netanyahu and the defunct peace process

In November 1995, two months after Oslo II, Rabin was assassinated by a Jewish religious fundamentalist, an act dramatizing the intense differences between orthodox and secular groups in Israel.[35] Shimon Peres took over the premiership and called for early elections in the summer of 1996. In a close vote, Peres lost to Likud's Benyamin Netanyahu, who had campaigned on a platform seeking to nullify the "dangerous" Oslo Peace Accords. Terrorist bombings provided an election boost for Netanyahu's no-accommodation position.[36]

Netanyahu has been described as having been "waiting all along for a way to get out of an arrangement he always held in disdain."[37] Like Rabin, security has been seen by him as a product of strength rather than peace negotiations and his distain has been linked not only to a "deep-seated distrust of the Oslo peace agreement [but also] of the Arabs."[38] Netanyahu's writings suggest a "vision of the Jew as perennial target who can never entrust his security to anyone, who must surround himself with what Jabotinsky called a 'steel wall.'" – that making peace peace with Arabs is like "keeping fish in a glass bowl until they learn not to bump against the glass."[39]

Foreign minister David Levy has criticized the prime minister for "destroying the peace" through actions seemingly designed to scuttle the Accords. These have included: tunnel-building in Jerusalem; a massive housing project at Har Homa; a dam project on Syria's doorstep;[40] the delayed Oslo II deployment of Israeli forces from self-rule areas; the punishment of Palestinians through harsh economic sanctions; the withholding of Palestinian tax monies from the Palestinian Authority;[41] and the sealing off of Israel from Palestinian labor and goods.[42] These actions could be expected to fuel Palestinian anger and only add to Arafat's inability to control terror.[43] Some have wondered whether Netanyahu has been the indirect source of the terrorism that he has used to disparage Palestinians and freeze withdrawal negotiations.[44]

The prime minister did make a concession in early 1997 of withdrawing the IDF from three-quarters of Hebron (virtually an all-Arab town). At the same time, his approval of the rapid expansion of Jewish housing at Har Homa (southern Jerusalem in the West Bank), some 6,500 new units in April 1997, drew condemnation from the UN General Assembly. Netanyahu declared: "We shall build in Jerusalem and everywhere, no one will deter us." He plans to enlarge Jerusalem to half again its current size and build many more Jewish homes in Har Homa by the year 2000 despite U.S. disapproval.[45] Netanyahu has been on the same expansionist track as Rabin and Peres who together increased settlements by 49 percent during their four-year rule.

Suicide bombings in Jerusalem in the summer of 1997 brought the "peace process" to a halt. Netanyahu refused negotiations about withdrawal and held Arafat responsible. Arafat accused Netanyahu of a "plot to stop and destroy the agreements."[46] Their mutual recriminations involved a circular linkage in which suicide bombings lead to halted negotiations which in turn lead to more suicide bombings. The United States has favored Netanyahu's side: "Only if the Palestinian side proves itself able and willing to comply with its security responsibilities is Israel obligated to transfer additional areas in the West Bank to Palestinian jurisdiction"[47] – confirmation to the terrorists that bombings are effective in sabotaging negotiations seen as submission to Israel

Conditions on the ground following the Oslo Accords

Settler violence in the occupied territories worsened after the 1993 Accords.[48] Settlers feared that limited self-rule would compromise what they considered rightful Jewish sovereignty over all of Palestine. Clashes accelerated. A settler massacred twenty-nine Palestinian worshippers in Hebron in February 1994.[49] This was followed by the killing of thirty Arabs by the IDF,[50] ushering in a wave of revenge suicide bombings by Hamas.[51] In January 1997, when settlers in Hebron brandished Uzi sub-machine guns and laid claim to Palestinian land, eight protesting Palestinians were shot by an off-duty IDF soldier. Two months

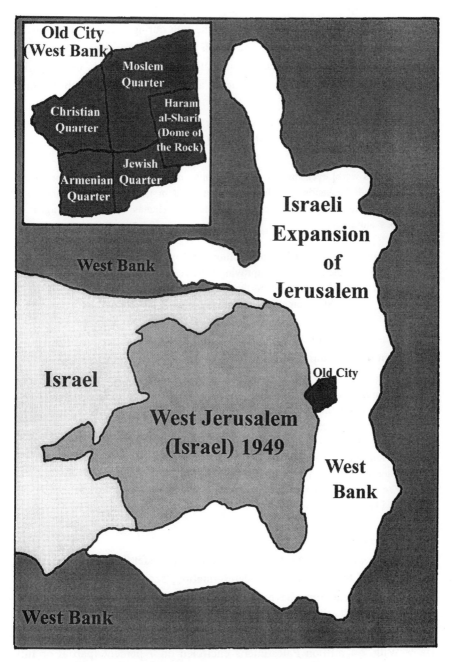

Expansion of Jerusalem into the West Bank (1998)

273

later fifty-eight Palestinians were shot by the IDF during a demonstration over Israeli construction at Har Homa. The Israeli government has been no more able or willing to curb the violence of the IDF, undercover agents or extremist expectedsettlers than has Arafat been able or willing to curb Islamic extremists.[52]

Self-rule and IDF withdrawal have not brought the Palestinians the relief they expected, even in the initial self-rule areas of Gaza and Jericho:

> [Conditions were] even made worse. Unemployment in Gaza increased, prices doubled and thousands of Palestinians remained in Israeli detention camps. Opposition to the peace process mounted and Hamas openly challenged Arafat's authority.[53]

> Gaza stagnates . . . most of the one million residents still search desperately for some sign that their lives are improving. The refugee camps remain mired in squalor. The result is a new mood that damns Israel and Arafat in almost equal measure. . . . Arafat's reputation has only fallen since his return.[54]

In Bethlehem, an Oslo II self-rule town, conditions in the summer of 1997 were reminiscent of those during the intifada:

> Black smoke billowed from burning tires and the crack of rubber bullets echoed through the streets of Bethlehem today as dozens of Palestinian youths hurled stones at Israeli soldiers to protest Israel's military closing of the town, which has now lasted nearly a month. The clashes reflected rising frustration among Palestinians at Israeli sanctions imposed after the suicide bombing in Jerusalem last month. . . . "There is no money, and no work. They're punishing two million people because of a bombing by two people whose identity isn't even known."[55]

Precedents and prospects

A sizable number of West Bank Palestinians have felt betrayed by Arafat's "surrender" of their right to self-determination, according to interviews by Norman Finkelstein. Some have admitted thinking the unthinkable – emigration from Palestine, a betrayal of Palestinian nationalist strivings and fulfillment of Israeli ultra-nationalist goals, yet a reflection of a need to finally live a normal life.[56] With 2.4 million Palestinians encircled on 7 percent (partial or full Palestinian political and security control) of what once was Palestine, and with 80 percent of West Bank water going to Israel and Jewish settlers, the future has seemed bleak to these people.[57]

What are the past, present and future solutions that have been proposed by Israel to deal with the "Palestinian problem"?

1. *Self-rule/autonomy in the occupied territories – an improbable solution*

Although Palestinian sovereignty has never been on the negotiating table, Palestinians initially experienced hope about economic exchange, mutual recognition and negotiating parity. Those hopes have not materialized. Rather, continued settlement-building in the West Bank and East Jerusalem have made future "permanent status" talks seem decreasingly relevant. Violent settlers have remained immune to authority.[58] IDF withdrawal has proved to be more encirclement with periodic reentry. Killing and torture of Palestinians has continued.[59] The prospect of economic cooperation soured in the reality of poverty and taxation.

Nor has the Israeli public found relief through the Oslo Accords, hopeful avenue of peace. Israelis hoped that Palestinians would provide their own internal security and that Arafat would suppress dissident terrorism. He has not. The peace process remains "on artificial respiration," "all but collapsed."[60]

2. *Annexation of the occupied territories – an improbable solution*

Could the Israeli government simply make annexational claim to the West Bank as it has the Golan Heights and Jerusalem? This alternative has not been seriously considered since Israel does not want possession of 2.4 million angry Palestinians. Incorporation of a large Islamic and Christian Arab population would clearly undermine a state established for the Jewish people.

Nor has "transfer" (voluntary or involuntary) of the Palestinian population followed by annexation, as demanded by the religious ultranationalists, ever been a policy officially accepted by the government – though debates about the possibility occurred in 1948, 1967 and 1987.[61] Sharon once advocated that all Palestinians be transferred to Jordan. Shamir invited Moledet, a party advocating transfer of Palestinians, to join his government in 1991. Yet, as a solution to Israel's demographic problem, transfer or deportation has not been considered an acceptable alternative. At the very least, an obvious parallel with Nazi deportations makes it obscene.

3. *The defunct Jordanian Option*

Rabin and others in the Labor Alignment preferred, rather than complete annexation, the Allon Plan, whereby Israel would retain its settlements and security areas in the West Bank while Jordan would rule over the remaining densely populated Palestinian areas. When Jordan relinquished claim to the

West Bank in 1988 and signed a peace threaty with Israel in 1994, this option was foreclosed.

Still, could Jordan be induced by Israel to once again annex or rule over the remaining islands of densely populated West Bank Palestinians? Or could Palestinians be paid to emigrate to Jordan or elsewhere? For that matter, could Egypt be induced to annex the Gaza Strip or Syria to accept emigrating Palestinians? The problem is that Palestinians are not generally welcome in Arab countries – posing political, economic and ethnic problems. Nor would it seem that Palestinians would welcome foreign, albeit Arab, rule. Could reparations or compensations paid to Palestinians to emigrate effect any change in the existing conflict? The money is there: ten years of U.S. aid to Israel (some $60 billion in government and nongovernment aid – equivalent to 6 percent of Israel's GDP for ten years) would constitute a Palestinian windfall.[62] Yet political identities, hatreds, injustices, humiliations and death are matters that can rarely be leavened with money.

4. *Separation under construction*

Rabin raised the "separation" option in January 1995: "We will continue on the path of peace since there is no alternative. . . . This path will lead us to total separation." Palestinian spokeswoman Hanan Ashrawi retorted that separation is acceptable "if it also entails sovereignty." Rabin did not have sovereignty in mind. He was proposing *physical separation* of Palestinians from Israelis as a security measure – a literal fencing off of Palestinian enclaves from Israel. This idea was a throwback to a plan proposed by Sharon in connection with the Oslo Accords, that 15 percent of the West Bank be divided into a dozen Palestinian islands, each encircled by the IDF and separated from each other and from Jewish settlements. This plan was, itself, a throwback to the *Drobles Plan* of Begin days (chapter 18).

In Gaza, self-rule areas are already surrounded by formidable electronic fences. However, the fencing off of all Palestinian areas in the West Bank seemed impractical.[63] More importantly, security experts pointed out to Rabin that impenetrable fences designed to hem in Palestinians and prevent terrorist attacks in Israel might in fact *fuel* terrorism because fencing in Palestinians or denying them access to Israeli jobs would lead to further economic impoverishment and anger. Jewish settlers and Greater Israel ideologues voiced a different fear: that walling off Palestinian enclaves might remove those areas from eventual Jewish control. Peace Now denounced separation on the grounds that it would herd Palestinians into South African-style apartheid "Bantustans," creating ghettoes destined to become storehouses of cheap manual labor.[64]

Another means of physical separation, one gradually and presently under construction, is the "bypass road" solution. The West Bank is now peppered with 140 strategically located Jewish settlements. The building of crisscrossing, wide roads that connect these settlements to each other and to Israel, bypassing Palestinian areas, could effectively separate Palestinians from Israelis since West Bank roads can legally be closed to Palestinians by the IDF.[65] This "ambitious project has a budgetary allocation of $330m and, together with the construction of settlements and infrastructure in and around Jerusalem, is expected to 'annex' more than 65 percent of the West Bank to Israel."[66]

Is the Middle East conflict over?

Given the future prospects for Palestinians, Palestinian terrorism cannot be expected to end. In that sense, the Middle East conflict is *not* over. As long as any Palestinian is willing to kill an Israeli and himself in protest or frustration over statelessness, injustice and poverty, Israel will have a security problem. And as long as any settler, Shin Bet operative or Israeli soldier is willing to kill a Palestinian for God, country or retaliation, Palestinians will have a security problem.[67] As long as both Palestinians and Jews terrorize and are terrorized by "sacrificers" against injustice and loss, Hamas and Gush Emunim alike, a *mutual* local security problem will remain. Attempts to stop terrorism through infliction of collective punishment or through bestowal of limited self-rule seem to have only fueled the problem. Nor has Israeli assassination of Palestinian figures such as Abu Jihad or Yahya Ayyash accomplished more than provoke counter-attack – as when, in March 1996, Hamas ended its self-imposed cease-fire. Palestinian terrorism cannot be punished away any more than could Jewish terrorism be punished away by the British in 1946-1948. "It is not easy to get a conquered person to resign himself to defeat."[68] Nor does moral condemnation work. When violence is the last bargaining chip of those feeling oppressed, it elicits little guilt. So as long as local terrorism persists, and given current conditions, it looks like it will, the Middle East conflict is not over.

Yet in important respects the Middle East conflict *is* over. There are no Palestinian military forces. There are no Arab states or superpowers importantly interested in the Palestinian cause. The United States, Britain and the Soviet Union no longer vie with each other for dominance through Middle East client states.[69] Nor is the United Nations involved in what is now treated as a matter for "out of court" settlement between the Palestinians and Israelis. The Middle

East conflict is not over at the local terrorism level, but the days of superpower arming and proxy wars in Palestine are done.

The prospects for negotiation

The optimists place their hopes in negotiation, believing that Israelis want peace, that diversity of opinion in Israel will break the current deadlock, that Netanyahu will be replaced in May 1999 by a more accommodative leader – that a "new Israel" (according to Glenn Frankel), comprised of younger, more progressive-minded citizens, will shape Israel's future. In short, peace negotiations will and *must* work.

The pessimists believe that Oslo autonomy negotiations are a stall strategy, that Israel's goal is incorporation of most of the West Bank, that terrorism, though politically sensitive, is tolerable to Israel (even helps to poison the Palestinian image internationally). These pessimists seem to have the better case in that few observers think that Israeli governments will turn accommodative any time soon.[70] Moreover, little territory is being offered in exchange for peace. For example, were the October 1998 Wye River agreements (attempted restart of Oslo II agreements stalled for eighteen months) ever completed, Palestinians would have control of security, but not sovereignty, over about 2.4 percent of Palestine with shared control over another 4.5 percent. Israel would have sovereignty and control of security over 93 percent of Palestine and shared control over another 4.5 percent. Regarding political control, the Palestinians and Israelis would have, respectively, 9 percent and 91 percent control of Palestine.[71]

The fundamental problem with negotiations is that the opponents are profoundly disparate in power. Negotiations between the powerful and the powerless are largely rhetorical and come down to gift-giving. And when the more powerful see themselves as righteous victims, there is little chance they will, on their own, make gifts to their past and future "enemies." And when those enemies see themselves, in turn, as victims, then they will never be grateful if there were ever any gifts. Nor will any outside government or agency be so indelicate or foolhardy as to confront the Gordian knot of mutual hatred in an effort to persuade either the victors or the defeated to simply give up.

Meron Benvenisti, former deputy mayor of Jerusalem, argues, following the Wye River agreements, that Israel has all the cards and has no need to negotiate – indeed, it could even accept a Palestinian state because *Israel* will define that state. "Let's say the Palestinians get even 50 percent of the West Bank. Think about water resources, land development, sewage. Israelis use five times the water of Palestinians. What happens when the Palestinians want more? Where will it come from? The Israelis will say: 'We gave all we could. No more. The rest is ours.' So what the Palestinians will get is exactly what the Israelis can live with, peace without any real price. That's why they don't care if there is a Palestinian state. That's why even Sharon and Netanyahu can accept a state, because of the way they will define it."[72]

The central political fact remains that the Palestinians have, until now, been effectively contained on island "reservations" without statehood in a quasi-apartheid existence, while a much larger number remain scattered as unwelcome refugees in surrounding Arab countries. One Middle East journalist and historian, Norman Finkelstein, parallels the Palestinian's fate to that of the American Indian. After the Jewish and American colonists defeated their overlord (in both cases, the British), they displaced and marginalized an indigenous population.

The dynamics of such dispossessions are well-known. The indigenous population resists dispossession and the colonizer feels himself to be the victim of terrorist attack.[73] Claims are made about the moral justification and higher good of the fight to dispossess ("Promised Land," "Manifest Destiny.")[74] and, after victory is achieved, the colonizer seeks peace. If the colonizer can impose his culture, the defeated population is presumed to profit despite loss of land, resources and culture. If that population is forceably removed, displaced or isolated, peace treaties bestowing autonomy are written and broken when the land is needed or natural resources discovered.[75] The conquest slowly winds down in continuing bouts of mutual terrorism.

This story is a familiar one because there does not exist a people who were *not* once conquerors.[76] The classic narrative story is that in which the conqueror, civilized and peaceable, somehow happens in self-defense to end up victorious over a lesser people who unwisely resisted the conqueror's civilizing mission and Providential taking. This biblical myth continues to influence our thinking about how both the American West and Israel were won.

Notes

1. $1 billion in 1991 alone. Under Shamir, 13,000 new residential units were under construction in 1991, 20,000 units having been built in the previous four years. By the end of 1991 there were 112,000 settlers in the West Bank and Gaza

(excluding East Jerusalem). Mark Tessler, *A History of the Israeli-Palestinian Conflict* (Bloomington: Indiana University Press, 1994), 745.

2. Rabin's election success partly stemmed from the vote of Russian immigrants (20 percent of the population) frustrated by neglect and second-class treatment by Likud. Serge Schmemann, "Outside In," *New York Times Magazine,* November 23, 1997, 76.

3. Rabin: "When it comes to Israel's security we will concede not a thing. From our standpoint, security takes precedence over peace." Avi Shlaim, "Prelude to the Accord," *Journal of Palestine Studies* (Winter 1994) 13.

4. While Rabin opposed new settlements in densely populated Palestinian areas for political reasons ("political settlements"), he built "strategic settlements" related to security.

5. The U.S. State Department's *Settlement Report* stated in April 1993 that Israel "made no commitment to halt or reduce construction in East Jerusalem [40,000 units since 1967 and] has affirmed its intention to continue settlement construction in . . . Greater Jerusalem." Donald Neff, "Jerusalem in U.S. Policy," *Journal of Palestine Studies* (Autumn 1993), 41. Housing construction surrounding East Jerusalem numbered 1,126 new units in the first quarter of 1995 (324 in all of 1994), according to Edward Said, *Peace and Its Discontents* (New York: Vintage, 1996), 151. For other sums see Clyde Haberman, "Loan Guarantees For Israel are Cut" *New York Times,* October 6, 1993, A3.

6. Shlaim, "Prelude to the Accord," 15.

7. Avi Shlaim, "The Oslo Accord," *Journal of Palestine Studies* (Spring 1994): 28.

8. Shlaim, "Prelude to the Accord," 18.

9. Meron Benvenisti, *Intimate Enemies* (Berkeley: University of California Press, 1995), 214.

10. *Edward Said,* "The Mourning After," *London Review of Books,* October 21 1993, 3.

11. The Accords invoked UN 242 as a frame for final, permanent status negotiations. Because the United .States had gutted UN 242 by deleting "all" (in reference to the occupied territories), UN 242 had no real teeth. Rabin was not absolutely against the idea of some territorial compromise. Yet he was constrained by the existing settlements built by previous Likud governments "intended . . . [to] limit the options of any future government oriented toward territorial compromise." Tessler, *History of Conflict,* 744.

12. Estimates vary as to how much of the West Bank was already under Israeli control (settlements, roads, "security" and "state" lands). At the time of the Accords, September 1993, it was about 65 to 70 percent, according to Israel Shahak (president of the Israeli League for Human and Civil Rights). *Ha'aretz,* March 26, 1993. One year *after* the Accords (due to a 70 percent increase in government expenditures) Israel had control of about 75 percent of the West Bank, according to Normam Finkelstein, *The Rise and Fall of Palestine* (Minneapolis: University of Minnesota

Press, 1996) 89.

13. Shlaim, "The Oslo Accord," 34.

14. "It is clear from the wording of this recognition that the Palestinian police force . . . is to protect Israel's security, responsibility for which will be shared by the Palestinian Council." Burhan Dajani, "The September 1993 Israeli-PLO Documents: A Textual Analysis," *Journal of Palestine Studies* (Spring 1994), 6, 7.

15. "It is clear that the PLO was not aware that through its unconditional recognition of Israel it actually affirmed Israel's sovereignty *beyond* the 1967 borders . . . allowing it to claim sovereignty over the occupied territory of the West Bank and Gaza Strip." Dajani, "September 1993 Documents," 19.

16. Haydar 'Abd al-Shafi, "The Oslo Agreement," *Journal of Palestine Studies* (Autumn 1993), 15. A "no-occupation" line of argument was advanced by some Israelis on the grounds that Israel has no *defined* borders. Without borders, the sovereign state of Israel cannot, it is claimed, exclude adjacent territories (West Bank and Gaza) that are not part of any other recognized state. By this argument, one contrary to international opinion, the West Bank and Gaza are not "occupied" but merely "disputed" territories – a formulation introduced by the Clinton administration.

17. The Fourth Geneva Convention, which Israel initially accepted as applicable to the occupied territories, prohibits: (1) establishment of settlements on occupied land; (2) deportation of inhabitants who are under occupation; (3) collective punishment such as house demolitions; and (4) collection of taxes. Israel imposed new taxes in 1976. One protesting village, Beit Sahour, was sealed off for six weeks and $1.5 million in property was confiscated.

The Hague Conventions include Article 46 (private property cannot be confiscated) and Article 50 (no penalty, pecuniary or otherwise, can be inflicted upon a population not responsible for individual destructive acts).

Other international law prohibits the occupier from using lethal force except in life-threatening situations. Official Israeli rules of engagement allow killing for wearing a mask, hoisting a flag or erecting road barricades.

International law prohibits torture, which, according to Amnesty International, has been "virtually institutionalized" in the occupied territories and has continued after the Oslo Accords, according to *Human Rights Watch/Middle East* (New York, June 1994):"Ill-treatment and torture have continued on a systematic basis . . . since September 1993." A follow-up report (November 1994) by *B'Tselem* concludes the same. See Finkelstein, *Rise and Fall*, 136n. The U.S. State Department (*Human Rights*, January 30, 1997) states that common interrogation practices reportedly include: "forced standing or squatting for long periods of time; prolonged exposure to extreme temperatures; tying or chaining the detainee in contorted and painful positions; blows and beatings with fists, sticks and other instruments; confinement in small and often filthy spaces, sleep and food deprivation; threats against the detainee's life or family . . . and violent 'shaking' [sometimes fatal]."

18. Dajani, "September 1993 Documents," 6.

19. Shlaim, "The Oslo Accord," 39.

20. IDF intelligence reported that Arafat's situation in the summer of 1993 was dire, possibly in danger of imminent collapse, making him the "most convenient interlocutor for Israel." Hamas and Islamic Jihad, on the other hand, were experiencing alarming growth. Shlaim, "The Oslo Accord," 31-2.

21. According to Meron Benvenisti, Gaza was a heavy burden on the Israeli conscience – a tiny strip inhabited by Palestinians uprooted from their homes by Israeli victory and flung into hardship and desperation. "For twenty-six years they [the Israelis] could have attempted to heal wounds in order to implant the roots of coexistence, equality, and mutual respect, but they did nothing." They made it Arafat's problem. Benvenisti, *Intimate Enemies*, 225-6.

22. Benvenisti, Meron, *Intimate Enemies*, 216.

23. In 1993, Palestinians controlled about one-third of the West Bank, i.e., 7 percent of historic Palestine.

24. Ethan Bronner, "Filling In Peace's Details Is the Painful Part," *New York Times*, October 25, 1998 (Sec. 4), 1, 6.

25. Palestinian police lack the authority to detain settlers committing crimes.

26. In Gaza, 1,100 of Israel's military laws are in force; 1,400 in the West Bank.

27. Israel controls commerce in and out of Gaza. Israel will not allow raw materials to enter Gaza. Nor are any significant number of Palestinian trucks given permits to leave Gaza and enter Israel. For example, tomatoes from Gaza must be transferred to Israeli trucks to be taken to the West Bank, a three-day process causing spoilage.

28. Rabin in a Knesset session: "Every agreement that concerns an arrangement with the Palestinians on the establishment of the transitional period . . . is then subject to change if it is violated significantly." Dajani, "The September 1993 Israeli-PLO Documents," 21.

Dissident terrorism is construed by Israel and the world as a reflection of Arafat's sympathy for, if not complicity in, terrorism and a violation of his Oslo obligations. After a suicide bombing (July 30, 1997) that killed fourteen Israelis and two unknown bombers, the Israeli cabinet secretary concluded, "The Palestinian Authority has yet to do the main thing – fulfill its obligation to fight the terrorist infrastructure." Danny Naveh, as reported in the Joel Greenberg, "Israeli Closing of Bethlehem Brings Tensions to a Boil," *New York Times*, August 27, 1997, A12.

29. Finkelstein, *Rise and Fall*, 92.

30. "I think this type of self-rule is in effect a kind of collaboration between the Israeli forces and the Palestinian police force, which strengthens the Occupation authority and does not lead to a Palestinian state. More clearly put, what I am saying is that the Palestinian Authority is slowly being turned into an instrument of the Occupation, and this will be its ultimate fate. . . . Self-rule is an extension of the Occupation by other means." (Interview, January 1995) Said, *Discontents*, 176-7.

31. "Hamas is not only a terrorist movement but also a social service provider, and it has the support of more than 20 percent of the population. The ministers of the Palestinian Authority have managed to secure for themselves reputations for

corruption and venality: in fact, the Palestinian Legislative Council recently criticized the Arafat regime for misusing more than $300 million in public funds. Hamas, on the other hand, is regarded as honest and charitable. A weakened Arafat lacks the strength to fight the Hamas infrastructure; he would be fighting, in some ways, the masses themselves." Jeffrey Goldberg, "From Peace Process to Police Process," *New York Times Magazine,* September 14 1997, 62-104.

32. Local interviews from Finkelstein, *Rise and Fall,* 93-96.

33 Neil MacFarquhar, "As Gaza Stagnates, Arafat Is Blamed as Well as Israel,". *New York Times* (International Edition), August 16 1997, 5.

34. Finkelstein, *Rise and Fall,* 93-6.

35. Difference concerning religious values and practices, not the handling of Palestinians, seems to have been the primary issue: "A serious danger exists that the divide between two irreconcilable Israeli political cultures [religious vs secular] may develop into cleavage with mutual acrimony sufficient to spur a minor civil war." Yoram Peri, *Davar,* March 25 1994. The assassination ended ongoing negotiations with Syria concerning the Golan Heights.

36. Terrorists killed 61 in Israel in February and March 1996, partly in revenge for presumed Israeli killing of Yahya Ayyash and other Hamas members. The IDF killed at least 75 Lebanese civilians in April in a UN refugee camp. Netanyahu insisted that the IDF operation continue, criticizing Peres for offering a cease-fire with Hizb'allah. See Serge Schmemann, "Peres Government Vows to Carry 'War' Into Palestinian Areas," *New York Times,* March 5, 1996, A1, A8; and Douglas Jehl, "Israeli Barrage Hits U.N. Camp in Lebanon, Killing At Least 75," *New York Times,* April 19, 1996, A1, A12.

37 Serge Schmemann, "Netanyahu's Hard Line Faces Rising Israeli Dissent," *New York Times* (International Edition), September 9, 1997, A3.

38. Schmemann, "Outside In," *New York Times Magazine,* November 23 1997, 58.

39. Ibid. 74.

40. Douglas Jehl, "Israel to Build Dam on Disputed Land Claimed by Syria," *New York Times,* August 26, 1997, A3.

41. Secretary of State Madeleine Albright declared, "It is beyond my understanding" how Israel's decision to withhold millions of dollars of taxes it owes to the Palestinian Authority could be a security measure. Steven Erlanger, "Albright Asks Israel to Take a 'Time Out' on Settlements," *New York Times,* September 12 1997.

42. To travel outside their villages (to work in Israel) Palestinians need an Israeli-issued identification card and a permit, both useless during closures. Students in Gaza are refused permits to travel to college in the West Bank. Joel Greenberg, "Travel Ban Burdens Students From Gaza," *New York Times,* October 11, 1998, 4. There were 200 days of total closure (100 of partial closure) during the two and three quarters years following the Accords. Nigel Parry, "Making sense of closure," *Middle East International* (*MEI),* September 20, 1996, 19. Gaza was sealed off for 82 days in 1996. Israel has recruited 200,000 guest-workers from East Europe,

Turkey and Thailand to replace Palestinian workers since the Accords. Graham Usher, "Closure, Likud style," *MEI*, August 2, 1996, 4.

43. Arafat was in trouble with Palestinians because of Israeli restrictions. "Palestinians are dismayed that so many aspects of their daily lives, including their food, their work and their travel, remain largely dependent on Israeli permits. . . . [Moreover] the aura of corruption around the entire peace enterprise has some local Palestinians suggesting openly that it might be better if Mr. Arafat left. . . . Criticism that once would have been considered astonishing is fairly common." MacFarquhar "As Gaza Stagnates," *New York Times* (International Edition), August 16, 1997, 1.

44. A mother whose daughter was killed by a suicide bomber charged that Israeli oppression of Palestinians was the root cause of terrorism. "They [the government] sacrifice our children for their megalomania – for their need to control, oppress, dominate." Schmemann, "Netanyahu's Hard Line," *New York Times*, September 9, 1997, A3.

45. Serge Schmemann, "Cabinet in Israel Decides Jerusalem Will Be Expanded," *New York Times*, June 22, 1998. Road networks will also be expanded.

46. Douglas Jehl, "Arafat Says Netanyahu Undermines the Quest for a Wider Peace," *New York Times*, August 31, 1997, 11.

47. U.S. State Department, "Note for the Record Concerning Oslo III on Reciprocity: entitled "Further Redeployment: The Next Stage of the Israeli-Palestinian Interim Agreement; Legal Aspects – January 1997." Cited in Naseer Aruri, "The US Role in the Peace Process," *MEI*, March 21 1997, 16. Later, however, U.S. Secretary of State Albright also cautioned Israel that Israel "should refrain from unilateral acts including what Palestinians perceive as the provocative expansion of settlements, land confiscation, home demolitions and confiscation of I.D.'s." Israel's response: "You can't ask us to stop expanding existing settlements, which are living organisms."Steven Erlanger, "Albright Asks Israel," *New York Times,* September 12, 1997, 1.

48. Since the Oslo Accords, 1994 through April 1997, Jewish settlers have killed Palestinians in a ratio of 2 to 1. *B'Tselem* (June 1997).

49. Rabbi Moshe Levinger, father of the settlement movement, responded: "I am sorry for everything that gets killed. I am not only sorry for dead Arabs, I am also sorry for dead flies." Finkelstein, *Rise and Fall*, 114.

50. Haim Baram, "Self-pity and Propaganda," *MEI*, January 10, 1997, 5.

51. A murderous car-bombing by Palestinians in Afula killed seven Israelis.

52. Israel actively sponsors undercover violence. "Death squads" kill Palestinians deemed responsible for attacks on Israelis. Tessler, *History of Conflict,* 758-9. Undercover Israeli agents have been involved in the killing of 161 Palestinians over the last decade. *B'Tselem* (June 1997). Israel's terror-saboteur-assassin unit (Flotilla 13) is known to have assassinated PLO leaders in Tunisia and Beirut and to have sunk a PLO ship. Serge Schmemann, "Israelis' Edginess Sharpened by Loss of 12 in Lebanon," *New York Times* (International Edition), September 6, 1997, 1, 8. The Mossad was recently caught in an attempt to poison a

Hamas leader in Amman. Joel Greenberg, "Gaza Gives Freed Sheik Welcome Fit for a Hero," *New York Times,* October 7, 1997, 1.

53. Benvenisti, *Intimate Enemies,* 223.

54. Douglas Jehl, "U.S. Envoy Leaves Mideast Without Sign of Progress," *New York Times,* August 14, 1997, A3.

55. Joel Greenberg, "Israeli Closing of Bethlehem," *New York Times* (International Edition), August 27, 1997, A12.

56. For interviews see, Finkelstein, *Rise and Fall,* 94-6.

57. Calculation (prior to Wye River agreement) of 7.0 percent: The West Bank comprises 22% of historic (mandated) Palestine; Gaza, 1.6%. Palestinians (1.5 million) live on and retain partial security control over about 24% of the West Bank (Area B) and full security control over 3% (Area A). 24% + 3% = 27%. 27% x 22% = 5.94% of Palestine. Palestinians (.9 million) have security control over about two-thirds of Gaza or 1% of Palestine. 5.94% + 1% = 7.0% of historic Palestine. Three million other Palestinians live in exile (refugee camps in Lebanon, Syria and Jordan or as citizens in other Arab states.

Israel controls "nearly all the water resources in the West Bank." Water is piped from three enormous underground aquifers under the West Bank, most of it going to Israel and Jewish settlers. Palestinians are permitted one-third the water that Israelis receive and less than half of what Palestinian experts say is needed. In Hebron, water has been rationed. Households run water no more than once every fifteen days. Digging wells in the territories is virtually prohibited to Palestinians but not to Jews. Douglas Jehl, "Water Divides Haves From Have-Nots in West Bank," *New York Times,* August 15, 1998, A3.

58. A factor in Palestinian support for Hamas is settler immunity to Palestinian police arrest. Hamas "make[s] them think twice before killing us." Finkelstein, *Rise and Fall,* 96.

59. UN Commission on Human Rights, March 28, 1998. Reported by Elizabeth Olson, "Arabs' Ordeal in Israeli Jails Scars Children, U.N. Is Told," *New York Times* (International Edition), March 29, 1998, 14. "Israel is holding an estimated 3,500 Palestinians in prisons and detention centers. They include 7 women and 70 to 90 youths under 18." The Finnish envoy reported to the UN Commission: "Torture is prevalent: placing hoods over prisoners' heads for sensory deprivation, sleep and food deprivation, exposure to loud music, forcing prisoners to maintain painful body positions, exposure to extremes of cold and heat, and violent shaking."

60. Schmemann, "Netanyahu's Hard Line," *New York Times,* September 9, 1997, A3, and Serge Schmemann, "Israelis Worry That Peace Effort Is Dead," *New York Times,* February 3, 1997, 12.

61. About half of the Israeli public leaned toward transfer in 1988. "Poll: 49% Lean Towards 'Transfer' of Arabs from Areas" *Jerusalem Post,* August 12, 1988, 1. In 1948, Ben-Gurion appointed a "transfer committee" (on June 5) and reported to the Jewish Agency a week later, "I am for compulsory transfer; I don't see anything immoral in it." Simha Flapan, *The Birth of Israel* (New York: Pantheon, 1987), 103.

62. If $60 billion were used to pay 2.4 million Palestinians to vacate the Gaza strip and West Bank ($25,000 for each man, woman and child), that would be 18 times the value of the products and services (GDP) produced by each Palestinian per year. Israel's economy is far larger than the combined economies of all its neighboring Arab states. William Orme, Jr. "Israeli Business Flies Like a Dove". *New York Times,* October 18, 1998, Sec. 4, 3.

63. Fencing, augmented by electronic sensors, mobile army units and dogs, would have cost $200 million according to Israeli estimates.

64. See Peretz Kidron, "'Separation' Set to Fail?" *MEI,* March 31, 1995, 7.

65. For more on roads, see Ghada Karmi, "Bearing Witness" *MEI,* November 17, 1995, 19. Rabin budgeted $330 million for this road project in August 1995.Also, Grahan Usher, "Israel tightens its grip on the terrritories," *MEI,* March 29, 1996, 6 $600 million was budgeted in January 1996, according to Said, *Discontents,* 41.

66. Naseer Aruri, "The Serious Challenges Facing Palestinian Society," *MEI,* August 25, 1995, 16. Mustafa Barghouti estimates 69 percent "Palestinians at the crossroads," *MEI,* January 19, 1996, 16.

67. Statistics reveal that a Palestinian is five times more likely to be killed by an Israeli than an Israeli to be killed by a Palestinian. Following the Oslo Accords (1994 through April 1997), 251 Palestinians have been killed (113 per million) in the occupied territories while 96 Israeli civilians have been killed in Israel (18 per million) – *B'Tselem* (June 1997). Over the last decade, 1,436 Palestinians have been killed in the occupied territories compared with 173 Israel citizens killed in Israel (a ratio of 8:1) – *B'Tselem* (May 1998). Historically, Israel has lost 16 to 23 civilians per year to terrorism (*Peace Watch,* 1997).

68. Maxime Rodinson, *Israel: A Colonial-Settler State?* (New York: Pathfinder, 1973), 96.

69. For pro-Israeli Clinton administration, some international issues do remain. U.S. containment of Iraq and Iran necessitate support of the Saudi monarchy, which is facing Islamic fundamentalist challenge. Were the United States to strongly condemn Arafat for failure to halt Islamic fundamentalists in Palestine (Hamas), the United States would provoke Islamic agitators in Saudi Arabia. For United States clear pro-Israeli policies see Donald Neff, "U.S. suspends its policy on Israeli settlements," *MEI,* September 20, 1996, 5 and Serge Schmemann's comment, "The President made no effort to balance his backing for Israel . . ." quoted by Neff, "'Peace summit' ends in tame compromise," *MEI,* March 29, 1996, 3.

70. "Even if Netanyahu is ousted by some crisis yet to come or if he is compelled to form a 'national unity' government with the Labor Party, the arithmetic of the electorate suggests the groups that dominate the Israeli government today – parties of Sephardim, the religious, Golan Heights residents, Russian immigrants, supporters of Foreign Minister David Levy or Agriculture Minister Rafael Eitan – will, in various configurations, determine national policy for some time to come." Schmemann, "Outside In," *New York Times Magazine,* November 23, 1997, 57.

71. If, as per the October 1998 Wye River agreement, 3.36% (14% x 24% =

3.36%) of Area B is added to the current 3% of Area A, then Palestinians will have political and security control over 6.36% of the West Bank. Under Palestinian political but *joint security control* will be 20.64% (24% – 3.36%= 20.64%) of the West Bank (Area B). Full Israeli political and security control(Area C) will be 63% (73% – 10%=63%) of the West Bank. The remaining 10% of the West Bank will go over to Palestinian political but remain under full Israeli security contro (Area D)l.

Given that the West Bank is 22% of Palestine (mandated Palestine minus Transjordan), West Bank Palestinians will thus have exclusive political and security (Area A) control over 22% x 6.36% = 1.4% of *Palestine*. Under Palestinian political control but *joint security* (Area B) control will be 20.64% x 22% = 4.5% of *Palestine*. Under full Israeli political and security (Area C) control will be (63% x 22%) + 77%(Israel) = 90.86% of Palestine. And Palestinian political control but Israeli security(Area D) control will be 10% x 22% = 2.2% of Palestine. Concerning Gaza, Palestinians have full political and security (Area A) control of 1% of Palestine.

In sum: If the Wye River agreements were to be fulfilled, then Palestinians would have *political* control over 1.4% + 4.5% + 1% +2.2% = 9% of Palestine; shared security control over 4.5 % of Palestine and *full security* control over 1.4% + 1% = 2.4% of Palestine. On the other hand, Israel would have *political* control of 90.86% of Palestine; shared security control over 4.5% of Palestine and *full security* control over (63% +10%) x 22% +77% = 93.06% of Palestine. See: Steven Erlanger, "U.S. Pessimistic Before Middle East Talks," *New York Times* (International Edition), May 4, 1998, A10; Steven Erlanger, "Arafat and Netanyahu in Pact on Next Steps Toward Peace," *New York Times,* October 24, 1998, A6; Ethan Bronner, "Filling In Peace's Details Is the Painful Part," *New York Times,* October 25, 1998, Sec. 4, 1.

72. Bronner, "Filling In," *New York Times,* October 25, 1998, Sec. 4, 1.

73. "As the Indians desperately fought to preserve the lands they lived on from white encroachment, their 'savage' actions were used to condemn them. . . . The violence engendered by the white advance was used to condemn the Indians who had been provoked to resist." Reginald Horsman, *Race and Manifest Destiny: Origins of American Racial Anglo-Saxism* (Cambridge: Harvard University Press, 1981), 115.

74. Thomas Jefferson was "confident that Americans were the new chosen people of God." The Doctrine of "Manifest Destiny" was that North America was "allotted by Providence for the free development of our yearly multiplying millions." Norman Finkelstein, *Image and Reality of the Israel-Palestine Conflict* (New York: Verso, 1995), 100.

75. The Indian Removal Act of 1830 called for the transfer of Indians. In an 1838 forced march (the "Trail of Tears"), as many as half of 15,000 Cherokees perished. Finkelstein, *Image and Reality,* 116. Count Bernadotte said of the survivors of the forced expulsion of the 1948 "Lydda Death March" (ordered by Ben-Gurion and executed by Rabin), "I have made the acquaintance of a great many refugee camps but never have I seen a more ghastly sight."

76. "In a sense, every modern nation is a product of colonization: it has always

been to some degree colonized or colonizing, and sometimes both at the same time." Etienne Balibar and Immanuel Wallerstein, *Race, Nation, Class: Ambiguous Identities* (New York: Verso, 1991), 89.

Appendix A

Government and Democracy in Israel

The Balfour Declaration of 1917 called for a home for Jews in Palestine on condition that the civil and religious rights of Moslem and Christian Palestinians not be violated. These rights came into question when Israel was founded as a Jewish state. Inequities and discriminatory practices were practiced against the Arab population living in Israel, and government and political party structures were designed for the benefit of Jewish citizens only. Most of the land in Israel remains state-owned, set aside for exclusive Jewish use in perpetuity. On the other hand, Israel adopted certain democratic structures, for example, all citizens have the right to vote in elections, hold political office and go to school.

The tension between democratic and undemocratic structures in Israel has been greater than it seems because, despite formal equities in the law, vast government bureaucracies and quasi-governmental institutions often discriminate sub rosa against Arab-Israeli citizens. Most of the draconian emergency (martial) laws adopted in 1948 are still in force, though since the 1980s have been less used against Arab-Israeli citizens. However, without a constitution, Israel has no fundamental legal protection of minority rights. And those specific laws which do prohibit discrimination lack mechanisms for enforcement. Power-sharing with non-Jews in Israel is also limited by tight control of government and social institutions by majority political parties.

The power of political parties

Historically, power in Israel has resided in the political party – more specifically, in the party's central committee which dictates the composition and practices of governmental authority at all levels. "Israel's political system is, in many ways, of and by, if not for, political parties."[1] Traditionally, parties have owned or sponsored newspapers, publishing houses, youth movements, banks, insurance firms, agricultural settlements, housing projects and educational institutions.[2] They have served as highly articulated debating platforms for ideology and mythology.[3] The party's oligarchical central committee has historically been the decision-maker concerning who will sit in parliament, who will be cabinet ministers and what governmental policy should be.[4] Moreover, party leaders fill multiple government positions simultaneously.

The diversity that does exist in Israeli politics arises from differences between parties. Israel now has primaries and direct election of the prime minister – prior to 1996 the central committee chose the prime minister. Otherwise, politicians do not run for political office as individuals. Their fate rises or falls with the party's percent of the popular vote. Each party fills governmental positions at all levels in proportion to its percent of that vote.[5] Members of the Knesset (M.K.) have little inclination to break away from party policy, being mindful of the source of their political position. "There is probably no other legislature in a democratic country in which the private member is quite so shorn of significance as he is in Israel, and certainly none in which he is so fundamentally reliant on his party."[6]

Three kinds of governmental authority

(1) The *official* governmental authority is composed of: *(a)* the executive branch – the prime minister, his cabinet and their bureaucracies; *(b)* the parliament (Knesset); and *(c)* the courts, both secular and rabbinical.

(2) The *"invisible"* quasi-governmental authority resides in a number of social, economic and political institutions dating from pre-state times,[7] including: *(a)* the Histadrut, *(b)* the Jewish Agency and *(c)* the Jewish National Fund.

(3) A separate *military* government was once responsible for security within Israel with focus on Arab-Israeli citizens – policing border areas and controlling Arab village life.[8] However, after 1966, these tasks of the military government were transferred to a number of other Israeli agencies, including the Office of the Advisor to the Prime Minister on Arab Affairs and the Arab Departments of the Histadrut, the Labor Party and Ministries of the Interior and Education.

(1) The official Israeli government

(a) Historically, the executive branch of the government has been filled by a stable group of top party leaders. In the early (first fifteen) years of Israel's existence, fewer than three of the thirteen or fourteen ministerial positions changed hands, despite eleven "changes" in government.[9]

In recent years, the need for coalitions between rival political parties has diffused that oligarchical nucleus. Nevertheless, a party is able to control ministerial positions by several means: Firstly, disagreements between ministers from different parties tend to be over legislative proposals, administrative practices or party patronage – not about *who* fills cabinet positions. Secondly, the powers and responsibilities of ministries are often manipulated. When a party insists on control of a particular ministry as a condition for coalition, the prime minister can simply transfer the function of that ministry to another under his own party's control. Thus, the negotiating power of coalition parties is less than it appears. The minister of a coalition party does gain some power by threatening to resign, but since the prime minister's party is ordinarily assigned the task of forming a new government, the coalition party has reduced leverage.[10]

Dominance by political parties in filling and defining cabinet positions has tended to turn government ministries into party functions that discriminate against Arab-Israelis.[11] Even ministries concerned with Arab affairs refuse Arab leadership. Historically, the vast civil service bureaucracies under the control of ministers and staffed by party members have created patronage systems of marked disadvantage to Arab citizens seeking civil service work.[12]

(b) The Israeli parliament has wide powers, theoretically.[13] In reality, the Knesset's power derives from the party which dictates membership and policy.

(c) The courts in Israel are of two types. Rabbinical courts apply Judaic religious law. Magistrate, district and supreme civil courts apply secular law.

The rabbinical courts rule on matters of family, marriage, divorce[14] and all issues covered by Jewish religious law. Parallel courts exist for Moslems, Christians and Druze. Rabbinical courts follow the policies of religious parties, which supervise expression of institutional Judaism in Israel.[15] These religious courts enjoy considerable independence from secular courts. Occasionally the Supreme Court will intervene, but generally it does not intrude on rabbinical rulings, e.g., concerning the validity of Jewish marriages outside the orthodox form or the prohibition of marriages of Jews to Moslems or Christians.

Secular courts rule over civil and criminal cases, applying a mix of Ottoman, British mandate and Knesset law.[16] English common law may be used if other law is inapplicable. Legislation is generally lacking in any number of matters connected with civil rights and civil liberties – a problem for the Arab minority.[17] Occasionally the Supreme Court will limit administrative abuse of Arab-Israelis by government ministries or their bureaucracies. The court will occasionally rule over matters in the occupied territories. For example, in 1979 when Sharon's Ministerial Settlement Committee elected to appropriate Arab lands in the West Bank for Jewish settlement on grounds of need for military defense, the Supreme Court judged that the real purpose was Zionist expansion and ordered the removal of buildings erected by the army. On the other hand, the Supreme Court has willingly flaunted accepted international law, including the Fourth Geneva Convention. In the opinion of most nations, Jewish settlements in the occupied territories violate that convention.[18] The Supreme Court brushed this aside on grounds that the Fourth Geneva Convention is not part of domestic Israeli law.[19] Rarely has the court questioned the appropriation of lands owned by Arab-Israeli citizens in Israel or the occupied territories.

(2) The "invisible" governmental institutions

The most powerful quasi-governmental institutions in Israel are the Histadrut, the Jewish Agency and the Jewish National Fund (JNF). Staffing is, as with the official Israeli government, politicized on the basis of party allegiance.

(a) Traditionally, the Histadrut has been a huge owner of heavy industry, thousands of businesses and the dominant labor union – a combination that, while strange to the American ear, harks back to a pre-state "socialist" ideology about government control of production and community. For many years, half of all Israelis were members. The Histadrut has maintained a health service, a vast pension fund for workers and one of the two largest banks in Israel. Since 1967, however, the power and membership of the Histadrut has declined with the declining fortunes of the Labor Party and a heightened entrepreneurial culture in Israel. In Israel's more privatized economy, workers can obtain health insurance through other insurance funds. International competition coming from the European Union has also put pressure on the Histadrut, traditionally a protector of jobs from foreign competition and a patronage facility for party members.[20]

Historically, the Histadrut has discriminated against Arab-Israeli workers.[21] Not until 1959 did it fully open its doors to Arab-Israelis labor. Still, only ten percent of the total membership in 1978 was Arab-Israeli, while in 1998 it has risen to fourteen percent (below the expected proportional 20 percent).

(b) The Jewish Agency is the political institution which governed the pre-state Jewish community – negotiating with British mandate authorities and foreign powers, raising an illegal army and facilitating immigration, both legal and illegal. In 1948 it became a strictly Zionist organization and later merged with, then separated from the World Zionist Organization (WZO). In 1952 the Knesset assigned the Jewish Agency the responsibility for encouraging immigration and settlement of Jews from all over the world – as well as supporting education in Israel and raising funds, mostly from the United States (e.g., the United Jewish Appeal and Foundation Fund).

Historically, the Jewish Agency has been compared with the Israeli government: run by a quasi-ministerial cabinet; functioning through the same party system; having a budget comparable to the development budget of the government; possessing a bureaucracy and patronage system that rival the government; and supporting immigration, rural settlement and coordination of a massive urban renewal program that the government might otherwise do. Because it is not part of the official government, the agency's discriminatory funneling of resources to Jewish citizens is less conspicuous. Nevertheless, the agency directs billions of dollars to the development of Jewish, but not Arab-Israeli villages. Virtually all Jewish villages in Israel are electrified; 40 percent of Arab-Israeli villages are not. Jewish villages have plentiful, inexpensive water, Arab villages do not.[22]

(c) The Jewish National Fund (*Keren Kayemeth Leyisrael*) was a privately owned land-purchasing agency prior to statehood. It used charitable contributions from the American public for goals "directly or indirectly beneficial to persons of Jewish religion, race or origin." The JNF was subsequently recognized by the Israeli government and made the sole instrument for the development of Israel's land.[23] JNF land is exclusively for Jewish use in perpetuity and cannot be sold. It is leased to Jews for forty-nine years, occasionally to Arab-Israelis for one year, though technically, Arabs cannot legally labor on these lands.[24]

In the early 1960s, before the Six Day War, the JNF owned 18 percent of the land of Israel. Another 7 percent was privately owned, mostly by Arabs. The rest, 75 percent of all of Israel, was considered by the government to be "abandoned" by Palestinian-Arabs during the 1948 war. The Israeli government "established" that this land belonged to no person and dubbed it "State Land." JNF and State Land together make up 92.6 percent of all of Israel – 95 percent according to the Histadrut secretary general.[25] This combined land is now called "National Land" and is under exclusive JNF control. It cannot be "alienated" to non-Jews – that is, is for Jewish use only. "This precludes Arab purchase or long-term lease of most land in Israel, and with the remaining non-JNF lands, there is still [in 1998] considerable de facto discrimination in favor of Jewish agricultural movements."[26]

(3) The military government

The military government of Israel was originally set up in 1950 to replace the Israeli army (IDF), which was eliciting UN censure for violations of armistice agreements in 1948.[27] This military government controlled the rural areas in Israel where three-quarters of Arab-Israelis lived.[28] In 1966 the military government was technically dissolved and many of its tasks transferred to the Office of the Advisor to the Prime Minister on Arab Affairs, an office typically recruited from Israel's Secret Service.[29] Other agencies controlling Arab behavior, especially political activities, are the Arab Departments of the Histadrut, the Ministry of the Interior and the Ministry of Education.

The legal basis for a military government derived from Britain's Emergency (martial) Laws, which Israel adopted soon after statehood and which remain largely intact today. The British adopted these Emergency Laws during the mandate period against Palestinian Arabs in their 1936-1939 rebellion and then again against Jewish terrorists in 1945-1948.[30] The power of these laws is virtually absolute. Theoretically they apply to all Israeli citizens. On rare occasions they have been used against a Jewish-Israeli. In practice, these laws have been used to deny Arab-Israeli citizens personal freedom, land and property, though since 1980 their use has diminished.

The Emergency Laws cut a wide swath.[32] They can force a person to remain in his house or village; put him under police control; impose a total or partial curfew in any area; cut telephone, mail and electric service; prohibit a person from working; forbid him from purchasing or using possessions; imprison a person without trial for fifteen days (six months in the occupied territories);[31] prohibit travel or use of certain roads; proclaim areas to be "closed" so that no one may enter or leave; permanently evict a person from a residence in "security" areas (appeals rarely considered); confiscate or destroy any property thought appropriate; censor the press; and treat personal speech as criminal. Authorities can no longer permanently deport a person without cause.

British Emergency ("Defense") Laws created a virtual police state in 1945-1948 and were branded as such by the international community. In 1958, a liberal Israeli-Jewish group argued unsuccessfully that the military government's oppression of Arab citizens through these laws was serving to endanger Israel's security:

> About 200,000 of the inhabitants of Israel, belonging to another religion and with a different nationality, do not enjoy equal rights and are the victims of discrimination and repression. The overwhelming majority of Arabs in Israel live under a system of military government which deprives them of their fundamental rights as citizens. They have neither freedom of movement nor of residence. They are not accepted as members with equal rights and obligations in the Histadrut or as employees in most concerns. Their whole life is dependent on the whims of the military governor and his assistants. . . . The state has other means at its disposal, in the civil laws and the ordinary security forces, to protect the security of the nation without discriminating against the Arab population. Ten years of discrimination and repression have created and fostered feelings of despair and bitterness, and the Arab population becomes prey of those wishing to exploit the situation for their own political purposes. The continuation of this situation could seriously endanger the security of the nation.[33]

Expropriation of Arab-owned land in Israel by all levels of government

Zionists wanted a Jewish-run state for the Jewish people on Jewish-owned land. But less than 10 percent of the land of Israel was owned by Jews or Jewish organizations at the end of the 1948 war.[34] Consequently, Israel sought to make the Jewish *state* the owner of the land. This effort proved very successful. Virtually all Arab-owned land in Israel (about 91 percent of the country in 1948) was eventually and seemingly legally transferred to the Jewish state or to the Jewish National Fund by 1966. Nearly all new Jewish settlements between 1948 and early 1953 were built on Arab land dubbed "abandoned" despite that fact that most Arab refugees were kept at gunpoint from returning.[35] This seizure was in violation of the UN Partition Resolution stipulation that "no expropriation of land owned by an Arab in the Jewish state shall be allowed except for public purposes. . . . In all cases of expropriation, full compensation as fixed by the Supreme Court shall be paid prior to dispossession." [36]

Israel designed laws to legalize state ownership ("redemption") of the land:

(1) *Law on the Acquisition of Absentees' Property.* Passed by the Knesset in 1950, this law stated that the land and property of a person declared "absentee" was to be transferred to the Custodian of Absentee Property. Such lands and buildings could then be sold to the government's Development Authority for Jewish immigrant settlements. An "absentee" was defined as any

person who had left his usual place of living, for however short a time, to go to another place within or outside Palestine *not* under Jewish rule between November 29, 1947 (the time of the UN Partition) and September 1, 1948 (the end of the fighting) – that is, *anywhere* in UN-designated Arab Palestine. By this law, Arab refugees who left their homes during the war for safer quarters in Arab Palestine or elsewhere (despite later returning home), were dubbed the "absent-present" and their land and property were expropriated. Moreover, any Arab-Israeli citizen who left his home in Arab Palestine (not *yet* under Israeli control during the war) to visit any part which *later* came under Israeli rule (by the 1949 armistice) was declared an "absentee."[37]

This law allowed for the expropriation of land and property of the vast majority of Arab refugees, as well as 40 to 65 percent of the land of Arab-Israeli citizens still in Israel, creating a new class of "internal refugees."[38] These rural Arab-Israelis turned to the cities to find menial work and encountered profound discrimination by the Histadrut and a Jewish public unwilling to rent housing.

(2) *Emergency Regulations (Cultivation of Waste Lands), 1949.* This law empowered the Israeli minister of agriculture to take possession of land when the minister was not satisfied that the owner was cultivating the land or would *continue* to cultivate it. This law was used in conjunction with Defense Laws. The minister of defense or a local military governor would declare an area "closed," expel the owner and then refuse him a permit to return for "security reasons." Since the owner could not cultivate the land, Israel could take possession by virtue of the law concerning "Cultivation of Waste Lands." The minister of agriculture would invariably turn this land over to neighboring Jewish settlements.

A direct military solution was an alternative. By declaring the land a "security zone" (by virtue of the Defense/Security Laws) the resident could be expelled indefinitely. For example, Arab-Israeli residents of Ikrit were to be expelled on October 31, 1948 for two weeks until "military operations in the area were concluded." After three years and multiple petitions, the residents sought Supreme Court permission to return to their homes. The court found in their favor, but the military government refused to comply. Six weeks prior to an additional trial, the army blew up the entire village and the government expropriated all the land. The fate of the village of Kfar Berem was identical.

(3) *Prescription Law, 1958.* Most large-scale appropriations of land were completed by 1958. As a result, many Arab farmers were working hilly, rocky patches that had never been surveyed.[39] By Ottoman and British mandate laws

(still in effect), an Arab-Israeli farmer working a piece of land for ten years (the "prescription" period) had a right to ownership after surveying his land. To subvert this right, the government proposed to change the prescription period to fifty years. Since few farmers had records to prove a half-century of residence, the land could be declared "state land." An Arab outcry eventually forced a modification of this proposed change.[40]

(4) *Nationalization of land.* The land of Arab refugees and Arab-Israeli citizens was converted into Israeli state-owned "public" land through the Jewish National Fund. Superficially, the conversion had the appearance of satisfying a UN proscription against expropriation of Arab lands "except for public purposes." JNF administration made the land "public" *by definition.* Because JNF land was reserved for Jewish use only, the Arab citizen lost his land.

There was a hitch in this last nationalization scheme. Nationalization by the state required *proof* of state ownership – ordinarily proved by payment of compensation. After a five-year delay, the government passed a law to compensate Arabs for expropriated land (Validation of Acts and Compensation Law, 1953) – perhaps out of fear that the whole question of expropriation would someday flare up.[41] At first the government offered 1947 land prices, then 1950 prices. Prime Minister Moshe Sharett considered the latter compensation to be a "scandalous robbery" since the Israeli pound was worth one-fifth its former value due to hyperinflation."[42] A large number of Arab-Israeli citizens refused to sign away their land for unfair compensation. To Palestinian-Arab refugees *outside* Israel, compensation for land and property was never offered.

The concept of democracy without minority rights

The government of the Jewish state attempts to balance certain *democratic* ideals and practices with certain *undemocratic* ideals and practices benefiting Jewish citizens exclusively. The Israeli Supreme Court took up the issue and determined that a Jewish state is not, by definition, undemocratic:

> The existence of the state of Israel as the state of the Jewish people does not negate its democratic nature, as the Frenchness of France does not negate its democratic nature.[43]

The flawed analogy: while all citizens of France are French by definition (just as all citizens of Israel are Israeli by definition), all citizens of a Jewish state are not Jewish. A democratic state exists for *all* its citizens, not just for its ethnic majority. Alternatively, a Jewish state could be seen to be democratic were it to have Jewish citizens only. Israel attempted to arrange this last by denying citizenship to Moslems and Christians by means of a 1952 *Nationality Law*.[44] This complex law effectively precluded the citizenship of either Palestinian-Arab refugees or Palestinians living in Israel unless they could prove their *former* Palestinian citizenship – an intentionally difficult qualification for most Palestinians.[45] As a result, some 40,000 Palestinian Arabs living in Israel were disqualified from citizenship. This Nationality Law, a violation of the UN partition resolution and the Balfour Declaration, embittered the Arab population and after years of dispute, many Palestinian-Arabs finally obtained citizenship.

The status of Arab-Israelis in the 1990s

Arab-Israelis, twenty percent of Israel's population, hold seventeen of 1,300 senior government positions, ten of 5,000 university posts and on average garner about five percent of Knesset seats. They are segregated into low-status jobs and constitute well over half of all those below Israel's poverty line. Though Israeli law "explicitly forbids discrimination in employment on religious, ethnic or national grounds, there is no enforcement mechanism outside normal criminal procedures. Consequently, such discrimination is basically unchecked and prevails widely: in practice it is sanctioned by the norms of Jewish economic and social life."[46]

Incongruities between the democratic ideal and practice

Israel considers itself to be a democracy. This fits with a traditional Jewish idealism centered on egalitarian socialism. That idealism, common to other homogeneous groups, faltered when the community, no longer solely Jewish, was forced to accommodate an ethnic minority. Some have argued that the government and laws of Israel reflect not a turning away from democratic values, but a necessary suppression of a minority that might well resent Jewish rule or intend to undermine the state. On the other hand, others have argued that the internal "security" issue is a cover – that Israel's true intent is to dispossess, marginalize or deport Arabs in an effort to make the Jewish state more Jewish. In either case, the Israeli government has not treated its Arab citizens equally, whether for security reasons or out of racial/religious intolerance – or both.

The final defining shape of Israel is dependent on the kinds of solutions it adopts to resolve the incongruities that now exist between its ideals and its actual practices. While Israel's stated values are democratic, community-oriented and redemptive through moral example, significant questions arise regarding democracy in Israel when unwelcome minorities are denied their civil rights, equal employment opportunity and use of most of the land.

One popular Labor politician in Israel, Shlomo Ben-Ami, observed: "Some [Israelis] no longer share the values of America – religious freedom, the civility of political discourse, democratic values."[47] It is an open question:

> The country is still very far from realizing these [power-sharing] ideals, and may indeed be heading in the opposite direction. . . . Israeli society is showing signs of increasing polarization, aggression and brutalization, both among its citizens . . . and against its real and perceived enemies.[48]

Notes

1. Leonard J. Fein, *Politics in Israel* (Boston: Little, Brown and Co., 1967), 67.

2. "The ideal movement [party] member lives in party housing (or in an agricultural settlement affiliated with the party), reads the party newspaper, handles his financial transactions through the party's financial institutions, attends seminars at party schools, reads books published by the party, belongs to his local party club and participates in its weekly or biweekly meetings, sends his children to the party's youth movement, and, perhaps most important of all, believes in the party's ideology as a comprehensive statement of political truth." Fein, *Politics,* 69. "Most newspapers, youth organizations, and athletic organizations are affiliated with parties, as are almost all collective and cooperative agricultural settlements" (97).

3. An example from the past might be Ben-Gurion's Mapai political party, which centered on programs combining Zionist and democratic socialist ideologies with special focus on pioneering as the central myth. To his political left was the Mapam party: communistic and pro-Soviet. To his right was Menachem Begin's Herut party: militant, expansionist, anti-Arab and capitalist.

4. The central committee controls disputes between cabinet ministers or other quasi-governmental institutions, e.g., the Histadrut labor and industry organization.

5. Each party presents a list of its candidates during the campaign so that, theoretically, individual personalities can have some sway over the popular vote – and say in party ideology. But the party decides on the candidate list and order. The number of candidates who gain government positions is based on the percent of popular vote the party receives.

6. Fein, *Politics,* 170.

7. "Invisible" quasi-governmental institutions were consistent with traditional Jewish emphasis on cooperative, decentralized, voluntary organization of communal life, with feelings of suspicion toward centralized, oppressive outside governments.

8. See Ian Lustick, *Arabs in the Jewish State* (Austin: University of Texas Press,

1980), 140.

9. Ben-Gurion – prime minister, leader of the dominant Mapai party (later called the Labor Party), the Jewish Agency and the Histadrut – created an oligarchy with colleagues Moshe Sharrett, Golda Meir, Moshe Dayan, Yitzchak Ben-Zvi, Berl Katznelson and Levi Eshkol.

10. The power of the prime minister is limited by the policies of *coalition* parties. At the same time, his or her own ultimate weapon, the threat of resigning (as in the British system), can bring down the entire government. Coalition parties must either accede to the prime minister's demands or return to the polls politically divided.

11. Howard Sachar, *A History of Israel: From the Rise of Zionism to Our Time,* Vol. I, (New York: Knopf, 1986), 370; Fein, *Politics,* 189.

12. Sachar, *History,* Vol. I, 362, 369-71.

13. The Knesset can force a government's resignation by a vote of no confidence, investigate governmental misbehaviors and set the governmental budget.

14. "For all practical purposes, civil *divorce* now exists in Israel, not through legislation, but by the creation of the Supreme Court." William Frankel, *Israel Observed: An Anatomy of the State* (New York: Thames and Hudson, 1980), 129.

15. Religous political parties control the religious education of immigrants, state sponsorship of religious schools, exemption of Orthodox girls from military or national service, imposition of religious law on public behavior and patronage through party clout. Sachar, *History,* Vol. I, 379-82.

16. The Supreme Court hears appeals and those cases not covered in lower courts.

17. Fein, *Politics,* 187.

18. *Human Rights Watch* (Washington, D.C., 1991), 67, n. 61. The international community, the UN Security Council and the United States disagreed with Israel.

19. The Fourth Geneva Convention prohibits an occupying power from colonizing captured territory through settlement of its own citizens.

20. The deputy defense minister in 1979 called the Histadrut "a Mafia which gives backing to parasites." For the Histadrut in 1980: Frankel, *Observed,* 194-5.

21. Ian Lustick found in 1980 that "of the thousands of Histadrut firms and factories not one is located in an Arab village." *Arabs,* 96. Noam Chomsky noted in 1976 that "Histadrut programs are overwhelmingly organized for the benefit of Jews. There are still no Arab members of the eighteen-man Central Committee of the Histadrut and no Arabs among the more than six hundred managers and directors of Histadrut-controlled industry." Sabri Jiryis, *The Arabs in Israel* (London: Monthly Review Press, 1976), xii.

22. Concerning land and water use, confiscation of Arab-owned land and use of water in Israel has meant that, per capita, Arab farmers produce only one-sixteenth as much as Jewish farmers. The Jewish Agency provides little support for agriculture, industry or commerce to Arab citizens compared with their Jewish counterparts. Income, infant mortality, school support, meaningful employment and housing are notably disadvantaged. See Howard Sachar, *History: From the Aftermath of the Yom Kippur War,* Vol. II (New York: Oxford University Press, 1987), 34.

23. The JNF is connected to the government through a covenant. The JNF's Board for Land Reclamation and Development establishes land policies in accord with the Israeli Minister of Agriculture and supervises the Land Development Administration. The JNF also continues to operate as an independent agency of the WZO. See Noam Chomsky, *Towards a New Cold War* (New York: Pantheon, 1973), 248.

24. Legally, Arabs may not be employed on national lands. However, some Jews have subleased land to Arab-Israels for profit. A Jewish farmer lost possession of his land in 1971 because an Arab bought and harvested tomatoes from his field (*Yediot Aharonot*, May 3, 1971). Clearly, enforcement is spotty, Arab labor being cheap and needed by Israeli farmers. The minister of agriculture denounced use of Arab labor in 1974 as an illegal "cancer." *Haaretz*, December 13, 1974; *Maariv*, July 3, 1975.

25. Report of Israel Lands Administration (in Hebrew) (Jerusalem, 1962), 6-7. See also, the JNF pamphlet, "Seventy Years in Facts and Figures" (Jerusalem, 1971). Both cited in Uri Davis and Walter Lehn, "And the Fund Still Lives," *Journal of Palestine Studies* 7, No. 4 (Summer 1978), 23. Histadrut 95 percent figure cited in Sachar, *History*, Vol. I, 742.

26. Alan Dowty, The Jewish State: A Century Later (Berkeley: University of California Press, 1998), 198.

27. For example, expulsion of Israeli Arabs living at Wadi Fukin and Baqa el Gharbiya. Avi Shlaim, *Collusion across the Jordan* (New York: Columbia University Press, 1988), 456.

28. Urban Arab-Israelis are handled by local police.

29. Lustick, *Arabs,* 66.

30. Israel justified retention of British Emergency Laws on the grounds that they were local law at the time of statehood. In fact, Britain revoked these laws *prior* to Israeli statehood. "Prison Conditions in Israel and the Occupied Territories," *Human Rights Watch* (Washington, 1991), 110 n. 19.

31. Meron Benvenisti, *The West Bank Handbook* (Boulder, Colo.: Westview Press, 1986), 58.

32. "Of the 170 articles in the Defense Laws of 1945, Article 125 is the most frequently employed. It grants the power to restrict liberty of movement by declaring 'closed areas which no one can enter or leave without a written permit from the Military Governor.' Articles 109 and 110 grant the right to restrict possession, the choice of residence, and the right to leave a location. They further provide for controlled access to homes. Under Articles 111 and 112 anyone can be detained for any reason whatsoever, for an unlimited period of time, without trial, and without declaring the charge. A person can be expelled from the country permanently and any person outside the country can be forbidden from returning. In addition, Article 124 confers the power to impose a total or partial curfew in any area. Among the most arbitrary powers are those regarding property. Article 119 grants the power to 'confiscate or destroy a person's property if the military governor suspects that a shot has been fired or a bomb thrown from such property.' Article 120 permits confiscation of an individual's property if the Minister of Defense is satisfied that

this person has broken these laws or has committed an offense for which he is liable to be tried by a Military Court." Cherif M. Bassiouni [Professor of Law, De Paul University], *Information Paper No. 22* (Detroit: Association of Arab-American University Graduates Press, 1978).

33. Statement of some Israeli kibbutzim representatives and university intellectuals. Jiryis, *Arabs in Israel*, 38-9.

34. In 1949, the Jews had possession of about 77 percent of Palestine (20.5 out of 26.4 million dunams) but owned only 8.4 percent of Palestine. In May 1948, Jews owned about 6.6 percent of Palestine (1.74 million dunams). Walter Lehn, "The Jewish National Fund," *Journal of Palestine Studies*3, No. 4 (Summer 1974), 74 n 2. UN estimates of Jewish ownership in May 1948 range from 6 to 15 percent. Stephen Green, *Taking Sides* (Brattleboro Vt.: Amana Press, 1988), 100n.

35. Don Peretz, *Israel and the Palestine Arabs* (Washington: Middle East Institute, 1958), 143. Thirty-five thousand were eventually allowed to return.

36. Cited in Sachar, *History,* Vol. I, 386.

37. The entire population of the "Little Triangle" area in the Galilee, annexed by the Rhodes agreement of April 3, 1949, was declared "absent-present, " and a great part of their land was confiscated despite agreement at Rhodes to respect the freedom and property of the inhabitants. All Arab property owners in the New City of Acre, even those who traveled only a few hundred yards to the Old City, were classified as "absentees"; similarly, in Lydda, Ramle and Jerusalem. Sachar, *History,* Vol. I, 387.

38. Sachar estimates 40 percent (*History,* Vol. I, 387). Also Peretz, (*Israel,* 142). Jiryis estimates 65 percent (*Arabs in Israel,* 130):"More than 1 million dunams of land belonging to Arabs who had remained in Israel was seized after 1948" (81).

39. Only about one-quarter of Israel was surveyed prior to statehood.

40. Yet other subterfuges were adopted. See Jiryis, *Arabs in Israel,* 112-14.

41. Jiryis, *Arabs in Israel,* 126.

42. Jiryis, *Arabs in Israel,* 127.

43. October 18, 1988, ruling. Anton Shammas, *New York Review of Books,* December 22, 1988 (letter).

44. Sachar, *History,* Vol. I, 383-4.

45. Sachar, *History,* Vol. I, 383-4.

46. Quote and preceding statistics from Dowty, *The Jewish State,* 195, 200. "Army service is another basis for discrimination. The military [forbidden Arab-Israelis] is a source of important benefits in employment, housing and education (198)." Many Arabs vote for Jewish parties, tactically, since Arab candidate lists are not likely coalition partners and thus not an effective route to influence (195).

47. Serge Schmemann, "Outside In," *New York Times,* November 23, 1997, 78.

48. Omer Bartov, "Helmet and rife at the ready," *Times Literary Supplement,* May 22, 1998, 26.

Appendix B

The Paradox of Nationalism

Jewish nationalism reflects a universal ideal, the right of a people to self-determination. Fulfillment of this ideal involved the taking and colonization of a territory, thereby precluding self-determination for the indigenous Palestinian Arab population. Some observers have seen the resulting struggle as one of right against right – not that there are angels on either side. Other observers have seen Palestinian resistance as a justifiable defense against aggressive Jewish colonial intrusion. Still others have demonized the Palestinians as would-be perpetrators of a second Holocaust.

Perhaps the Middle East struggle is, however, best understood as a nationalistic struggle like those of nationalism generally.[1] The Jewish people, deeply injured, seeking self-determination, prizing and protecting their national identity above that of the Palestinians, have, in the manner of other nationalistic people, conquered an opponent in the name of security and self-defense. That opponent has come to be seen as an alien and fanatical aggressor overcome through courage and use of regretable but necessary force. This is the self-portrait of nationalists, generally.

Nationalism, the cornerstone of the modern political world, is a two-sided affair – liberal as well as illiberal. On the one hand, it is associated with democracy, liberalism, the value of the common man and a people's right to be free of domination by others. Typically it centers on the right of national *self-determination* as, for example, by overthrow of a monarch or a foreign colonial power. National liberation movements in Africa have changed European colonies into independent states. Dissolution of the Ottoman Empire after World War I led to new Arab states in the Middle East and Jewish nationalism led to the establishment of Israel.

On the other hand, nationalism is associated with the imperialistic conquest of weaker, alien peoples. For example, the French Revolution began in defense of the liberty of the people but developed under Napoleon into wars of conquest and empire-building throughout Europe. Similarly, the American colonists, seeking self-determination and freedom from European rule, carried their national zeal westward in conquest of indigenous native populations and southward in conquest of Mexico, Cuba, Central America and the Philippines.

The basic tenet of nationalism is that a people should have their own state because, lacking a state, they will be abused by others. Woodrow Wilson hoped that nationalism, in its liberal, idealized form, could end this abuse. He envisioned separate peoples advancing their interests in their own sovereign states, free of interference and in cooperation with other states. But the ideal of a league of independent nations foundered on the reality of political and military power – nationalism in its illiberal, imperialistic form. After World War I, the Allied powers feasted on the spoils left by the dissolution of the German and Ottoman empires. Britain and France carved out client states in the Middle East in a division that violated the self-determination of Arab peoples.

The Wilsonian ideal assumes that a nation, arising from a compelling urge for liberty and self-determination, will be a *self-limiting* entity (or at least one constrained by international pressure). But in concrete application, "self-determination" is a vague and expandable concept, ranging anywhere from modest self-regulation and self-defense to aggressive conquest of those who stand in the way of the peoples' self-perceived needs or potentials, as in Hitler's quest for *Lebensraum* in Poland. Like the concept of freedom, self-determination is a concept open to illiberal use. Adam Roberts recently noted:

> Claims for self-determination, and resistance to those claims, have been one element in the causation of practically every war this century – including two world wars, countless regional conflicts, and most terrorist campaigns.[2]

Moreover, the concept of "the people" (the nation, ethnic group, race) can also be put to illiberal use because its indefinite scope may be used to exclude or oppress minorities from within ("internal racism") or foreigners from without ("external racism").[3] Those ill-fated persons judged not to belong to "the people" are considered to lack certain essential and prized traits, the peoples' *unified core.* Most often this core involves some claim about the *past,* a claim that there exists historically a constant and unchangeable group. This claim may be naive or spurious, but is powerfully affecting.[4]

In sum, when "self-determination" is expansively defined and "the people" is narrowly defined, then nationalism tends toward the illiberal exclusion of minorities and conquest or colonization of foreigners.

What, then, are the basic elements of the nationalistic mentality that account for both its liberal and illiberal aspects?[5]

The features of the nationalistic mentality

(1) *Ethnocentrism.* Nationalistic movements are classically infused with notions about the value of belonging to and possessing the preferred if not prized traits of one's own people or nation. These traits are understood to be *unique* to one's people and thus lacking in others who are necessarily viewed as lesser. This pride/xenophobia quotient may justify aggression toward other peoples taken to be undeveloped or uncivilized. Conquest may even be construed as bringing progress to the other. Early English colonials in North America justified their seizure of Indian land on grounds that the inhabitants "run over the grass, as do the foxes and wild beasts, [lack] the art, science, skill or faculty to use either the land or the commodities of it."[6] William Henry Harrison saw America as the "haunt of a few thousand savages" in a land "destined by the Creator to be the seat of civilization, science, and true religion."[7] Similarly, Theodor Herzl portrayed the future Jewish state as "an outpost of civilization against barbarism."[8] Perhaps the clearest expression of ethnocentric superiority was Theodore Roosevelt notion that the extermination of the American Indians and expropriation of their land "was as ultimately beneficial as it was inevitable":

> Such conquests [are] sure to come when a masterful people, still in its raw barbarian prime, finds itself face to face with the weaker and wholly alien race which holds a coveted prize in its feeble grasp.[9]

(2) *Unity of the people.* A second basic feature of the nationalist mentality is an assumption (and requirement) that the national group be *homogeneous.* All those who share the common language, ethnicity, culture or national identity are presumed or imagined to *equally* possess the group's important and prized traits:[10]

Every member of the "people" thus interpreted partakes in its superior, elite quality, and it is in consequence that a stratified national population is perceived as essentially homogeneous, and the lines of status and class as superficial. This principle lies at the basis of all nationalisms and justifies viewing them as expressions of the same phenomenon.[11]

That *every* belonging member of the group is said to partake of the positive traits of the group – i.e., possesses some sort of inner superiority – accounts, of course, for the great popularity of nationalism. Whatever the individual's personal failing or class, he shares equally in the national pride. "Regardless of the actual inequality and exploitation that may prevail . . . the nation is always conceived as a deep, horizontal comradeship."[12] On the other hand, conspicuous ethnic minorities, those assumed to lack the desired national traits, palpably spoil that national identity. They are the pariahs, the Jews, the Blacks, the "natives" in the colonies. They, too, are assumed to be homogeneous, that is, "*equally* contemptible."[13] Nationalism and democracy make a uncomfortable mix.

(3) *Moral justifications for the conquest of outsiders.* Nationalistic zeal about the special worth or entitlement of one's own kind may lead to heroic acts of patriotism. It may also lead to oppression of minorities and conquest of outsiders, in which case, various sorts of self-justifications are invoked to maintain a sense of national goodness:

(a) The *altruistic* justification, a benevolent infusion of progress, religion or culture into the untutored or uncivilized – i.e., "white man's burden."

(b) The *economic* justification, the claim that a people will profit from being conquered. The people of India were to gain through purchase of finished goods from Britain; the Palestinians to profit from Jewish investment. The destruction of an indigenous culture seems to the colonizer to be of economic advantage to an otherwise backward people.

(c) The *wilderness* justification, the notion that the conquered land is essentially empty. The British claimed in 1622 that "it is lawful now to take a land [America] which none useth" – like the Zionist slogan: "A land without a people for a people without a land." The wilderness myth implies either that the inhabitants are few in number, fail to use the land productively,[14] or lack a European-style political identity (in which case the territory is *politically* empty).[15]

(d) The *metaphysical/religious* justification, the conquering people's belief

in their divinely sanctioned or historical mission. For example, "Manifest Destiny" in North America was the idea that the continent was "allotted by Providence for the free development of our yearly multiplying millions." This rationalization sprung directly from the biblical notion that a people could be sanctioned by God to dominate, conquer or displace others.[16]

(e) The *ends-means* justification, a quasi-terroristic viewpoint in which the means employed are less important than the end result. Unsavory means and injury to others are accepted for the sake of a greater good. Typically, a "purity of arms" (minimum force necessary) is claimed.

(f) The *Social-Darwinian* justification, the notion that "survival of the fittest" refers to victorious might as "Nature's way":

> The earth is awarded by providence to people who in their hearts have the courage to conquer it, the strength to preserve it, and the industry to put it to the plough. Hence, every healthy, vigorous people sees nothing sinful in territorial acquisition, but something in keeping with nature.[17]

(g) Justification by *selective attention*. The victor, as victim, attends to *his* costs and injuries and bemoans *his* brutalization in brutalizing others.[18] Golda Meir insisted that she would never forgive the Arabs for causing "our boys" to act as they did (kill Arabs).[19]

(h) The *self-defense* justification. This universal justification for nationalistic conquest is a unique feature of the modern world, according to Joseph Schumpeter:

> Every war is carefully justified as a defensive war by the government involved, and by all the political parties, in their official utterances.[20]

Nations normally conceive or represent their own agression as defensive or preventative.[21] Even Adolf Hitler portrayed his war against the Jews as "defensive," against Bolshevik barbarism as "preventative."[22] Psychologically, it is the *other's* aggression that one is forced to take up.

David Ben-Gurion saw into this rhetoric:

> When we say the Arabs are the aggressors and we defend ourselves – that is only half the truth. . . . The fighting is only one aspect of the conflict which is in its essence a political one. And politically we are the aggressors and they defend themselves.[23]

Nationalism– liberal and illiberal – an inevitability?

> How we act toward the Arabs will determine what kind of people we become:
> either oppressors and racists in our turn like those from whom we have
> suffered, or a nobler race able to transcend the tribal xenophobias that afflict
> mankind.[24]

I. F. Stone here implies that tribal xenophobias are not inevitable, that Jews
need not join in the kind of oppression of Arabs that, ironically, the history of
the oppression of Jews so compellingly illustrates. Yet the premise of
nationalism (and Zionism) is otherwise – that conflicts between diverse peoples,
whether related to greed, self-inflation, racism and disdain, are inevitable; and
that sovereign statehood affords protection from that abuse and curbs one's own
temptation to abuse. The implication is that tribal xenophobias, whether
directed at Arabs, Jews or any other people, are expectable if not inevitable and
that statehood is some kind of necessary answer.

Is there reason to postulate some sort of universal *psychological need* to
believe that one belongs to a group endowed and entitled because of favorable
traits lacking in others, in which case xenophobias would be inevitable? I refer
to a need that goes well beyond a simple desire to find dignity of place within
the small variations that exist in the human family – but rather, to a
vainglorious need to search out and fix on tribal differences between peoples,
however fatuous or imaginary those differences. One does regularly observe, more
or less everywhere, an impulse to scent out differences (insufficiencies) in others
and a tendency to take pride in one's own (better) people. Even when the
differences appear to be largely inconsequential, accidental or otherwise non-
essential, they often become an inflated object of focus. Psychologists call this
need to find and exaggerate differences the *narcissism of small differences.*[25]

Belief in a tribal identity or national origin bearing favored endowments,
whether or not ficticious, creates a psychologically satisfying sense of and value
in belonging. It often inspires great patriotism and sacrifice in defense of people
and place. Yet its dangerous corollary, its illiberal flip side, is one of entitled,
xenophobic nationalism.

Jewish Nationalism

Special circumstances surrounded Jewish nationalism (Zionism). Most
obviously, it gained a momentum, a special sense of urgency and a moral

permission from the trauma of the Holocaust. Furthermore, the specter of the earlier Nazi Goliath was preserved and displaced to a later time, circumstance and Eastern people, fashioning the Middle East struggle on the past in the minds of Jews and Western observers alike.

Yet Jewish nationalism is not unique. The colonization of Palestine and dispossession of its indigenous people is a familiar story – indeed, it is both biblical and an example of what historically has been the way of the world. Familiar is how forceful resistance to dispossession is seen as unwarranted attack and how the victor seeks peace only after the conquest is completed. Jewish nationalism follows the features of nationalism generally – ethnocentrism, belief in the unity of the people and moral justification for the dispossession.

Zionism is neither better nor worse than the other nationalisms which characterize modern political life. It bears all the earmarks of a working-out of both the freedom-seeking, positive aspects of nationalism and its illiberal, negative aspects, intolerance and conquest of alien peoples. The Arab-Jewish struggle, then, is not so much a Manichean drama in which demons are pitted against angels, nor a lofty struggle on the alabastrine heights of Greek tragedy – right versus right. It is more directly the application of a nationalistic ideal by a Western and favored people concerning their self-determination and security – fueled by the nightmare of the Holocaust and illusions about the unimportance of an indigenous people – that resulted in an illiberal and disquieting conquest.

Notes

1. To see Jewish nationalism as falling into the class of other forms of nationalism is not to ignore specialized interpretations that have been advanced to explain concrete Israeli behavior. Avner Yaniv has sorted these explanatory interpretations into five types: (1) *Anti-Zionist* – "Israel is the product of an aggressive ideology and therefore cannot but act aggressively towards its neighbors"; (2) *Zionist Fundamentalist* – "Israel is the innocent victim of a fanatical pan-Arab drive for hegemony in the Middle East"; (3) *Psychological-Cultural* – Israel reflects "the personality traits and the historical-psychological 'baggage' of Israeli decision makers [who are] . . . prone to act harshly because they cannot help observing their Arab environment through the distorting lens [Holocaust syndrome] of their Jewish legacy of suffering and persecution"; (4) *Domestic-Political* – Israel's conduct "is chiefly determined by the pulling of political forces to which Israeli decision makers have to respond at home"; (5) *Security* –"nations are impelled to take care of their

security unilaterally." Avner Yaniv, *Dilemmas of Security* (New York: Oxford University Press, 1987), 5-7.

2. Adam Roberts, "When in the Course of Human Events," *Times Literary Supplement*, April 11, 1997.

3. Collective terms such as "nation, ethnic group, race or people" are highly ambiguous in meaning and denotation, but have shaded differences. *Nation* refers either to a nation-state (a geopolitical concept linked to goeographic boundaries) or a nationality (an ethnic concept). An *ethnic group* is a cultural category in which certain continuing behaviors are allegedly passed from generation to generation and is *not* normally linked to state boundaries. *Race* is supposed to be a genetic category which has a visible physical form, but is sometimes defined more broadly to include *all* forms of exclusion and depreciation, whether or not they are accompanied by biological theories. The definition of *people* usually *follows* rather than precedes the creation of a nation-state. Thus, the existing population, or its preferred majority, *becomes* "the people" – for example, the white population in America in 1776.

4. "The power of myths of national origins and national continuity resides in their capacity to convince individuals to function politically as representatives of a genuine social reality, that is, a continuous and historic community. . . . A 'people' is said to be or act as it does because of either its genetic characteristics, or its socio-political history, or its 'traditional' norms and values. The whole point of these categories seems to be to enable us to make claims based upon the past against the manipulable 'rational' processes of the present. We may use these categories to explain why things are the way they are and shouldn't be changed, or why things are the way they are and cannot be changed . . . [or] conversely . . . .to explain why the present structures should indeed be superseded in the name of deeper and more ancient, *ergo* more legitimate, social realities. The temporal dimension of pastness is central to and inherent in the concept of peoplehood. . . . [This] pastness is a mode by which persons are persuaded to act in the present in ways they might not otherwise act. Pastness is a tool persons use against each other. Pastness is a central element in the socialization of individuals, in the maintenance of group solidarity, in the establishment of a challenge to social legitimation. Pastness therefore is preeminently a moral phenomenon, therefore a political phenomenon, always a contemporary phenomenon." Immanuel Wallerstein, "The Construction of Peoplehood: Racism, Nationalism, Ethnicity," in Etienne Balibar and Immanuel Wallerstein, *Race, Nation, Class: Ambiguous Identities* (New York: Verso, 1991), 78.

5. By "basic elements of the nationalistic mentality," I am not referring to the causes or necessary conditions that give rise to nationalism, but to the content of nationailist thinking. Those historians who *do* focus on the causes and conditions for nationalism stress: (1) the development of a vernacular language, (2) popular literacy and high culture, (3) occupational mobility in an industrial economy, (4) a centralized educational system and (5) a centralized state. See Ernest Gellner, *Nations and Nationalism* (Ithaca: Cornell University Press, 1983). Benedict Anderson explains the illiberal or imperialistic turn which nationalisms tend to take

to the usurpation of state policy by residual dynastic/aristocratic groups in the society *after* populist nationalism begins to threaten their power. Benedict Anderson, *Imagined Communities* (New York: Verso, 1983)

6. David Stannard, *American Holocaust: Columbus and the Conquest of the New World* (New York: Oxford University Press, 1992), 235.

7. Norman Finkelstein, *Image and Reality of the Israel-Palestine Conflict* (London: Verso, 1995), 91. "Savage" was the accepted usage even in legal decisions. James Smith, *Seventeenth-Century America: Essays in Colonial History* (Westport, Conn.: Greenwood Publishing, 1980), 27.

8. Finkelstein, *Image and Reality*, 101.

9. Theodore Roosevelt, *The Winning of the West*, Vol. IV (New York: Peter Smith, 1889), 200. Hitler saw a parallel between his and the American need to take living-space from the Indians and praised "the efficiency of America's extermination of the red savages who could not be tamed by captivity." John Toland, *Adolf Hitler* (Garden City, N.Y.: Doubleday, 1976), 702.

10. Race, as distinct from language and culture, often figures powerfully in a people's sense of identity, despite being a highly dubious biological concept. But even linguistic and cultural identities involve fictional elements. "Every social community reproduced by the function of institutions is imaginary, that is to say, based on the projection of individual existence into the weft of a collective narrative, on the recognition of a common name and on traditions lived as the trace of an immemorial past (even when they have been fabricated and inculcated in the recent past)." Balibar and Wallerstein, *Race, Nation, Class*, 93.

11. Liah Greenfeld *Nationalism: Five Roads to Modernity* (Cambridge, Mass.: Harvard University Press, 1992), 7.

12. Anderson, *Imagined Communities*, 7.

13. Anderson, *Imagined Communities*, 122.

14. Concerning failure to use the land productively, Chief Justice John Marshall concluded in 1823 that the usual laws were inapplicable since the Indians were fierce savages whose occupation was war and whose subsistence was drawn chiefly from the forest – that indian-occupied land was "vacant." Robert Williams, *The American Indian in Western Legal Thought* (London: Oxford University Press, 1990), 308-9. Hitler justified the seizure of Poland on the grounds that his was not a conquest of the Polish people but a settlement of a wilderness. See Finkelstein, *Image and Reality*, 89-98.

15. Maxime Rodinson, *Israel: A Colonial-Settler State?* (New York: Pathfinder, 1973), 12.

16. The biblical notion that God sanctions and assists in making war has been used to sanction the British conquest of North America, Ireland and Australia; the Dutch conquest of South Africa; the Prussian conquest of Poland; and the Zionist conquest of Palestine. Arnold Toynbee, *A Study of History*, Vol. VIII (London: Oxford University Press, 1987), 310.

17. Adolf Hitler, *Secret Book* (New York: Grove Press, 1961), 15-16.

18. "The strain was far heavier in the case of our men who carried out the executions than in that of their victims" – Paul Blobel, leader of Einsatzkommando 4A during World War II. Cited in Finkelstein, *Image and Reality*, 118-9.

19. Omer Bartov, "Helmet and rifle at the ready," *Times Literary Supplement*, May 22, 1998, 26.

19. Finkelstein, *Image and Reality*, 107.

20. Raul Hilberg observed: "The theory of world Jewish rule and of the incessant Jewish plot against the German people penetrated into all offices [of the German bureaucracy]. . . . In the minds of the perpetrators, therefore, this theory turned the destruction process into a kind of preventive war." Raul Hilberg, *The Destruction of the European Jews*, (New York: Holmes and Meier, 1985), 284-5.

21. Raul Hilberg, *Perpetrators, Victims, Bystanders* (New York: Harper Perennial Library, 1993), 10.

22. Simha Flapan, *Zionism and the Palestinians* (London: Croom Helm, 1979), 141. Cited in Finkelstein, *Image and Reality*, 205.

23. I.F. Stone, "Holy War," in *The Israel-Arab Reader: A Documentary History of the Middle East Conflict,* Walter Laqueur and Barry Rubin, eds. (New York: Penquin, 1984), 324.

24. Identification with and loyalty to a group can be based on surprisingly *arbitrary* criteria. For example, people will take fierce pride in arbitrarily selected teams in a parlor game. A sense of belonging and need to prove superiority in that belonging requires little objective basis – hence, Anderson's "imagined communities." While some real political, economic or cultural criteria may justify assignment of differences to others, this mostly seems to be based on self-inflation and questionable evidence. After a war, for example, when propagandistic differences are no longer useful, shared traits with the enemy are mysteriously discovered.

Just as small differences with outsiders are exaggerated in nationalisms, so, differences within the national group are denied. For example, the difference between an Oriental and a European Jew would have to be seen as less fundamental than that between an Arab and a Jew. Otherwise, the state's raison d'être, based on the notion of a unitary Jewish people, would be undermined. This notion of a unitary Jewish people, like that of the Aryan *Volk*, is a romantically and nationalistically flavored idea that is accepted by many Jews and anti-Semites alike.

Bibliography

Books

Abu-Lughod, Ibrahim, ed. *Transformation of Palestine*. Evanston: Northwestern University Press, 1971.

Anderson, Benedict. *Imagined Communities*. New York: Verso, 1983.

Aronson, Geoffrey. *Creating Facts: Israel, Palestinians and the West Bank* Washington: Institute for Palestine Studies, 1987.

Balibar, Etienne, and Immanuel Wallerstein. *Race, Nation, Class: Ambiguous Identities*. Chris Turner, trans. New York: Verso, 1991.

Ball, George. *Error and Betrayal in Lebanon: An Analysis of Israel's Invasion of Lebanon and Its Implications for U.S.-Israeli Relations*. Washington: Foundation for Middle East Peace, 1984.

Begin, Menachem. *The Revolt: Story of the Irgun*. New York: Nash Publications, 1977.

Benvenisti, Meron. *Intimate Enemies*. Berkeley: University of California Press, 1995.

———. *The West Bank Handbook*. Boulder, Colo.: Westview Press, 1986.

Bowle, John. *Viscount Samuel*. London: Gollancz, 1957.

Brecher, Michael. *Decisions in Israel's Foreign Policy*. New Haven: Yale University Press, 1975

Brenner, Lenni. *Zionism in the Age of the Dictators*. Westport, Conn.: Lawrence Hill, 1983.

Buffet, Cyril, and Beatrice Heuser, eds. *Haunted by History: Myths in International Relations*. Oxford: Berghahn, 1998.

Carter, Jimmy. *Keeping Faith: Memoirs of a President*. New York: Bantam, 1982.

Chomsky, Noam. *The Fateful Triangle*. Boston, Mass.: South End Press, 1983.

———. *Towards a New Cold War*. New York: Pantheon, 1973.

Cohen, Michael J. *Palestine and the Great Powers, 1945-1948*. Princeton: Princeton University Press, 1982.

Dowty, Alan. *The Jewish State: A Century Later*. Berkeley: University of California Press, 1998.

Dupuy, Trevor. *Elusive Victory: The Arab-Israeli Wars, 1947-1974*. New York: Harper and Row, 1978.

Eban, Abba. *An Autobiography*. New York: Random House, 1977.

Elon, Amos. *The Israelis, Founders and Sons*. New York: Penguin Books,

1984.

Ennes, James M. *Assault on the Liberty.* New York: Random House, 1979.

Ernst, Morris. *So Far So Good.* New York: Harper and Brothers, 1948.

Fein, Leonard J. *Politics in Israel.* Boston: Little, Brown and Co., 1967.

Finkelstein, Norman. *Image and Reality of the Israel-Palestine Conflict.* London: Verso, 1995.

———. *The Rise and Fall of Palestine.* Minneapolis: University of Minnesota Press, 1996.

Flapan, Simha. *The Birth of Israel.* New York: Pantheon, 1987.

———. *Zionism and the Palestinians.* London: Croom Helm, 1979.

Frankel, Glenn. *Beyond the Promised Land: Jews and Arabs on the Hard Road to a New Israel.* New York: Touchstone Books, 1996.

Frankel, William. *Israel Observed: Anatomy of the State.* New York: Thames and Hudson, 1980.

Fromkin, David. *A Peace to End All Peace: Creating the Modern Middle East, 1914-1922.* New York: Henry Holt, 1989.

Gellner, Ernest. *Nations and Nationalism.* Ithaca: Cornell University Press. 1983.

Gilbert, Martin. *The Macmillan Atlas of the Holocaust.* New York: Macmillan (Da Capo), 1982.

Glubb, Sir John Bagot. *The Changing Scenes of Life: An Autobiography.* London: Quartet Books, 1983.

Goldmann, Nahum. *Sixty Years of Jewish Life: The Autobiography of Nahum Goldmann.* New York: Holt, Rinehart and Winston, 1969.

Green, Stephen. *Taking Sides: America's Secret Relations with a Militant Israel.* Brattleboro, Vt.: Amana Books, 1988.

Greenfeld, Liah. *Nationalism: Five Roads to Modernity.* Cambridge, Mass.: Harvard University Press, 1992.

Gresh, Alain. *The PLO: The Struggle Within, Toward an Independent Palestinian State.* London: Zed Books, 1985.

Halevi, Ilan. *A History of the Jews.* London: Zed Books, 1987.

Hersch, Seymour M. *The Price of Power: Kissinger in the Nixon White House.* New York: Summit Books, 1983.

Herzl, Theodor. *Complete Diaries.* Marvin Lowenthal, ed. and trans. New York: Dial Press, 1956.

———. *The Jewish State: An Attempt at a Solution of the Jewish Question.* Sylvie d'Avigdor, trans. London: CentralOffice of the Zionist Organization, 1946.

Herzog, Chaim. *The Arab-Israeli Wars.* New York: Vintage Books, 1984.

———. *The War of Atonement.* Tel Aviv: Steimatzky's Agency, 1975.

Hilberg, Raul. *The Destruction of the European Jews*. New York: Holmes and Meier, 1985.

———. *Perpetrators, Victims, Bystanders*. New York: Harper Perennial Library, 1993.

Hitler, Adolf. *Secret Book*. New York: Grove Press, 1961.

Horsman, Reginald. *Race and Manifest Destiny: Origins of American Racial Anglo-Saxism*. Cambridge: Cambridge University Press, 1979.

Hurewitz, J.C. *The Struggle for Palestine*. New York: Schocken, 1976.

Hutchison, Elmo. *Violent Truce: A Military Observer Looks at the Arab-Israeli Conflict, 1951-1955*. New York: Devin-Adair, 1956.

Jiryis, Sabri. *The Arabs in Israel*. London: Monthly Review Press, 1976.

Kapeliouk, Amnon. *Sabra and Shatilla*. Belmont, Mass.: Association of Arab American University Graduates Press, 1984.

Khalidi, Rashid. *Under Siege: PLO Decision-making during the 1982 War*. New York: Columbia University Press, 1986.

Khalidi, Walid. *Before Their Diaspora*. Washington: Institute for Palestine Studies, 1984.

———. ed., *From Haven to Conquest: Readings in Zionism and the Palestine Problem Until 1948*. Washington: Institute for Palestine Studies, 1987.

Khouri, Fred. *The Arab-Israeli Dilemma*. Syracuse, N.Y.: Syracuse University Press, 1985.

Kimche, Jon and David. *A Clash of Destinies*. New York: Praeger, 1960.

Kimmerling, Baruch. *Zionism and Economy*. Cambridge, MA: Schenkman Publishing, 1983.

Kissinger, Henry. *White House Years*. New York: Little, Brown and Co., 1979.

———. *Years of Upheaval*. Boston: Little, Brown and Co., 1982.

Lamb, Franklin, ed. *Reason Not the Need: Eyewitness Chronicles of Israel's War in Lebanon*. Nottingham, England: Bertrand Russell Peace Foundation, 1984.

Laqueur, Walter and Barry Rubin, eds., *The Israel-Arab Reader: A Documentary History of the Middle East Conflict*. New York: Penquin, 1984.

Learsi, Rufus. *Fulfillment: The Epic Story of Zionism*. Cleveland: World Publishing Co., 1951.

LeFeber, Walter. *The American Age: United States Foreign Policy at Home and Abroad, 1750 to the Present*. New York: W.W. Norton, 1994.

Lenczowski, George. *Soviet Advances in the Middle East*. Washington: American Enterprise Institute, 1972.

Lorch, Natanel. Edge of the Sword: Israel's War of Independence, 1947-1949.

New York: Putnam, 1961.

Lustick, Ian. *Arabs in the Jewish State*. Austin: University of Texas Press, 1980.

Meir, Golda. *My Life*. New York: G.P. Putnam's Sons, 1975.

Mishal, Shaul. *The PLO under Arafat: Between Gun and Olive Branch*. New Haven, Conn.: Yale University Press, 1986.

Morris, Benny. *The Birth of the Palestinian Refugee Problem, 1947-1949*. Cambridge: Cambridge University Press, 1987.

———. *Israel's Border Wars, 1949-1956: Arab Infiltration, Israeli Retaliation, and the Countdown to the Suez War*. New York: Oxford University Press, 1993.

Neff, Donald. *Warriors against Israel*. Brattleboro, VT: Amana Books, 1988.

———. *Warriors at Suez*. Brattleboro, Vt.: Amana Books, 1988.

———. *Warriors for Jerusalem*. Brattleboro, Vt.: Amana Books, 1988.

Nixon, Richard M. *The Memoirs of Richard Nixon*. New York: Touchstone Books, 1990.

Parker, Richard B. *The Politics of Miscalculation in the Middle East*. Bloomington: Indiana University Press, 1993.

Parkes, James W. *A History of Palestine from 135 A.D. to Modern Times*. New York: Oxford University Press, 1949.

Peretz, Don. *Intifada: The Palestinian Uprising*. Boulder, Colo.: Westview Press, 1979.

———. *Israel and the Palestine Arabs*. Washington: Middle East Institute, 1958.

———. *The West Bank: History, Politics, Society and Economy*. Boulder, Colo.: Westview Press, 1986.

Peri, Yoram. *Between Battles and Ballots: The Israeli Military in Politics*. Cambridge: Cambridge University Press, 1983.

Pryce-Jones, David. *The Closed Circle: An Interpretation of the Arabs*. New York: Harper and Row, 1989.

Quandt, William. *Decade of Decisions: American Policy toward the Arab-Israeli Conflict*. Berkeley: University of California Press, 1977.

Quandt, William, Fuad Jabber, and Ann Mosely Lesch. *The Politics of Palestinian Nationalism*. Berkeley: University of California Press, 1977.

Rabin, Yitzhak. *The Rabin Memoirs*. Boston: Little, Brown and Co., 1979.

Rodinson, Maxime. *Israel: A Colonial-Settler State?* New York: Pathfinder, 1973.

Rokach, Livia. *Israel's Sacred Terrorism*. Belmont, Mass.: Association of Arab-American University Graduates Press, 1986.

Roosevelt, Theodore. *The Winning of the West*. New York: Peter Smith, 1889.

Sachar, Howard. *Diaspora: An Inquiry into the Contemporary Jewish World.* New York: Harper and Row, 1985.

——. *A History of Israel: From the Rise of Zionism to Our Time.* Vol. I. New York: Knopf, 1986.

——. *A History of Israel: From the Aftermath of the Yom Kippur War.* Vol. II. New York: Oxford University Press, 1987.

Safran, Nadav. *Israel: The Embattled Ally.* Cambridge, Mass.: Belnap Press, 1978.

Sahliyeh, Emile. *The PLO after the War.* Boulder, Colo.: Westview Press, 1986.

Said, Edward. *Peace and Its Discontents.* New York: Vintage, 1996.

Said, Edward, and Christopher Hitchens, eds. *Blaming the Victims.* London: Verso, 1988.

Schiff, Ze'ev. *Security for Peace: Israel's Minimal Security Requirements in Negotiations with the Palestinians.* Washington: The Washington Institute for Near East Policy, 1989.

Schiff, Ze'ev, and Ehud Ya'ari. *Israel's Lebanon War.* New York: Simon and Schuster, 1984.

Schumpeter, Joseph. *Imperialism and Social Classes.* New York: A. M. Kelly, 1951.

Shafir, Gershon. *Land, Labor and the Origins of the Israeli-Palestinian Conflict, 1882-1914.* Cambridge: Cambridge University Press, 1989.

Sheehan, Edward R.E. *The Arabs, Israelis, and Kissinger: A Secret History of American Diplomacy in the Middle East.* New York: Reader's Digest Press, 1976.

Shehadeh, Raja. *Occupier's Law: Israel and the West Bank.* Washington: Institute for Palestine Studies, 1988.

Shimshoni, Jonathan. *Israel and Conventional Deterrence: Border Warfare Between 1953 and 1970.* Ithaca: Cornell University Press, 1988.

Shipler, David. *Arab and Jew: Wounded Spirits in a Promised Land.* New York: Times Books, 1986.

Shlaim, Avi. *Collusion across the Jordan.* New York: Columbia University Press, 1988.

——. *The Politics of Partition.* New York: Columbia University Press, 1990.

Smith, Charles. *Palestine and the Arab-Israeli Conflict.* New York: St. Martin's Press, 1992.

Smith, James. *Seventeenth-Century America: Essays in Colonial History.* Westport, Conn.: Greenwood Publishing, 1980.

Spiegel, Steven L. *The Other Arab-Israeli Conflict.* Chicago: University of

Chicago Press, 1985.

Stannard, David. *American Holocaust: Columbus and the Conquest of the New World*. London: Oxford University Press, 1992.

Stein, Kenneth W. *The Land Question in Palestine, 1917-1939*. Chapel Hill: University of North Carolina Press, 1984.

Stein, Leonard J. *The Balfour Declaration*. New York: Simon and Schuster, 1961.

Stone, I.F. *Underground to Palestine and Reflections Thirty Years Later*. New York: Pantheon, 1978.

Sykes, Christopher. *Crossroads to Israel*. Cleveland: World Publishing, 1965.

Tessler, Mark. *A History of the Israeli-Palestinian Conflict*. Bloomington: Indiana University Press, 1994.

Thomas, Hugh. *Suez*. London: Weidenfeld and Nicolson, 1967.

Tibawi, A.L. *A Modern History of Syria*. London: Macmillan, 1969.

Tillman, Seth. *The United States in the Middle East*. Bloomington: Indiana University Press, 1982.

Timerman, Jacobo. *The Longest War*. New York: Knopf, 1982.

Tivnan, Edward. *The Lobby: Jewish Political Power and American Foreign Policy*. New York: Simon and Schuster, 1987.

Toland, John. *Adolf Hitler*. Garden City, N.Y.: Doubleday, 1976.

Toynbee, Arnold. *A Study of History*. Vol. VIII. London: Oxford University Press, 1954.

Truman, Harry S. *Memoirs: Years of Trial and Hope*. Garden City, N.Y.: Doubleday, 1956.

Vance, Cyrus. *Hard Choices: Critical Years in America's Foreign Policy*. New York: Simon and Schuster, 1983.

Weizman, Ezer. *On Eagles' Wings: The Personal Story of the Israeli Air Force*. London: Weidenfeld and Nicolson, 1976.

———. *The Battle for Peace*. New York: Bantam Books, 1981.

Williams, Robert. *The American Indian in Western Legal Thought*. London: Oxford University Press, 1990.

Yaniv, Avner. *Dilemmas of Security*. New York: Oxford University Press, 1987.

Journals, Periodicals and Reports

Amnesty International Country Reports

The Association of Arab-American University Graduates Press, information Papers

Aviation Week and Space Technology
The Beirut Massacre: The Complete Kahan Commission Report
B'Tselem (Israeli Information Center for Human Rights).
Christian Science Monitor
Foreign Affairs
Foundation for Middle East Peace, reports
George Washington Law Review
Human Rights Watch
Information Regarding Israel's Security, reports
Institute for Public Policy Research
International Herarld Tribune
Jerusalem Post
Journal of Palestine Studies
Le Monde diplomatique
London Review of Books
Middle East Insight
Middle East Institute
Middle East International
Middle East Journal
New Outlook
New York Review of Books
New York Times
Peace Watch
Perry-Castenada Library Map Collection, University of Texas
Times Literary Supplement
Washington Post
Washington Report on Middle East Affairs

Index

About the Author

Baylis Thomas, Ph.D. is a freelance journalist and clinical psychologist in New York. His graduate training in philosophy and psychology at Haverford College, Harvard University and New York University led to a career examining the sources of individual and group conflict, psychological and political, particularly where myth plays a role for participants and observers alike.